C0-AUY-833

RADICAL EVIL
AND THE
SCARCITY OF HOPE

Indiana Series in the Philosophy of Religion
Merold Westphal, editor

Radical Evil and the Scarcity of Hope

Postsecular Meditations

MARTIN BECK MATUŠTÍK

Indiana University Press
Bloomington and Indianapolis

LORETTE WILMOT LIBRARY
NAZARETH COLLEGE

This book is a publication of

Indiana University Press
601 North Morton Street
Bloomington, IN 47404-3797 USA

http://iupress.indiana.edu

Telephone orders   800-842-6796
Fax orders   812-855-7931
Orders by e-mail   iuporder@indiana.edu

© 2008 by Martin Beck Matuštík

All rights reserved

No part of this book may be reproduced or utilized in any form or
by any means, electronic or mechanical, including photocopying and
recording, or by any information storage and retrieval system, without
permission in writing from the publisher. The Association of American
University Presses' Resolution on Permissions constitutes the only
exception to this prohibition.

The paper used in this publication meets the minimum requirements of
American National Standard for Information Sciences—Permanence of
Paper for Printed Library Materials, ANSI Z39.48-1984.

MANUFACTURED IN THE UNITED STATES OF AMERICA

Library of Congress Cataloging-in-Publication Data

Matuštík, Martin Beck, date
Radical evil and the scarcity of hope : postsecular meditations /
Martin Beck Matuštík.
p. cm. — (Indiana series in the philosophy of religion)
Includes bibliographical references and index.
ISBN-13: 978-0-253-35104-3 (cloth : alk. paper)
ISBN-13: 978-0-253-21968-8 (pbk. : alk. paper) 1. Good and evil. 2.
Hope. 3. Good and evil—Religious aspects. 4. Hope—Religious aspects.
I. Title.
BJ1401.M27 2008
170—dc22
2007035573

1 2 3 4 5 13 12 11 10 09 08

170
mat

To my three maternal great-aunts
Murdered in Auschwitz with their husbands and young children
To my firstborn great-aunt who lived through
Auschwitz with her daughter
To my two great-uncles who survived the war on the
Russian front and with the Slovak partisans
To my maternal grandfather and grandmother who outran
transports and capture in Slovakia with their entire family
I never knew any of them
Yet their stories taught me about the faces of evil and hope

Love is as strong as death
—Solomon's *Song of Songs,*
chapter 8, verse 6

CONTENTS

ACKNOWLEDGMENTS

The origin of this book project can be traced to lectures on the scarcity of hope I delivered at the Conference on Social and Political Philosophy at the Inter-University Center in Dubrovnik and at the Sartre Society meeting in Waterloo, Ontario, in 2000. My research culminated in a series of engagements with Kant's notion of radical evil, in lectures delivered in 2003 and 2004, and studies of violence in relation to religious phenomena. In April 2005, I helped organize at Purdue University a philosophical conference, The Problem of Evil, that brought together analytic and Continental philosophers, critical social theorists, and biblical scholars.

I am grateful to the grant from the Center for Humanistic Studies at Purdue that allowed me to take a full year sabbatical leave to work on this book during the academic year 2005–2006. The Philosophical Institute of the Academy of Sciences of the Czech Republic invited me to spend my Purdue sabbatical year in Prague and for this purpose provided me with an office and a stipend covering overseas housing.

All previously published or presented material was substantively revised for this book:

Chapter 1
Previously unpublished. Partly presented in lectures on The Scarcity of Hope.

Chapter 2
"Singular Existence and Critical Theory," *Radical Philosophy Review* 8/2 (2005): 211–23. Revised for this book and with a new introduction.

Chapter 3
"Between Hope and Terror: Habermas and Derrida Plead for the Im/ Possible," *Epoche* 9/1 (2004): 1–18. To Jacques Derrida in memoriam. Revised for this book.

Chapter 4
Previously published material was substantively expanded and revised for this book: "Violence and Secularization," in *Modernity and the Problem of Evil,* ed. Alan Schrift (Bloomington: Indiana University Press, 2005).

"Progress and Evil," in *Imagining Law: On Drucilla* (Cornell: SUNY Press, 2007).

Chapter 5
Previously published only in Czech. The material was substantively revised for this book: "Vydávání svědectví a otázka uznání v antivykupitelské době: vyhlazované národy a *náš* problém uchování paměti." [Witnessing and Recognition in an Antiredemptory Age: Destroyed Peoples and Our Memorial Problem] *Filosofický časopis* 50/5 (2002): 811–28. Translated from English into Czech by Ota Vochoč. Comments by Michael Pullmann, pp. 828–30. Additional material in this chapter was developed in the lecture, "Genocida paměti i odvážné vzkříšení" [Genocide of Memory and Courageous Resurrection] delivered in Langhans Galery, Prague, April 11, 2006, on the occasion of the exhibit on memory. Short version of the lecture appeared in *Právo,* Salon sec., May 18, 2006.

Chapter 6
Previously unpublished. This chapter develops themes introduced in chapter 4. The following lectures provided an opportunity to raise and draft the new questions discussed here: "Radical Evil: Is It a Religious or Secular Phenomenon?" Discussion panel with Prof. Václav Bělohradský," Conference on Moral and Political Philosophy, Czech Academy of Science, Prague, November 28, 2005.

"Derrida and Lévinas on Religion and Violence," International Congress on Person and Society: Perspectives for the 21st Century, the Faculdade de Filosofia da Universidade Católica, Braga, Portugal, November 16–20, 2005.

Religion and Violence, major discussion panel with Dean Jan Sokol and Prof. Tomáš Halík, Charles University, Prague, October 20, 2005.

Chapters 7–10 and the three part introductions are published here for the first time, though some material was initiated earlier in "Sorrowing Loneliness, Joyful Solitude," *Listening: Journal of Religion and Culture* 40/3 (2005), 207–27, and developed in lectures delivered in the Czech Republic during 2005–2006.

Epilogue
Previously unpublished. Partially developed as an afterplay lecture for the discussion of the dramatization of Dostoyevsky's *Brothers Karamazov* at the Czech theater, Husa na provázku, Brno, Czech Republic, April 13, 2006.

RADICAL EVIL
AND THE
SCARCITY OF HOPE

Part 1

●

IMPOSSIBLE HOPE

There was a time I used to reject those who were
not of my faith, now.
My heart has grown capable of taking on all forms.
A pasture for gazelles, a convent for Christians.
A temple for idols, a Kaba for the pilgrim.
A table for the Torah, a book of the Koran.
My religion is love.
Whichever the route love's caravan shall take,
that path shall be the path of my faith.

—Ibn Arabi (1165–1240)

The Messiah will only arrive when we
no longer need him.

—Franz Kafka, *Octavo Notebook G*

Philosophers of religion, social thinkers, and political thinkers, as well as various truth commissions and communities coming to terms with human atrocities are confronted with humanly engendered moral evil. Kant coined the term "radical evil," if not the problem. Yet he shrank from the implications of his discovery. Is there anything like radical evil and if there is, what kind of phenomenon is it? I situate my question at the intersection of two contemporary fields of the humanities: critical theory and philosophy of religion. What theoretical and practical difference does our affirmation or denial of the phenomenon of radical evil make? Answers we offer impact us personally and publicly; they affect multiple ethical, political, and religious spheres.

I will develop a figure of human evil according to its four intensities or modalities, considering practical evil as at once banal, morally radical, paradoxical, and diabolical. Do-gooders tranquilize themselves on the trivial pursuit of the good: theirs is the banality of evil. Practical evil in Kant's sense distorts the human capacity for free development, and so evil comes to be apprehended as morally radical. When our deferred desire for the impossible (antinomical, aporetic, incomprehensible) confronts our pursuit of the good life with insurmountable conceptual and linguistic dissonance, a sort of malignant sublime, then even goodwill becomes implicated in its undoing, and we engender a paradoxical, ethico-religious sense of evil. But in our times we know that even human-all-too-human acts of cruelty can exceed the bounds of reason in ways Kant thought could never happen. This second-order desire of the "impossible"—second because not only paradoxically (or conceptually) deferred but also positively willed—reveals that human evil exceeds itself and so reaches diabolical intensity.

As anxiety is to fear and evil is to wrong, so is hope to hopes. I speak of evil and hope in the first, intransitive sense. Any excess or saturation also has transitive and intransitive modalities. Allain Badiou and Jean-Luc Marion hold very different notions of excess or "saturation." Badiou (2006) means a certain exhaustion of possibilities (for "saturated" read "tired of possibilities"), while Marion (2000, 2002) means an intuitive excess of conceptual intentions (for "saturated" read "energized with possibility"). Badiou's saturation records a historical exhaustion of transitive hopes such as the party-class experiment; Marion's saturation reveals an intransitive excess of hope in intuitive givenness that is bereft of object, language, or meaning to fulfill intention. "Radical moral evil" in all four intensities—like its intransitive apposite modality, hope—exceeds in intuition what it intends in concepts. Human evil according to its four intensities or modalities (banal, morally radical, paradoxical, and diabolical) represents intransitive levels of saturation.

Why at its greatest intensity does human evil's excess aim at the objectless dimension of hope in defiance? This book is a sustained meditation on the intransitive, excess dimension of human evil, whereby the scarcity of hope reveals itself as what I call *a negatively saturated phenomenon*. There are many hopes won, and perhaps even more hopes lost; there are many goods pursued, and perhaps even more such pursuits exhausted by experiments gone bad. In this book I am not primarily concerned with transitive hopes or fears, goods or evils, but rather with the intransitive scarcity of hope. While we can name moral wrongs and pursue hopes, we find no adequate language, concept, or meaning for evil's own excess of cruelty and lost hope.

The loss and recovery of hope mark the core phenomena for my meditations.

In part 1, I speak about impossible hope in the first degree: hope desired yet deferred. Paradoxical, aporetic, at times hidden and other times incomprehensible hope maximizes its intention for the wholly other than this unjust world only to discover that its desire does not meet up with an adequate gift. Inspired by Kofman, Sartre, Marcuse, Jonas, and the Frankfurt tradition of critical theory, yet with Derrida going a step further, I apply the material weight of scarcity (the first-order desire of the "impossible" we confront in our intentional aims) to the intransitive spirit of hope.

In part 2, I broach the possibility of the second-order desire of impossible hope. Deferred hope is deemed impossible on account of overflowing intentions that cannot be satisfied. But the aggravated scarcity of hope makes hope "impossible" because one positively wills it so. I mean by radical evil an aggravated scarcity of hope. Yet what can one desire without concept, object, and beyond the first order of maximizing an unfulfillable, deferred intention? Can one will the impossible in the unlimited givenness of intuition released from intention? Can one will oneself to hope negatively? This aggravated possibility of the impossible is one's willed despair revealed in acts of radical evil. Drawing on Schelling's discovery of inverse possibilities of human freedom, Kierkegaard's and Dostoyevsky's descriptions of defiant despair, and Lévinas's notion of evil as not being directly synthesizable, I will introduce the notion of radical evil as a negatively saturated phenomenon. Taking off from yet going beyond Kant and Arendt, I will harness the language of radical evil to name the phenomenon of excessive, irreparable violence.

In the figure of the uncanny, part 3 joins the two—paradoxical and exceeding—meditations on the scarcity or impossibility of hope. How does forgiveness heal the despair of the unforgivable? How does tragic beauty bless us so that unforgettable suffering can ever be bearable? How does silence fill the solitude crushed by unspeakable loneliness? How does the gift of unconditional love mend the annihilation of hope wrought by the excess of cruelty? With Derrida, Kierkegaard, Lévinas, Marion, and Ricoeur, I will meditate on the uncanny—*teshuvah* (from Hebrew, turning), *tikkun olam* (from Hebrew, mending of the world), *chashmal* (from Hebrew, speaking silence), and *berakhah/barakah* (from Hebrew/Sufi, blessing)—that takes what was irreparably breached and makes it whole again. The possibility of mending the world lies at the apposite of the entropic, absurd, nonresponsive and unreceptive universe. This very hope is defying the antiredemptory nothingness, which Derrida inspired by Plato's *Timaeus* describes as *khôra*, that unformed surd of space and time that makes room even for creation out of nothing as well as for any redemptive or liberating possibility, groundless ground, yet in itself an *impassible* impossibility and religiously tone-deaf exteriority or empty spacing of space (cf. Caputo, 1997: 35–38, 58f., 167ff.; Derrida, 1995 and FaK 57f., and in Sherwood, 2005: 297f.).

WAYS OF RAISING
THE PROBLEM OF EVIL

I am concerned in this work with humanly generated evil. Belief in the reality of evil and the numerous metaphysical and conceptual ways of dealing with such belief have been equally if not more widespread throughout human history than belief in God's existence. The classical way of posing the problem of evil is to challenge God's coherence or one of God's attributes of omnipotence, omniscience, or goodness, or to justify God's coherence with those attributes intact. There are at least three pre-Kantian ways of raising the problem of evil:

- *Metaphysics offers theodicy:* justification of good, omniscient, omnipotent God with evil in the world.

- *Theoretical arguments offer proofs:* cosmological, ontological, and moral cases for or against God's existence.
- *Propositional analysis offers evidential arguments from evil:* analytical restatement of classical arguments.

These three ways have evolved and intertwined over time. The first two developed in the early and high Middle Ages, integrating Greek metaphysics (first of Plato and then with the mediation of Arabs and Jews on the Iberian Peninsula; also of Aristotle) with Judeo-Christian-Muslim theology. The third way, albeit emerging after Kant in contemporary analytical philosophy of religion, restates the pre-Kantian ways of approaching the problem of evil in theodicy and evidential arguments. With Kant's critique of all rational theodicies and proofs for God's existence, there appeared yet a fourth way of dealing with moral evil:

- *Moral arguments offer postulates:* ideal moral requirements needed for the exercise of practical reason.

Kant postulated what he could no longer prove—immortality, God—as he still needed to buttress moral virtue against the nihility of freedom not backed up by cosmic justice. The fragility of the Kantian moral "God" and human agency operating in the radical openness of its free will would be revealed in full force with Nietzsche's proclamation of the "death of God."

The fifth way arrives with the post-Kantian raising of the problem of evil, and this one comprises all approaches that take less issue with God's coherence and attributes and more with human flourishing and capacity for sustained free development. In part 2, following Marion but also Schelling, Kierkegaard, Dostoyevsky, and Lévinas, I develop the notion of *radical evil as a negatively saturated phenomenon.* This fifth way is at once post-Kantian and post-Nietzschean, postmetaphysical and postsecular:

- *Existential-transformative way reveals the phenomena of despair and hope:* this evidence is lived in one's positive or negative relation to hope.

By "existential" I do not mean an ontological structure of being-in-the-world, but rather the passionate care for one's soul found in Job, Socrates, Jesus, Buddha, Augustine, Pascal, or Buber. Care for existence becomes a philosophical topic for the nineteenth-century precursors to existentialism. Kierkegaard defines self as spirit. I read this view in a Lévinasian manner: the self is a performative site of difficult freedom wherein I live by caring responsibly for myself, others, and the Other who always already names the possibility that I live by either hope or despair. For Nietzsche the "death of

God" is a spiritual event of existential-social proportions, an occasion for the rise of "new gods" as well as for self-overcoming. The possibilities of hope and despair define my existentially transformative self-and-other relation. The "existential" is thus something always lived, singularly personal, ethically interpersonal, social, and political.

While the classical and the analytical approaches to the question of evil are for the most part preoccupied with metaphysical, conceptual, or propositional analysis, the post-Kantian approaches do not primarily raise validity claims but speak to a mode of existence or through raising an injunction to a certain way of existence. It is in this sense that I call them existential-transformative. Instead of discussing theodicy, proofs, postulates, or evidential arguments, one is confronted with the quality of hope or despair as those categories qualify one's entire mode of existence. From an angle of this distinction, one cannot fail to notice the peculiar despair of those strains of contemporary philosophy of religion which even after Kant avoid self-confrontation in the ways they limit the "problem of evil" for human to the "problem with God."

The nature and scope of *radical* evil has come under scrutiny since Kant's moral defense of autonomous free will. Kant places in doubt the human capacity for diabolical volition, even as he ironically invokes the term "radical evil." Thus radical evil for Kant can never be "diabolical." Kant's moral de-differentiation between *radical* (he admits) and *diabolical* (he denies) evil in human willing is rooted in his theoretical architectonic that protects human freedom from ever harming the moral law. Yet in our post-Kantian times, "radical evil" has all but exceeded the transcendental condition set for rational freedom. Kant's speculative limit on human volition has thus produced an abyss between the rational freedom he defends and the diabolical freedom he denies.

Adorno ponders whether or not we can write poetry and philosophy after Auschwitz. Benjamin (1968:256) considers most monuments of Western culture sunk in barbarism: "There is no document of civilization which is not at the same time a document of barbarism." With ethnic and religious wars and the permanent war on terror in the twenty-first century, philosophers might doubt the reality of the most radical evil, but ordinary people no longer do. At least since the twentieth century we can say with certainty that everyone knows what is *radical* about "radical evil"—it strays from the bounds of mere reason. We have witnessed the wanton mass annihilation of human beings for the sake of ascertaining the superiority of one group of people over another, no less than the mass killings occurring in the cataclysms of the Soviet, Chinese, or Cambodian attempts to create social paradise. In mentioning these historical events here I am less concerned with defending or judging this or that transitive attempt at revolutionary change, be it Mao, Stalin, or Pol Pot, than with the failed learning curve among the social theorists and activists who confuse hope with hopes and thus teach or otherwise propagate revolutionary progress as a sufficient self-transformative way *for us*. With Benjamin we must remember the notion of progress as disaster. As I noted with regard to Badiou above, this book is not about transitive hope, and thus not about the historical past or future of Judaism, Christianity, or Marxism. My book aims to forge redemptive critical theory by challenging the political economists, social theorists, and activists with certain spiritual questions concerning intransitive hope they always already presuppose but can never rationally guarantee or master.

"Radical evil" is defined by common sense (although Kant limits the concept to unrestrained self-interest) as gratuitous destruction and invidious violence. A thief might commit murder to avoid being caught in the act of robbery, betrayed lovers might kill in the heat of passion or out of anger and jealousy, and wars might be waged for political and economic gain. Yet mass murders have no such reasonable *telos*. Killing the Hungarian Jews in 1944, when the Nazis had all but lost the war, served no gain but murder. The sniper alleys in Sarajevo or the hacking of limbs in Rwanda pursued no aim but human carnage. Individual rape is often motivated by sexual violence, but the mass rape of women in the Balkan wars served neither sexual lust nor a strategy for winning the war; it was underwritten by a "religious" motive of destroying the identity of the women and their possible offspring. Islamist terrorists are yet to formulate constructive civilizational aims besides those formulated by Iranian President Mahmoud Ahmadinejad as erasing Israel from the map of the world or by fringe groups as destroying the Occident. With aimless evil, it is difficult to negotiate reasons or pursue normative goals. Shaming radical evil's logical self-contradiction or rational and moral incoherence does us existentially no good. Radical moral evil lies in humans willing destruction even at the cost of their own downfall. In his late work on the limits of religion within the bounds of mere reason, Kant wishes to explain away the dangers free actions pose to the rational nature of human intellect and will. He thus saves our respect for moral freedom by demoting evil's effect on the rational core of free will. A hundred years later, Nietzsche questioned whether or not our good moral will masks within itself will to power. Nietzsche suspected that at the heart of Kant's moralized religion lies nihility waiting to be awakened.

THE POSTSECULAR LANGUAGE
OF RADICAL EVIL

Evil that I call "radical" distorts intelligence and free will in their capacity to guide and sustain human development and well-being. If radical evil cannot be attributed to ordinary mistakes in judgment or erroneous decisions, then it is not enough to narrate evil in terms of moral wrong (cf. Lara, 2007). What is its ground cause? Evil's "radicalness" consists in purposelessness that exceeds ordinarily bad and morally wrongful actions. This added "something" exercises a contrarian effect on the purposeless play of sublime beauty that brings about joy or tragic beauty that promises rebirth even in death. This book offers a sustained meditation on the faith claim that *love is as strong as death* found in the opening epigraph (cf. Rosenzweig, 2005:169, 213–20, 345). "Radical evil" exceeds the commonsense errors or badness with willed meaninglessness, nihilism, and destruction. Humans experience the phenomenon of radical evil not in mortality but in cruel death. The atrocities—like the gulags, Srebrenica, Darfur, 9/11, targeting of civilians—overflow with such excess. To state this succinctly: *cruelty has no ordinary political or economic utility.* Yet the word "evil" not only emigrates into many fundamentalist vocabularies but also forces its spelling onto modern secular lips. Social-political thinkers have difficulty using the word "evil" in discourse because even in vernacular it bears overdetermined religious connotations. Yet they press thought to evil's extreme limits.

Critical social theorists and activists presuppose that we know how to narrate radical evil. They presuppose as unproblematic what is in no way an obvious phenomenon. Lara (2007) seeks to open a space for coming to terms with human atrocities and cruelty through reflective judgment about experiences that cannot be directly communicated or conceptualized but can be narrated, for example, in truth commissions. But she a priori limits her theory of any such narration to the secular horizon of Kant's "moral wrongs." She stays decidedly within the secular domain because she conflates the adoption of postmetaphysical reflective judgment with her rejection of the religious perspective. Yet to come to terms with cruelty, must not our narrations and self-understanding come to terms with the distinctly postsecular modality of the phenomena? What is cruelty? The answer will be wanting if we arbitrarily restrict the phenomena to the moral universe of Kant's narration of evil. Thus my work begins where Kant, Habermas, or Lara end, or better, their narrations of evil presuppose what my meditations on radical evil attempt to fill. By narrating evil as excess that breaks the bounds of mere secularity or the rational horizon of moral wrongs, critical social and ethical theorists and activists are prompted into a fruitful, indeed necessary dialogue with philosophers and practitioners of religion.

If we cannot spell the word "evil" in our theorizing, should we then jettison the word altogether in order to avoid its political and religious abuses, as many philosophers and critical theorists propose we do? Yet if the phenomenon of "cruelty"—purposeful or manipulated nihility—revisits us with even greater intensity in our times, philosophers, whether religious or secular, would be wise in my view to elucidate the persistent phenomenon of radical evil rather than brush it aside. This phenomenon marks out the domain on which I set out to meditate in my work.

Meditating earnestly on radical evil in the twenty-first century calls for postsecular sensibilities. Postsecular is to secular as postmodern is to modern. These pairs of terms offer broad descriptive umbrellas. The first terms in each pair can house such diverse phenomena as are religious fundamentalisms, Derrida's "religion without religion" (Caputo 2001:109–42), and radical orthodoxy's self-reference. Sociologists describe by the term "postsecular" any coexistence of secular and religious forms of life. Put in another way, insofar as our age is plagued by the myriad phenomena of willed human destruction (some religious and secular forms of life contribute to radical evil, while others heal its sources), we live in the *postsecular condition*. The term "postsecular" designates the coexistence of various religious and secular phenomena, and I count radical evil among its chief exemplars. No social theory of globalization can disregard the stubborn resurgence of these phenomena. The subtitle of my work, *Postsecular Meditations,* signals that radical evil appears even in the secular context as the uncanny phenomenon.

I adopt the postsecular angle of vision because it is natively better disposed to unmask the impetus to holy wars insofar as their underlying motives feed on the phenomenon of evil or its conquest. I hold out for an internal critique of radical evil—or what I will call *redemptive critical theory*—to harness the advantage of living in the postsecular condition. "Redemptive" or "redemptory" awaits the possibility of healing the world crushed by hopelessness. The entropic nothingness of the *khôra* is religiously deaf, mute, and even free of existential anxiety's nothingness, and so as wholly exterior to the possibility, it neither can explain the excess of radical evil nor await hope. Fragments of intransitive redemptive hope are always already redemptive as Benjaminian chips of messianic now-time, as interrupted eschatology; the transitive teleology of redemption always already destroys hope (cf. Derrida and Tracy in Caputo, 1999:182ff.).

The possibility of hope exists for the sake of those without hope, that hope can be granted even when all reasonable conditions or resources for its return have been exhausted. By redemption I mean the very opposition of cruel annihilation. To hope against the antiredemptory situation of the world is the first essential act of radical resistance to evil. Redemptive critical theory or critical theory of redemption is a discourse about the possibility of hope. An internal or redemptive critique of radical evil as a religious phenomenon does not advance external critiques of religion. A redemptive critique does not rely on classical arguments explaining how God and evil coexist. Postsecular meditations apprehend the return of various religious phenomena as the excess of radical evil *after* the "death of God"—the death of the classical ontotheological and modern rational critiques as well as Kant's "moral God" (cf. Marion, 1991:16, 25–49, 58f.; Derrida, FaK 49–52).

RADICAL EVIL AFTER THE "DEATH OF GOD": THINKING WITH KANT AGAINST KANT

The "death of God" was not first announced by Nietzsche's madman and then made famous among disenchanted theists. It has been proclaimed in every liturgy since the first Good Friday and White Saturday, the two Christian holy days when the body of Jesus of Nazareth was wrapped and laid in the tomb. During Passion Week, Christians replay and relive the "death of God": God is absent (incomprehensible in a Pseudo-Dionysian, mystical sense) as well as hidden (crucified, dwelling in darkness, reachable by struggling faith in the Lutheran sense). Only lamentations over the Pietà of God's suffering incarnation are sounded; no liturgy of Eucharist is celebrated until the Easter Vigil. Eastern Orthodox iconography shows the transfigured as well as the risen Christ decked in white robes; his brightness eclipses the sun disc rising behind him in black colors of natural eclipse. This is not an idol of the divine; the icon reveals an inverse eclipse of natural sunlight by the spiritual sun, and such eclipses do not occur in nature. On the resurrection iconography, the spiritual light of transformation descends for two days to hell. (And what does the messianic light do for these two days between God's death and resurrection in hell? Would there be any purpose to such descent if hell were as practico-inert as the *khôra*, that is, if no prayers or hope could ever be sounded from hell and be heard?) Christ breaks the seal of death with its dark sun of nihilism, vanity, and melancholia, as the New Adam extends the liberating hand to the First Adam and Eve (Eve means literally "life"), along with all fallen humans (on the dark sun, see also Marion, 1991:16, 122, 128, 134).

The Hegelian philosophical reading of the paschal mystery that inspired Nietzsche introduces a threefold secularizing interpretation of the "death of God" by way of Martin Luther's hymn for the Good Friday liturgy. There is a *civilizational or cultural death* of the West's effective belief in God. Our concept of God has become abstract, ineffective, unreal, estranged from the mainstream culture. There is an *allegorical or dialectical death* of Christian appreciation of suffering and death as ways to overcome human alienation and find a richer life. St. John's Gospel narrates the Passion in ways that recognize the resurrection always and already revealed in Christ's death on the cross, but even this Johannine prophetic angle of vision (and some would read into it already dialectical atheism) grows alien to disenchanted theists. There is a *metaphysical or speculative death* of God, whereby the God of religion must die in order to give way to God's philosophical resurrection. That third death announces Hegel's speculative Good Friday. Hegel stands at a crossroad where one can read the "death of God" in either emphatically religious or methodologically atheist terms. The theism of natural and revealed theology becomes sublated (or surpassed?) by Hegel in a nonsectarian and nonviolent reconciliation of religious belief with philosophical critique. Art and religion recognize in each other the same content and goal, reaching their resurrection historically and developmentally in a philosophically reconciled, rational form of life.

Nietzsche's claim, placed on the lips of a madman, "God is dead," the cry later completed by Heidegger's critique of ontotheology, accentuates the civilizational death of God. We have killed the living God. What are the cultural artifacts of Christian practices and morality but empty tombs of Good Friday and White Saturday, those rituals offered to a God in whom practically nobody believes and before whom the despairing theists and philosophers neither dance nor worship? For Nietzsche, will to power and the morality of those who have the courage to embrace their freedom as sources of all values lead to a life beyond nihilism. Whereas Nietzsche located nihilism in positing of values, Heidegger unmasked the positing of a God as value or belief to be nihilism. One's will to power worshiped as absolute value could become a decadent God. Neither thinker awaits Judeo-Christian resurrection, though Nietzsche holds out for self-overcoming and Heidegger for meditative thinking. In this sense, too, they allow for some return of the religious phenomenon after God's cultural death. Defining human beings by their desire to be God, Sartre took over the dialectical meaning of the "death of God." The idea of human as omnipotent God is self-contradictory, contrary to finite freedom. There is either God or human freedom. God must die in order for the human free self to be born.

Freud and Marx, both secular Jews, took over Hegel's philosophical secularization of the Christian kerygma as well as Nietzsche's proclamation of the good death of that secularized, moral divine. Their announcement of the "death of God" applies to secular Judaism. Freud suggested that God is but a prosthetic illusion, thereby uniting Hegel's cultural and dialectical senses of the "death of God." After losing the security of mother's womb, after being disappointed by the paternal authority of teachers, politicians, and even traditional morality, after embracing various projects to replace those losses, after artistic and erotic ways of simulating God, for some even after taking drugs as a form of religious ecstasy, God returns as the grand prosthetic illusion of the anxious child-in-the-adult still desiring the parent. Religion is a creative invention for how to treat the shock of our birth and adulthood; it is a compulsion-repetition of rituals and worship that are akin to obsessive neurotic behavior. Attributes of God are those items we project in our infantilism onto parents. Placing the conflict we have with parents on the shoulders of a deity releases a psychic pressure valve and simulates reconciliation. As most psychoanalytical theory after Freud confirmed, all our behavior—theistic or atheistic—is subject to an awakening that is at once religious in its longing and illusory in its object relations.

Marx transformed Hegel's speculative "death of God" into revolutionary action that will deliver us to a socially just form of life. Religion is an ideological reflection of current economic alienation—relations of inequality, oppression, and social injustice. The idea of God serves as a convenient apology for the capitalist lifestyle. Religion is the opium of the people that falsely addresses the cry of the heartless world, while money is our only visible God, relic, and pimp among the nations. The religious longing projects a human ideal of liberated and just society that only communism satisfies. Social revolution brings the true Sunday, that is, our social resurrection from the dead; communism is thus the riddle of history resolved. We do not need the religious projection of a just future while living in an unhappy and oppressive world once we actively bring about social change that delivers us to just social relations. In place of priests and churches who mediate our unhappy world, we become our own mediators; instead of the future postponement of the kingdom of God, we establish justice among us.

The Grand Inquisitor, the literary character presented by Ivan Karamazov to his religious brother Alyosha in Dostoyevsky's novel *Brothers Karamazov,* harnesses in his ideology all three meanings of the "death of God." The suffering servant interrogated by the Grand Inquisitor is Jesus of Nazareth, who visits seventeenth-century Spain and is apprehended by its religious inquisition. No longer blaming the Jews for Christ's death, the chief Christian Pharisee sentences the suffering witness to death because God has become inconvenient to Christendom. There is no Roman Empire to blame either. The religious power has taken over all secular duties and hopes for a regime change of God's creation. I see in Jesus standing before the Inquisitor also the biblical Job, whom the Inquisitor counsels to live free of pain if he is willing to give up religious conscience. The Inquisitor is the figure of radical evil, and for this reason I return to his portrait in the epilogue. He provides humans freedom from suffering and permits them to aggress each other (engaging in "just," "holy," "humanitarian" wars), while he redistributes the basic material things and symbols of allegiance, yet without demanding *religare,* acts of religious self-transformation.

In Nietzsche's footsteps thinkers have proclaimed the death of a "God" fashioned by classical philosophical arguments or buttressed by moral teachings. Luther's and Bergman's (1962) crucified and kenotic (albeit often despairing) faith gives way to Schellenberg's (1993; cf. Howard-Snyder, 2002) analytically eviscerated, argumentatively atheistic apprehension of a hidden God. From Luther to Nietzsche, this was to be a salutary death of the "moral" and "rational," ontotheological "God," and so this dying should not jettison all religious phenomena per se. We were supposed to transvalue or secularize our search for the ultimate. We were to become like the new gods—creators of our own destiny. Our inability to live up to the postreligious hope gave rise to new forms of nihilism. When the Paris philosopher André Glucksmann writes about Dostoyevsky's atheists and religious adherents wreaking terror in Manhattan, he portrays contemporary nihilism turning back upon itself. Humans, fearful of nothingness, have adopted new values and beliefs to replace the idols carved by religious integrations. Innocent victims of history are just as overwhelmed by this excess under the guise of radical evil as the notion of the Holocaust becomes overdetermined. That added "something" breaks the bounds of reasonableness. Evil evinces excess in that it reveals itself as a mode of a saturation whose intensities can be banal, radical or moral in Kant's sense, paradoxical or aporetic in Derrida's sense, and, contra Kant, diabolical.

Following in general contours Kierkegaard's classification of existential spheres, throughout and especially in part 2, I assign the four intensities of evil to four existential stages or spheres on life's way: aesthetic sphere (banal evil), ethical sphere (morally radical evil), ethico-religious sphere (paradoxical evil), and religious sphere (diabolical evil). Of these only the last intensity amounts to what the post-Holocaust common sense understands as "radical evil." To offer some working definitions for each pair of relations: aesthetically, one operates with no principle of evil, except that one's boredom is experienced as an excess of ordinary sense experience, the sensualist's root of all evil. One searches for what is interesting and pleasurable, while avoiding boredom and pain. Aesthetically speaking, incidence of human evil at this level is banal; philosophically speaking, the abstract way of grasping the problem of evil lies at the greatest remove from one's concrete existence. Radical evil in its intelligible forms and in Kant's moral sense appears for the first time as a possibility when the aesthete desires to become ethical. What is deemed good and bad, right and wrong is discernible by normative criteria. By the same moral criteria even a murderer can repent and resume an ethical life (e.g., by being punished and by expiating the crime). This intensity of evil acquires the moral sense in Kant, who defines all radical evil through moral categories. His moral postulates of hope, immortality, and God are to protect free agency from outright despair in pursuing virtue without proofs of God's existence or immediate rewards for acting with good will. Postmodern thinkers, let us say Derrida, Caputo, or Marion, discovered how to speak of God even after the "death of God" and otherwise than through the affirmative denials of negative theology—they discovered the impersonal, ethico-religious domain of aporias, or the paradoxical religion without religion. They share their post-Kantian pathos for the impossible (and we shall see how Derrida's and Caputo's deferred impossible differs from Marion's saturated impossible) with the paradoxical irony of Kierkegaard's Johannes Climacus who makes an effort to become religious in his theocentric age.

Yet what I call "radical evil" in this book appears at first, contra Kant, in a religious intensity bursting through the bounds of mere reason. At this level banal boredom, moral weakness, and even paradoxical Lutheran hiddenness and the Pseudo-Dionysian incomprehensibility of God morph into one's will to meaningless self-and-other destruction. A cruel agent can be punished, just as a morally wicked one can repent. But no amount of repentance and even accepted and completed punishment can in and of itself restore shattered human bonds. Theodicies justifying God and proofs for God's existence are too weak to carry the day, and moral postulates do not console with hope. One can pay with one's life for murder, and kings and states can declare amnesty or grant pardon. But for radical evil, which negatively exceeds all rational bounds, one cannot morally win or legislate forgiveness. The annihilating and cruel will shatters the moral. Such will is more than aesthetically banal, morally weak, and paradoxical or aporetic: it is religiously *diabolical.* Its appearance and overcoming must be grasped as also a *religious,* rather than just moral-political, phenomenon.

I take up the Kantian irony of the term "radical evil" in part 2. The irony consists of the formal and normative contradiction in the term. If by "radical evil" is meant "evil for evil's sake," then we find ourselves in this conundrum. Either radical evil is so rarefied as to be more an exception than a norm, or evil for evil's sake is never the case. In both regards, "radical evil" would be describing something marginal or nonexistent. The marginal case would be that of a pervert who finds pleasure in another's pain. Yet even in these extremes, as the other side of the conundrum points out, we cannot avoid that strange sense of evildoers enjoying their acts and thereby willing some good. The cruelest master is not acting for evil's sake but for the sake of aesthetic and normative gains. Even as there is justice among thieves, is there lust among devils for the ultimate?

If we have such difficulty in defining radical evil, why even use the term "evil," let alone "radical evil"? Kant could not wish to recreate the Manichaean world in which the figure of radical evil served as an even match to absolute good. If evil is not a divinity equal in power to good—and this is the chief motive behind Arendt's demoting the sacral sense of evil into something banal—then is evil, even radical evil, a form or a privation of the good? This is in general terms what classical theodicies thought (classical theodicies justified a good God in the face of evil in the world and portrayed evil as privation of the good).

Taking off from Schelling and inspired by Kierkegaard and Marion, I wish to think the category of radical evil through the Judaic inspiration of the early Frankfurt School thinkers as well as Jonas and Lévinas (cf. Scholem, 1991:56–87). Evil—at once aesthetically banal, morally radical, ethico-religiously paradoxical, and religiously diabolical—is not a negation but rather, as I explain in greater depth in part 2, a negatively saturated position. It is not to be thought of as privation but rather as excess. I am not preoccupied with formal contradictions of evil for evil's sake any more than with justifying God in the face of evil or entering analytical debates about the evidence against God arising from the "problem of evil." I meditate on evil rather than pursue arguments about it. The purpose of meditations on radical evil is existential-transformative, rather than metaphysical-conceptual or for the sake of propositional analysis. While one can speak of religion within rational bounds, I will claim that there is nothing wholly secular about cruelty and annihilation. Radical evil attempts to create absolute values; however, in the case of fundamentalist terror or war on terror (unlike medieval holy wars), it fails to act as a constructive cultural force. The values erected with zealotry arise as so many warring gods and demons against the twilight of religious and secular idols. This excess is communicated in the language and action of radical evil, which is a postsecular, postmodern, and increasingly global phenomenon.

THE RELIGIOUS TURN AND
METHODOLOGICAL A/THEISM

What is the significance of the religious turn of contemporary philosophical thought? In the wake of 9/11, public discussions of the ubiquity of evil intensified. Janicaud (2000, cf. 2005) wrote in the early 1990s a widely discussed essay, "The Theological Turn of French Phenomenology," in which he acknowledges a turn toward the "religious" among French thinkers like Marion, Derrida, and Lévinas, or American scholars Caputo, Westphal, and Kearney. He also contends that philosophy and religion "make two." This would be a nonproblematic and rather classical view, such as found in Aquinas's distinction between faith and reason. But Janicaud defends phenomenology's emphasis on "methodological atheism" (to admit transcendent phenomena, we must grasp them immanently, i.e., reduce transcendence to experience given in the world). He insists that Husserl and Heidegger elaborate an "atheist phenomenology." For Janicaud, there are no "religious" phenomena to investigate.

Can philosophy be deployed in immanence yet become a phenomenology of religion? Marion answers this question affirmatively by describing the "saturated phenomenon." This saturation of experience is what above I called the "excess." We need not venture into special religious revelation (epiphany or theophany) in order to meet such excess, since we find it in philosophy: Plato's good beyond being, Descartes's infinity, or Kant's aesthetics of the sublime. Marion (2007) admits that the "banality of saturation" reaches all the way to sense experience, where I have located aesthetic intensities of human evil. Whereas Arendt introduces the notion of the "banality of evil" in order to resist the apotheosis of the Nazi deeds, as I will discuss in chapters 1 and 4, Marion's notion of the banality of saturation reveals that low-level epiphanies occur in excess of ordinary or natural sense experience. Or as Derrida would have it in his paradoxical version of the impossible, speaking of Abraham's sacrifice of Isaac, every other is wholly other, every face-to-face encounter carries us to an Abrahamic ethico-religious aporia. Marion replies to Janicaud that phenomenology remains faithful to Husserl's "principle of all principles" (everything offered to us in experience has the right to be taken as it gives itself) even when it is describing the saturated phenomenon. In its natural modalities the saturated phenomenon offers banal albeit infrequent counterexperience (2007:397, 400). Marion allows us to disconnect the God question from descriptions of the saturated phenomenon (391). "*The majority of phenomena, if not all,* can undergo saturation by the excess in them of intuition over the concept of signification" (390). The phenomenology of religion reveals in ordinary counterexperience "possible," generic religiosity, not some really existing religion, some historical or mystical revelation.

What is the category that could institute *the religious*? Traditionally the domain of the religious is defined by acts of religion (e.g., prayer or rituals or worship), religious texts, and religious institutions as reservoirs of culture and tradition. I meditate from the vantage point in which Benjamin, among others, suspects all remnants of religious culture to be barbaric. In that constellation, impossible hope discussed in part 1 and the aggravated scarcity of hope discussed in part 2 offer two postsecular entries into the religious. One way to describe *the religious* would be to call it counterexperience, Marion's saturated phenomenon; the other way would take us via hermeneutics, deconstruction, and infinite midrash about God into Derrida's aporetic religion without religion as eschatological desire for the impossible; and yet another way would confront us with Lévinas's infinite ethical responsibility for the other. Apart from mythical counterexperiential epiphanies or theophanies, what could institute the religious within ordinary human condition? Is it the holy midrash of undecidables or the iconic trace of the wholly other in face of the human other? In part 3, under the figure of the uncanny, I demarcate impersonal fields that exceed secular experience and also describe corresponding personal and interpersonal modalities of "excess." As the uncanny of existential nausea and freedom is to anxiety, so the uncanny of the

divided self and faith is to despair. Both figures of the uncanny are phenomenological, not theological, disclosures, both are revealed in certain stepping
back from transitive hopes or values to questions concerning human existence. The first uncanny marks the nonproblematic human condition of existential guilt and homelessness in the cosmos. If this human condition of
nausea, uneasiness, absurd, and existential nullity is not evil or even moral
wrong, then certainly our coming to terms with existence could carry ethical implications; however, it would not be "religious" in the ways I articulate
that phenomenon. "In anxiety one feels '*uncanny*'" (Heidegger, 1962:233;
cf. 295f., 322, 325, 331, 333, 393–95; 1969:64f.). Yet this existential mood
is not the second sense of the uncanny, of which I speak under the figures of
intransitive evil and hope. The latter brings us face-to-face with the religious, both as the worst—the impetus to cruelty—and the best—its *impossible* healing. In this second nontheological disclosure of the phenomenon
of the uncanny, hope is never a futural longing (unhappy hope) or past nostalgia (unhappy remembrance) but rather a counterexperience of the religious revealed as the messianic now-time. Heidegger (1962:395f.) distinguishes the nostalgic yearning hope (like fear, it is a futural phenomenon)
from the existential mood of "hoping itself" in which one always already
inhabits ecstatic temporality. By awakening to hope I mean Benjamin's
messianic (1968:263) and Tolle's more Buddhist-like time of the now
(1999:61).

I apprehend the religious through postsecular descriptions of radical
evil. I learn a great deal from Kierkegaard's study of despair, itself anticipated by Schelling's study of freedom. Kierkegaard is the only one in Western thought whom I have discovered to offer performative, experimental
evidence (not rational proofs or moral postulates) for a "religious" mode of
existence by attending to the form of despair he named defiance. Kierkegaard discovered the category of existence, whereby I am able *in despair* to
will to be myself. In this modality—in contrast to the banal, aesthetic intensities of evil, Kant's moralized "radical evil," and *after* Nietzsche's paradoxical claim to have gone beyond good and evil—I can exceed morally
radical evil in a diabolical sense. Not being merely an absence of good,
every act of an aggravated scarcity of hope becomes freely posited. As one's
despairing will of the impossible, evil becomes one's demonic self-asser-
tion.

Since the possibility of radical evil both institutes and destroys the religious, the entropic universe or the *khôra* can institute neither. One can neither dance nor sing before the *khôra*, one can pray from hell but cannot
hate or love the *impassible* space bereft of face. The will to annihilation
paves the way to hell, and in that excess it acts unlike the *khôra*. In the mar-

gin between the nothingness of cruel will and the nothingness of unresponsive emptiness, there lies the possibility of hope.

The reader might ask at this point to what extent my meditations are a form of theism or philosophy of religion. *The religious as the phenomenon of excess,* which I ponder in these meditations, is not instituted through the ontotheological frame of reference (metaphysical, propositional, evidential way) but rather existentially (self-transformative way). Some contemporary thinkers have insisted on the category of theism in order to defend the personal as opposed to impersonal view of God, for example, Paul Tillich's or Calvin Schrag's post-Heideggerian language about God beyond the God of theism. I endorse the view that God cannot be conceived of as an object, a validity domain, or some ordinary phenomenon. If there is a God worthy of worship, the One before whom I can dance and sing (Heidegger, 1969: 72), God cannot be an outcome of a syllogism. The God to whom I pray and relate in my heart—the God of Abraham, the biblical prophets, Ibn Arabi, Augustine or Anselm, Buber or Kierkegaard—is not necessarily best defended by *theism* as the only path to personal religiosity.

Theism teaches about nature and attributes of God, and atheism about the failure to establish proofs or postulates regarding God objectively. If God is not an object, then God cannot exist in an object domain or in an object relations theory. If conceptual a/theism cannot but seek objective proofs regarding God matters, proofs cannot be about the living God (cf. Marion, 1991:32f.). It is this *religious* hiddenness or, better, absence of the objective God (the true twilight of idols), Kierkegaard's objective uncertainty of faith, that positive conceptual a/theism as well as the moral "God" fail to appreciate. Nietzsche's "death of God" is quintessentially announced as a "Christian" event to Christian West, yet with the techno markets it has become globalized, or as Derrida (FaK 50) says, globalatinized or mondialatinized. If Christianity lives and dies with all versions of the death of God, announced in the Easter proclamation, "recalled by Kant to the modernity of the Enlightenment," and harnessed as Nietzsche's and Heidegger's non-Christian good news about the end of ontotheology, then Judaism and Islam are "two non-pagan monotheisms that do not accept death any more than multiplicity in God, two monotheisms still alien enough at the heart of the Graeco-Christian, Pagano-Christian Europe, the only forces that seem to resist the death of God" (51). Sacrilege at the highest altars of religion requires of the secular West, and increasingly of us all globally, that we relearn spiritual life otherwise than by relying on the conceptual a/theism or on moral postulates of "God." Many are today who suffer boredom, caducity, and melancholia (Marion, 1991:115–38), failing to rely even on existential anxiety to guide them with easy conscience through the world filled with artifacts of religious culture, institutions, and bankrupt traditions from which the gods have long fled.

I write from the perspective of someone born in a communist regime that proclaimed atheism as its state religion and who became a convert to Christianity against the oppressive state in my teens. Once in exile, I spent five years of my late twenties in the Jesuit order only to suffer a crisis of faith. In my forties I returned to religious questions after a decade of philosophical atheism as I belatedly discovered that I was the child of a Holocaust survivor; it has ceased to be crucial for me nowadays to articulate religious phenomena in terms of theism. Some will object that this makes my account of the religious vulnerable and weak. Is the religious that is not articulated as theism worthy of faith? I do not want to quibble over words. What I articulate here might come for some close to their living theism, and maybe some disenchanted theists will be free to think freshly about these matters.

Horkheimer, a neo-Marxist proponent of the Frankfurt School, after he returned from his U.S. exile to Germany, wrote in his 1963 essay, "Theism and Atheism," that both theism and atheism have their martyrs and tyrants. Ideology is a legion, and most theoretical integrations do not escape its cancer. We should not one-sidedly condemn the religious, but it is doubtful, at least historically, how good a fruit the concept cluster of "a/theism" produced. It is time to complete the quote from Benjamin (1968:256) that I cited earlier, "And just as such a document [of civilization] is not free of barbarism, barbarism taints also the manner in which it was transmitted from one owner to another."

The roots of the word "theism" are not without ambiguity. A quick perusal of linguistic and religious encyclopedias reveals that the word for God, *theos, thea,* which was used in the Greek New Testament text, was *a mere Greek word,* and was not used especially of the true God in heaven. There were many *theoi* in the Greek idol worship system, and even kings and others could be called *theoi.* The Greek *theos* was in no way "holy" as it had many kinds of uses, and it mostly referred to Greek idols. Christian rulers appropriated the ambiguous legacy of *theos* under the notion of the divine right of kings, and ever since the cults of personality and tyranny followed that dangerous route of political apotheosis. *Theos* was never a *personal* name of the God in heaven, just as little as the Germanic word *Gott* (*gut,* god) was. So historically the etymological linkage between "personal God" and "theism" is suspect on all fronts. The root meaning of the name "God" (from Gothic root *gheu*) is either "the one invoked" or "the one sacrificed to." *Deus* is the Latin translation from the Greek *theos.* The supreme *theos* among the many Greek (male and female) *theoi* was *Zeus* (genitive *Dios*), and he was possibly a wicked, diabolical *theos.* Italian, Spanish, and French words for "God" derive from this genitive form of the wicked *theos* Zeus (gen. form *Dios*), and not from the Greek *theos* or Latin *Deus* (Italian for God is *Il Dios*, Spanish *Dios*, French *Dieu*).

Most encyclopedias of religion derive the word "religion" from the Latin verb *religare*, to bind oneself back with piety to God. Lactanius, *Divine Institutes* 4.28, says, "We are tied to God and bound to Him *[religati]* by the bond of piety, and it is from this, and not as Cicero holds, from careful considerations *[relegendo]*, that religion has received its name." Augustine, *City of God* 10.3, writes, "Having lost God through neglect, we recover Him *[religentes]* and are drawn to Him." In *Retractions* 1.13, he endorses Lactanius's definition: "Religion binds us *[religat]* to the one Almighty God." Crucial for the one concerned with *personal* dimensions of religious life is, however, that the original etymological meaning of "religion" is an action verb, not a noun: *religare* denotes a way of life, not a doctrine or belief system. "To religion" is not the same as to "have" or "lose" a religion (as in the song by R.E.M.). One cannot "have" a religion; one can "be" or live religiously or in a religious way (Tao Te Ching: Tao is the Way; the Gospels: Jesus is the Way; Kierkegaard: Christianity is not a doctrine but existence-communication). The noun form of religion emphasizes the right (orthodox) doctrine versus the heterodox (heretical, deviant) one, or a correct proposition, or the evidential proofs for or against God's existence or attributes. I prefer speaking of "religiosity" as a way of spiritual self-transformation, not some fixed station. For this reason, I do not identify a *personal* God with holding to *theism*. Rather, the difference between verb and noun forms is obvious in their uses: "to religion" is to *inhere* in one's existence spiritually in every moment of life. "To be a theist or atheist," one espouses or rejects beliefs, one *adheres* to the right teaching (orthodoxy), one lives on the adopted conceptual plateau, one holds a doctrinal platform or plank, and so on (cf. Cooper, 1997).

Etymologically, an atheist is someone who does not believe in *theos*. In ancient times, I would be an atheist if I did not believe in the *theos* Zeus; in our times, an atheist is anyone who does not honor the gods of one's tribe or of the powers that be. A dissident in the Soviet regime with its divinized state communism was deemed by definition an *atheist*. By the same measure, a modern theist invoking God's name in every sentence could easily be an ideologue, nationalist, fundamentalist—a zealous adherent who has little in common with *religare*, the life of spiritual self-transformation. Atheism was Socrates' capital offense. Yet he, like religious Jews, prohibited the positive idols or images of the divine and so philosophically resisted idolatry. I embrace this nonidolatrous, (inter)*personal* sense of religiousness for which Socrates was considered to be an apostate of the state gods.

The happy error of mistaken identities that elevated Pseudo-Dionysius the Aeropagite to be viewed as an apostolic follower of St. Paul granted an almost scriptural authority to his writings on negative theology. For the Aeropagite, who wrote in medieval France, any theism stands on a negative ground that exceeds the positive. Luckily, even arguably the most rational of the medieval theists, St. Thomas Aquinas, cited Pseudo-Dionysius over a thousand times. I call my way of speaking a negative phenomenology of the religious, I invoke in my meditations a negative utopian hope, and I write here a genre of redemptive critical theory. I meditate on the negatively saturated phenomenon of radical evil, the excess of divine hiddenness. Meditation teaches not just how to pray but also how to invoke holy names without idolatry.

Practically, these meditations begin with the saturating postsecular "excess" that underwrites the uncanny public expectations of social theorists. Social thinkers and activists presuppose yet do not know how they get beauty or forgiveness that would grant injured communities a new hope in the aftermath of human atrocities. These meditations contribute to social-political and moral theory and empower waiting on hope among the fieldworkers.

Unlike thinkers who prefer to delete the word "evil" from political and religious vocabularies, I think that by understanding it better we can bring a margin of sanity into public matters. Terror emerges in the wake of the "death of God" and thus in existential despair over one's powerlessness in the face of tragedy.

Hopelessness has a Janus face: nostalgia for the passing away of time and future-oriented longing for lost innocence. Understanding the upsurge of hope and joy has a tremendous impact on the work of truth commissions. They form networks of solidarity working for and waiting on the impossible: sublime beauty, enchantment, a new beginning beyond the devastating historical situations.

There are unforgivable deeds. Cruelty cannot be legally redeemed by just punishment. As I heard one field-worker say, all social theory fails on the killing fields of Rwanda. All democratic theory presupposes but does not know how to achieve healing, how to purchase pardon and then blessing on a new start after acts of unforgivable cruelty.

Sorrow and mourning are politically and religiously manipulable. The standpoint of victims can be easily turned into a platform for revenge or holy war. Yet as both Benjamin and Adorno show, an intergenerational reconciliation contains messianic expectations. Memory work cannot give us back those who were annihilated, yet each act of coming to terms with the past—whether it is Daniel Libeskind's Jewish Museum in Berlin or his winning proposal for Ground Zero in New York—shapes the future present.

The postsecular economy of the "gift" corrects as well as restores exchange economies.

The book of meditations invites a response, not necessarily arguments; it is intended for edification, not for a library shelf or the accumulation of knowledge. That said, the book I have written moves back and forth between dialogues with various thinkers and positions and is a self-transformative journey of reflecting faith, hopeful witnessing, and love. The prose has a decidedly contemplative tonality, yet it also imparts a deeply activist tenor. I wish the reader some of the astonishing self-discovery I have made in my quest, that the more one delves into hidden and at times dark recesses of the human odyssey, the more audibly and persistently the beckoning of hope calls.

ONE

Job at Auschwitz

●

How do surviving neighbors continue to inhabit a village after they have engaged in deliberate acts of pillage, rape, and murder against one another, or stood by as others engaged in them? The space of our global village has grown fractured. Its lived time languishes in desperation. Another way of posing the opening question is, How do we apprehend that loss which humans experience as even more violent than material deprivation? Let us name this intractable dimension of loss the *scarcity of hope*.

Hope's disconsolation does not result from an ordinary loss of possibilities or from human demise. As difficult as disease and death can be, they do not of themselves produce this type of violence. Finitude and mortality motivate tears or inspire works of tragedy, but they do not yield the bitter fruit of hopelessness. That graver condition arises from a type of action that affects meaningful human flourishing at its heart. Lévinas (1983:160) reopens this wound of our age by raising anew Job's fundamental question; it "is no longer Leibniz's question *why is there something rather than nothing? But why is there evil rather than good?*" The past hundred years have provided spaces and times that have become thoroughly disconsolate. I take *Auschwitz* to be the single name that stands for all others—the gulags, Rwanda and Darfur, Sarajevo and Srebrenica, Kosovo and Grozny, the Twin Towers, to name the more notorious.

With Job in Auschwitz, we ponder in all times and places of scarce hope the same question. Nobody will deny nowadays that the phenomenon of lost hope exists globally, even though each case represents an event of a singular kind. Searching for intelligible meaning and human flourishing while abandoning any search for a theological theodicy, the secular mind-set has at its disposal no name for this type of injury. If there is a dimension of violence that injures the very capacity of humans to sustain free development—to hope—must we not speak of it boldly as an *aggravated scarcity of hope*?

Can life regain its innocence after a deep moral disaster? How can people come to terms with the truths of a criminal past without having to either reenact them or ignore the perpetrators, bystanders, and victims? How can one begin in time and space in which both reparative forgetting and remembering are required for restoring hope's living sense of innocence? This paradox of impossible hope marks memory as well as its mending. Can any mind, but especially the secular one, confront the aggravated scarcity of hope—that shattering anomie and entropy of possibility—without recourse to the uncanny?

I begin with Job in *Auschwitz,* meditating on the post-Holocaust horizon that challenges us to face evil and ask whether one can do so without despair. The following two chapters will take up anew the possibility of what I name the redemptive critical theory of hope. In part 2, I will ponder how it is possible at all to corrupt the hope dimension of time. This is why I depict radical evil in ways Kant dared not consider: inhumanity that aims to cleanse our lived time of its dimension of hope would also smother words and crack silence. In part 3, I will meditate on radical evil that, albeit no longer viewed as a privation of the good, parasitically draws its force from the uncanny.

KANT'S READING OF JOB

Kant (1973) considers all philosophical theodicies that rationally plead "God's cause" in face of both moral and physical evils to have failed. This is for Kant the failure of "a reason which presumptuously ignores its own limits in these matters" (283), but not of Job's "authentic theodicy" rooted in a faith response (291). Yet is not theodicy Job's prime temptation to explain away his suffering? Theodicy is offered in the guise of a God who bets with Satan about Job's fate; it is provided by Job's three friends who suggest, among other things, that there must be reasons for Job's suffering. Job is a happy and good father and member of his community who is stripped of his riches, health, and family. Only his believing conscience before God remains his own. However hard he protests his innocence, since he apparently has committed no crime, his friends comfort him by providing rational cause-and-effect explanations sought in views of divine justice that punishes our transgressions. He must have done something to justify the afflictions sent to torture him. In that Job rejects these explanations as less than honest, the projects of mythical or rational theodicies are revealed as presumptions to know God's ways. Job, while questioning the hidden God who does not respond to his appeals for justice, accepts his ordeal as God's decree. The God who finally answers Job is the Creator who now asks Job in turn, Where were you when I made heaven and earth? One cannot answer the Creator's rhetorical question, though in itself it does provide a form of self-justification—a theodicy.

In Kant's dramatization, Job handles his case right because he responds with faith rather than by seeking a rational evaluation of his ordeal. Kant's pietism sympathizes with Job's elemental conscience that eschews rational explanations of suffering in order to make room for faith. What Kant calls Job's "authentic theodicy" is "not an interpretation set forth by *ratiocinating* (speculative) reason but by an *authoritative* practical reason, which having in itself authority to legislate can be considered to be the immediate expositor and voice of God in charge of the interpretation of the book of creation" (291). As if anticipating Dostoyevsky's Grand Inquisitor who produces on God's behalf an anti-Job theodicy that allows humans to sin in exchange for their clear conscience, Kant writes, "If Job were to appear before some tribunal of dogmatic theologians, some senate or inquisition, some worthy presbytery or some high consistory today . . . he probably would have met with a worse fate." Kant's Job never receives a rational explanation of suffering but embraces a theodicy in the form of a faith response (293).

But must not even an "authentic theodicy" be an *impossible theodicy*? Neiman draws this paradoxical lesson when she, echoing Kant, notes that "God Himself condemns the impulse to theodicy, for He says that not the friends but Job spoke truth." Yet she concedes that our spiritless age is unable to live without some source of meaningful hope. "Job's speeches are no systematic justification but a response to the same impulse that gives rise to theodicy: the need to face evil in the world without giving in to despair" (2002:291). Neither modern reactions to the Lisbon earthquake of 1755 nor post-Holocaust thinkers seem to find hope without meeting the *deep-seated need to face evil without despair.* Don't we need and desire something impossible?

What seems impossible is a rational formula underwriting any, even an authentic, theodicy.

In what sense does the biblical story embrace a Kantian, authentic faith theodicy? Goodhart (1996:168–212, 2005) in his fine commentary on Job drives home the rabbinical intent for including this text among the twenty-four books of the Hebrew Scripture: the book of Job dramatizes four failed theodicies. They correspond to what Martin Buber (1982:188–98; Goodhart, 1996:174–82; and 2005) identifies as four idolatrous sketches of God: *a mythic theodicy* with the God who spars with Satan about Job, *a theodicy of sin* of Job's three friends, Job's own *negative theodicy*, or what Goodhart labels an atheist theodicy of social justice, and an *elemental creationist theodicy* with the rhetorical accusation against Job. Unlike Kant's rationalized Job tucked within the bounds of pietist morality, the biblical Job only gets negative answers. He finds no rationale for his suffering or evil in the world, for, as Goodhart (2005) notes, "all of the explanations are forms of accusation." Deconstructing four failed theodicies can have but one edifying purpose, defining the Judaic faith as the "law of anti-idolatry," warning that "Jews have become non-Jews," that "Judaism understood as the law of anti-idolatry is absent." If we ask with Goodhart, What is the core of the commandments? we step beyond Kant's announcement of the failure of all philosophical theodicies to his failure of ascribing to Job a religious theodicy bound within the horizon of the possible for the sake of rational faith. "To question suffering as a problem," Goodhart warns, "is to question Judaism, to question the law of anti-idolatry, to question creation itself, which is constituted in Judaism as a response to that problem." Goodhart (1996: 180f.) finds the earnest biblical message about human suffering addressed to the lament of God's hiddenness:

> We must function *as if* there is no God, as if all responsibility for human behavior and human relations falls upon man himself. . . . The hidden God, . . . far from a stumbling block to Job's lament, is in fact its very answer, an answer we may want to argue God explicitly reveals by appearing to offer Job the discourse of His otherness, His exteriority to man. . . . The Answer to Job's question . . . is Judaism itself. The God of the sufferers (to use Buber's phrase) is the Jewish God, and has in fact never been other.

Lévinas (1988:161) prompts us to read Job from Auschwitz and from there to embrace our radical responsibility for the world and one another. Auschwitz has definitively ended all theodicies of the God who rewards good and punishes evildoers. Lévinas accepts Nietzsche's word that "God is dead" insofar as it refers to the childish notions of God deconstructed in the book of Job. A certain salutary atheism links Job to Lévinas, yet this linkage appears at first as a dialectical atheism. Lévinas affirms the radically transcendent God, the one we might apprehend as absent and shrouded in divine incomprehensibility (hence the Judaic prohibition on idols). At times hidden and dark, and other times incomprehensible and transcendent, Lévinas's God is present as a trace in our care for the neighbor. This core religious intuition is shared by Jews and Christians in the second central biblical commandment, the love of neighbor. Kierkegaard is as ethico-religious here as Lévinas and Buber, and all three, while espousing the prophetic ethics of neighborly love, teleologically suspend (critically apprehend) the Hegelian communitarian social ethics, or what Heidegger would call the third-person perspective of the conventional "they." With the biblical Job rather than Kant's, Lévinas considers not just Leibniz's attempt in 1710 but any rational or religious theodicy to be a "temptation" (Bernstein, 2002: 169). Lévinas's "why is there evil rather than good?"—moving from theodicy to responsibility—defines our troubling times (2002:166–83; Neiman, 2002:291).

An intuition that radical evil is becoming the defining question of our times haunts many post-Holocaust thinkers. Arendt (1965) became famous with her controversial thesis about the "banality of evil" with which she describes Eichmann's duty-bound comportment and pseudo-Kantian conscience during his trial in Jerusalem. Evil's banality was supposed to preclude eulogizing an evil genius, and this is what originally worried Jaspers, who used the notion of "banality" in his letter to Arendt in 1946 (Arendt, 1992:62). But its banality was also to drive the nail through the coffin of all theodicies. Neiman (2002:302f.) begs to differ with Arendt on this. Calling evil banal offers at once "a piece of moral rhetoric" and also "the aestheticization of evil as one way to respond to the absurd. . . . To call evil banal is to offer not a definition of it but a theodicy." Arendt hoped that if evil could be stripped of its inscrutability and magnitude, rendered finite and boring, we would grasp and face it without despair. Arendt's demythologizing intent was to view even radical evil as banal in some sense.

Arendt (1994:134), like Lévinas, views the twentieth century through the prisms of the problem of evil. Kant's pious admission of Job's authentic religious theodicy—and the suffering Job would be relating to God in this way according to some rabbinical readings—seems just as hopeless as it is impossible to philosophically justify at Auschwitz. Pressing the critical side of Kant, Neiman (2002:314–28) concludes that in facing evil without despair we might be regenerating a continually secular need of theodicy if not of finite theism. "The impulse to theodicy is not a relic of monotheism but goes deeper than either. Indeed, it is part of the same impulse that leads to monotheism itself" (318). If the collapse of all attempted philosophical theodicies were to lead to a failure of comprehending evil, then, she submits, we would abdicate honest, nondespairing ways of facing evil (325). This thought concedes much to Kant's Job.

We stand between the relentless, critical drive of reason for the unconditioned and the law of anti-idolatry that prohibits all positive representations of the redemptive. Reason demands answers to all relevant questions in search of the unconditioned in which it could rest its quest. The monotheistic prohibition of idolatry, as in genuine Buddhism, proscribes divinity that could be paraded as an object, conceived of as an answer to arguments or problems. Between a critical redemptive theory of hope and prohibitions of its positive images, what must our honest, nondespairing response to evil be? It benefits us to meditate on hope available in the secular milieu. Jonas formulates an impossible, desert-like theodicy; thinkers in the early Frankfurt School of social criticism introduced in dialectical atheism a possibility of redemptive critical theory.

IMPOSSIBLE THEODICY

Buber (1993:178) poses the question most poignantly for the survivors of Auschwitz by identifying them with "the Job of the gas chambers": "How is it still possible to live with God in a time in which there is Auschwitz?" Jonas (1996:133) reveals Job's "paradox of paradoxes":

> it *was* the ancient people of the "covenant," no longer believed in by those involved, killers and victims alike, but nevertheless this and no other people, under which the fiction of race had been chosen for this wholesale annihilation—the most monstrous inversion of election into curse, which defied all possible endowment with meaning.

Every theodicy, even the authentic one praised by Kant, of a God who would consent to Auschwitz or its continuing incarnations would seem to both a critical and a pious mind to be nothing but perverse. To answer Job from Auschwitz, while not giving up on God altogether, Jonas decides to square the circle of theism and atheism. He requires of us nothing less than to rethink God otherwise than presented under the guise of the Lord of history who is an omnipotent sovereign.

Jonas brings us to two intuitive openings. In the first he adopts the prophetic voice of Etty Hillesum (1984); in the second he conjures up the myth of a self-limiting God. Hillesum was a young Dutch Jew who went of her own will in 1942 to the Westerbrook concentration camp in order to partake in the suffering of her people. She died in the Auschwitz gas chamber in 1943. Jonas (1996:192) cites her diary testimony:

> I will go to any place on this earth where God sends me, and I am ready in every situation and until I die to bear witness . . . that it is not God's fault that everything has turned out this way, but our fault. . . . And if God does not continue to help me, then I must help God. . . . That is the only thing that matters: to save in us, O God, a piece of yourself.

Inspired by her, Jonas narrates the myth of a suffering, becoming, and caring God. Rather than borrowing from the Christian myth of the suffering God, Jonas retells the Kabbalistic myth of the intelligible Creator who gives up power in order to suffer with all creation. Not unlike Whitehead's Christian process God, who is our fellow sufferer, Jonas's God, now revealed to Jews from Auschwitz, "abandoned Himself and his destiny entirely to the outwardly exploding universe and thus to the pure chances of the *possibilities* contained in it under the conditions of space and time." This deity "had to renounce His own power," and with it went out the classical attribute of omnipotence (189f.). "In the beginning," Jonas mythologizes, "for unknowable reasons, the ground of being, or the Divine, chose to give up itself to the chance and risk an endless variety of becoming." In an ongoing *kenosis,* God has been "effacing himself for the world" (134). Creation "involved suffering on the part of the God" who is "a *becoming God* . . . emerging in time . . . and affected by what happens in the world" (136f.)

Self-limiting divinity is really related to its creation, and so "bound up with the concept of a suffering and a becoming God is that of a *caring God*" (138). God who cares also suffers. God's suffering is "useless" (Lévinas, 1988) in the very same sense as all suffering of the innocent victims of history. Yet in God's co-responsibility for Creation this suffering is redemptive without underwriting another theodicy. In this koan of useless-because-unjust suffering of the innocent and redemptive-messianic suffering of those who have become responsible, whose messianic power has been expected by the previous suffering generations, lies a hidden key for the rapprochement between the Jewish law of anti-idolatry and low Christology. By low Christology I mean Jesus who just like Job in refusing all theodicy reveals the God of Abraham, Isaac, and Jacob. This God of whom Hillesum (1984, in Jonas, 1996:192) demanded "no account" is powerless. This God is unlike Kant's Job and unlike God the Creator who speaks to Job about the beginnings of the universe. This God is a suffering, becoming, and powerless God who "cannot help" but through, what Václav Havel discovered in the dissident years, the power of the powerless. Humans must redeem and protect the divinity of God within them, and must in turn help God be God (cf. Gross, 1992; Moltmann, 1967; Wiesel, 1990).

Inspired by Hillesum, Jonas demands no positive theodicy, "knowing there is no *proof* of God" (1996:132). I venture to call his myth—seeking the intelligibility of a good God in the face of evil beyond the drive of relentless reason for the unconditioned—an *impossible theodicy.* If not Kant, certainly Plato allowed us to take recourse in the imaginary domain beyond the sphere of the knowable (134). "Only a completely unintelligible God can be said to be absolutely good and absolutely powerful, yet tolerate the world as it is" (139).

What can lift an existential sense of our "cosmic loneliness" (196) side by side with the God who may not be powerful enough to redeem us if we fail to save "a piece of God" in us? One can hear distant echoes of Sartre that even if God existed it would make no difference to our responsibility, indeed even if C. S. Lewis's science fiction were true and incarnations of God occurred on other planets, it would make "no difference at all" to know there is other life in the universe (195). We can know honestly only one thing for sure, "that with us and in us, in this part of the universe and at this moment of our fateful power, the cause of God trembles in the balance." This "wager of creation" poses an existential either/or: in us creation will "either be preserved or betrayed" (197).

On the other side of Job's demand, there arrives a Pelagian temptation to replace God, to suffer the hubris of an Atlas who thinks humans can carry the world from which God is absent or hidden. Jewish thinkers who imagined a finite, becoming, suffering God who now needs our help offer one way of taking the burden off Job's shoulders without demanding a positive theodicy. Jonas turns the demand for intelligibility into an *impossible theodicy.* Following the same Platonic license for mythologizing beyond the known, going with Jonas beyond Jonas, I venture with a Judaic reading of the Christian finite prototype of the suffering God. In a similar venture, Kierkegaard's pseudonyma often reinvent Christianity within Christendom. With Jonas we return to Job only to rediscover the Lévinasian infinite responsibility for the world and one another. Therein lies the core Judeo-Christian commandment to love God in loving one another. Our love is under injunction to imitate the suffering, becoming, powerless God. God's suffering could be redemptive for us not vicariously, as if a powerful God magically bore evil and pain for us from some omnipotent stance of indifference, but rather that we are to become, suffer, and care as God does. Low Christology at once rejects theodicy and defends the Jewish law of anti-idolatry (cf. Metz, 1995; Schuster, 1999).

I will take up Schelling's myth about God and human freedom, which anticipates as well as parallels Jonas's myth, when I turn to radical evil in Kant and Kierkegaard in part 2. Suffice it to say here that it was Schelling who brought the Jewish Kabbalah into the Protestant philosophy of German idealism (Cahnman, 1981; Scholem, 1991:56–88; Rosenzweig, 2005: 25, 34). Kabbalistic wisdom inspired Jonas's (1996:142f.) myth about God after Auschwitz. The Lurianic Kabbalah operates with the notion of *tzim-tzum* whereby the infinite Creator (Ein Sof) withdraws and self-contracts in order to make room for the "Nothing" out of which God creates the world. Jonas extends the Kabbalistic contraction of the Infinite in order to define the core of divine power. What remains the heart of the human-divine relations is our task, as if redemption of the world depended on us. The Pelagian (or Sartrean) temptation of the desire to be God, and the parallel desire for positive theodicy, is averted when God is revealed as powerless. With Camus, at the end of his *Rebel,* we can now say that none of us is omnipotent. Jonas insists that both his and Job's answers to the question of evil actually praise God. Job praises God's creative power, Jonas (1996) praises the Creator's self-renunciation of power for the sake of creation. "This, too, so it seems to me, is an answer to Job: that in him God himself suffers" (143).

Lawrence Vogel's introduction to Jonas (1996) helps us discern with greater nuance how Jonas's answer could satisfy Neiman's demand (that we face evil without giving in to despair) and yet do so without the need for even Kant's authentic or her secular theodicy:

> Like Jonas, Hillesum answers Job's question by invoking the chosen avoidance, not plenitude, of God's power. But this radical version of *tzimtzum* is a song of praise, not despair, for God suffers with the victims of injustice as He hands responsibility over to us that we may complete His work. (26)

The gratuitous suffering of innocents is not something to be intellectually explained but rather borne by our coresponsibility. A self-transformative response to the divine *tzimtzum* (withdrawal from power) is human *teshuvah* (return to one's true self). Return to oneself heralds at the same time return to God. Yet return to God marks neither an answer to a syllogism nor an outcome of a proof, nor is the terminus identifiable with the unconditioned of reason's search for intelligibility. In our *teshuvah* of self-transformative responsibility for one another, the divine *tzimtzum* reveals the all-powerful Creator as hidden, dark, and incomprehensible.

It is from this Judaic critique of power and sacrificial violence that low rather than triumphant Christology draws its genuine inspiration. Goodhart's (1996:186) reflections on Job and René Girard conclude as much: "If Jesus is particularly powerful for us . . . it is because he is 'prophetic' in the Jewish sense, because he shows us where our violence is leading . . . because he announces the end of the sacrificial and violent road upon which we are traveling." Or said in words that go to the heart of Judaism: Job's genuine problem is "idolatry, namely, that sooner or later, all social structures, all sacrificial structures, will become identical with violence." We must thus read Job as announcing "the law of anti-idolatry" and offering an "ethical response" to suffering (199). Post-Holocaust ethico-religious and social thought, whether secular or religious, Judaic or Christian, gathers from Job the following core intuition: *If God is not an object in the world, some theism or Buddha to be proved or disproved, how could evil ever be an evidential (accusatory) argument against God rather than a matter of responsibility left for us?*

HOW IS SECULAR HOPE POSSIBLE
AFTER THE "DEATH OF GOD"?

In the philosophical memoir to her father's death in Auschwitz, Kofman's (1998) words suffer from lack of air. Smothered words express the unspeakable. *The* disaster (i.e., the Holocaust) is made of something unutterable and unimaginable yet lived through. What can neither be spoken of nor imagined, that cannot even take up its temporal beginnings.

> Knotted words, demanded and yet forbidden, because for too long they have been internalized and withheld, which stick in your throat and cause you to suffocate, to lose your breath, which asphyxiate you, *taking away the possibility of even beginning.* (39; italics added)

The disaster: When one cannot begin in innocence and live in one's historical time and space without experiencing a wretchedly disconsolate existence. Kofman's biographical lamentations express *an aggravated scarcity of hope;* that hope's radical disaster names "radical evil":

> Since Auschwitz all men, Jews (and) non-Jews, die differently: they do not really die; they survive death, because what took place—back there—without taking place, death in Auschwitz, was worse than death. . . .
>
> Because he was a Jew, my father died in Auschwitz: How can it not be said? And how can it be said? *How can one speak of that before which all possibility of speech ceases?* (9; italics added)

Describing incommunicable hopelessness, one does more than circumscribe the ontological condition of one's finitude or anxiety of one's being toward death:

> How then can one tell that which cannot, without delusion, be "communicated"? That for which there are no words—or too many—and *not because the "limit-experience" of infinite privation, like all other experiences, cannot be transmitted?* How is it possible to speak, when you feel a "frenzied desire" to perform an impossible task. . . . *Impossible, without choking.* (38; italics added)

In describing her smothered words, Kofman becomes a second-order witness of her father:

> *Auschwitz:* the impossibility of rest. My father, a rabbi, was killed because he tried to observe the Sabbath in the death camps; buried alive with a shovel for having—or so the witnesses reported—refused to work on that day, in order to celebrate the Sabbath, to pray to God for them all, victims and executioners, reestablishing, in this situation of extreme powerlessness and violence, a relation beyond all power. (34)

Yet her smothered speech breaks the suffocating silence. On the nether side of hope's scarcity, she is speaking the unspeakable (*chashmal,* from Hebrew, *chash*—silent, *mal*—to speak) in the silences and words of a witness.

To speak: it is necessary—without (the power): without allowing language, too powerful, sovereign, to master the most aporetic situation, absolute powerlessness and very distress, to enclose it in the clarity and happiness of daylight. (10)

Kofman refuses the death of the story, poetry, philosophy, ordinary speech acts. In all modes of speaking, she refuses the entropy of hope choked in disasters. She refuses hopelessness by invoking "a duty to speak, to speak endlessly for those who could not speak because they wanted to safeguard true speech against betrayal" (36).

Profane Illumination of Hope

On the level of ordinary lived experience, the central question arises for democratic and liberation theorists who are faced with the historical instances of hope lost. How are political ideals of cosmopolitan citizenship or the economic ideals of redistributing goods even thinkable in the same time and space occupied by the experience of disaster? Must not *here and now* all our attempts to overcome disastrous memory become in turn disastrous forms of progress drenched in shameful forgetting of victims? How is hope, once it has been lost, found? The twentieth-century variations of the Adorno-Benjaminian question, What does coming to terms with the past mean? have been repeatedly brought to the order of the day. Confronted with a disastrous past, we are questioning concerning our hope now (Adorno, 1986). Will questioning that comes to terms with lost hope prepare us for the possibility of hope now? Preparatory questioning of lost hope is not yet the granting of hope.

Hope is indispensable for the projects of human flourishing. Secular thinkers of hope associated with the Frankfurt School of social criticism in the early part of the twentieth century knew as much. Bloch (1959), who was not a member of the Frankfurt Institute, wrote several volumes on the principle of hope. A materialist, Bloch wrote of hope after the "death of God": "Hope is able to inherit those features of religion which do not perish with the death of God." Bloch's decidedly secular theorizing of hope does not build on theism, and with the exception of the Christian theology of Tillich and the materialist Jewish theology of Benjamin, a secular angle of vision seems to guide all Jewish thinkers from the Frankfurt School, from Horkheimer and Adorno to Marcuse. Even Habermas, who comes from a Protestant home, inherits this search for hope along with the Judaic prohibition on the carved images of God. Bloch's principle of hope arises from a secular meditation on material scarcity. Akin to the Latin American theologians of liberation and Marx's own critical relation to the religious lamentations of suffering, Bloch's hope is to resist ideology. "Where there is hope there is religion, but where there is religion there is not always hope: not the hope built up from beneath, undisturbed by ideology" (Bloch 1972:272f., from Mendieta, 2005:50f.). The messianic Judaism of the atheistic theologians of suspicion and hope—that vintage negative theology of critical theory *avant* Derrida's *impossible* religion without religion—permeates Bloch's relation to Christianity when he says that "only an atheist can be a good Christian; only a Christian can be a good atheist" (Bloch, 1972:9; from Mendieta, 2005:11).

Yet it was Benjamin's negative materialist theology of anamnestic and messianic hope (hope of remembrance and expectation) that had perhaps the most profound impact on the atheistic-cum-redemptive strain of critical theory in Adorno and Marcuse, as well as late Horkheimer. Two sources of his thought are pivotal for my meditation on the possibility of redemptive critical theory. First, there was Benjamin's famous letter exchange with Horkheimer from March 16, 1937, whether or not history is complete, whether or not the past is closed and the victims of history are without hope (Benjamin, 1999:471, N8, 1). Second, there are Benjamin's "Theses on the Philosophy of History" (1968). Benjamin sought a "profane illumination" (Tiedemann, 1999:934) in order to transform the secular domain of history and rescue the passing away of time with something akin to religious illumination or awakening. In his corrective to early Horkheimer's objection that "past injustice has occurred and is completed. The slain are really slain," Benjamin held that "in remembrance we have an experience that forbids us to conceive of history as fundamentally atheological, little as it may be granted us to try to write it with immediately theological concepts" (1999:471, N8, 1).

In this materialist mysticism of time and history Benjamin passes near the genuine spiritual insight that the past is never past. Though it is doubtful that as a materialist he would have meant it in the pregnant spiritual sense of self-transformation whereby, as Ezekiel prophesied, the dry bones will rise and so the past will be resurrected. Our generation must exercise the healing of *tikkun olam* of the Lurianic Kabbalah, or as Benjamin wrote (1968:254f.), make whole by "a *weak* Messianic power, a power to which the past has a claim." That claim to healing and blessing (*berakhah/barakah*) may be *redeemed* by *our* acting in the now-time, whereby we rescue the hope of preceding generations. Only thus we become endowed with "the gift of fanning the spark of hope in the past," that is, if we become "firmly convinced that *even the dead* will not be safe from the enemy if he wins."

Because transformative or messianic time is neither cosmological nor linear, and so "chips of Messianic time" become "the time of the now" (263), redemptive hope cannot be ascribed to historical progress. Redemptive time cannot be projected as a positive utopia or party program either. To what degree the now-time could be identified with a historical revolution or national Zionism, on this late Horkheimer might differ from Benjamin. Yet any gate, not just the ones prescribed by historical and dialectical readings of the forces of production and material history, "every second of time" can be the "straight gate" through which messianic transformation enters our existence (264), which Benjamin admits in his revisions of utopian socialists, Marx, and social democracy alike (256f., 1999:944).

Secular Assumptions of Hope

Could human flourishing get off the ground without hope? Would it continue? It all depends on hope that *our* coming to terms with historical and future presents is possible. Do not democratic and liberation theorists tend to assume this hope as always and already settled without considering it on its own terms? The presumption of theoretical innocence overlooks how the scarcity of hope threatens *our* democratic and cosmopolitan projects of recognition and redistribution. This is the unaccounted presumption of a social theorist: that liberation is possible after disasters with which we have burdened our time and place. "Where we perceive a chain of events, . . . [Angelus Novus] sees one single catastrophe which keeps piling wreckage upon wreckage and hurls it in front of his feet. The angel would like to stay, awaken the dead, and make whole what has been smashed. But a storm is blowing from Paradise. . . . That storm is what we call progress" (Benjamin, 1968:257f.). How honest is the celebrated "death of God" with its presumption of innocence in social theory? Does the secular mind take for granted the possibility of hope? "The concept of historical progress of mankind cannot be sundered from the concept of its progression through a homogeneous, empty time. A critique of the concept of such a progression must be the basis of any criticism of the concept of progress itself" (261).

Sustained Scarcity of Hope

Hope's lived *scarcity,* to borrow Sartre's language of the material scarcity of goods in order to speak about hope (Sartre, 1976; Catalano, 1986), has been sustained by the contingencies of our history. This scarcity has been entrenched by our practices, and this experience of hope lost has taken on a form of something almost historically necessary. Hope is scarce not merely because of some basic (ontological) sense of finitude and mortality; hope has become scarce because we have made it rare in history and sustained its scarcity by our praxis. The practico-inert weight of unfree history and victimage of the innocents is not just some entropic *khôra* but rather an unhappy fruit of human praxis. One does not sing a Magnificat at its annunciation, yet one does not need to yield to its mute nothingness either.

Hope is not available to our mastery as the ongoing projects of human history are. If hope could be equally distributed to all, then one could safeguard speech against betrayal by appealing to democratic procedures. One could take recourse to an ethic of discourse with its symmetrical conditions of raising and evaluating validity claims. One could even appeal to cosmopolitan world citizenship. But the blindness of social and political theory—albeit written *with illocutionary power*—is revealed in its presumed innocence. This presumption is dangerous. The illocutionary power of speech, when blind to its conditions of possibility, betrays victims of history with a kiss. The blindness consists in embracing the progress in history. No wonder Benjamin did not hesitate to unmask this naive belief in progress as our democratic disaster. For him, then, hope (if it is given in the first place) must rescue us from all naive senses of progress.

Praying for a Good Death

Horkheimer, who late in life reversed his opposition to Benjamin's thinking, wrote in 1963 (1974) that "if the great had taken the conflict of Christianity and Christendom as seriously as Kierkegaard did in the end, there would exist no monument of Christian culture." Herein lies the salutary sense of the "death of God," the good death that Kierkegaard would share with Nietzsche and they both would share with the thinkers of the Frankfurt Institute. This sense is salutary in the same way it can be redemptory in its critique of the present age. Horkheimer deconstructs the "opposition between theism and atheism" in order to drive home their very alliance. Atheists profess courage to think critically during periods of authoritarianism, yet it is "honest theism" that overtakes that very role in totalitarian regimes. Both theism and atheism, he says famously, have not only their martyrs but also their tyrants. Theism can support temporal injustice, just as atheism can thwart hope in the wholly other than this unjust world. "Dialectical atheism" no longer abuses the religious because its critical thorn is more akin to the unmasking of failed theodicies in the book of Job. Dialectical atheists and Job at Auschwitz share a negatively utopian pessimism by adhering to the Judaic law of anti-idolatry. Harnessing the commandment against idolatry, critical theory holds some crucial keys to redemptive possibilities: *Unlike the utopian and state socialists, thou shalt not profess a positive material utopia! Against the conservative status quo, thou shalt critique relentlessly falsely positive utopian hopes! Against hope lost, thou shalt hope for the wholly other than this unjust world!*

Speaking to Speak

Kofman makes trouble for democratic and liberation theorists: What is the speech that smothers and betrays true speech? Which speech restores speakability and imagination to our interruptions, silences, and words? I trace unspeakability and unimaginability to what I named a sustained scarcity of hope. Meditating on hope's scarcity exposes a certain blindness in critical theory even as it holds some keys to redemptive possibilities.

> To speak in order to bear witness. But how? How can testimony escape the idyllic law of the story? How can one speak of the "unimaginable"—that very quickly became unimaginable even for those who had lived through it—without having recourse to the imaginary? (Kofman, 1998:36)

Against the blind power of speech, the illocutionary "hell of language" and the "betrayals of the 'true speech'" (42), Kofman invokes the "ethical exigency" of witnessing the "silence of those who could not speak." A witness speaks and writes "without power" (41). A witness restores the validity basis to language. Witness's silence restores the once betrayed binding power of speech (*chashmal*).

Inertia or Reversibility of Hopelessness?

An open question posed for my first series of meditations by secular social theorists Sartre and Marcuse is the degree to which sustained material scarcity is reversible and to which its inertia has, so to speak, become our second nature. If we accentuate the conservative status quo, the notion of inertia, then possibilities of genuine existential freedom and social liberation (redeeming another human future than our historical present) are nil. If we stress the possibility of reversal, then we must account for its conditions under sustained scarcity. Our untimely meditation applies this double-edged insight to the phenomenon of impossible hope. Halfway hope is like a part-time lover. Hope against the scarcity of hope already refuses hopelessness. Any crack in the inertia already partakes of that new human sensibility of reversal.

When hope is assumed by the secular social theorists and so intoned as cheap grace, to paraphrase Dietrich Bonhoeffer, does this not beg the question of its initial possibility? Or to invoke Benjamin (1968:254), the "weak" power of anamnestic or messianic solidarity of the present generations with hope of the past generation, "that claim cannot be settled cheaply." How is hope possible for us now—any now? The secular visionary of hope in new sensibility, Marcuse, harkened to Benjamin who in one of the most disastrous moments in our modern history, in the era when the Nazis made a pact with Soviet power, invoked hope for the sake of those without hope (Marcuse 1991:257). Though he was a tough secular optimist, Sartre likewise invoked "hope now" (1996) against worries of fraternal and revolutionary terror; he designated it as the ethical heart of human flourishing. The issue of hope lost and found that stands before us is not an empirical or applied one. So it cannot be solved after normative theory has been put in place. This is why *postsecular* meditations on hope after the "death of God" function as a prolegomena to thinking about the future of human flourishing. Their untimeliness lies in questioning of the secular ethical heart, questioning concerning hope's aggravated scarcity.

THE SARTREAN CHALLENGE

I continue with a phenomenological questioning concerning hope found and hope lost. Since material scarcity is a key notion in both Sartre and Marcuse, their secular considerations provide a good entry into meditation on the scarcity of hope. But if scarcity refers to basic material needs, how can we apply it to intangibles such as hope? The Sartrean challenge will yield fruit only if we can establish such a link. The tension between material and spiritual dimensions of scarcity is already apparent in the expression "postsecular meditations" with which I approach these secular social theorists.

Sartre (1976:122–52; Catalano, 1986:108–16, 245, 255, 262, 266) distinguished between abstract material scarcity, resulting from the given finitude of goods and human life, and sustained material scarcity, which is brought about by human praxis in human history as we know it. The scarcity of finitude is necessary for the type of existences we are and for the concrete material world we inhabit. I call it ontological scarcity. The sustained scarcity is more paradoxical: it did not have to come about (it is contingent in principle). Yet it always already appears necessary in human practice (it seems to us as if it were just as necessary as death).

We can conceive of a possible world in which the material finitude of goods and human mortality could lead to mutual cooperation rather than strife. This imaginary meditation allows us to distinguish the two levels of material scarcity. But *our* lived history has never evolved outside of the conditions of material scarcity and the human struggle against it. And so the meditation on human progress prompts us to collapse the two levels of material scarcity. Strictly speaking, only the abstract level of scarcity is ontologically necessary, while sustained scarcity is principally contingent and yet paradoxically *becomes necessary* in a concrete historical sense.

When we ponder the fruit of both meditations, we reach a new level of awareness. Sustained scarcity has become and remains historically necessary, but only in our free praxis that has always already confronted the established conditions of scarcity. The history of struggle against scarcity and of humans struggling against one another in its milieu created that second necessity of sustained scarcity. The past praxis of sustained scarcity confronts our present freedom with a counterfinality and, if you will, an inertia fashioned out of our historical strife. Our freedom runs against the record of noncooperative struggle against scarcity. In our experience, human freedom, just like Kofman's words, is often choked by this weight of history.

Enter all secular appeals to the historical evidence of human failure: Are human flourishing and liberation all but impossible? Must the forces of counterfinality and inertia prevail over the projects of human flourishing in liberation struggles, in existing socialisms or democracies? In their skepsis, secular critical and postmodern theorists reinvent the notion of original sin; in their assumption of cheap grace they reinvent shortcuts to redemption. *Khôra* names something like the scene of original sin-consciousness. Yet this is the desert not of desert-fathers but Derridean desert of desert without any name to invoke in prayer. Still more, this denegation of the redemptory does not necessarily save the name of possible liberation, it only faintly hopes to leave the spacing of space open. The price to be paid is to concede the last word to the aporetically impossible, that cold nothingness which does not even stir up in us the self-transcending anxiety of creative possibility (cf. Caputo, 1997:37).

The question concerning the inhumanity of sustained scarcity goes to the heart of the liberation and democratic projects of human flourishing. Let us say that we can distinguish with Sartre between the two dimensions of scarcity. The one dimension is necessary in the ontological sense. Here I can meditate on the realization that I am not God, my experience of space and time is finite, we all are mortal beings, and the earth has limited resources. The other dimension has become necessary by our historical praxis and its temporal character. Here I learn to meditate on the failure of freedom to sustain human flourishing.

What Is to Be Done? First, Hope!

The issue before us remains how our existential freedom and social liberation are possible at all, given the inhuman praxis that we confront in the sustained scarcity of our lived history. It is the struggle against the oppressive division and distribution of the given material scarcity that affects our collective meaning- and will-formation from within. Benjamin spoke of disaster within the very notion of historical progress. With this questioning of social optimism he registered a keen sense of the inhuman counterfinality of historical time and space, a counterpraxis distorting our free and rational praxis. Appealing to an ethic and rationality of communication, to political struggles for recognition, or to economic struggles for redistribution—these appeals do not explain how freedom and liberation are possible in the first place. How do such appeals reverse counterfinality, inertia, and more aggravated counterpraxis? Such appeals to free and rational praxis must answer Sartre's deeper doubts about the vicissitudes of human freedom and rationality, about meaningful historical progress, and about the possibilities of liberation.

Once we are compelled to explain the very possibility of existential freedom and social liberation, satisfying our material needs turns on the question of hope: How can I act at all? In human freedom and rational praxis, starting with hope carries existential priority over dealing with actual material scarcity, since hope motivates the very possibility of satisfying material needs and acts against the weight of sustained scarcity. Freedom and hope are Janus-faced dimensions of possibility. Secular social theorists of material needs, revolution, utopia, regulative or other ideals are never entirely free to dispense with the intangibles of hope. If they do, they imbibe cheap grace. If hope is ignored at the material base of needs, how can free praxis reverse the inhuman inertia of history?

How Hope Disappears from Time and Space

Sartre's distinction between ontological and sustained scarcity becomes applicable to hope once it too is sought at the basis of material needs and not in some reality abstracted from existence. In our sense of time and space, we inhabit an ontologically necessary scarcity of hope. Since historical progress and consciousness of time are radically finite, both our remembering and forgetting are marked by irretrievable losses. Just as our finitude and death, so also time and space are vehicles of strict scarcity. In principle, it is possible for a human world to exist in which this sense of radical temporality could lead to cooperation. Yet the world we have fashioned in our time is marked by the struggle against the passing of time. Our praxis operates within historical time, which is always already lost to us in the counterpraxis of inherited history. This historical struggle weighs down our present human praxis of existential freedom and social liberation with an inhuman inertia. History becomes the key conduit to hope's disappearance from the world.

Remembering as well as forgetting become new vehicles of this counterfinality. Both remembering and forgetting contribute to sustaining the scarcity of hope. Nationalism and literalist religious integrations cluster around the counterfinality of institutional life and inhabit the practico-inert time. This temporal inertia is often fixed either through selective memory or by erasures of history. The cycles of counterpraxis build on one another, each aggravating the condition of sustained hopelessness as the nationalist, religious, democratic, and economic projects of human flourishing variously try to arrest the passage of time.

How Can Hopeless Inertia Reverse Itself?

The scarcity of hope is an outgrowth of human praxis anxious about the passing of time. This is not an abstract hopelessness or ontological anxiety about death, not even the desert of the desert, the nothingness of *khôra,* but rather hopelessness brought about by ethno-genocide, such as in Rwanda or Darfur. Since this contingent scarcity confronts us as something that has now become necessary, the question turns on how to struggle against our own praxis of hopelessness for another historical future present.

Sartre helps us differentiate ontological or abstract from sustained or historically concrete scarcity. I apply the notion of material scarcity to the scarcity of hope. While he might at times speak of necessary scarcity, this can be misleading in cases when Sartre means something contingent. Sustained scarcity *has become necessary* through free praxis. As paradoxical as any becoming of necessity might appear, Sartre shows that we confront its inhuman inertia not as some merely external obstacle to be removed or overcome by free praxis, but as the practico-inert resulting from our prior free counterpraxis (cf. Catalano, 1986:109).

The struggle for a more humane future cannot overcome finitude and death, and so cannot free mortals from the passage of time. Transcending all forms of inhuman scarcity may not imply becoming in time and space something other than human, finite, temporal beings either. Overcoming the scarcity of needs as well as of hope would require changing how we individually and socially apprehend our finite human existence and how we individually and socially pass through our material history and time. I meditate on that precise moment of possibility for self-transformation required for any lasting confrontation with all dimensions of material scarcity. This is the existential question that every social theorist must ask in order to motivate any other kind of change: How do we come to terms with the past that has injured our sense of hope and how do we begin innocently, albeit not naively, at our renewed beginnings?

THE MARCUSEAN REVERSALS

Sartre and Marcuse were preoccupied with material scarcity. Both also invoked hope by admitting the possibility that things could be otherwise. If hope were not conjured up even by secular thinkers, then, as Benjamin insists, there would be no way to cross the shadow of the past and win a new beginning. My meditation is postsecular and thus untimely in this precise sense. It witnesses the upsurge of hope where none can be theorized by a secular social theorist and historian who always already assumes it as something granted.

It is Marcuse who helps Sartre reverse sustained scarcity. Marcuse's innovation comes from his Marxist rereading of Freud. To be sure, these are equally paradoxically secular resources for generating hope. What further complicates this consideration is that Sartre was not very excited about psychoanalysis, and Marcuse, after his failed beginnings with Heidegger, seemed disenchanted with existential philosophy, even Sartre's. Yet for reversing sustained scarcity, a Marcuse-Sartrean, psychoanalytic-existentially inflected critical theory might be what the secular doctor ordered.

Enter Marcuse's advantage: an in-depth psychoanalytical dimension of existential freedom and social liberation allows him to develop a concrete dialectic of reversal. By the reversal I mean a new beginning (e.g., from hopelessness to hope). The inhuman praxis of counterfinality and inertia is overcome by the praxis of existential freedom and social liberation. But how? Let us dwell on this miraculous feat and witness the upsurge of hope.

Surplus Scarcity

Marcuse (1955) explains the reversal of inertia by distinguishing between necessary and surplus repression. By surplus repression he refers to an outgrowth of human history. What is historical, unlike the necessary repression we need vitally in order to perceive and pacify the terrifying cosmos, can be altered. Repression becomes surplus when it serves the systems of sociopolitical and economic organization of domination. Surplus is extracted by the logic of acquisition and its performance imperatives; and for Marcuse, surplus is extracted all the way down to the structure of sense experience, drives, needs, identity, and language formation. Opening up the free space of imagination (Marcuse's secular name for incarnate hope is a new sensibility), we can witness the upsurge of possibility and thus win the beginning for the reversal of sustained scarcity. By imaginatively conjuring up this free space uncontaminated by counterfinality, Marcuse unmasks the cultural spaces of the practico-inert or decadent praxis.

How can our free praxis further our own domination? What Sartre calls inhuman counterpraxis and Marcuse surplus repression can be rendered more intelligible with the notion of repressive desublimation. Marcuse elaborates this at greater length in *One-Dimensional Man.* Our freedom does not confront some external obstacle to itself, but rather runs into a structure of inertia that invades its willing as if from within. Marcuse explains what every marketing and political genius knows all too well: we are excited by ads promising us freedom and social liberation only to be offered a product to buy instead. The term "repressive desublimation" refers to arousal resulting from the shape and color or power of new cars; infantile arousal in response to the heavenly shapes and fragrances suggested by Victoria's Secret; or aggressive arousal by the moralized fragrances of surgically precise bombs. The repression of true needs and desires is the inner fabric of our sustained scarcity. Our free praxis is already, necessarily, repressive.

Self-Transformation for Liberation

Marcuse noticed the introjection of false needs, thereby articulating in repressive desublimation a secular equivalent of struggle within existential inwardness. Because of this discovery, he is keenly aware that no reversal can last without changing that repressive dimension of self. He envisions that an undoing of surplus repression requires the transformation of the entire mode of human existence. In this move he would be in agreement with Sartre, but only to make an even greater demand for this transformation to facilitate the reversal of sustained scarcity, which has become necessary in a derivative, that is, temporal and free sense.

Moving with Marcuse to Freudian interiority—and here I remain on strictly secular terrain—we may begin meditating with greater nuance. Now I introduce into Sartre's discussion of scarcity Marcuse's distinction between necessary and surplus repression. Necessary scarcity refers me to human finitude in the overwhelming universe; surplus scarcity defines the inhuman counterpraxis, which clusters around historical modes of life, culture, production. Marcuse allows me to imagine that a new structure of human needs could open up the possibility of a new sensibility. I move to creative imagination in order to break with the inertia of sustained scarcity and launch its reversal.

Marcuse's notion of great refusal embodies a form of free praxis with which we could struggle against the inertia of sustained or surplus scarcity. This refusal would begin to reverse the original project of human history—any performance built on organized scarcity. Sartrean hope remains silent about the form that human consciousness and embodiment could take outside of the context of scarcity. Must not a true end of our history signify a radical change in the mode of human existence? What this all comes down to is that sustained scarcity represents a repressive surplus that our historical praxis entrenched as its inhumanity. Awareness gained in this meditation reverses the view of the practico-inert *khôra* as a necessary Janus face of humanity.

Hope Now

Surplus scarcity clusters around necessary scarcity. Does unmasking the former eliminate the latter? By human necessity we can, strictly speaking, mean only finitude, death, and the passage of time. Sartre (1996:53–57) spoke on this in his last interviews with Benny Levy when he insisted on "hope now." In his impatience for freedom and liberation, Sartre joined Marcuse's Benjaminian invocation of hope given for the sake of those who live radically without it—who inhabit hope's scarcity. Sartre envisioned a human transformative project along two axes (91): in struggles against material scarcity and in our striving for ethical humanity. The scarcity of hope also clusters around two axes. We confront our striving for solidarity in its perverted forms as fraternal terror, and our struggle for material abundance strains against the historical conditions of sustained scarcity. Marcuse's vision of human flourishing intertwines freedom and necessity, play with work. He refuses surplus repression as something necessary. Both thinkers strive to reverse surplus scarcity because both begin to apprehend material scarcity as well as intangible scarcity through a dimension of "hope now."

THEODICY OF SCARCITY?

Commenting on Antelme's *The Human Race,* Kofman (1986) launches a phenomenology of Auschwitz that would allow her to come nearer to her father's life in the camp. She gropes for the margin of humanity. Speaking of Antelme's camp experience, she thinks of her father: "In all his time there, he never ceased experiencing what is possible for the human race, what is possible for it beyond all possibility: to remain men to the end" (57). Reduced to the basic biological functions of finding something to eat, of pissing and shitting--these "were ways of triumphing over the torturers who could not prevent these *acts* any more than they could prevent death" (65). At the latrines prisoners could find a rebellious freedom and solidarity: "It was the only place where he could feel free, linger for a moment without being watched. . . . The place, too, where he could exchange questions and answers with others, share with them some kind word . . . like someone who is not oneself and who does not threaten you, but responds" (65f.). For those who were excluded from all humanity, the defecating acts could express no greater abjection. Even abject humanity contains something akin to a phenomenological reduction to its own irreducibility—no matter that a human face was denied them by the torturers.

With Kofman we may meditate once more about the prisoner sitting in the camp latrine. The prisoner embodies a testament of hope by preserving the unity of the human race here and now. Kofman underscores the opposite of the sacrilegious. She does not mean by the ordinary the same as Arendt does by the banal. Rather, she witnesses to the uncanny at the site of the abject:

The joy of being in the latrines, beyond the reach of the Nazis, of escaping their power; the place, too, where this power was undermined, because there one could see them lose their pseudo-divinity and dignity . . . because they [Nazis] . . . did it [shitting] in an indecent way, showing off their strength, their fat thighs and their white undershorts. (66)

Neither demons nor gods, the circle of perpetrators and victims reveals their shared humanity and thus ultimately their powerlessness. "To give the name *man* to everything that assails him as if it were his fate, such was the last recourse that remained to the deportee" (69).

Salutary Atheism

How is a reversal of sustained scarcity possible and available to us in the first place? Neither Sartre's sobering challenge nor Marcuse's imaginary reversals ask this critical question. Neither the philosophical analysis of freedom nor the acts of great refusal explain the upsurge of hope. They presuppose theoretically what lived hope dramatizes. Democratic and liberation theorists assume that we can always already begin (i.e., hope now); they do not realize that hope cannot be taken for granted. Existentially and psychoanalytically inflected critical theorists unwittingly trust that we can reverse domination and achieve free beginnings in spite of scarcity; they do not reveal how hope is possible once it has been lost to us.

Since the turn of the past century we have been undergoing the persistent breakdown of any theodicy—a justification of divine goodness in the face of sustained scarcity—that could account for spirit in the world in the midst of human inhumanity and hopelessness. These meditations inevitably pass through an *a-theism* of those who have become responsible for the human history they make, for one another, one for the other. Lévinas wrote the most consistent meditation on this paradoxical atheism, teaching us to pass through our sustained scarcity of hope as a salutary bath in order to rediscover our difficult freedom. No longer intoning God's name as a prosthetic rescue from responsibility, one finds divine traces within the encounter with the other. When Lévinas struggles against inhumanity, he does more than rejuvenate Marx with an ethical heart; his impossible hope becomes even unlike that of Sartre—hope is an epiphany of the infinite. The ethical struggle for humanity is a spiritual matter because a Lévinasian reversal, unlike that of Marx, Sartre, or Marcuse, requires self-transformative transcendence. In Sartre's hope, one hears an echo of that false god who has been unmasked as humanity's useless passion for self-divinization. That echo brings back a theodicy of scarcity that wishes to postpone its own overcoming.

Can One Hope within a Thoroughly Secular Horizon?

The question of hope now does not cease to perplex me. How is its motion against scarcity, a kinesis for another future and for another beginning, possible, given the utter destruction of hope in the hell holes of human history? How does our free praxis move here and now given not only material immiseration but also disconsolation of so many people? Sartre and Marcuse invoked hope and a new sensibility, but did they explain their possibility? However innerworldly their hope might be, does it not express at its core another sensibility? Does not hope, to be worthy of its name, bespeak a postsecular promise? A new sensibility has antennas for uncanny promises. I do not fathom what it means to hope now in the midst of its scarcity. How do we struggle against our destructive historical praxis and inhumanity, that inertia haunting our present from the past, appearing as our future?

Hope passes through a Nietzschean atheism (that our disenchantment with hope has killed God) along with a Lévinasian atheism (that God is not available in arguments but in ethical relationships). This twofold atheism accounts for the reason why hope fails to justify itself or its poetic vision and philosophizing in the mode of a theodicy. This meditation returns us to ourselves. My question returns: How is responsibility for oneself and for the other possible in the midst of hope's desolation? The question foreshadows its answer, as in it we are already witnessing a promise. The promise of hope is taken for granted yet expected, not only by democratic and liberation theorists but also by those who set up various reconciliation and truth commissions. Those who can speak publicly about past disasters act as if they want to restore validity to their and our speech. How come their words do not become choked by the unspeakable? This is the epiphany of the uncanny within the ordinary, and the meditative questioning is its witness. There is an upsurge of hope in our midst; at the limits of human degradation, we bear witness to the reversal of its scarcity.

Secular Witness

Sartre and Marcuse become secular witnesses to the emergence of hope-filled speech. Hope is granted to speech out of a silence that is not spoken directly. This hope cannot be secured under the conditions for reciprocal recognition of difference or by redistribution of scarce goods. For this reason hope ultimately cannot be fathomed by a secular sensibility of democratic speech and material justice, though each in turn presupposes it. Marcuse witnesses the Benjaminian granting of hope for the sake of those without it. Sartre witnesses hope in the ethical injunction of acting so as to hasten the promise of another humanity. Both secular acts witness to another beginning. Only acts allow for the possibility of mutual recognition and equal redistribution. When possibilities are choked by the weight of history, then even secular witnesses can become the gates through which the promise may arrive.

Phenomenological Clues to Hope's Possibility

How does one become free to speak as a witness after experiencing an unspeakable horror? How can Sartre and Marcuse overcome that performative gap between their secular witness and the postsecular sensibility to the reversal of scarcity? Their irreligiously paradoxical postsecular sensibility to the mode of validity in speech offers us but meager clues to the restorative relation of witnessing to recognition. Neither they nor Oliver (1998:xii–xiii, 79f., 88–94, 173f.), who takes up the post-Holocaust theme of witnessing and recognition, can explain how this reversal is possible. I want to meditate on the experientially available clues to this counterexperiential possibility. These are the clues:

- Mutual recognition without hope is blind and empty
- Hope requires us to recognize that mutual recognition is neither possible nor desirable in all dimensions of singular human experience
- Witnessing concrete instances of hope's scarcity (e.g., radical suffering of innocents) can restore the validity basis to speech
- Witnessing to disasters cannot be achieved by acts of mutual recognition; rather, witnessing is what any recognition of trauma already presupposes
- Humans strive for a twofold transcendence—of the unnecessary material scarcity and of inhuman counterpraxis
- In our world of sustained scarcity, in our struggle for human future, witnessing can restore the possibility of and competence for mutual recognition and equal material redistribution

Disasters of the past two centuries bar us from theodicies for justifying God. But are we safe from a secular theodicy for justifying sustained scarcity as our original sin? We cannot but acknowledge the shattering and materially weighty nature of hope's scarcity in our history. There are nights without stars that make human beginnings impossible, unthinkable, unimaginable, paralyzed, always already late, never innocent, never happy. This phenomenology of disaster infuses our global historical present, and we suffer from a sustained scarcity of well-being and hope. We only have clues to hope now, hope for the sake of those without it. All of *us* now hope for the impossible.

Difficult Hope

This is the essential difficulty of meditating on hope: the clues to hope lie within the phenomenological field of our experience. Yet the way we are moved from the scarcity *of* hope to a beginning *in* hope is not of this same field of experience. If an upsurge of hope were part of the same phenomenological field as our experience of its scarcity, rather than a counterexperience, then human history marked by our free counterpraxis could never hover on the brink of hope's impossible return. If hope were a pimp or a slut, then transcendence in revolutions and organized religions alike would be like hurried one-night stands. One could get rejuvenated in political action or church rituals as if dropping by McDonald's. Hope promises otherwise than by having. Hope *is:* that there is possibility, that there is a beginning for me in relation to others, a beginning for concrete humanity. There can be no such thing for us as mastery of hope. Hope is lost, hope is given. Whether we do it singularly or communally, striving to own hope cannot overcome hope's scarcity either.

THE PASSAGE OF TIME

We are meditating in the gap between the phenomenological field of experience and the critical theory of hope, on the one hand, and the counterexperiential upsurge of hope in a witness to the traumatic or disastrous event, on the other. To bridge that gap calls for an awareness that is neither a theodicy nor argument nor postulate, nor another space and time to take the place of the one in which we act hopelessly. Since intransitive hope is not another space and time, one cannot think against hope from the apposite of our space and time, the radically exterior space of the *khôra.* One can only hope to hope against hope, for the sake of those endowed with face, those who are without hope. But faceless *khôra,* never having had hope, never suffering its loss, its outer condition of impossibility for all possibility lame when it comes to hope, has no language to hope for itself or for the sake of others.

Hope is not to be found along the ride from hopeless cities to the frontier. We stand in the gap between our passage of time (our field of experience) and new beginnings (a counterexperience to which we have but scattered clues). In this space and time, how are we ever given hope where there was none? In becoming responsible for our space and time, we renew our praxis with such hope. On the mountains of corpses and in the oceans of blood in this disaster, we witness how we begin. Standing next to our fellow humans, after betraying them and ourselves, how do we hope?

From the foregoing Sartrean challenge and Marcusean reversals on necessary and surplus scarcity, I can discern three dimensions of time. They pertain to the question of negative theodicy—as if elevating scarcity into a quasi-divine horizon of time—and its overcoming.

- I live my historical time marked by scarcity due to my finite memory and mortality, both expressed in forgetting and irretrievable losses. Remembering and forgetting represent the modalities of historical time. They are the modalities of my striving for existential freedom and social liberation. Any pacification of scarcity—Marcuse's term for overcoming domination and transcending unnecessary toil—must respect this lived sense of historical time.

- I experience time in its historical inertia. Anxiety at once arrests and hurries time's passing. Counterpraxis tries to fix time at its best in institutional and cultural life and at its worst in nationalist and religious fervor to solidify memory or to forget. Ethnic cleansing takes forms of injurious amnesia or weighty historical consciousness. Both historical amnesia and weight are dangerous as they issue in the cycles of doubly lost time. Each dimension of temporal inertia makes the time of lived hope scarce. Each loss occurs through our own continuing historical time and its free counterpraxis.

- Hope now, if one is granted to us, would assume yet a third, intransitive dimension *in* time. For the lack of better expression, I call it a dimension in time, or existential now-time, and not a third kind of time. Hope arises in gaps between the passage of time (our field of phenomenological experience) and another beginning (granting). That beginning, if it is to merit the name of hope, dawns otherwise than our once-forgotten past or anticipated future. That dimension breaking into lived time is experienced neither cosmologically, immemorially, nor linearly within its ordinary or historical flow. It is a counterexperience. Such beginnings are absolutely past, "the unforgettable," and yet still radically future, "unhoped for" (Chrétien, 2002). Such beginnings are neither unhappy remembering, nor unhappy longing. We witness in hope's upsurge this uncanny nonphenomenological variation of every lived historical present of which we have, however, some phenomenological clues. Hope arrives in time's flow, yet, unlike hopes and fears, it is not of time's passage.

Worse Than Death

Why should I ever find anything wanting in the ordinary passage of time if hope could arrive by way of historical progress? Finitude and mortality belong to our field of experience; they make us human. Finitude is not a surplus repression or surplus scarcity. To lose hope over the passing of time, perhaps even over the *khôra*-like unresponsiveness and coldness of the universe, would be to misunderstand myself. In that self-misunderstanding I would want to become other than human among mortals. When I meditated on Kofman's portrayal of her father's humanity in the midst of Auschwitz, I approached with Job the radical limit of any secular reflection on time's passage and the nothingness or entropy that empty space and time evoke in us. The death camps were factories fashioned to murder innocent living humans. Yet more essentially, they were designed to arrest human time in its intransitive dimension of hope; they were places and times of willed despair.

The nothingness of *khôra* wields no power of the demonic, and so it cannot effect despair. Hell is excess even of *khôra,* and so its despair is worse than death. Yet what is worse about *khôra* is that one can neither make love nor pray to it. But there is still something worse than *khôra* about human hell, knowing oneself as unable to love. But, if Augustine is right that nobody has lived who has not loved, and if Solomon is right that love is as strong as death, then hell, unlike *khôra,* is also a condition that saves in itself hope-filled possibility. The entropic and practico-inert *khôra* knows no possibility, it suffers *nothing,* it redeems nothing. More useless than suffering, *khôra* can never suffer redemptively, and every ethics of substitution in it would be just as pointless. One can descend to hell for another. Hell *is* hell, and for that it remembers and hopes hope.

Kofman and other witnesses and survivors of atrocities teach that *hopelessness is worse than death,* and that is why the iconography of Eastern Orthodox Christianity portrays prayers for a good death. That is why the intentionally produced impossibility of hope (though never human finitude or historical time or death alone) intends to make the human heart desolate and render human beings superfluous.

TWO

Redemptive Critical Theory

●

Marcuse, echoing Benjamin's relentless critique of the Hitler-Stalin pact, invoked hope against hope, thereby introducing the possibility of redemptive critical theory. I am harkening back to that possibility with the first-order desire of the "impossible." I set my next untimely (and in that postsecular) meditation on impossible hope within the secular horizon and its maximized (and in that aporetic and paradoxical) desire for liberation. I will muse on Habermas's lifework in order to witness how hope is given to singular existence and how its question is situated in critical theory today.

I do not believe in heroism, but I esteem greatness. Writing a biography of Habermas as an "existential hero" (Pensky, 2005) would stage a comedy of errors. His lifework inspires not by superhuman qualities but because it aspires to hope despite setbacks, failures, and dead ends that every human being undergoes in time, thought, and action. Greatness of lifetime achievement does not render human existence immune to finitude and even blindness. Heroism serves politicians who need to march nations to war; greatness belongs to courageous singularity in the face of trials and opposition.

Habermas delivered a singular address on November 11, 2004, after receiving the Kyoto Award for Lifetime Achievement. Blume (2004) wrote about the speech, "For the first time he presented himself as a person, and for the first time he reflected on his philosophy in biography." On the road to Purdue, Indiana, to speak on the critical ideal of cosmopolitan law, Professor Habermas described his reluctance to delve seriously into my published biography of him for two years after it appeared in 2001, but now he was writing his autobiographical essay for the Kyoto ceremony.[1] He was glad his autobiographical musings would be delivered in a faraway corner of the world rather than before the home audience in Germany. Habermas's revelations during our ride to Purdue suggested that his Kyoto self-disclosure provided an affirmation of and a fitting afterword to my philosophical-political profile of him.

A key question regarding why and how one goes on living is, *How is hope given in a singular life?* In Habermas's lifework, I was confronted with two similar questions. Is any use of existential categories to discuss critical theory compatible with a recovery of the publicity of facts and norms? Can one concede a secular reading of solidarity with the victims of history and yet retain this very conception to sustain, against the objection leveled by early Horkheimer against Benjamin, hope in the openness of history?[2] The best answer for oneself has to be sought in inwardness, and so the best answer is provided in Habermas's astonishing autobiography (ORpO). The second-best will be first to situate his text and then meditate on the above questions in light of his personal self-presentation of hope.

HABERMAS'S AUTOBIOGRAPHY:
TRAUMATIZED SPEECH,
HOPE-FILLED COMMUNICATION

Habermas distinguishes two types of public sphere: the one intrudes into the private life of celebrities; the other allows for an open exchange of views. The focus on topics replaces in the latter one's personal narrative. The public is no longer a passive hearer and onlooker but rather transforms into speakers and addressees in a conversation. The private sphere moves to the background of the public sphere, as speakers "need not speak about themselves" (ORpO). Habermas has a view about the relationship of philosophy and biography that is not so different from Heidegger's: "As philosophy professors we limit ourselves in our lectures about Aristotle or St. Thomas or Kant to bare life dates: when they were born, lived, and died." The events from the life of philosophers fall behind the work and do not of themselves make it into a classic.

Yet "every obsession has autobiographical roots," he declares openly and as a proof introduces his reflections about the "relationship between theory and biography." Habermas distinguishes four relevant autobiographical situations that provide the contexts for the emergence of his thought. First, after birth and in early childhood he underwent a traumatic palate surgery. He intimates that this medical intervention impacted his natural trust in the environment. "But this intervention could have woken up the feeling of dependence on and the sense of relevance of the relationship with others." His theoretical starting point comprises an insight into the social nature of humans. Humans are "animals existing in a public space." The palate surgery was repeated when he was five, and this sharpened his sense of human interdependence. Habermas locates in these formative experiences the

LORETTE WILMOT LIBRARY
NAZARETH COLLEGE

experiential roots of his interest in Humboldt, hermeneutics, American pragmatism, and late Wittgenstein's philosophy of language. "The intuition of deep-reaching reciprocal dependence of one on another" defines the core of his later communication theory. As his corrective to vintage textbook existentialism, Habermas describes human interiority as "an inner center of the person" that is always already built on the basis of achieved communicative and interpersonal competencies. One is capable of uttering the *I* of the first person singular because one was addressed by an originary *you* first.

Second, during his early schooling, Habermas had difficulty communicating with his peers on account of his disability. He recalls two experiences: not being understood by others due to his speech disability (a cleft palate) and the characteristic nasal articulation that made comprehending his spoken words difficult without careful attention from the hearers. And there was a subsequent and repeated rejection by his peers. Significantly, Habermas's school experiences as the Other occurred during the Nazi period and thus among the cohort that comprised his age-group when ten-year-old Habermas entered the Hitler Youth in 1939. Given the Nazi penchant for physical fitness, his birth defect and speech handicap must have had a pronounced effect on Habermas's alienation from others in his immediate surroundings. He writes, "Only those who speak can be silent. Only because we are from the beginning connected with others, we can become individuated." The trauma of speech hindrance provided the seeds for his later reflection on the communicative medium as the ground of individuation. "Language does not mirror the world," he says, "but opens our entry into it."

Habermas notes two further effects of his struggle with the speech impediment. He developed a marked preference for the written word and its precise discursive form. It is in discourse that we exchange grounds and require examination of problematic claims to validity in order to reach a better argument. He grades students on the basis of their written work and to this day prefers a written interview form. Furthermore, globalization comes to mean that we can imagine what it is to be a stranger or excluded from the human community. The need for reciprocal recognition is inscribed into our interiority as that fragility to which we are introduced through empathy. Moral sensibility offers protection against the injury of those who have been communicatively socialized and individualized; and hospitality and solidarity emerge as moral protection against marginalization. During adolescence Habermas confronted the break of 1945.

While I was not free to write about his first two experiences in my biography before Habermas summoned the courage to speak about them openly in his own voice, I did begin his profile with the phenomenological figure of his *existential philosophical-political birthday* at age fifteen. May 1945 saw Germany's defeat and liberation, Habermas's death and rebirth. From here on Habermas's self-presentation basically parallels the structure of my biography of him. When Habermas acknowledges his "luck of late birth," he ascribes to himself an intergenerational position: too late to commit the crimes of his parents' and teachers' generation but old enough to suffer the trauma of the Hitler Youth time and the national breach. Given both his handicap and age, he had no chance of becoming an enthusiastic Hitler Youth member. The young Habermas was not a victim, but given the eugenic policies planned by the Nazis he probably would have become one eventually had the regime prevailed. The chapter on so-called hereditary diseases in his school textbook was illustrated with three photographs, one showing a cleft palate.[3]

I brought Habermas's core intuitions and motives under these generational umbrellas. The postwar generation lived through Germany's Nazi dictatorship and its defeat. As a teen, Habermas witnessed Germany at once freed by the Allies and turned upside down overnight by them. As a mature thinker, he affirms the first core motive of his lifework in *an uncanny intuition of hope:* Reason even with its life world catastrophically injured is able to act against its failures from within its own resources. I say this secular hope is uncanny because after Auschwitz its warrants as well as those of reason inhabit a "double ground" of normality and civilizational breakdown. Habermas, not unlike Jonas discussed in the previous chapter, takes this secular recourse to hope by way of the modern Judeo-Christian, at once pietistic and Kabbalistic, notion of the absentee God brought to life through human cocreation. *Nihil contra Deum, nisi Deus ipse.* Nobody can act against God but God alone. This is the mystical phrase adopted by the rationalist Habermas on numerous occasions. In the most hopeless situations, such as the postwar Europe, reason rises from its ashes utilizing its own resources for renewal.

The contemporary relevance of Habermas's work is that he turns the defining aspiration of the 1945 generation into a lifelong search for the nonideological foundations of a democratic, constitutional, and lawful state. "Democracy," not Anglo-Saxon liberalism, is for him the postwar "magic word" (ORpO). In his view, only a democratic polity can survive in today's pluralist, multicultural, and multireligious societies.

The third significant autobiographical situation was his disappointment with the preceding generation of parental and teacher authorities. With Heidegger, ironically, political biography and philosophy come together for Habermas for the first time. If the link between existence and theory matters in Heidegger's case, since he also theorized it, that link is pronounced in Habermas's surprising autobiographical reconstruction of the sources of his own thinking. Among the chief objections to Heidegger's generation is its heroic call to creative power, the cult of German mandarins, the antimodern attitude, and the failure of responsibility for and distancing from the Nazi ideology. Habermas absorbed early Heidegger "through Kierkegaardian lenses," but for this same reason he neither espoused the heroic ideal nor became an existential hero. National, religious, or even personal heroism would be alien to Kierkegaard's notion of greatness. As a budding philosopher of communication, at age twenty-four risking his Ph.D. and career, Habermas confronted in Heidegger's unrepentant 1953 republication of his 1935 Nazi-flavored lectures the incomprehensible if not guilty silence of the German elite. Habermas's act was not some romantic heroism but a seed of singularity, what I called his *signature event.*

Fourth, his adulthood was marred by the slow and endangered process of Germany's postwar democratization. Against the horizon of Germany's disaster, the second core motive of his lifework was inspired by the generation of Habermas's students. In 1968 they were protesting against the fascist continuities that had survived in the values of their parents, teachers, political authorities, and in the general culture. From the student revolt, Habermas adopted the intuition that no human culture or tradition can claim for itself an original innocence. His reflection on the past and future of national founding myths is marked by profound ambivalence toward the nationalism that impacted his youth and by the fresh need to engage in public discussions concerning bankrupt traditions that we must jettison and life-giving traditions we need to affirm. This existential either/or projects into the public sphere as the question for both *I* and *we*—How to safeguard democratic institutions today?—highlights the second aspect of contemporary relevance of Habermas's lifework. He envisions political culture maturing into a postnational attitude that sheds raw, emotive, sectarian nationalism for the civic virtues of constitutional patriotism. Kierkegaard's existential distancing from bankrupt traditions, be it Christendom or nationalism, offers Habermas the category, existential and social at once, of singular existence that is rooted in the attitude diametrically opposed to both religious and secular heroism.

Although I was only eleven in 1968 when the Soviet empire under the pretext of brotherly help and liberation invaded my native Czechoslovakia, I was privileged to study with Habermas as a Fulbrighter in 1989 just as the Berlin Wall crumbled and the Velvet Revolution in my native country symbolized new beginnings. In those historic months, I discovered in Habermas not only a bold thinker but also a great teacher and passionately engaged intellectual. Habermas's third motive arose from this most recent world constellation in which the fall of the Iron Curtain, Germany's unification, the European Union's expansion, and the global impact of the state of international relations all tested anew the generational aspirations. The '45ers founded the democratic state on a patriotism that rallied around constitution and law, while the '68ers resisted cultural restoration of authoritarian regimes at the heart of democracy. Habermas's third core intuition comes to life in the *hope now* that against all odds we may rescue ethical communities by rooting them in our solidarity with the victims of history. The third aspect of contemporary relevance of his lifework consists in guiding our learning how to sustain global institutions in a more robust democracy of world cosmopolitan citizenship and international law.

Habermas's theoretical articulation of the first core motive and intuition points us to his philosophical-political origins—integrating the securing generational sensibilities of the '45ers. In the articulation of the second motive and intuition, he learns from the student rebellion against the fear of open society. His third articulation comes from a post-1989, future-projected ideal that completes this entire equation: *Habermas's lifework integrates the constitutional-democratic needs of the securing '45ers and the revolutionary core of the protesting '68ers.* He inhabits a soberly critical ground between the conserving and progressive interests. In short, the contemporary relevance of Habermas's lifework is a thorough articulation of what must be at once conserved institutionally and protected by nonviolent forms of civil dissent when endangered—the deliberative democratic checks and balances on the strategic dominance of power and money.

SHOULD CRITICAL THEORY
BE AFRAID OF INWARDNESS?

Two things become indisputably clear from Habermas's autobiography: First, Heidegger's momentary lapse into national heroism as a form of authentic resolve becomes a key political argument against existential categories such as inwardness. Thanks to his *existential* confrontation with Heidegger, Habermas does not conflate singularity with heroism. Greatness is a category distinct from heroism, as the latter alone can be celebrated en masse and thus foster abusive power. As greatness is to intransitive hope, so heroism is to devaluation of all transitive values. Heroism is incomplete nihilism. It is the value-positing of heroism that, according to Nietzsche's madman, occasions the "death of God" or kills God. Positing hope as value kills hope. Redemptive critical theory can have no truck with heroic or *causa sui* projects or with liberation or revolution projects if conceived as so many value-gods. With fidelity to the Judeo-Christian law of anti-idolatry and the ethico-religious injunction of substitution or redemptive suffering, the critical theory of hope resists the worship of progress in the very place vacated by theodicy (justifying violence against and the suffering of the innocents on the way to paradise) and ontotheology (i.e., God as the first or final cause or value). The harm self-inflicted on the innocents on the way to redemption is always already useless suffering (read: never justifiable in a theodicy), and so how can it ever be made good as an ethico-religious substitution or redemptive suffering on behalf of the future generations? Before the heroic, liberation, or revolutionary projects that have not become responsible to the singular other one can neither dance nor pray. Victory parades for the heroes sacrificed and substituted by the powers that be to appease death and the illusion of mastery become but so many scenes of obscene secular theodicies. Indeed, "useless suffering" is worse than death, and worse than the nothingness of the *khôra*. (See Lévinas, on substitution 1987:ch. 4; on the end of theodicy and "useless suffering" as calls to ethical responsibility, see 1988).

For this reason I speak of Habermas's greatness but never refer to him as an "existentialist hero" (Pensky, 2005). Habermas (ORpR) underscores this difference in a key distinction between the divided roles of the intellectual as a critical professional and a public figure. The critical role of influence should never have truck with political power. He writes about this because he feels the need to learn from his own failures as much as from those of his predecessors. "In the public office the intellectuals cease to be intellectuals." The possibility of failures or mistaken influence should turn intellectuals neither into mandarins nor into "cynics." Second, Habermas's autobiography puts at rest the truncated view of him as an aloof formal theorist bereft of singular and robust motives and intuitions. If anything, his Kyoto self-disclosure confirms my view of his normative theorizing arising from his existential singularity.

Academic thinkers on the left often hide behind cases such as Heidegger's to mask their own propensity to misconceive the category of singular greatness. With that confusion between heroism and inwardness, critical theory grows too weary to resist religious as well as secular forms of modern fundamentalism. But it is those very forms (and the religious or secular veneer plays no difference) that fall into the category of the heroic. *Pity the lands that need heroes; pity the critical theory that robs itself of resources to critique them!*

Pensky (2005) examines the question from Habermas's 1987 Copenhagen lecture (NC 261), the very question on which I based my earlier book (1993:5–20): "What would group identities have to be like to be capable of complementing and stabilizing the improbable and endangered type of ego-identity that Kierkegaard outlines?" I addressed the issue of compatibility between and even mutual requirement of communicative ethics and radically honest existential attitude, a requirement Habermas acknowledged in my first conversation with him on this topic (1993:250–

64). The fear that existential categories are incompatible with the recovery of the publicity of facts and norms rests on mistakes typical among social theorists.

The first mistake is the equivocation between 'existential' and 'existentialist.' Most often they are either viewed as the same category (Owen, 2005, n. 1) or used equivocally as in locutions "existential hero" and "existentialist hero" (Pensky, 2005). I consider only the word "existentialist" as referring to the twentieth century, mostly textbook readings of radical self-choice as a validity domain divorced from social situations. This is how the ascriptions of unsituated freedom often become the container for the acosmic readings of inwardness. I reserve the term "existential" for inwardness, but then this can never designate a choice of this or that value, belief, worldview, or even doctrine.

The second mistake is made by almost all critical theorists following in this regard Habermas, who identifies existential self-choice with the clinical or narrative questions of the good life *(eudaimonia)*. Habermas and his commentators distinguish the ethical domain from moral autonomy and self-determination. There are three domains of practical questions. Besides pragmatic questions about how things are done, there are ethical and moral types of questions. The dimension of inwardness is subsumed by the Habermasian architectonic under the ethical domain, understood as the Aristotelian or Hegelian good life. Pensky's description of inwardness is a vintage example: "'Ethical discourse' in its *existentialist reading*—in which the isolated individual, alone in her conscience and her life-history, must confront herself honestly and ruthlessly is the derivative, secondary form of an ongoing ethical discourse, in which we are always already involved." Pensky (64) concedes that there is a dialectic between the first-person singular (inward self-choice) and the first-person plural (publicity of norms). Yet he corrects the perceived ambiguity of this relation in Habermas by insisting that "this primacy of inwardness is only relative, perhaps even deceptive" (61–62).

The bugbear of asocial inwardness comes from a common superficial reading of Kierkegaard, minimally, for whom this category neither describes psychological states nor the philosophy of mind, nor is it some *validity claim* in competition with the publicity of the ethical, moral, and legal discourses. In order for inwardness to function as a "mediating moment between an unreflective and a self-reflective form of publicity" (Pensky, 2005: 63), it would have to become *a mode* of inwardness that is capable of critical distance on the received practices, institutions, and cultural ethos. But if all distancing is derivative from one's being born, socialized, and individualized as a German or an American, that is, if all terms of self-reflectivity are preset by received individualization through socialization, then no such distance from one-dimensional thinking could occur. Kierkegaard begins where Hegel, Mead, Peirce, late Wittgenstein, and Habermas end: with well socialized citizens, in his case Christian Danes, cultured and sagacious offspring of the nationalist-cum-esthetic religiosity of their (not unlike our) times. Kierkegaard's requirements of *becoming subjective* and *becoming sober* call for a mode of radically honest and open inwardness requisite of the demand for the critical publicity of facts and norms. His combined requirement attacks the false religious publicity of Christendom in ways that unmask its ideology and strip its socialized hold on the self-deceptive mode of one's self-relation.

My view has been all along that critical theory with liberation intent (i.e., if it is to speak of hope, if it is to be, therefore, a redemptive critical theory) needs the self-transformative category of inwardness as a mode of existing. I defined this category as the fifth way of raising the problem of evil in the introduction to part 1, as well as my use of the "existential" as transformative self-and-other relation. This is the missing third category of mode (between ethical and moral categories of validity) that accounts for the ability of socialized adults to take distance on bankrupt religious and secular traditions. This modal category is distinct from the ethical-clinical questions of the good life and the moral-normative questions of self-determination. Habermas's lifework and self-reflection open access to sober inwardness in creative ways that my prior biographical work on him explored without adulation, reductionism, or vain suggestion that he succeeded in carrying it through. It is by witnessing Habermas's singular struggles for truthfulness, as a critical theorist of his in-between generation, that we also meet his existential greatness. We do best to unmask heroism in those who are blindsided by unrepentant "military philosophers" (Anderson, 2005).

SHOULD CRITICAL THEORY BE AFRAID OF THE POSTSECULAR TURN?

Is there a postsecular turn in Habermas's profane architectonic? I did not encounter this term in Habermas prior to 2001, though I applied it in my biography of him (Matuštík, 2001:142, 146f., 149, 223, 226f., 265–74). But it emerges suddenly in his now voluminous writings on tolerance and religion after 9/11 (AW, ETC, FK, FT, GW, ID=RT, LG, ORSR, RR). Should critical theorists be afraid that the great thinker has gone soft or even *neoreligious* (Pensky, 2005:69)?

The meaning of witnessing must be located in what I name the *countermonumental quality of Habermas's uncanny hope* that propels his active critical work. But in the face of unforgivable and radically evil deeds, any such hope, however it profanes its illumination, always and already moves on the postsecular terrain. Following the announced "death of God," *our* hope-to-come is expected after our unforgivable deeds and so denotes what Derrida and others call a religion without religion (Matuštík, 2006; Habermas AW, LG). The uncanny here names *our* waiting that historical present can rescue its future from the past of the victims of history—*whether or not we can bring the dead back to life* (cf. Pensky, 2005:71). That such hope could ever be in our possession is neither a true meaning of the Buddhist awakening, nor of Ezekiel's prophecy that the dry bones shall rise. Hope is a granting whether or not one invokes it with a secular or religiously inflected tongue.

The notion of redemption holds for Habermas a Janus-faced ethico-religious status of *redeeming* rational claims to validity in public discourse and *hoping* that things do get better where disasters destroy the human capacity to forgive and repair. I do not dispute the contention that Habermas avoids all strictly theological implications found in Benjamin's rescue for the victims of history. Yet by rendering human solidarity in political rather than spiritual terms, *our* hope now (e.g., that after Auschwitz our smothered words will speak and write again with joy) becomes no less uncanny. Critical theory's disconsolate and countermonumental hope (and this sobriety I never denied to Habermas) arrogates to itself a robust postsecular expectation. By hoping against hope, critical theory assigns to itself a dual task of existential responsibility and waiting for or redemptive witnessing of hope-to-come. We may be just waiting for Godot (that possibility one need not deny to secular thinkers), but if hope comes, is that just because of our doing? It is not so much my articulation of the notion of redemption that reintroduces religious consciousness into critical theory; it is reason's faith in its recovery of reasonableness, hope that hope is to be given even where it became utterly disconsolate, that turns performatively postsecular.

These questions are addressed by Habermas's Frankfurt Paulskirche speech (FK) and his lectures on secularization (DS, ID, ORSR, RT, cf. RR, ZNR). Perhaps under the impact of 9/11, he speaks for the first time in his work about the 'postsecular' constellation complementing his 'postnational' constellation (cf. DIL). The 'postsecular' adjective appears in his Frankfurt speech three times at crucial junctures (FK 103f.). After admitting that "the boundaries between secular and religious reasons are fluid" (109) and even "mined ground" (113), he not only calls for the translation of the religious into the secular discourse but also admits the need for their mutual cooperation. Translation and cooperation are two contrarian moves reinforcing the new postsecular sensibility. He revisits the dispute between Benjamin and Horkheimer and stakes out his place (with a typical Habermasian ambivalence) between the open and irreversible senses of history, between the "true impulse and its impotence" (FK 111) of our coming to terms with the past. To bypass this ambivalence is to neutralize the hidden intuitions that underwrite the uncanny status of hope itself; indeed, without the at once critical and redemptive role of hope, critical theory makes itself irrelevant to the aspirations of the age.

Rather than plugging what he self-mockingly terms his religiously "tone-deaf" ears (FK 114), Habermas affirms against the genetic engineers the "absolute difference that exists between the creator and the creature" (115)—and this not so veiled heeding of the ancient commandment against the idolatry of human reason is hardly a secular claim. So when he concedes that the "unbelieving sons and daughters of modernity seem to believe that they owe more to one another, and need more for themselves, than what is accessible to them, in translation, of religious tradition," one must read between the lines his indirect acknowledgment of a loss of that redemptive hope that secular social theory, like the inarticulate Godot, expects to arise where disasters strike, yet may not supply from its own "exhausted" sources (111).

That acknowledgment is most indicative of his reading of Kant against Kant on radical evil. While Kant attempted a "critical *assimilation* of religious content" of evil into his rationally bound moral religion, this "may seem less convincing" in the face of the modern forms of annihilation. Deliberate cruelty is not simply "morally wrong" but "profoundly evil." And something was lost, Habermas concedes once more, in the translation of radical evil into the secular moral-legal categories. Neither ethical discourses nor normative moral and legal discourses can grant forgiveness, for the publicity of facts and norms can at best present moral culpability and punish. As I noted in the Introduction, modern social theory with its talk of tolerance and deliberative democracy is intellectually useless and existentially helpless in the face of Rwanda or Darfur.

Here we need to ask what is gained by critical theory becoming so flat-footed that it cannot unmask the heroic-aesthetic religiosity underpinning sectarian hatred? It has no resources to name, and so render powerless, religious-demonic cruelty, for it has translated away religiosity as a critical resource. Yet we need this resource to be able to grasp the upsurge of willed unreasonableness (and this phenomenon is more than intolerance) in human affairs. Without such a resource, critical theory has at its disposal no religious critique of the demonic—the notion that has become the trope for every fanaticism and religious ideology. Can critical theory thus impoverished point us to the sources of hope or, minimally, to what after dastardly deeds grants human affairs their reasonableness?

Wallis's book (2005) provides a fitting subtitle to answer these rhetorical questions: *Why the Right Gets It Wrong and the Left Doesn't Get It*. Michael Lerner's *Tikkun* call for critical religiosity should be at least seriously considered by the progressives as it fills this lacuna. In the absence of *redemptive critical theory,* progressives vacated the space to the bigoted forms of religiosity, the new Grand Inquisitors, and their hate-filled holy wars. Social theory begins with the background condition of reasonableness, yet this assumption that humans are reasonable is at best unwarranted and at worst idolatrous. Adorno was an intellectually more honest atheist in prohibiting positive images of hope and voicing doubts about doing philosophy and writing poetry after Auschwitz. Social theory justifies in vain its rational hope in the face of deliberately evil (I call them demonic or diabolical) acts such as genocide.

Many often ask, What are the sources of Habermas's unwavering, to twenty-first-century tone-deaf ears more and more uncanny, secular optimism that a margin of reason may prevail in the midst of human destruction and insanity? His own remarkable journey through the twentieth century bears witness to the fact that things did get better in postwar Europe. Habermas's theory of communicative action expresses this fact by locating the resources for learning on this side of the world—in human linguistic competencies—that is, in our ability and willingness to rise up from the ashes of our dastardly deeds and rebuild the fragments of fragile social bonds. As long as we do not go entirely mad or cease to communicate with one another as humans about something in the world, what other options do we have (so he questions skeptics as they question him, and so he would also confront his own unbelief), than take recourse in hope lodged in our very speech, communicative action, and want of mutual recognition?

I recognize in Habermas's hope, vested in the power of mutual understanding, a voice crying in the wilderness. In the next chapter, I will ponder how in 2003, Habermas (PWE; cf. LA, IFM, NWE) joined with Derrida (who passed away on October 8, 2004) in worldwide antiwar protests against the unilateral war on Iraq. The two of them crossing the modern/postmodern divide strove to resurrect Kant's dream from two hundred years ago of perpetual peace and the league of nations. In his sober hope, Habermas never pretends to deliver us from death or offer his theory as redemption. Yet his very sobriety is a recognizable *religious* act, and I mean here the Judaic law of anti-idolatry, proscribing the carved images of redemptive hope.

In that nuance of Habermasian ambivalence and self-limitation, I situate my meditation on the disconsolate and so paradoxically impossible desire for hope as it is revealed in his singular existence as well as in critical theory. Nowadays his at times secular Jewish and at times almost Lutheran hidden hope is perhaps even more sober than that of many a secular politician or religious leader alike. In a Camusesque *atheistic declaration of the postsecular phenomena* of the unforgivable, a good centurion, Habermas, writes, "There is no devil, but the fallen archangel still wreaks havoc—in the perverted good of the monstrous deed, but also in the unrestrained urge for retaliation that promptly follows" (FK 110). Perhaps in this self-limitation, questioning radical evil in the postsecular sensibility still available to our wit, huddled in solidarity under the earthly sun, a new redemptive critical theory may become a placeholder where genuinely nonideological questions of how or to whom hope is granted can still be asked.

THREE

Between Hope and Terror

●

I want to stage a conversation between a religiously tone-deaf Habermas and religiously irreligious Derrida in order to illustrate how their intentions of hope fare after the "death of God." In this meditation, I aim at the postsecular heart of hope appearing under the paradoxical, at times regulatively disconsolate and other times deferred, first-order desire of the *impossible*.

HOPE AS MULTICULTURAL ENLIGHTENMENT

Care for one's soul and city raises a Socratic as well as democratic requirement of self-constitution. To constitute oneself and the city in justice, we cannot geographically privilege any nation, continent, hemisphere, or world axis. *Hope as care for the psyche and polis* embraces minimally five core curriculum subjects of just constitution. On these Habermas and Derrida largely agree:

- Multicultural and postcolonial world without imperial ambitions
- Receptivity to the radical otherness of the other
- Decisive opposition to the violence of terror
- Secularized politics
- Ancillary role of critical theorists, philosophers, deconstructors

Multicultural Other

The first two core subjects should deflect any easy condemnation of the alliance between Habermas and Derrida as just another recentering exercise. For Europe and North America, to become responsible for one's history of exclusion, violence, and promise means to account for oneself in humility before one can say anything to anybody else. When Derrida invokes a "new figure of Europe," he already relinquishes all *terra,* territory, or terror as part of this figure. Decisions on the future of Europe's traditions involve the struggle against Europe's demons—exclusion, assimilation, and murder. The idea of Europe must draw on its dangerous memory of failed empires, colonialism, religious intolerance, and the Holocaust. Such dangerous remembrance of its victims both deconstructs the gestures of hegemony waived from the other side of the Atlantic and invites hope (Derrida, A 116). The heart of *this* Europe hurries the incomplete transatlantic Enlightenment against its imperial temptations (A 117). Only in this sense may Derrida and Habermas (PWE 292, cf. TUSE) prompt the "avant-gardist core of Europe" to become a "locomotive" of the greater inclusion of the other. The shared experience of struggle produces a "postnational constellation" that lends life to a new mentality, but with the following anti-imperial centers of gravity: self-limitation of state sovereignty, care for social welfare to resolve class conflict, and trust in the achievement of international law (PWE 294). The new multicultural enlightenment raises an imperative of learning: "Europe" must become other than its imperial heading (Derrida, OH), thus allowing the formation of the common European identity that would be in solidarity with worldwide antiwar demonstrations:

> A culture which for centuries has been beset more than any other by conflicts between town and country, sacred and secular authorities, by the competition between faith and knowledge, the struggle between states and antagonistic classes, has had to painfully learn how differences can be communicated, contradictions institutionalized, and tensions stabilized. The acknowledgments of differences—the reciprocal acknowledgment of the other as Other in his otherness—can also become a feature of a common identity. (PWE 294)

Each European nation underwent its history of bloody empire striving and the "loss of its empire" and colonies. With that loss, most Europeans, Derrida and Habermas conclude, are able to "assume a reflexive distance from themselves." This is elusive for the North American experience because of its young history and incomplete secularization. The European mentality is borne of witnessing its uprooting violence in modernity, apprehending victories "from the perspective of the defeated" (PWE 297). The plea is a vanishing point of self-corrective, "old" European learning for a new figure of Europe. "This could support the rejection of Eurocentrism and inspire the Kantian hope for a global domestic policy" (PWE 297).

Nonviolent Activism

In the third core subject of their plea and new alliance, Derrida and Habermas's opposition to terror emerges as more consistent than the hegemonic war on terror they oppose. Habermas (FT 34) drives home that there is no moral excuse for terror. Since terrorism is neither a war nor a private criminal act, it should be treated more like a political deed. Communicative action can have essentially (in the *telos* of speech oriented to an understanding with another) no truck with violence. Communicative ideality requires that we can overcome the structural violence issuing from material inequalities and distortions by power politics. Habermas argues that there are no alternatives to the uses of violence except developing "world citizenry" and strengthening its requisite institutions like the United Nations and World Court (FT 35–39). He offers no kind words for the "self-centered course of a callous superpower" with its strategy of unilateral war. Habermas (PWE 296) and Derrida (A 117) not only refuse all normative bases for the death penalty, viewing it as a covert survival of religious fundamentalism in politics, but also show how the core curriculum inscribes the "ban on capital punishment as a condition for entrance" into the ideal polis. Should decentered Europe ever require accepting the retributive and fundamentalist virus back into the core? The U.S. death penalty and the language of crusades were snubbed by most commonsense modern Europeans as at best medieval and at worst barbaric, and yet these critical attitudes are normative rather than anti-American.

Derrida notes that terror brings "semantic instability" to concepts, borders, as it is "self-escalating" (A 102, 107). Terror uses the worst of "technocapitalist modernity for the purposes of religious fanaticism." He judges that terror carries "no future . . . for the 'world' itself" (A 113). Bracketing all theoretical undecidability, Derrida decisively enters into the post/modern binary and in so doing joins Habermas on the side of democratic institutions:

> If I had to take one of two sides and choose in a binary situation, well, I would . . . take the side of the camp that, in principle, by right of law, leaves a perspective open to perfectibility in the name of the "political," democracy, international law, international institutions, and so on. . . . Even in its most cynical mode, such an assertion still lets resonate within it an invincible promise. (A 114)

Salutary Secularization

In the fourth core subject of their plea and new alliance, Derrida and Habermas detect the key issue between terror and hope in one-sided, incomplete secularization. Derrida defends

> "Europe," even if in quotation marks, because, in the long and patient deconstruction required for the transformation to-come, the experience Europe inaugurated at the time of the Enlightenment . . . in the relationship

between the political and the theological or, rather, religious . . . will have left in European political space absolutely original marks with regard to religious doctrine . . . over the political. (A 116f.)

In this instance (Matuštík, 1993:2001), Derrida (A135, GD) distinguishes with Kierkegaard religious doctrines or belief systems from faith. Derrida shoots a Socratic torpedo into the permanent terror alerts by claiming that the demarcation between belief and faith exists neither in Arab, Muslim, or Far East nations, nor in North America and Israel.[1] The "post–September 11" division comes down for him to "two political theologies" of the terrorists and the U.S. war on terror at one end, and "Europe" that has opted out of the "double theologico-political program" at the other end. In place of the intolerant, provincial, and dangerously global U.S. discourse on evildoers, axis of evil, infinite justice, and the civic religious pledges of allegiance and appeals to "God bless America," the core subjects of secularization inaugurated a discourse beyond the empire centrism of the theological politics (A 117f.).

Derrida and Habermas (PWE 296) do not cover over the sense in which they behold the "old" European politics as more sober than the "new" regime changes exported by the United States, whose values they consider Eurocentric in the pregnant sense: "For us [Europeans], a president who opens his daily business with open prayer, and associates his significant political decisions with a divine mission, is hard to imagine." Europeans "possess a keen sense of the 'dialectic of enlightenment,'" they no longer believe naively the gospel of technological progress and unregulated markets to deliver the world to justice (PWE 295). Habermas judges universalism sought by all empires as a transfigured, depraved political way of recapturing the singular cosmologies of world religions. Fundamentalism, as well as the unilateral global policy that opposes it, can be defined by the very same claim as "a stubborn attitude that insists on the political imposition of its own convictions and reasons." Fundamentalism and hegemonic politics are postmodern phenomena that repress "cognitive dissonance" of the plural world through a "holy" or nationalist intolerance. Secularization can stabilize a "nonexclusive place within a universal discourse shared with other religions" (FT 31, cf. FK 102).

Redemptive Critique without a Vanguard

In the fifth core subject of their plea and new alliance, Derrida's philosopher aspires to be neither a king nor an idealistically aloof adviser to the king nor a materially pedestrian consumer of the myth of the given. A deconstructor inhabits the discipline of responsible self-reflection, demands accountability from the powers that be, and contributes critical reflection to the life of the polis (A 106). A deconstructor waits with the critical theorist when both act as witnesses (Matuštík, 2001:139–56). The new alliance between deconstructor and critical theorist grounds no new philosophical or political hegemon.

HOPE AS RADICAL QUESTIONING:
WHAT IS TO COME?

A more than superficial difference between Derrida and Habermas turns on the nuance of how each invokes hope after Nietzsche's death of God. This contrast is thought against the backdrop of Western Christian majority, for neither Jews nor Muslims consider the religious or secular possibility of the "death of God." That idea and anguish come entirely from Europe's self-reflection. Yet even as Nietzsche's claim is quintessentially addressed to Christian culture and its demise, paradoxically, globalization spreads the now secularized Christian message under the fig leaf of its own fundamentalist beliefs as well as unbelief. Both Islamic and Jewish fundamentalism share with Christian zealots their horror of the modern value emptiness. Religious terror becomes one of the chief epiphenomena of the "death of God." When radical questioning fails to hope, then *horror vacui* yields to terror.

Even as they invoke the Judaic expectation of the messianic future—Habermas appeals to the regulative ideal of communication and Derrida to democracy-to-come—their gestures are affected by Nietzsche's disconsolation. Habermas hopes with Kant's Enlightenment for the possibility of discursive democracy. Derrida denudes even this disenchanted hope and begins to hope for the *impossible*. That latter hope comes *after* secularization, yet Derrida's *impossibility* does not simply oppose Habermas's possibility. I ponder this nuance lodged between *im/possible* under three umbrellas: secularization, radical democracy, and postsecular hope (RR 152; Matuštík, 1998:40, 49–64, 135–41, 228, 247).

Secularization

What the two thinkers secularize is an already secular exile of God—the God who was first sent out from the monastic enclosure to attend the world of needs and then, along with church property, was handed over to the secular affairs of the state. Secularization of cultural and social modernity completes the exile of God from the public sphere. Habermas (RR 159, cf. FK 103–105, 109ff.), always already irritated with Heidegger for gesturing toward that God who alone can save us now, proposes a cooperative, translatable relationship between the claims of knowledge and those of faith. Habermas values religion as a semantic reservoir of meaning. The boundaries, at once porous and treacherous (FK 109, 113), between secular and religious claims—like the tracks in the sand left by the desert wanderings of the exiled God—require mutual perspective taking and from it issuing mutual recognition between faith and knowledge. The secularizing reflection supplants the exiled God (FK 104). Reflection evinces the capacity to raise and defend unconditioned validity claims to truth, rightness, and sincerity. This linguistified God becomes but the placeholder of the vanishing point traversed by reflection. Into the empty space vacated by transcendent divinity, Habermas projects the ideal communication community. The ideal exists neither in the world (God has been gradually exiled from it) nor in some beyond (the vanishing point of secularizing reflection closed the gap between this world and transcendence beyond it). This exiled, secularized, *dead God* undergoes, however, repeated social resurrection of what is to come *after*. The ideal comes back to life in actual discourses when the formal-pragmatic placeholder acts as the final court of appeal to which speakers and hearers offer reasons for their claims. Habermas's transcendence on this side of the world betrays the neurotic compulsion-repetition (Freud would be suspicious of its linguistified ideality) even if there is no higher court of appeal than an infinite communication community. This wish appeal is the surviving phantom limb of a religious longing (cf. FK 111).

When he confesses the disconsolate character of communicative reason, Habermas closes ranks with the secular theologians of the "death of God." That a translation relationship ought to be possible between such different modes of existence as faith and reason is something that the secularizing reflection optimistically assumes. Reflection gradually strips religions of their self-enclosed claims to be the comprehensive worldview: "Religious consciousness itself undergoes a learning process . . . [and becomes] modernized by a way of cognitive adaptation to the individualistic and egalitarian nature of the laws of the secular community." This learning ought to accomplish the "renunciation of violence" that used "to push forward religious beliefs inside or outside the community." We replace violence with the "acceptance of the voluntary character of religious association" (Habermas, ID 6). Reflection exists side by side with the absolutizing imaginary of belief systems. Beliefs continue to raise absolute claims to truth, rightness, and sincerity. Secularization demands that the belief claims learn mutual tolerance. Tolerance also demands its price: the abdication of missionary zeal toward infidels or heretics (ID 7).

Derrida depicts September 11 as an incomprehensible, unpresentable "event" of "nonknowledge" and "pure singularity" that we can neither name, date, nor utter (A 90–94). He shows how this radical "limit" on experience and knowledge completes the "death of God." It likewise limits what may be hoped for as possible. Terror's wounding is "infinite" because it cannot be mourned or redeemed by any known or possible future to come. While secularization yielded reflection on the possibility of the Enlightenment hope to come, terror inflicts a threefold suicidal destruction of reflection's autoimmunity.

The first moment aggressively attacks the "symbolic head" of modern economy and power from within its own ground and with its own means (A 95f.). The second moment wounds without granting a future, ushering the present age into trauma without the possibility of earthly consolation at least through mourning. The third moment moves in the vicious circle of terror renewed with every attempt to fight it. All three moments arrive at the unnameable and "impresentable to come" (A 97–100). To clarify this nuance, I borrow from Kant the concept of radical evil. This possibility *is* of "the worst" to come. Its terror, rather than hope, lies in "the repetition to come—though worse" (A 97). Acts of terror/war on terror deliberately move in the circle of a "suicidal autoimmunity" (A 95). The "death of God" self-escalates. With Derrida I begin to think against Kant and Habermas of the "diabolical" acts as something humans will to do freely. Indeed, the question before us is why humans effort to be cruel despite the doubts whether they are acting in defiance of a god or to overwhelm the deafening silence of the *khôra*. Since one can neither pray nor make love to the entropic nothing, it makes even less sense to act up against it with some diabolical intent, that is to pray in hell and hate as a demon or devil would. I return to this in part 2. Suffice it to say now, Derrida pleads for the impossible against the grain of the human failure to be God, against this desire's irreversible wound.

Radical Democracy

Whereas Habermas (DIL) presents democracy as a disconsolate regulative ideal of deliberative and procedural justice, Derrida says that democracy-to-come requires faith and hope (A 119). Habermas reforms national sovereignty in the direction of popular procedural sovereignty. Derrida's waiting for democracy does not envision an arrival of a political regime. Democracy-to-come is a contested space, an event without history or visible horizon. Habermas redresses the violent effects of one-sided secularization (FK) by enlarging the sphere of public tolerance (FT 37–41, ID, DIL). Derrida insists on "gift, forgiveness, hospitality" in the public sphere (A 120f.).

Let us consider Habermas's concepts of democracy side by side with Derrida's:

- Habermas's regulative ideal with Derrida's event
- Habermas's tolerance with Derrida's hospitality
- Habermas's world citizenship with Derrida's democracy-to-come

- Habermas's self-limited sovereignty with Derrida's alliance beyond sovereignty
- Habemas's Enlightenment's possibility with Derrida's gift's impossibility
- Habermas's procedural justice with Derrida's forgiveness

The key nuance in each pair pivots between Habermas's world cosmopolitanism, which assumes shared, divisible, and self-limiting sovereignty, and Derrida's deconstruction of the state form itself for the sake of "an alliance . . . beyond the 'political.'" In Derrida, democracy-to-come gathers singular beings beyond the limits of cosmopolitanism and citizenship (A 130, cf. SM). Habermas's democracy radicalizes the Stoic, Pauline, and Kantian ideals of human sociality under the regulative limits of secular globalization. Derrida secularizes the horizon of sovereignty that those same ideals still assume. For him the Greco-Roman, Pauline, and Kantian imaginaries of world citizenship (along with Carl Schmitt, who so worries Habermas) transmit the legacy of the political ontotheology (A 121ff.). Democracy-to-come after the "death of God" for Derrida sheds even the popular aspirations to sovereignty and strives for "a universal alliance or solidarity that extends beyond the internationality of nation-states and thus beyond citizenship" (A 124).[2]

Derrida is neither an antidemocratic prophet of the "death of God" nor a cynical power politician advising the elites how to use the pseudoreligiosity of the Grand Inquisitor to induce intoxication in conservative moralists and pliable masses (cf. Postel, 2003). Derrida's alliance with Habermas guards against the new political ontotheology of sovereignty. Derrida cautions Habermas that "tolerance" can become but "a conditioned, circumspect, careful hospitality" of the religiousness of those in power. He invites into community "whomever arrives as an absolutely foreign *visitor,* as a new *arrival,* nonidentifiable and unforeseeable, in short wholly other." This is hardly an abstract otherness. A new figure of Europe, more than an "invitation" into the regulative-ideal club of the possible, is a "visitation" of the unexpected and uninvited (A 129) and a task to welcome strangers beyond duty and law (A 132f.).

Postsecular Hope?

The coming of the *im/possible* turns on the margin between what was secularized without violent reminder of ontotheological-political programs and what is left over after acts of terror/war on terror. The former programs refer to the grand religious and metaphysical narratives of great religious syntheses and their political equivalents (e.g., the Christian mission to and the conquest of the New World). The latter acts designate the vacuum resulting from the collapse of those grand narratives. The slash stands for an invisible margin, not undecidability between Habermas and Derrida. That margin is faith purified of imaginary's belief in its power. If Derridean visitations conjure up angels, if hospitality echoes the biblical prophets, then even the secular plea must be more than a spiritless prayer. How secular can prayer be? Is this the untimely moment in any secular meditation? I recognize in this uncanny post-Nietzschean guest a postsecular return of the religious without religion (Caputo, 2001, 109–12, 132–41), hope given for the sake of those without it (Marcuse, 1991:257).

Habermas's impassioned plea for a fallible Enlightenment harkens back to a nondestructive secularization that *invited* reason and faith to coexist in tolerance and freedom from terror (FK 108–11). Now that the terror of the twenty-first century has revealed the fundamentalist abyss of Nietzsche's death of God, coming to terms with hope becomes our difficult task. After too many genocides, we grasp with greater acuity what Nietzsche's madman meant by saying that we were not yet up to our own deed. Fundamentalism marks a disconsolate return of this abysmal god in the form of a punishing superego and a longing imaginary; together they demand our adherence to power, doctrine, and discipline. In my postsecular meditation what differentiates fundamentalism from religious faith is *adherence* to beliefs in the former and *inherence* in spirit by the latter. Habermas views as "fundamentalist"

> those religious movements which, given the cognitive limits of *modern* life, nevertheless persist in practicing or promoting a return to the exclusivity of premodern religious attitudes. Fundamentalism lacks the epistemic innocence of those long-ago realms in which world religions first flourished, and which could somehow still be experienced as limitless. (RR 151, cf. FK 102)

For Derrida, fundamentalism responds to the "death of God" in acts of terror/war on terror, and this is why terror has no *terra* and no future (A 118).

It is here that I press my untimely postsecular meditation to its vanishing secular horizon: Derrida and Habermas venture into the desert of religion without religion. Not what but how they venture defines their difference. Habermas's religious discourse (we can agree a bit with Freud here) is a phantom limb—a "musically tone-deaf" (FK 114) and unredeemable absence of the impossible. What alone can be redeemed for him lies in human solidarity—the profanized religious ideal of communication community. Nondestructive secularization must translate religious and rational claims into the language of communicative freedom. Equal freedoms shared among humans require, more than the death of God, that the divine throne remains empty. Not a psychoanalytically vacuumed desire for oneself as *causa sui,* Habermas's communicatively responsible atheism resists both terror and fundamentalism that try to appropriate the place of God (FK 113ff.). After depth psychology revealed that our desire to be God died on the analyst's couch in at once transferred and disappointed desire, that dying divinity can still save by absence. Habermas's communicative ideal of community is disconsolate but not inherently predestined to celebrate the human failure (Žižek, 2003:145–71).

Can Heidegger's own postsecular absencing of God come to a truce with Habermas's disconsolate ideal? Or must we interpret even *this* dimension of Heidegger's silence—humans not speaking with the mandate of the God whom they exiled, killed, and psychoanalytically amputated—as an evasion of responsibility for our disasters (nights without stars)? Or are not those who proclaim the past closed saying too much, as if their claim could be more than a belief imposing mythical hopelessness on the victims of history? Is not speaking of what one should be silent, just as staying cowardly silent about failure, nothing but one's evasion of responsibility?

Questions like these allow Habermas to make a political alliance *with* Derrida. He concedes that what binds him with Derrida philosophically is a certain reading of Kant. What continues to divide them is Derrida's late Heideggerian inspiration, which Habermas finds, even when viewed through Derrida's Lévinasian angle of vision, betraying both the Judaic prophetic and the Socratic enlightenment legacies of the West (Habermas, IEM). Questions like these prompt Derrida to hold reservations about regulative ideals (Derrida, A 134f.). Hope is not impossible because of some counterfactually deferred or imaginary ideality. Hope's urgency cannot be ideally projected onto abstract otherness. Hope "precedes me—and seizes me *here now,*" or I have never been infused with hope. Political theorists and activists, even Habermas, assume hope when they set up truth commissions to deal with war crimes and unforgivable human disasters. Yet their assumption is wrong, as hope is never available as a regulative ideal. Camus declares in the opening pages of his *Myth of Sisyphus* that he has never seen anyone die for the ontological argument, in the same way one could reiterate that to hope in regulative ideals would be odd rather than impossible. If Habermas does not want any truck even with Derrida's (or Lévinas's) Jewish transformation of Heidegger, then the same angle of vision can be had with Marcuse's appeal to Benjamin at the end of *One-Dimensional Man,* indicating hope as a granting, a gift, not an ideal or a pragmatic presupposition. The visitation of hope arrives as "what is most undeniably real." Responsibility (spoken of or not) cannot be settled by a norm or rule. What comes after the death of the God of ontotheology may never be a regulative ideal but must always remain concrete, albeit aporetic, reality (A 115).

Derrida saves his most playfully irreverent reading of Nietzsche's death of God against the grain of Heidegger's saving God for a footnote (A 190 n. 14; cf. n. 16). Derrida's postsecular God names "an ultimate form of sovereignty that would reconcile absolute justice with absolute law and thus, like all sovereignty and all law, with absolute force, with an absolute saving power." This impossible God names "a new international" without institution or party. Such "improbable institution" requires "faith" rather than a zealot, St. Paul, or a vanguard, Lenin. The impossible is the gift of "messianicity without messianism," "democracy-to-come," and the "untenable promise of *just international institution.*" Neither Heidegger, in his critique of technological age, nor Nietzsche, lamenting the nihilism of all value positing, held hope for radical democracy; but Derrida does. Echoing Benjamin's theological materialism, Derrida's democracy-to-come solicits "faith in the possibility of this impossible and, in truth, undecidable thing from the point of view of knowledge, science, and conscience," and such faith "must govern all our decisions" (A 115). Hardly even noticed, two years before issuing their joint plea, Habermas writes approvingly of Derrida: "Today, Jacques Derrida, from different premises, comes to a similar position [of the early Frankfurt School]—a worthy winner of the Adorno Award. . . . All he wants to retain of Messianism is 'messianicity, stripped of everything'" (FK 113; cf. Derrida GD, FaK 18).

UNTIMELY POSTSECULAR MEDITATIONS ON IMPOSSIBLE HOPE

Michal Žantovský, former Czech ambassador to the United States, commented on the end of Václav Havel's presidency (Remnick, 2003) by citing Bertolt Brecht. I cited the same Brechtian jeremiad in the previous chapter, as it concluded Habermas's (FT 43) philosophizing in a time of terror: "Pity the land that needs heroes." Žantovský, Havel's long-term associate, gave a diplomatic toast to the outgoing Czech president at the Prague Castle farewell party by adding a wish to Brecht's lament, "I hope we don't need another." That U.S. culture and politics are not up to Brecht's secular sobriety might have motivated Habermas's recourse to this citation. Yet is either Havel's or Habermas's Europe more up to this sobriety?

I conclude with preparatory meditations for parts 2–3. They will begin to seek to add a crucial redemptive edge to the relentless drive of critical thought which wants to hope against hope. In a Christian language, the deferred desire becomes a desert faith of the hidden God, and the maximized intention of hope becomes perpetually deferred, crucified faith. In a Judaic language, critical hope must always honor the law of anti-idolatry. In a Buddhist language, if hope presents itself under the guise of hope, reject it.

I deem a redemptive critical theory well suited for our global scene with its strange admixture of fundamentalism and hopelessness. The first meditation names the return of evil by its name. In the second meditation, I come to terms with the realization that even critical ideals cannot heal all wounds of history. In the third, I learn from secular masters of suspicion to expose the false prophets who blaspheme by speaking about vanquishing evil and delivering hope as if these could be achieved by heroic acts. With its postsecular sensibility, the first meditation grasps that evil can be called radical for the first time when we mean by it acts that deliberately suspend goodwill; the second meditation begins by mourning the trauma of the human condition for which hope is always already *simply* impossible; the third meditation ventures with a risky, uncertain faith against both personal and social projects of the heroic.

First Meditation: Radical Evil Is Diabolical

We need no "devil" to personify the diabolical in deliberate acts of destruction that intend no future. The truly problematic for the present age is Kant's harnessing of evil, not that of religion, within the bounds of mere reason. The beliefs of rational religions can be easily translated into secular terms to yield the moral point of view. Habermas completes Kant's task brilliantly. By translating and assimilating Kant's notion of radical evil within the bounds of mere reason—a secularizing project that Habermas (FK 110, ORSR) inherits from Kant—we rob ourselves of naming critically the coming of the worst. Derrida's (A) three moments of suicidal autoimmunity restore the postsecular edge to our critique of the present age of terror. Moreover, learning from Kierkegaard (yet for him unlike for Habermas in his secular translations), Derrida names willed ignorance by its true name as stupidity.

Radical evil is an act willed by not so good will; it is one's self pledged and one's acts willed in despair. Radical evil presents the existential (untranslatable either/or) boundary that "both destroys and institutes the religious" (FaK 100). This nuance makes me meditate on what Derrida, like Kierkegaard yet unlike Kant and Habermas, finds in radical evil—the demarcation between the religious and the ethical spheres of existence. Habermas (FK 110) translates sin into guilt and hence fuses forgiveness into an ethical repentance or righting of social injustice. Would there be any need for forgiveness if it were in our power to repent evil ethically and to undo all wrongs socially?

Meditating on the sources of forgiveness—a capacity that does not lie in human power alone—intimates the most offensive though nonetheless spiritual logic. In another telling footnote, Derrida (GT 165–66 n. 31; cf. SP) shows that the weakness of Kant's watered-down definition of evil is a reduction of forgiveness to repentance. Unforgivable cruelty and willed stupidity are called radical evil because by bursting rational bounds of guilt, they cannot be repented ethically. *The human possibility of diabolical evil revisits us as a religious phenomenon after the "death of God."* This phenomenon invokes forgiveness. If need for forgiveness did not arise, would any evil ever be "radical"? Without the uncanny phenomena of evil and forgiveness there could be no phenomenology of the "religious" after the death of the God of ontotheology. If such evil never arose, would there be a philosopher's need for its rational translation? Kant and Habermas cannot have it both ways, and Nietzsche does not live up to this task.

Second Meditation: Hope Is Impossible

Truths that lie beyond our rational horizon of what is known or not yet conscious, from this ignorance humans can be delivered by a self-corrective process of learning. What is not known, that rational enlightenment can cure. Rational criticism, learning, and communication are the greatest possible hope for the continual progress of the human race. If Kant, Hegel, and Marx as well as Habermas are wrong, and therefore some wounds cannot be healed by progress or learning projected under the regulative ideal of communication community, then hope that could still deliver or redeem us carries the name of the *impossible*. The sheer lack of human possibility can be ignored or repressed, or one can despair of the impossible. Yet all second-order ignorance, repression, and despair are willed by us, and in that intensified willing act, and this is more than a deferred, first-order desire or maximized intention of the aporetic or paradoxical impossible, we acknowledge the exceeding appearance of the *impossible* itself. Two impossibles of hope are in play: one shatters on the inadequacy of concepts, another reveals excess of intuition. To go on pretending that all wounds of history can be healed rationally is to ignore, repress, or despair of the impossible. The ultimate pretense reactively defies all healing by placing deliberate accents on the transitive *im*possibility, celebrating human trauma, confusing hope with hopes. The convex mirror of theism is atheism held dogmatically as a belief in the *im*possibility of hope. But *impossible* hope is not an objectifiable phenomenon of *belief* (hopes) and hence not a rational validity claim against what is humanly possible. To stop pretending altogether, one must complete the death of that God who survives not just in our grammar, as Nietzsche once thought, but in all atheistic beliefs we imbue with false reverence.

The religious phenomenon returns after the completed "death of God" under the figure of impossible hope. No amount of talking or learning or force can break the boundary that protects unmourned trauma from what rational enlightenment or possible hope can deliver. The unmourned, to be accessible, requires self-acceptance and forgiveness. Negatively, redemptive critical theory calls evil by its name and shows how rational enlightenment fails to heal all wounds of history or forgive. Positively, now without despair's defiance of the *impossible,* the new sensibility of self-forgiveness opens to the cosmos and oneself with uncanny hope.

Third Meditation: Heroism Is Idol Worship

Heroism is the other face of the human terror of possibility or its loss. Self in terror of its freedom either searches for and imposes fundamental(ist) certainties or puffs up with war on its terror externalized. The idols of broken emptiness on either side usher the terror-stricken self into heroic projects. There one bolts and takes a last stance. Heroism—whether religious or secular—is idolatrous precisely because its worship of self lies opposite of faith. If Abraham or Job were heroes, we could celebrate them with national songs of victory. They were prototypes of faith, not idols.

Derrida (A 135) drives this point home with his Benjamin-Lévinasian view of Kierkegaard: "I always make *as if* I subscribed to the *as if*'s of Kant . . . or *as if* Kierkegaard helped me to think beyond his own Christianity, *as if* in the end he did not want to know that he was not Christian or refused to admit that he did not know what being Christian means." Habermas learns from Kierkegaard's existential ethics how to adopt the either/or decision of Euro-American traditions that would foster the democratic political culture and identity (PWE 295). But his public either/or does not help us unmask the sacral language of heroism emerging anew in postsecular political culture. Derrida resists all conflation of the ethical-political sphere with the religious because he grasps religion without religion as contrary to heroism. We know better why we should take heed from Brecht's profane lament. *Hero worship is the most spiritless not because it is godless but because in its appearing pseudoreligious phenomenon we recognize an idolatrous divinization of human projects.*

Heroism emerges in the anxiety of freedom's possibility. Ripened anxiety masks the despair of the weak will as it embraces the heroic crowd. Ultimately the hero's will to power manifests the full-blown despair of religious-cum-political defiance. The defiant self feeds the life of empires that in turn celebrate the hero's deeds. To grasp the nature of terror we need to supplant the death of God by the category of spiritlessness. In this way we deliver the requisite blow to heroic religiousness—whether couched in a fundamentalist or patriotic mission—as the most dangerously desperate of all in its spiritlessness. Any religiosity can become spiritless when it worships itself. The role of critical theory with a postsecular edge—redemptive critical theory—suited to our desperate times must expose not only secular but most of all the religious false prophets. They are false who speak the language of vanquishing evil and delivering hope through heroic projects.

This meditation is needed most when divine blessings on a country are counted by the deeds of its heroes. Intoned in hymnals or as religious and national flags, along with civic prayers for national victories, are raised side by side, to pity all lands that need heroes; this prayer of blessing all creation (*berakhah/barakah*) would become the most devastating public performance in any international forum (Matuštík, 2004).

> *Baruch Atah Adonai Elohenu Melech haOlam . . . Sanctus, Sanctus, Sanctus Dominus Deus Sabaoth . . . Allah Akbar . . . Pity the land that needs heroes.*

We should chant in synagogues and at the Wailing Wall, in churches and in bully pulpits, and from the loudspeakers of great mosques, in all places where humans call God's name great but dress it in the heroic caricature of greatness. The meditation that could breathe life into a new redemptive critical theory inhabits the self that rests transparently in the work of mourning one's unhappy remembering and unhappy longing, and in the work of one's recovery from yielding to the sirens of the practico-inert and entropic *khôra*. Knowing all along that the human race cannot heal all wounds of history yet, freed from all pretensions to heroism, one's faith yields now not just to the deferrals, aporias, and paradoxes of, but also to the exceeding, indeed saturating visitations from impossible hope.

Part 2

●

THE NEGATIVELY SATURATED PHENOMENON

In order for evil not to be possible, God would
have to be impossible.
—Schelling, *Freiheitschrift*

We actually have nothing to fall back on in order
to understand a phenomenon that nevertheless
confronts us with its overpowering reality and
breaks down all standards we know.
—Hannah Arendt, *The Origins
of Totalitarianism*

Perhaps the most revolutionary fact of our
twentieth-century consciousness—but it is also
an event in Sacred History—is that of the
destruction of all balance between the
explicit and implicit theodicy of Western
thought and the forms which suffering
and its evil take in the very unfolding
of this century.
—Lévinas, "Useless Suffering"

I want to think through "radical evil" as a special instance of the saturated phenomenon. By freely developing Marion's notion of the saturated phenomenon beyond where he took it, learning from Schelling, Kierkegaard, and Lévinas, I mean by "radical evil" the negatively saturated phenomenon of a positive act of defiance. Humanly generated evil dramatizes a special case of saturation not because its levels of excess or intensity could not be deemed at times banal, but rather because in human agency doing evil always reveals a positive excess and yet this positive is at the same time something done in a negative mode.[1]

When Marion (2000:176–216; 2002:28f., 189–212, 225f., 234–47; 2002b:chaps. 2–5; 2007) introduced the figure of the "saturated phenomenon" in order to describe the modality of the religious, Janicaud (2000:17; cf. 2005) objected that all such "spiritualist" moves mix phenomenological apples with religious oranges.[2] Janicaud (2000:35; cf. Marion, 2002:184) appeals to Husserl's principle of principles (1998:par. 24), according to which one ought to respect phenomenal immanence, while intentional transcendence ought to be apprehended and explained in terms in which it appears in the world. Following Husserl, phenomena given to us in intuition ought to be received as they give themselves, and that means within the limit and in the world horizon in which they give themselves. There can be no "phenomenological theology," Janicaud objects (2000:100), for Husserl requires that "the suspension of the natural attitude ought not to lead to a flight to another world or to the restoration of absolute idealism, but to a deepening of the transcendental regard vis-à-vis experience and for it" (35).

Marion's "new phenomenology" remains faithful to Husserl's principle of principles by developing its precept of attending to givenness against the grain of phenomenal immanence. Janicaud's objection to the theological move in phenomenology raises serious concerns. How could a religious phenomenon appear out of the bounds of horizontal immanence or, echoing Kant, bursting the bounds of mere reason? Marion (2000:176) says that religious phenomena "would have to render visible what nevertheless could not be objectivized." The religious would reveal an "impossible phenomenon." He considers precisely this "radical possibility" that there could be given to us a phenomenon that would be neither restricted by a given immanent horizon nor reducible to a constituting I. This would be the case of "an unconditioned and irreducible phenomenon" that breaks the rational bounds of the immanent horizon of experience as well as one's constituting intentions (184f.). The phenomena that shatter the poles of experience—immanent horizon and constituting ego—would be saturated by intuition, rather than a common phenomenon that is always poor or inadequately fulfilled in intuition. The saturated phenomenon would exceed conditions of possible experience because it would deliver more intuition than I ever intended in the first place. It would overfill and overflow the original intention with excess (195).

The saturating "excess" of the first order (197) marks out four ways in which an *impossible phenomenon* breaks the subject-object poles of possible experience and the bounds of rational categories. The saturated phenomenon exceeds both Kant's limit placed on all phenomena to stay within the bounds of mere reason (his four categories of the understanding—quantity, quality, relation, and modality) and Husserl's principle of principles (his two poles of experience—the immanent horizon and the constituting ego). Undoing the four categories of the understanding Kant requires for *possible* experience, the saturated phenomena of the first order come in four basic generic types: events, flesh, the idol, and the icon.

- Quantity-event: Being "unforeseeable" in our aims, the excess of incomprehensible event becomes "visable" without anticipation by anything prior. Hence an event without a prior privileged perspective of seeing announces itself in our "amazement" (198, 202).
- Quality-flesh: Excessive intensity of pleasure or pain exceeds our conceptual power, and so the quality is unbearable to the point of "blinding" the direct gaze and so producing "bedazzlement" (200).
- Relation-idol: As a sui generis event, for example, in colors, sounds, or forms of art—the idol—the saturated excess cannot appear directly by drawing on analogies with prior events in the field of experience (202f.).
- Modality-icon: The invisible face of the visible other—the icon—reverses my direct gaze and intention; neither can the saturating excess be apprehended directly (208f.).

The saturated phenomenon of the first order in its four types "appears in spite of and in disagreement with the conditions of possibility of experience—by imposing an impossible experience (if not already an experience of the impossible). Of the saturated phenomenon there would be only a counterexperience" (210). While Derrida's possibility of the impossible deconstructs intentions or desires that can never be fulfilled, "a gift that can never be given" (Caputo, 2007:78), Marion's possibility of counterexperiencing the impossible reveals givenness that saturates the fulfilling pole of intentional consciousness. Marion's impossible gives itself without conditions, restraint, or reserve. Derrida's impossible maximizes intentional and messianic desire through constant deferral. Derrida's impossible task marks the dark night of *kenotic* faith and the darkness of God on the border of conceptual a/theism and professes religion without religion, which in its darkest and most inaudible prayers becomes overwhelmed by the mute silence of the *khôra*. In both dimensions, bereft of a congregation or synagogue or nation, Derrida's at times messianic religion without religious messianism and at other times his irreligiously deconstructive spacing of the *khôra* is more akin to Martin Luther's hidden God (crucifying ego's fulfillment in the epoch and the exilic desert of faith), than to Pseudo-Dionysian overflowing yet incomprehensible God (cf. Tracy, 1999). Derrida responds to Richard Kearney: "I would share your hope for resurrection, reconciliation and redemption. But I think I have a responsibility as someone who thinks deconstructively to obey the necessity—the necessity of the possibility—that there is *khôra* rather than a relationship with the anthropo-theological God of Revelation. . . . My own understanding of faith is that there is faith whenever one gives up not only any certainty but also any determined hope" (Sherwood and Hart, 2005:297). Marion's (2000:212) impossible maximizes "the possibility that surpasses actuality" as well as the rational bounds of possibility. Instead of deferring the advent of the messianic desire, it proclaims its own advent; instead of delving into the dark night of crucified faith and even that darker hiddenness of Ingmar Bergman's "spider God," the saturated advent of messianicity awaits redemption in transfigured faith (cf. Caputo, 2007:77–79).

Hence this book speaks in two voices of two scarcities of hope, two paths that aggravate it in radical evil, two messianic gates at which one hopes against hope to arrive. While part 1 walked us through the secular desert of hope, part 2 brings us to the postsecular gate of excess, and part 3 will meditate on both.

Infinity in Descartes, Lévinas, and Pseudo-Dionysius and the sublime in Kant antedate Marion's four modes of appearing of the saturated phenomenon (2000:213ff.). That phenomenon appears neither as visable event (it arrives without a perspective of the agent) nor as bearable intensity (it blinds and bedazzles); it appears singularly (without analogy to experience, hence as counterexperience) and indirectly (the Lévinasian face-to-face encounter is an ethico-religious encounter because the trace of the Other in the face is iconic, not visible).

While these four modes of the first, natural order of saturation reach all the way down to the banality of sense and common experience (every ordinary phenomenon is thus amenable to saturation, says Marion, 2007), the fifth dimension or the saturated phenomenon of the second order arises from an intensification or reduplication or resaturation of the first order (Marion, 2007; 2002:234–47). When the saturated phenomenon gives itself by revealing itself, we arrive at impossible counterexperiences of the second order. Phenomenologically, the possibility of counterexperiential revelation can prescribe or prophesy neither historical (Jewish, Christian, Muslim, Buddhist) nor contemporary mystical forms of revelation (cf. 367 n. 90); it can at best describe the condition of their phenomenal *impossibility* or excess or resaturation.

I describe radical evil as a form of the negatively saturated phenomenon. In doing so, I wish to bypass both the Janicaud- and Caputo-type objections to Marion. Janicaud worries that Marion's "new phenomenology" violates Husserl's principle of immanence. Caputo (2007:79–83) quizzes Marion, as if after Heidegger he had now smuggled in an onto-phenomenology, as if Marion were retracing the trajectory of Hegel or Karl Rahner; he questions him for "phenomenologizing of theology": Does religious revelation have to be grasped on the phenomenologically described grounds of pure counterexperience, namely, as the saturated phenomenon of the second order? For Janicaud, a strictly Husserlian phenomenology prohibits any theological turn of phenomenology; for Caputo, a correlational, nonliteralist theology prescribes certain hermeneutical conditions of possibility for receiving any revelation, and thus it prohibits a reified, counterexperiential phenomenological turn of theology. There is an ironic sense in which Janicaud's phenomenologically methodological atheism joins with Caputo's Derridean religion without religion. And from the opposite sides they try to limit Marion's "hyperbolic" phenomenology in order to leave room for the venture and risk of crucified, dark, struggling faith that here and now sees only the hidden God. Indeed, as St. Paul said, this faith sees through a glass and darkly. For Janicaud, not unlike Schellenberg and Nietzsche, a hidden God is always already not just incomprehensible but also a "dead God." For Caputo (2007:89), "the excess in faith is not that of phenomena saturated or doubly saturated with plenitudinous givenness, but of venturing out beyond the limits of givenness into deeper and uncharted seas, out upon the sixty thousand fathoms as Kierkegaard used to say."

Moral evil saturates the garden variety of natural (common and banal) phenomena, the paradoxical, as well as the higher-order phenomena of defiance and cruelty. The latter, I claim, must be comprehended in "religious" terms. Yet any description of the second order of saturation in radical evil requires neither theology nor sacred texts to be revealed. Gods have fled, yet cruelty prevails. Radical evil reveals itself as a type of counterexperience; and yet as the negatively saturated one, it is revealed "correlationally," that is, in human situations and hermeneutical contexts in which it is performed. Radical evil reveals the exceeding impossibility or saturation of the second order yet without denying its own banality or hermeneutical situatedness in everydayness; it happens in a phenomenological field of experience yet exceeds it by counterexperience; it reveals the religious precisely in the eclipse of its melancholy despair, that is, by and in relating to the absent sun defiantly, rather than like the *khôra*—mutely, deafly, without heart, not at all. Radical evil manifestly rages in this world; yet is what it reveals in its deeds of this world or of the unmoved, unaffected, and unresponsive nothingness only? "If God was absent in the extermination camps, the devil was very obviously present in them" (Lévinas, 1988:163).

FOUR

Job Questions Kant

●

We pray to be delivered from all evil; we hope we can avoid temptation to do iniquity, and that evil deeds will be wiped clean with the rites of atonement, fasting, or pilgrimages to holy places. But in our prayers and hopes, do we comprehend how *radical* is the "radical evil" that darkens our intellect and weakens our will?

The problem of evil has been for the most part associated with the slew of logical and evidential arguments for or against theism (Howard-Snyder, 1996:xi–xx). This literature treats evil as a problem for any coherent theodicy. Is it not then curious that analytic philosophers of religion would accept Dostoyevsky's last novel, *The Brothers Karamazov*, especially the chapters on Ivan Karamazov's and the Grand Inquisitor's rebellion, as a literary version of such deductive and probabilistic arguments (Howard-Snyder, 1996:286)? But the Grand Inquisitor is not an atheist; rather, he is someone who has come to divine good and evil in God's place. Ivan is not an atheist either but rather someone in despair. Dostoyevsky does not pose the problem of evil as a challenge to God but to human existence as well as to the idea of progress. Kant's (no less than Job's or Ivan Karamazov's) horror at the suffering of the innocent is not driven by rational arguments for or against theism. As ascertained in the opening chapter; neither Kant's nor Job's discussions of evil and hope are aimed at establishing philosophical theodicy. In order to bring all these considerations into a meditation, I must leave aside analytic debates about the "problem of evil" as largely marginal to the existential issues raised by post-Kantian reflections on radical evil and human freedom.

Kant argued in his late work *Religion within the Boundaries of Mere Reason* that evil must be imputed to the weakness of human will. In this series of meditations, anticipating the full discovery of radical evil as the negatively saturated phenomenon, first, I ponder Kant's insight that moral evil attests to the dignity of human freedom. Second, straining against Kant with penetrating questions posed by Arendt and Silber, I wonder whether his defense of moral reason suffices to sustain freedom. Third, I consider Cornell's (2002, 2003a,b,c,d,e) confrontation of Kant's discovery of radical evil with Adorno's and Benjamin's notions of progress. How can we conceive of the ideal of humanity in a manner that is at once open and critical? This challenge makes evil not only banal in Arendt's assessment of Eichmann and morally radical for Kant, but also disastrous for Benjamin. If Adorno and Cornell are right—that we must resist radical evil without becoming totalitarian in turn—should we leave this requirement to those whose view of original sin as predestination justifies domination? In this meditation, Job fully confronts Kant about what radical evil discloses concerning the progress of humanity.

KANT'S YES AND NO
TO "RADICAL" EVIL

Kant laments the fact of "radical evil" in international politics. When we consider the "state of constant war" among "civilized peoples" and how they "have also firmly taken it into their heads not to get out of it," then we become aware of the fundamental contradiction between our promulgated moral principles and the realpolitik. In his "Religion" essay, he presciently describes the disdain that is expressed for the relevance of the United Nations at the start of the twenty-first century: "So *philosophical chiliasm,* which hopes for a state of perpetual peace based on a federation of nations united in a world-republic, is universally derided as sheer fantasy as much as *theological chiliasm,* which awaits for the completed moral improvement of the human race" (Kant, 1996, 6:34). A telling footnote explains that the human race is guided by the raw progress of nature through force rather than by the other-regarding categorical imperative to treat humans as ends in themselves:

> So long as a state has a neighboring one which it can hope to subdue, it strives to aggrandize itself by subduing it. It thus strives for . . . a state constitution in which all freedom would necessarily expire. . . . Yet after this monster . . . has swallowed up all its neighbors, it ultimately disintegrates all by itself. [And] instead of striving after a union of states (a republic of free federated peoples), in turn begins the same game all over again, so that war (that scourge of the human race) will not cease. (6:35)

Kant confesses the "incomprehensible" (6:44) reality of radical evil—hateful distortions of friendship, cruelty, savagery, sectarian violence, warfare among states—only to save humans from misanthropy, indeed, to bid them instead to become enlightened through tolerance (6:33). Good and evil originate in human free will as our choice of fundamental maxims we give ourselves. We alone are authors of good or evil choices (6:21–22, 25). This high level of deontic responsibility is the price humans must pay for the dignity of their free will. There is no other original sin—another "beginning in time" of evil—than its subjective origin in lived will (6:42).

Radically evil for Kant is the human reality that while we have the disposition *(Gesinnung)* to good and evil, our intellect and will suffer a certain propensity *(Hang)*—there are only negative ones—or weakness that predisposes us to adopt evil rather than good maxims to guide our conduct. Kant attributed this propensity *(Hang)* not to some original depravity—in talking of certain innate negative propensities he inherited and then turned away from the doctrine of original sin—but to the free will of the "good or evil heart." Weakness, impurity, and perversion of our actions are the three modalities of evil to which this freely adopted propensity gives rise (6:29–30). Thus the propensity is a remote negative influence if not a causal link, yet the evil act is morally attributable to free will that adopts it. One can be called evil *by nature* in all but a derivative sense (6:32). The acts of free will alone, not persons as such or races of people, can be imputed good or evil (6:31). If we cannot observe the maxim giving in others, then we can hardly detect its upsurge within our free will. We do not possess access to the originating ground of *any* maxims in a person. Ergo, "the judgment that an agent is an evil human being cannot reliably be based on experience" (6:20).

Radical evil—so named by Kant—is never so "radical" that it could destroy human dignity. Human dignity comprises free will and its transcendental (i.e., rationally inescapable) conditions—the respect for moral law inscribed into our hearts and every exercise of freedom. Free will is inscribed into the rational requirement to always act in consistency with the reciprocal recognition of freedom of others. Not that we always act morally, that is, in accord with the categorical imperative to universalize our maxims for action, not that we always emphatically respect the moral law in our actions. For Kant the crucial is the a priori, transcendental respect for the moral law from whose categorical power even its transgressor unwittingly draws strength.

The weakness, impurity, and wickedness of the heart—and these are the three modalities of moral evil admitted by Kant—all arise from freely acting will. They arise neither from sensuousness nor from reason that is never cut off, Kant insists, from our respect for the moral law within. Just as for Newton gravity defines the laws of physics, so for Kant, following Rousseau, respect for the moral law defines the laws of practical reason. Just as Newton defined planetary motions by the laws of gravity that are never invalidated by natural disasters, so Kant insists that an evildoer cannot but act—transcendentally speaking—for the sake of some good. Respect for the moral law is Kant's rational (albeit not thereby necessarily motivational) and only so inescapable transcendental conditions of free action (Allison, 2001:87; Neiman, 2002:5; cf. Baynes, 2005).

Sensuous desires offer us too little to qualify for free human acts, and reason holds too much ideality to qualify for radical evil. So we may not root radical moral evil in the core of rational humanity, as that would transform any one of us into "a *diabolical* being" (6:35). "Despite a corrupted heart" the human person can "always" possess "a good will" (6:44).

In a nuanced move intended to save the human dignity of practical reason even in evildoers, Kant softens the radicalness of evil insofar as it could never shatter our rational ability to recover free will *as* goodwill. He calls only the "perversity of the heart" radically "evil."

By locating the radical root of evil in human "depravity" *(Bösartigkeit),* that is, in something that does not prevent me from repenting myself back into ethical life, Kant (1996, 6:37) avoids rooting "malice" *(Bösheit)* in willing as such. He absolves the legislative will *(Wille)* that never wavers in its respect for the law and assigns the root of evil to free choice of the lived will that is never fully coincident with itself *(Willkür).* Radical evil—this "foul stain of our species" (6:38)—never destroys our respect for the moral law within, and Kant shies away from admitting this possibility out of fear of crippling rational freedom's access to moral light. That one could in principle "incorporate evil *qua* evil for incentive into one's maxim" and *do* things "diabolical" (6:37), but in that doing still remain human and not becoming thereby a "*diabolical* being" (6:35), this Kant rejects without explanation or persuasive argument.[1]

WITH KANT AT AUSCHWITZ

In attending to the moral evil we know today, how should *we* grasp its radicalness? In this question, my meditations on radical evil have since the beginning moved beyond the limit Kant places on radical evil (and not just religion!) by setting it within the bounds of mere reason. By "radical evil," I mean what Adams (1999) calls "horrendous evil." She defines "horrors as evils the participation in (the doing or suffering) of which constitutes *prima facie* reason to doubt whether the participant's life could (given their inclusion in it) be a great good to him/her on the whole" (2001:871). Horrendous evil destroys the "meaning-making structures" and value of persons (872). "Horrors resist domestication in terms of 'morally sufficient' reasons" (873). By radical evil I mean also what Arendt (1992:166) wrote to Jaspers on March 4, 1951: "making human beings as human beings superfluous." This act does not just treat humans as means to ends but destroys our capacity for freedom and spontaneity. Kant locates radical evil in human weakness and self-love, so he aims to preserve the human dignity of evildoers, thereby insisting on the inescapable transcendental conditions of every human action. Arendt's study of radical evil revealed that even Kant's "apparently *transcendental* condition of a human life *can* be eliminated *empirically,* by totalitarian means" (Bernstein, 2002:208).

John Silber Joins with Job

A recent challenge to Kant is found in Silber's (1960, 1991) commentary on Kant's religion work. "It is time that Kant, in particular, comes to Auschwitz" (Silber, 1991:180). After taking Job to Auschwitz, with Kant we have the advantage of applying the imperative of the Judaic anti-idolatry law (none of us is God) to correct Kant's moral law (that in positive deployment of human freedom one can only act by respecting the moral law). Kant rejects the cosmological (causal) and design (purpose) proofs for God's existence, as all variations of these classical and modern proofs require an intermediary step in an ontological argument for God's existence, which illegitimately infers from an innate idea of God to positing of God's existence. So at best Kant allows us to hope for God, immortality, and final judgment as moral postulates warranting the ultimate coincidence of happiness with moral virtue. Is not postulating even *moral* hope but a form of rational theodicy, albeit rooted in a belief in the moral and lawful universe of absolute freedom?

Silber (1960:cxxviii) identifies two flaws in Kant's theory of radical evil. One of these is Kant's rejection of diabolical will; the other is the issue of forgiveness. The first flaw appears even though Kant rejects the Socratic view that sin is ignorance and concedes that humans at times knowingly do evil. Yet why they do evil does not devalue rational freedom; their evil act is explained by human weakness. "Devilishness was shown to be an illusion, because no one can deliberately reject the law since the power (the freedom) to reject anything is derived from the law" (cxxix). Defiance of rational freedom is impotence for Kant, never something in itself positive. I believe that the view we find from Kant to Hegel, Marx to Habermas—that radical evil is moral weakness or impotence, rather than a positive mode of power—differs in crucial ways from the line of modern thought running from Schelling to Kierkegaard to Dostoyevsky to Lévinas and Derrida that admits the possibility of radical evil as power that can be positively asserted. I will return to the latter in my meditation on the negatively saturated phenomenon.

Kant remains classically Platonic in his rejection of the possibility of a diabolical agency that could empower a positive rejection of the moral law. Silber draws on Pauline misgivings about the Greek optimism that we have at our disposal the rational ability to establish harmonious coincidence between knowing and willing. Even though both the Greeks and Kant consider the evidence of *akrasia* (incontinence, weakness, moral impotence), they doubt the possibility that humans could knowingly violate what they know is rational and good. This feared possibility would mean that radical evil arises in the human heart that is split within itself, and arises regardless of one's knowledge of the moral law or one's intentions (Payne, 2005:84, 121, 212). The Pauline and in this I believe also Job's corrective to Kant finds its existential articulation in Kierkegaard's notion of defiant despair no less than in Nietzsche's will to power.

Silber (1960:cxxx–cxxi and n. 122) sums up the first flaw as a failure to admit "that the power of volitional rationality can be fully asserted either in irrationality or in sound rationality." But practical reason does not destroy its own power to act against the moral law. One can ascribe impotence to theoretical irrationality (i.e., incoherence), Silber shows, but "volitional irrationality can derive its power elsewhere. . . . in a parasitic use of theoretical reason . . . [and in] other non-rational sources for the power of freedom and personality." Silber concludes his analysis of the first flaw by showing that there is no ground for rejecting the possibility that I could be free to fulfill myself, finding my purpose, precisely by rejecting the moral law. If my freedom can empower itself "apart from its observance of the law"—if defiance is possible—then not all power of freedom must come from the observance of the law. Disobeying the moral law, while illogical and even transcendentally or performatively self-contradictory, does not necessarily lead to the destruction of one's freedom and thus of the self whose foundation is freedom. Dostoyevsky's portraits of moral defiance—whether Ivan Karamazov or his alter ego in the Grand Inquisitor or the man from the underground—are not guided by logic. Nor are they morally impotent and powerless in some perverse fulfillment of desire or intention. They intuitively exceed what can be grasped conceptually; they defy moral logic to defend freedom!

We can mark the exact juncture at which Dostoyevsky and Lévinas part ways both with Kant's rationalized moral religion and Derrida's yielding to the aporetic possibility that the impossible hides behind the curtain of the holy of holies the secret that there is no secret but the unvocative nothingness of the *khôra* (on the curtain between the holy of holies and the holy that used to be in the Jerusalem Temple until its Roman destruction, and on Derrida's *tallith*, his prayer shawl, see Derrida, S 314–319, 326–328). In their parting from Nietzsche's transvaluation of all values as well as Ivan Karamazov's nihilistic response to the useless suffering of innocent children, each in his way affirms Job's antitheodicy and Jesus's low Christology, that is, in both instances they provide an ethico-religious responsibility as the answer to suffering. All innocent suffering for Lévinas remains useless until or unless one responds to it ethically; for Dostoyevsky innocent suffering remains scandalous until or unless one bears it for the other redemptively or in an act that Lévinas calls substitution. Bernstein is right on the money when he makes the following observation: "When Lévinas speaks about the scandal of useless suffering, he sounds as if he is uttering the very words of Ivan [Karamazov]" (2002:171). Indeed, "Each of us is guilty before the other for everything, and I more than any" (Dostoyevsky, 2003:374, 386). "We are all responsible for everyone else—but I am more responsible than all the others" (Lévinas, 1981:146; cf. 1988:179; and Lévinas's response in Kearney, 2004:82). This core claim of human ethico-religious solidarity with Adam, Job, and the crucified Jesus, is spoken with equal strength by Father Zossima describing the youthful impact of his brother's conversion from hatred to forgiveness, Alyosha Karamazov confronting Ivan's nihilism, and Lévinas who in his Kaunas years in Lithuania learned the heart of his Judaic philosophy from Russian Christian novelists.

The second flaw in Kant's treatment of radical evil is the antinomy of freedom and forgiveness (Silber, 1960:cxxxi–cxxxiv). Forgiveness absolves of moral guilt only to weaken the absoluteness of deontic freedom, yet unabsolved and aggravated guilt can in its despairing freedom collapse into itself. Grace and freedom, the need for forgiveness and the inescapability of the moral law, stand in antinomical positions. How will one's lack of goodness, one's evil, be overcome—will it be by active moral repentance or by the gift of grace? Ahead of Sartre and Lévinas, Kant places on human shoulders absolute responsibility as the price for difficult freedom; yet the finite guilty will has no power to acquire innocent freedom. Lost innocence and so lost hope represent a second level of difficulty for which finite guilty freedom has nothing in its rational toolbox. Innocence and hope are not transcendental conditions of freedom even for Kant; they are at best moral postulates. But what can guilty freedom postulate of its own accord unless it is empowered to do so in the first place? If humans have absolute freedom, Silber contends, then Kant must agree with Ivan Karamazov that "there can be no forgiveness." For Ivan, and, as we shall see in part 3 with Jankélevitch, every forgiveness of the unforgivable violates the moral law itself; forgiveness is a "moral outrage" (cxxxiii). The either/or posed by Dostoyevsky's novel is either sensuality, suicide, insanity, or the gift of forgiveness (cxxxiv). In sum, the two flaws Silber identifies in Kant lead us to ponder whether or not human freedom is ever either fully rational or absolute.

Arendt: Is Moral Evil Radical or Banal?

Silber takes up the possibility of the demonic in relation to Arendt's thesis of the banality of evil. Arendt's treatment of radical evil is both consistent and evolving, though she never means by it what Kant does, as Bernstein explains (2002:205–24). Arendt's (1951) early position is formed by her study of totalitarianism. Radical evil is characterized by the following aspects: it makes human beings superfluous, it destroys their spontaneous freedom and "natality," it prompts individuals to strive for omnipotence that eliminates human plurality, and its horrors pale with what Job and Kant had to face. She agrees with Kant on spontaneity being one of the transcendental conditions for effective freedom; she disagrees with him that those conditions could not be destroyed (Bernstein, 2002:208). Totalitarianism kills both the juridical and moral in human persons and destroys all human creative ability to act newly, singularly, and spontaneously (Arendt, 1951:438, 447, 451, 455). Bernstein (2002:213) identifies a "theological aura" in Arendt's early view of radical evil, or with what I identified in chapter 1 as the core violation of the Judaic law of anti-idolatry:

> What is it about superfluousness that makes this evil so distinctive and so radical? It is not exclusively the humiliation, torture, and systematic murder of millions (Jews and non-Jews). It is also the *hubris* of those totalitarian leaders who think they are omnipotent, that they can *rival* a God who created a plurality of human beings.

Echoing these dangers, Habermas (2003:115), another post-Kantian centurion witnessing to the secular translation of the anti-idolatry law, warns against making humans superfluous by positive eugenics or cloning. His tone-deafness to the music of the heavenly spheres does not preclude his earnest, honest atheism to work as a salutary curb on the human desire to play God: "Would not the first human being to determine, *at his own discretion,* the natural essence of another human being at the same time destroy the equal freedoms that exist among persons of equal birth in order to ensure their difference?"

Arendt (1965) shifts her language from radical evil to the banality of evil in her consideration of the special case of Eichmann kidnapped and then tried in Jerusalem for orchestrating the Final Solution. But it was Jaspers in correspondence with her in 1946 (Arendt, 1992:62, Bernstein, 2002:214f.) who introduced first the notion of banality to correct for any dangers of glorifying a "satanic greatness" of the Nazis or "the 'demonic' element in Hitler." She responded by vowing to "combat all impulses to mythologize the horrible" (Arendt, 1992:69). The notion of evil's banality should be viewed through the prisms of the anti-Manichaean, Judaic law of anti-idolatry: one ought not worship the diabolical by ascribing to it an aura of greatness. In her report on Eichmann's trial, she came to terms with the horrendous acts done by ordinary citizens, not by a race of devils from another planet. Her thesis of evil's banality, which replaced her language of radical or even demonic evil, is to account for Eichmann's respect for Kant's moral law while also judging his acts as crimes against humanity. Bernstein (2002:218) clarifies what changed and what remained the same in her position:

> Arendt *never* repudiated the thought-trains that went into her original discussion of radical evil, especially the claim that radical evil involves making human beings as human beings superfluous, as well as systematic attempt to eliminate human spontaneity, individuality, and plurality. On the contrary, the phenomenon that she identified as the banality of evil *presupposes* this understanding of radical evil.

Evil is not sought in some hidden depth (it is not radical for her in that root sense); it is found among ordinary and even surface phenomena. Yet its radicalness follows that same aim Kofman, just as Arendt, identifies with Auschwitz—to destroy the human in the human person.

Eichmann made a perfect test case for Kant in Auschwitz because he cited Kant's categorical imperative during his trial: always act in such a way that the *Führer* would approve!

What Arendt does not spell out in her report is that Eichmann's banal little-German appeal to the moral law violates the anti-idolatry law. Evildoers are not monsters or a race of devils from another planet. Yet the nice boy next door who drops the bomb on Hiroshima, albeit his act of military obedience is banal, deliberately exercises an idolatrous freedom of his superiors to render humans superfluous. It is not a perverted moral freedom that still holds out respect for Kant's moral law that must be deemed evil (appeals to Kant too might be called banal); it is the unrepented freedom that suffers no guilt and thus appears in no need of forgiveness that is radically evil. Kant's three modalities of evil—frailty, impurity, and wickedness—do not go to the heart of Eichmann's absolute freedom to play God to human beings in his self-defense in Jerusalem. Could Kant's morality resist Auschwitz as well as Job's anti-idolatry?

Civil Disobedience of Evil Authority and the Possibility of Free Defiance

Bernstein (2002:33, 36f.) finds Kant at war with himself and judges Kant's "analysis of evil and radical evil" to be "disappointing." How could Eichmann defend his conduct by appealing to Kant's categorical imperative (Arendt, 1965:136)? While we would be unfair to accuse Kant's (1996b: 18f.) answer to his own question, "What is Enlightenment?" to exonerate Hitler's or Eichmann's conduct, Kant did prohibit dissent against legal authority: "There is no right of edition (*sedition*), much less a right of revolution (*rebellio*), and least of all a right to lay hands on or take the life of the chief of state when he is an individual person on the excuse that he has misused his authority." And even if Kant would judge the Nazis to be criminals, he offers no alternative to evil authority. Its subjects must "endure even the most intolerable abuse of supreme authority."

Baynes (2005) should not be surprised that Kant's critics (Copjec, 1996; Bernstein, 2002:38–45; Silber, 1960, 1991) question his emphatically rationalistic account of human evil. Does Kant actually show that humans cannot *become* diabolical beings? He demonstrates at best what must be a priori (rationally, transcendentally) required for a consistently free agency; he does not prove what could become the case. Does the transcendental limit of what one in principle cannot freely and consistently reject—the moral law within—exhaust the possibility of what one can become—for example, a diabolically free agent? Eichmann, contrary to Fackenheim's (1994) wish, provided Kant with the best a posteriori defense by acknowledging the categorical imperative both in his execution of Hitler's Final Solution and by his self-defense in Jerusalem. In this he demonstrated that even the Nazis could not repudiate the moral law as such even as they chose to violate it. This is good for Kant, but is it enough for Job?

Bernstein (2002:39), confirming in this regard Silber (1991:198f.), contends that Kant's theory of free will requires admitting the perverse possibility that remains categorically undertheorized if not rejected without an argument by him: "It must be possible for an individual to *become* a devillish person. . . . to defy and repudiate the moral law in such a manner that he freely adopts a disposition *(Gesinnung)* in which he consistently refuses to do what the moral law requires." Contrary to Baynes (2005) and Allison (2001), Kant's critics do not conflate the transcendental conditions of freedom with empirical facts of human motivation. Critics are not defining human nature or the race of humans as diabolical, nor are they denying that someone like Eichmann could be at once clever and banal enough to offer and believe in his commonsense respect for the moral law. The key critical claim is that what is missing in Kant's rational architectonic set for free will as well as in the transcendental conditions of the possibility of freedom is the possibility of free defiance. Silber (1991:199) drives this crucial point home:

> Kant not only ignored all literary and imaginative efforts to describe devilish beings who defiantly and powerfully reject the moral law, he even ignored demonic personalities of his own times such as Robespierre, although they are admittedly pale examples in comparison with those that were to emerge with the rise of totalitarianism in our time.

The reasons for Kant's rejection of diabolical volition in humans are conceptual. Such volition is either beyond experience (and that goes for the

literary portraits of Milton's Satan, Macbeth, Richard III, Faust, Ivan Karamazov, or the Grand Inquisitor), or in their wickedness, humans are but
weak, impotent. Doing evil—irrational use of freedom—can never be for
Kant a positive expression of human freedom. Silber (1991:200) contends
that Kant does not detect limits of human freedom, but only the limits of
his own conception of it. Yet, Bernstein rejoins, Kant overlooks consequences of his articulation of free will. "There is no free choice *(Willkür)*
unless there is the free choice to be morally evil, and even devilish" (Bernstein, 2002:42).

PROGRESS AS DISASTER: FROM KANT TO ADORNO VIA BENJAMIN

> Through war, through the taxing and never-ending
> accumulation of armament, through the want which any
> state, even in peacetime, must suffer internally, Nature
> forces them to make at first inadequate and tentative
> attempts; finally, after devastations, revolutions, and
> even complete exhaustion, she brings them to that
> which reason could have told them at the beginning
> and with far less sad experience, to wit, to step from the
> lawless conditions of savages into a league of nations.
> —Immanuel Kant (1963:18f.)

Moral Evil as a Radical Limit

Cornell adopts a positive ideal of humanity from Kant and reads it through
Adorno's (1973) negative delimitation of all totality or utopian concepts.
Her philosophy of limit (1992) critically informs the task of recollective
imagination (1993) as well as the conceptuality of the imaginary domain
(1995) wherein we are to face our humanity (2003b) as our critically open
and always reimagined task (2003a). If there is progress, it must respect
Kant's insistence that ideals remain regulative (not nameable in a metaphysical sense). It must likewise heed Adorno's corrective to all striving for
assimilative closure of ideals in identity logic or totality thinking. With
Adorno (1998), Cornell reconsiders Kant's (1996) moral notion of radical
evil, but, like most post-Holocaust thinkers, she includes under "radical
evil" more than Kant's moral weakness or propensity to self-love. Her notion of cruelty lies much closer to Arendt's worry about making human superfluous than to Kant's saving the rational face of evildoers.

What is the promise of progress, she queries with Adorno (1998:143f.)?
Progress can overcome evil only without progressive ideal becoming itself a
homogenizing concept or static achievement. Progress lies in the margin

between cruelty that holds no relationship to historical idealities, and violence that still contains a relationship to ideals of humanity. Cornell (2004) illustrates this distinction in the first and second Persian Gulf wars: "Progressive idealists in the global antiwar movement are insisting on the mediation of violence by ideals . . . [against] the cruelty that treats the citizens of Iraq as disposable people." By labeling some groups or individuals as evil, politicians make it possible (1) to dehumanize the enemy through raising the "fear of the evil they" (and this is her learning from Kant's moral definition of evil), (2) to raise emblems and fetishes so that they can rally people around God and country (this emphasis appears in Kierkegaard's religious critique of Christendom), and (3) to blur the line between violence and cruelty in the cleansing of evil (this courts the danger of diabolical evil).

Cornell (2004) underscores Kant's point with the case of a Palestinian mother whose suicide bomber daughter killed two Israeli civilians: even the terrorist who commits wrongful violence has a human face. Kant's moral tenor is worth repeating. Evil can be imputed to human will, but never to our humanity. Hence Kant (1996, 6:37), unlike politicians who stir passions against evildoers, affirms "depravity" *(Bösartigkeit)* but downplays "malice" *(Bösheit)* of willing. He absolves our self-legislative will *(Wille),* since it always respects the moral law, and locates evil in our free choice *(Willkür).* This move is replayed against Kant's denial of diabolical in human conduct when Cornell introduces the distinction between violence that still carries its umbilical cord to human ideals and cruelty that appears to have fallen into nonhuman bestiality. Whether or not humans can commit diabolical evil is another question that Cornell (2004), unlike Kant, does not even raise. She wants to "return to the battle over ideals and attack the cruelty" that underwrites all dehumanization of the sources of human evil.

Adorno (1998:153) unmasks our "false reverence" for evil with which we deride hope for perfectability of human nature and condemn human civilization. He (144) defends Kant's perpetual peace in order to wrestle the ideals of progress from mere struggle for self-preservation. Cornell (2004; cf. 2002) harnesses the ideal of humanity to overcome the civilization of cruelty. Here we find ourselves at the heart of her new critical theory. She productively deploys the antinomy between the transhistorical ideal of humanity and concrete historical humans. She corrects for the positivism of a fully rationalized progress and yet retains its ideality as a critical ally against cruelty. This alliance between critical ideals and suspicion becomes possible thanks to what Cornell (2004) invokes as "Kant's negative dialectic of unsocial sociability." The term "unsocial sociability" comes from Kant's "Idea of Universal History," thesis 4 (1963:15). Its characterization as "negative dialectic" marks Cornell's reading of Kant through Adorno. She speaks of *moral evil as a radical limit* that presents us with the task to reimagine human ideals. A narrow passage between limit and human ideals—a free play of imagination—enables progress. Even if we were a race of devils, here echoing Kant, we might be able to resist the fate of a self-destructive dialectic of enlightenment. Because we are primitively "unsocial," we become sociable in order to protect ourselves from nature and each other. Even as a race of devils, humans could come to control what is other than them. Social harmony would emerge through a self-corrective process of learning. We would stop resorting to warfare when nations have completely exhausted their unsociable ways of coexisting. Perpetual peace would arise as a dystopian utopia. This Kantian view of history allows for social progress within the margins of rationality winning through unsociable discord and even against our weak and selfish moral will (Kant's definition of radical evil).

Cornell (2004) echoes Kant's mixed assessment of "human beings who have only come together in order to preserve themselves against endless violence and yet cannot seem to avoid being the bullies on the playground." Progress is never something positively normative but is a dialectic of progress and evil. At the limit of our self-destructiveness, we project the regulative possibility of "a redeemed humanity" that would reconcile self-preservation and ideal sociability. Formerly excluded groups would find it possible to represent and reconstitute this ideality. A human ideal, to be normative in a critical sense, cannot be ontologically immanent to what always already is: "Symbolic universality thus always carries within it a moment of transcendence since it tries to represent what does not yet exist." Even as unrepresentable metaphysically, humanity as a multiple ideality can become "deliberately resistant and inconclusive." The imaginary domain exists by our birthright (human as well as moral and legal right) as a field of possibility through which we both relate to received traditions and envision new ways of being in them (2003c). The task of the critical theorist is to raise one's consciousness that alone must engage the imaginary domain through what it reimagines, performs, and embodies in existence. Cornell (2003b) updates the "Kantian lesson" through Adorno's dialectic of enlightenment and radical evil: "We do not deserve to be human and cannot lose our humanity"; "we need to learn today that a crime against humanity does not justify further crimes against humanity."

Radical Evil as a Limit

> This storm is what we call progress. The concept of
> progress must be grounded in the idea of catastrophe.
> —Walter Benjamin (1968:258, 1999:N9a, 1)

Kant apprehends *moral evil as a radical limit* on the positive ideals of humanity. If we are not to leave discourse on evil to those who use original sin to justify dividing the human race into essentially good people and subhumans, then we need to face *radical evil as a limit* of the received notions of progress. I return from Adorno to Kant by way of Benjamin.[2]

Adorno (1998:153) worries about those antiprogress arguments that by the "translation of historical desperation into a norm" legitimate domination. Views such as "radical evil legitimates evil," or "progress from the slingshot to the megaton bomb may well amount to satanic laughter" reveal "false reverence" for evil. They falsely revere evil as if it were some object or face to be destroyed externally. Kant depicts evil as a quality of free will, and Adorno sticks with Kant (1996, 6:21–25): evil must be imputed to a human will that is free to be either good or evil. Evil acts do not disconnect one from human respect for the rational moral law.

Yet is there not also a false reverence for progress? Adorno (1998:160) concedes this possibility partially when he invokes the Judaic prohibition of carved idols to redeemed life. After Auschwitz any genealogy of human progress is implicated in the dialectic of evil and enlightenment. Echoing Kant, he foreshortens the triumph of radical evil: "If progress were truly a master of the whole, the concept which bears the marks of its violence, then progress would no longer be totalitarian. Progress is not a conclusive category. It wants to cut short the triumph of radical evil not to triumph as such itself." The concept of progress remains productive for Adorno as a negatively dialectical "resistance to perpetual danger of relapse." "Progress can begin at any moment" (150); "at all stages" it exists in forms of "resistance" (160).

Adorno rightly worries about predestination inscribed into the conservative reading of original sin. Cornell helpfully emphasizes the productive ideal of humanity. But can we close our eyes to what radical evil teaches us about ideals of humanity and progress? I want to intensify the question whether or not one can hold a false reverence for progress and I name three temporal limits placed by radical evil on the ideals of humanity and progress. If these limits affect everyone in every generation, then disregarding them here and now would attest to one's false reverence for the ideal of progress. First, there is evil of past unredeemed suffering. Second, there is the disconsolate present of reason and will. Third, there is a willed dimension of evil—cruelty—that closes off all prospects of a liberated future.

We run into the first limit with Benjamin's (1999:471, N7a,8) rebuttal to Horkheimer's letter of March 16, 1937. Is human history closed or open? If it is closed, then the suffering of the victims of history remains unredeemed. The finality of unjust death of those who were murdered is a consequence of a consistent materialist historiography. But does not crude materialism hold a false reverence for both evil and progress? It regards history as a science that investigates determined facts; it envisions progress as another set of facts. There pivots only an external relationship between the two sets. An unredeemed suffering inflicts a qualitative wound on the happiness and progress built on the blood of the dead victims. With a mixture of bad faith and faint smile, a crude materialist imagines to have escaped and now claims that because the "slain are really slain," one must move on. Benjamin offers a theologically materialist corrective to Horkheimer when he invokes anamnestic solidarity (mindful remembrance) that later generations ought to exercise for the sake of unredeemed suffering. In his "Theses on the Philosophy of History," he develops this idea: "The past carries with it a temporal index by which it is referred to redemption. There is a secret agreement between past generations and the present one. Our coming was expected on earth. Like every generation that preceded us, we have been endowed with a *weak* Messianic power, a power to which the past has a claim. That claim cannot be settled cheaply" (1968:254).[3]

The second limit placed by radical evil on the ideals of humanity and progress arises if we assume our ethical liability as members of later generations for past injustices and begin to act responsibly in the present. An existential reading of original sin that respects human freedom, notably by Kierkegaard and Jaspers, shows that no collective guilt for past injuries may be imputed, but collective liability can be accepted in the present historical tense by later generations. Responsibility, just like good and evil, is imputed solely to freely acting will. Reason and will become thus doubly disconsolate in the present. First, just as one cannot be collectively guilty by living in a nation that embarks on an unjust war, so also by living within a generation that has assumed liability for the past evils one cannot become responsible en masse. Insofar as imputing good and evil to anyone is possible, one stands alone regardless of whether one is a member of a generation that regresses or progresses. One neither escapes the generational failure without any liability (a sober rendition of original sin without a false reverence for evil) nor becomes responsible by simply closing ranks with a progressing generation (a sober existential corrective to a false reverence for progress). Second, no historical progress (even anamnestic solidarity) is able to fill the void of the injurious acts of annihilation or guarantee future outcomes of responsibility. This limit is not the same as the crude materialist's closing the book of life and hope on the past. Progress can infuse our responsible acts today, but it can never guarantee the harmonization of human ends in the future. Indeed, enlightened reason and responsible freedom remain doubly disconsolate. There is a form of atheism that can stand guard against a false reverence for progress, and we are falsely reverent whenever we reimagine or reinvest humanity with religious connotations and beliefs.[4]

The foregoing limitations of the ideals of humanity and progress turn into an aggravated third limit when human cruelty blossoms into flowers of evil. Adorno (1998:150, 160) is right that progress is available to us at any moment in a manner of human resistance. Benjamin (1968:261–64) is furthermore right that progression through empty present time is always catastrophic, while progress through the messianic gate of the now-time ("the time of the now," "messianic time") is available to us "every second of time." Until I face my ability to close off future hope at any moment—and this is what Job discloses in heeding the law of anti-idolatry—no resistance from within or without, no redemption can overcome my willed ignorance. Free will that binds itself in cruel joy of self-destructiveness lives by catastrophic freedom. Cruelty is the disaster of progress for everyone and in every generation.

Kant is frightened to admit the "diabolical" (1996:6:35, 37) into enlightened reason and will. This admission would demonize the human person beyond human recognition. The strength of Kant's moral sense of radical evil, underscored by Cornell's reading of the ideals of humanity and progress through Adorno's philosophy of the limit, is that they save the human face of the evildoer against dehumanizing racism. The humanity of the evildoer is also preserved by Arendt's (1964) emphasis on the banality of evil, with which she repudiated her earlier view (1951) conflating Kant's radical moral evil, he affirms, with diabolical evil, he shuns.[5]

Yet the most pedestrian form of the radically diabolical will is the cruel *human* face of the presumed do-gooder. From this combined angle, evil acts can be as much morally radical in the Kantian sense as also cruel and thus diabolical in the negatively saturated sense to be explained later, yet without those very acts becoming thereby nonhuman (Kant's worry) or satanically great (Jaspers's and Arendt's worry). The thesis of banality of evil only affirms that a good citizen—not a demon—can become perpetrator of monstrous deeds. Admitting the possibility of monstrous deeds does not require redefinition of human deeds as something other than human.

One does not need to go far to witness the grimace of a religiously bloated goodwill that rejoices in carrying out capital punishment, marching the nation to a war on evil, or cleansing one's ethnic neighborhood of those deemed other. For Kant no less than Adorno or Cornell, no triumph over evil can be called just that excludes part of the human race from humanity. Adorno lamented writing philosophy and even poetry after Auschwitz, yet only Benjamin admitted the possibility that historical progress is often disaster. Squaring Kant and Benjamin, Cornell follows Adorno to use his negative limit category itself as a form of resistance.

But facing one's capacity for cruelty at the heart of the desire to inhabit truth and do good requires courage to grasp *radical evil as limit of the ideal of humanity and progress.* This portends not only the Kantian limit of rational theodicy but also the limit on the idolatry of human progress. To think of progress as a developmental achievement that can be passed from one generation to the next is just as naive and dangerous as thinking of sin as some fixed inheritance. Here the progressivists share the existential blind spot with conservatives, and Adorno is not off the hook in his own argument against the latter. Both harbor an equally false reverence for abstract human existence, an abstraction that the sui generis thinker of human existence, Kierkegaard, unmasks as radical evil, indeed, the sin of Christendom. Because evil must be resisted in free will, and because cruelty can be resisted only by willing to be oneself without despair, no generation can resist or act on behalf of another. This limits further Benjamin's weak messianic force and our adoption of collective liability for the past and responsibility for the future generations. In human existence we begin in radical equality—always at the beginning. That realization offers a humble ideal of humanity and progress, but one that can better guard against its own disaster. Knowing one's humanity marks progress on the spot where one is pinned in existing. Progress becomes knowing oneself in a pregnant sense.

I think that progress is falsely revered when, like evil in reverse, it is projected outwardly as evolution of human history in sync with larger designs of nature. We can admire Kant's (1963:18–21, 23, 87f.) optimistic pessimism that "unsocial sociability" of the humankind would deliver us, let us say if the planet can stomach a few more wars, to a more workable U.N. Security Council. We can press his thought further that if moral evil must be imputed to free will, and not externally to evildoers who would have to be destroyed, then progress must be imputable only to free will. We must then grasp the radicalness of radical evil not as a negative limit of the human intellect and will hampering their progress externally but leaving them internally intact. We need to discern in evil a category that hemorrhages intellect and will inwardly, affecting even progress nurtured by goodwill and negative resistance. In the process of affirming the humanity of evildoers—thus the sheer banality of evil—we must not water down human evil, speaking of it as negative limit, as finitude or fallibilism, merely intellectually inscrutable something, but never as evil. If we are not to vacate the field to the conservatives who invoke God and sin but name evil by national and sectarian names, we must confront radical evil in the sense Kant and early Arendt conjured up and then hushed away, namely, as cruelty chosen positively—for its own sake. Human evil is more than ignorance; indeed, radical evil is at once banal, morally radical, paradoxical, and diabolical. Still, as I will drive home in the next two chapters, only that last sense of evil reveals its willed stupidity (Derrida, 1994:165 n. 31) which is echoed in that irreverent vision of progress as catastrophe by Angelus Novus (Benjamin, 1968:257f.).

The very possibility of humans freely defying the moral law is not easily read off from the transcendental conditions of freedom set within the rational bounds of respect for the moral law. But that *second-order possibility of impossibility*—defiance of creation and forgiveness—is detected and addressed by the Judaic law of anti-idolatry. This is why in meditating with Job at Auschwitz we have already journeyed further than if we arrived there alone with the Kantian philosophy of limit or with the knights of the paradoxical or aporetic transgression of limit or the deferral of the conceptual impossible, what I call *the first-order possibility of impossibility.*

To meditate on defiance as a negatively saturated, second-order possibility of the impossible, I turn to Schelling's rather mystical treatise on freedom. To bring this defiance closer to home existentially, that is, home in self-transformation, I spend some time with Kierkegaard's penetrating study of despair. Before explaining thus the theoretical and phenomenological possibility of the negatively saturated phenomenon in chapter 6, I will describe in the next chapter three cases of recent struggles for memory as the site of the best and the worst. The cases speak the words of *annunciation* by the angel of disaster, Paul Klee's painting, *Angelus Novus,* whose image is invoked by Benjamin (1968:257) speaking of horror wrought in the name of progress. It is for the sake of those without hope that one must invoke at this scene the words of Solomon, "love is as strong as death," indeed stronger than the faceless, hence uncaring silence of the *khôra* (cf. Derrida K with Rosenzweig, 2005:169).

FIVE

Redemption in an Antiredemptory Age

●

The destruction of a people raises for its contemporaries and later generations an urgent problem of memorial, memorialization, and memory. The question of memory opens the window onto a dimension of redemption. This dimension is intrinsically linked to the possibility of healing and making whole what has been smothered. If to hope is to resist cruelty from having the last word, then it means also to resist the cold unresponsive nothingness of the universe by our ethical responsiveness to the face of the other who commands me to do the works of love. *Khôra,* having no face and so being tone-deaf and unvocative, neither ethically commands nor religiously calls me. Redemptive critical theory or critical theory of redemption articulates the possibility of this ethico-religious resistance to cruelty and the nothingness of uncreation as hope.

I enter this meditation as a witness to the problem of memory in its existential and social dimensions. Both are expressed in cultural and artistic artifacts (memorials) as well as in social acts (politics of recognition). How can one speak of human annihilation with remembrance that bespeaks hope? That the present age is drenched in an aggravated scarcity of hope is yet another name for its antiredemptory attitude. *Our* memorial problem has become acute in an antiredemptory age. But how global is this situation? The wars of annihilation, the fundamentalist terror, and the wars on terror marking our era offer diminishing formative civilization values.

I meditate on three twentieth-century cases that witness to what I later explain by the concept of the negatively saturated phenomenon. The Jewish Central Museum in Prague during 1942–1945 dramatizes the site where the excess of negatively saturated phenomenon and the excess of impossible hope stand at the juxtaposition to each other. This site during the Nazi period houses the worst and the best, and so it poses the initial question of *our* memorial problem. The Mayan struggle for integrating the San Andrés Accords on Indigenous Rights and Culture into Mexico's Constitution illustrates the memorial problem at the limits of the politics of recognition. The creation of antiredemptory countermonuments in Germany's coming to terms with the destruction of the European Jews highlights the limits of both art and the politics of memorialization. Given the limits of recognition and memorialization in all three cases, what reparations for destroyed hope are possible in an antiredemptory age?

MEMORIALIZATION: THE SITE
OF THE BEST AND THE WORST

The subject of this meditation is the twentieth-century museum that has become the paradigm site of the best and the worst. In 2006 the Jewish Museum in Prague celebrated one hundred years of its founding in the heart of the ancient Jewish Quarter. Built as the third-oldest Jewish museum in Central Europe (Chateau, 2004), it grew from 1906 through 1926 even as most of the old Jewish town disappeared during the Austrian-Hungarian modernization of Prague (1897–1921). The Jewish Museum was radically refashioned under the plan hatched after Hitler's takeover of Bohemia and Moravia on March 15, 1939. Was the secret project for the Jewish Central Museum in Prague conceived by forces of resistance or annihilation? Even though the curators of various centennial exhibits of the museum have been curiously silent about this fact (Veselská, 2005), the wartime museum was most likely spearheaded by both, thereby becoming at once the site of dissent and destruction.

The Twofold Origin of the Museum

By the end of 1941, all synagogues in Bohemia were closed and Jews were forbidden to sell or otherwise transfer their property. Jewish religious communities in Bohemia and Moravia were the main depositories of religious objects, but in 1942 Prague's Jewish religious community became the only functioning community. According to the most cited version of the museum's wartime history, sometime early in 1942 lawyer Dr. Karel Stein, then director of the department for affairs of countryside of in Bohemia and Moravia and later a member of the Prague Jewish religious community, proposed to the Nazis creation of the Jewish Central Museum in Prague, which would gather in one place all religious and museum objects from around the country (Chateau, 2004). This story is defended by some Czech scholars working in the museum today and is presented in museum brochures. The Jewish plan, it is stressed by this version, was to resist and save religious and cultural objects for future generations (Brandner, 2001). If

Stein's initiative marks the true inspiration and origin of the central memorial project (and his activity is not in question), then this feat took place under the nose of Reinhard Heydrich, the main architect of the "Final Solution of the Jewish question," who was also Himmler's right hand in the Protectorate of Bohemia and Moravia. The Zentrallstelle für Jüdische Auswanderung—Center for Jewish Emigration—was created in Prague in July 1939. It was renamed in August as Zentralamt für Regelung der Judenfrage in Böhmen und Mähren—Center for the Regulation of the Jewish Question in Bohemia and Moravia. The center reported directly to Department IVB4 of Reichssicherheitshauptamt in Berlin, headed then by Adolf Eichmann. In early 1942 the Prague Jewish religious community began to gather all public Jewish property from the religious communities in Bohemia and Moravia. On May 27, 1942, Heydrich was assassinated in Prague by the Czech paratroopers sent from Britain, and he died on June 4. From May and June of the same year, we find sporadic written evidence that the museum project was directed by the SS Untersturmführer Karl Rahm. In a letter dated June 17, 1942, the director of the Prague Jewish religious community wrote to the Zentralstelle with a request to begin collecting all public Jewish religious and cultural objects from Bohemia and Moravia in Prague. The museum authority in the letter was, however, ascribed to Rahm. The day before Heydrich's assassination, May 26, Rahm ordered all valuable Jewish artifacts to be gathered in Prague (Petrášová, 1988:10). He wrote, "All historically valuable objects of religious cult found outside of Prague should be sent to Prague and gathered in the Jewish Museum" (Brandner, 2001; cf. Volavková, 1968:33, 72; Altshuler and Cohn, 1983:24; Lieben, 1912).[1]

Why would the Nazis in Prague agree to a memorial site for the same people their immediate superiors, such as Heydrich and Eichmann, intended to erase from existence? The few surviving written documents about the museum plan do not suggest an answer. Was this idea for the central museum an act of resistance by a small group of Jewish intellectuals, among them the philosophers Salomon Hugo Lieben and Dr. Josef Polák, and the museum architect, František Zelenka (cf. Veselská, 2005)? Or should we accept the verdict of Kisch (1986:331), one of the famous German-writing Jews in Prague, who calls the Jewish Central Museum from 1942 to 1945 the "mausoleum" created by the Nazi murderers for their Jewish victims? Kisch opens his journalistic essay on the wartime museum story with a strong claim that contradicts the official Czech historians: "The plan was this: To destroy the million-strong people" and build the museum testifying to their extinction.

Interestingly, two Czech graduate works seem to give more than a nod to Kisch, and so take on the one-sided official Czech version presented during the museum's centennial in 2006 as well as in the regular museum history today. Petrášová writes in her dissertation, defended during the last year of the communist regime (1988:8f.), that while Dr. Stein had the idea to gather Jewish artifacts in Prague in order to preserve them, "without some effort to preserve them from the side of the SS there could be no such gathering of Jewish memorabilia in Prague." She raises the doubt that "it is impossible to exclude [the possibility] that the first impulse [to gather the objects in a museum] came precisely from the Zentralstelle." Indeed, on April 24, 1941, Heydrich himself came up with the idea of transporting the Jewish collections from the Mikulov Museum to Prague. Petrášová suggested the other possible motive for the museum's origin: "The Nazis wanted to erect a museum of the extinct race and document in it their idea of anti-Semitism and racism" (9). She is forthcoming in interpreting all the sparse historical evidence without downplaying the possibility of the best and the worst:

> The Jewish Central Museum was an institution that originated from the encounter of two antagonistic and disjointed views and interests. At one side stood the Nazis, whose aim it was by means of this museum to catalogue and document the memorabilia of the annihilated Jewish communities, in order to gradually create a museum conceived in the spirit of racism and serving the Nazi ideology. At the other side stood Jewish specialists, the very creators of the museum, whose aim it was to preserve for the future generations by means of this museum the cultural and artistic testimony of the Jewish communities of Bohemia and Moravia. (71)

In her master's thesis Veselská (1999:25) largely confirms Petrášová's findings that whether the decisive impulse for the Jewish Central Museum came from Stein or the SS is unclear. She concedes that the first impulse to centralize Jewish artifacts came from the Zentralstelle. Regardless of who gave the first impetus, she does not hesitate to interpret the continuing motives of the Zentralstelle that "the Jewish museum was supposed to be anti-Jewish, the museum of 'the destroyed Jewish race'. . . . It was supposed to serve later as one of the educational centers for new generations of German national specialists." The Jewish leaders hoped to preserve Jewish life in face of extermination; the Nazis memorialized the race condemned to death. The museum became for a time at once the site of the best and the worst. Veselská (1999:30f.) ascribes it a double meaning. For its wartime director Polák, who died with most other curators and specialists in Auschwitz, the museum was a true science institution. On account of his resistance work, Polák was detained by the Gestapo in August 1944, and he was last seen alive in Auschwitz in January 1945. For the Nazis it was a "'dead' institution, whose existence was limited by time and which should serve mainly for gathering of objects and for creation of ordered 'products'—propaganda exhibitions." However, Veselská (2005) is silent about this painful history in her Polák catalogue.

Duplicity of Memorialization: Genocide and the Genesis of Hope

How do we come to terms with the double message of hope and anomie lodged in a single moment dedicated to redemption and destruction of memory—some 213,000 objects under 110,000 inventory numbers belonging to 153 Jewish communities? This is *our* memorial problem: the Nazis intended to enshrine in the Prague Museum their annihilation of the Jewish people. The museum, with Jewish artifacts collected by the curators as their act of resistance to annihilation, would stand in perpetuity as an antiredemptory act of witnessing and recognizing that very annihilation. Volavková (1966: 9) finds in the Nazi intent for the Prague Museum and its collections the "role of a deceptive witness." I dwell on this case of the negatively saturated phenomenon in order to discern a corrective framework for any future reparative politics of recognition and memorialization.

The Nazi Planning Commission of the Prague Museum compelled about thirty Jewish art historians, collectors, archivists, and custodians to prepare exhibits documenting the gradual extinction of the Jewish people. The Jewish Central Museum was situated in the Spanish synagogue built in 1868 in a Moorish style at the site of a former Jewish school, Stará škola, at Jáchymova street. Its operation was kept secret (Petrášová, 1988:47). Jewish objects from Bohemia and Moravia were received and catalogued there beginning on August 3, 1942, when the secret work began systematically (Volavková, 1968:36). In the first two months almost 8,000 Jewish items were processed: "The warehouses stuffed with shoes in Auschwitz and Maidanek are the result of the same policy that produced the Jewish Central Museum in Prague. All are simply testimonies of crime." Volavková sums up the "role . . . ascribed to the collection of the Jewish Central Museum in Prague . . . [as] that of silent witness. The fact that there was to be a museum at all implied that the original owners of the exhibits were dead and is part of the nightmare which started on March 15, 1939" (9; cf. 27ff., 33).

Even as curators "were inheriting the legacy of the dead," they practiced what Volavková calls "an act of spiritual resistance" during the four exhibits opened in 1942–1943 for the elite group of the SS (Altshuler and Cohn, 1983:29). For the November 1942 exhibit, museum curators, chiefly Polák and Zelenka, chose to organize and interpret various items for the display of Jewish ritual imagery and observances with the veiled intent of subverting the Nazi's primary aim of annihilation: "Items associated with the Jewish festivals of Passover and Purim, which celebrate freedom and express thanksgiving for the joy of redemption from slavery and near-annihilation in ancient times, were shown alongside labels that in Hebrew quoted biblical passages on hope and deliverance" (35; cf. 36). This and other exhibitions that followed in the spring of 1943 were

> secret and not open to the public—just as the entire simulated museum existed in secrecy. When the Germans entered the exhibitions for the first time they were "full of arrogance and murderous brutality"; but their expectation of finding something to mock at was already dampened in the ante-room by a Hebrew inscription. They hoped to find right at the beginning the solution to some secret riddle or mystery but all they found were words saying that "a gift in silence appeases wrath." (Volavková, 1968:132f.)

When the exhibition in the Klaus synagogue was completed in March 1943, SS Sturmbannführer H. Günther informed museum curators that only he could view it. On April 6, Günther visited the exhibit with two leaders from the Jewish Council. He immediately suspected subversion in the celebration of the book of Esther, the story of the fall of the tyrant Haman, who failed in his own attempt at the Final Solution of the Jewish problem. Günther demanded that all Hebrew captions be translated and the exhibit be altered with caricatures of Jewish life (133–137).

The exhibits, that active yet secret performance of museum life, struggled for their own interpretation. What today the Prague Jewish Museum and worldwide Jewish community call the *precious legacy* was at once the site of the best and the worst. The magnitude of the precious legacy received at Prague's Jewish Central Museum can be measured day by day against the dates of deportations to the concentration camps. In 1943–1944 these accelerated to the point of consuming the Jewish curators of the Prague museum. By May 1945, four museum guards and one conservationist remained from those had who worked on the Jewish Central Museum in June 1942. By the end of the war in 1945, the Jewish Central Museum overflowed into eight buildings and some fifty storage facilities in Prague's old Jewish Quarter (Altshuler and Cohn, 1983:38). I cite in full Volavková's (1968:220) shattering description:

> In Terezín only the present was seen with clarity, in Prague, in the Museum, only the past. But in the store-rooms of the Museum, at close range and in contact with the subject matter and so many reminders of the past, this remote, historical, reconstructed time slowly began to disintegrate. In this great burial ground the present was being replaced by the future, and this in an almost intangible way. Here a man could almost see with his

own eyes what connections existed between the various columns of figures, namely the departure of living beings and the arrival of dead objects. Here you could practically touch the dreadful reality that people still refused to believe with . . . hands and fingers. In 1943 the connection between the overflowing store-rooms of the Museum and the shrinking population of Terezín became more and more apparent until in 1944 it became almost a certainty, when all mail from Auschwitz began to dry up.

Kisch's stark judgment does not differ (1986:339): "The evidence for the criminal origin of the Museum" lies in the plurality of objects thrown together not as a collection but as mass theft.

The Will to Annihilate

On a summer Friday in 2005, I was attending Sabbath services at the Spanish synagogue in Prague. The rabbi's opening words made a strong impression on me: "This glorious space was once intended to be part of the Museum to the Extinction of the Jewish race, and look at us today!" The rabbi turned to the international body of visitors with a rhetorical question that penetrates in a shattering way the heart of our meditation: the museum stage, even if intended and lovingly performed by the Jewish resisters who were already on the way to their own death, makes little pragmatic sense if allowed as a memorial to Jewish resistance. Their would-be annihilators meant to destroy the Jews physically as well as spiritually. What more than the banality of evil is to be gleaned from this insane pedantry of destruction? Why would a will to destroy an entire people inspire a museum site rather than erase their memory? Would not any such museum have to cite and exhibit the lives and beliefs of the destroyed people in such a manner that would fail to relinquish them into oblivion for generations to come? This question aims at the core of my deep concern about the intensified will to annihilate hope: first by genocide of memory, then by resurrecting genocidal memory (cf. Altshuler and Cohn, 1983; Volavková, 1968:36).

What sense could there be in performing this site other than to aggravate hopelessness, creating a site saturated by genocide? This somber meditation must consider what propels the will to annihilate: the radical evildoer comprehended that the so-called Final Solution required not only a genocide of a people, and so genocide of their memory, but also perpetual erasure of their future return—an actively genocidal memory of the annihilating will.

Benjamin (1968:255) writes that dead victims are not safe even from the enemy if he wins. How could dead victims return and make the victors unsafe? Why would the Nazis feel unsafe from their victims? Could the dead haunt atheistic regimes as their memorial problem? Annihilation of a people revisits future generations as a memorial problem because death and memory bring everyone face-to-face with the question of hope. The human will to annihilate deals a second-degree death to possibility—to hope. We must meditate on this hope-destroying act, for it reveals the kernel of radical evil—an excess of what we ordinarily mean by bad or wrong. Radical evil is any act aggravating the scarcity of hope. This act goes beyond wrongful death to commit second-degree of death, that is, to preclude hope's future return.

In the idea of a museum to the destroyed Jews of Europe, the Nazis invented a theodicy to their superhuman act. Worse than death, eternally more horrible than the icy embrace of the unloving mother and unkind father that *khôra* is, in the terror imitation of the Easter *Exultet,* an antiredemptory god was to rise up after the proclamation of saving god's death. This Eurocentric theodicy of radical evil would perpetually justify its will to annihilate in an act that J. Young (1990:189) calls a "calculated resurrection" of a destroyed people: "Hitler never planned to 'forget' the Jews, but rather to supplant their memory of events with his own."

In their destructive deed the Nazis grasped and inverted Benjamin's redemptory hope, echoed by Marcuse in the 1960s. That is the main clue to why their public policy, politics, and art of memorialization had to be emphatically (i.e., positively) *antiredemptory:* contrary to Horkheimer's materialist rebuttal to Benjamin's materialist theology of messianic hope, the Nazis considered the past open to the messianic claims of later generations. Benjamin and the SS planners of the Jewish Central Museum paradoxically shared certain postsecular proclivities: neither he nor they could judge the past to be closed. The past is the site of the best and the worst, and for this reason the past can never become dead for later generations. There is a messianic dimension of now-time of which the past is also part. Benjamin hopes for the messianic time to redeem the claims of the past victims. The Nazis acted beyond ordinary atheism, and their diabolical deed was meant otherwise than positing theism as well. The will to annihilate wants to close off all messianic gates through which hope could enter any future historical present. Ergo the victors—then the Nazis—did not feel safe from their victims (Benjamin 1968:254f.; Marcuse 1991:257). "Hitler planned to substitute Nazi memories of Jews for Jewish ones through monuments that commemorated his acts of destruction and oblivion" (La Capra, 1992:125).

Only a memorialization of destroyed peoples *qua* destroyed (making them alive today but in their annihilation) could prevent another memory from undoing their obliteration. The Nazi intent for the Jewish Central Museum was to perform this antiredemptory theodicy of its godlike act of destruction and do so by remembering what cannot come to life again. The total act of annihilation had to unite two temporal dimensions in one. The first dimension would be the *genocidal politics of recognition and redistribution.* It comprises laws that gradually stripped the Jewish people of their rights, citizenship, economic and sociopolitical participation, living identity as well as their burial stone, advancing them from exclusion to total physical destruction. The second dimension would be the ongoing performance of *antiredemptory memorialization.* Its will to annihilate would be enshrined in art and public acts that repeatedly bring destroyed people back to life but in their unredeemed suffering and always already as *the* destroyed people. The historical erasure of peoples would be followed by their active erasure in memory. The final act, the "museum," lets the dead be born again in the memory of their destruction.

Dangerous Memory of Resurrection

No historical present can restore our dead to life through political recognition, artistic memorialization, or monuments. Yet memory work aims to redress the misrecognition and physical destruction of people. Death and memorialization raise the question not addressed by a struggle for recognition: Whence our memory of redemption? The will to annihilate the other extends beyond physical destruction to a second degree of death in order to remember genocidally and so to destroy redemptive hope. This antiredemptory act even *khôra* is unable to carry out! And so what the Nazi plan for the Jewish Museum intended was worse than physical death, it was eternally more horrific than entropy. That will always wanted more than to misrecognize, dangerous memory of hope always wanted more than every struggle for recognition. The annihilating will reveals the negative saturation of radical evil that celebrates in hopelessness the positive void of destroyed peoples. The witness of immemorial possibility of redemption reminds us of the dangerous memory of hope.

RECOGNITION AND ITS LIMITS

I want to ponder the limits of the politics of recognition by discussing one core demand raised by the Mayan indigenous people of Chiapas, Mexico. During my January 2000 trip to La Realidad in Mexico's Lacandon jungle, I saw a banner displayed at the political heart of the community. The words on the banner were striking, given the fact that since 1995 La Realidad has been suspended between the two largest military encampments of the Mexican Federal Army, one at San Quintin and the other at Guadalupe Tepeyac.

> Luchamos por el miedo a morir la muerte del olvido. [We struggle against the fear of dying the death of oblivion.] Luchamos para hablar contra el olvido, contra la muerte, por la memoria y por la vida. [We struggle to

speak against forgetfulness, against death, [but] for memory and life.] El mundo que queremos es uno donde quepan muchos mundo . . . todos los pueblos y sus lenguas. [The world that we desire is one in which many worlds . . . all peoples and their languages, fit.] (*La Revuelta,* 1999:177; all translations mine)

These words, taken from the celebration of the second anniversary of the Zapatista uprising in January 1994, sum up the key intuition of the indigenous struggle. This struggle for memory is echoed a year later: "No habrá paz mientras el olvido siga siendo el único futuro" (There will be no peace as long as oblivion continues to be the only future) (174).

From February 24 to March 12, 2001, representatives of the indigenous struggle, retracing the path of the Mexican revolution, embarked on a bus caravan from San Cristóbal to Mexico City for the implementation of the San Andrés Accords on Indigenous Rights and Culture (*Acuerdos,* 1996). They reiterated their core intuition at the opening of the march: "Somos la dignidad rebelde. Somos el corazón olvidado de la patria. Somos la memoria más primera." [We are the rebelling dignity. We are the forgotten heart of the country. We are the most ancient memory] (Monsiváis, 2001:11). At the stop in Puebla: "In our memory we keep all the colors, all the paths, all the words, and all the silences. We live so that memory may live, and so that which is alive shall not be lost" (Mexico Solidarity Network, February 27, 2001).

The San Andrés Accords endowed this indigenous intuition with political speech. But the things that went wrong between February 16, 1996 (the day the accords between the Mexican government of President Ernesto Zedillo and the Zapatista National Liberation Army were signed) and April 30, 2001 (the day the Mexican congress approved, with the approbation of President Vicente Fox, the altered accords) reveal the limits of the politics of recognition. The key is Mexico's inability or unwillingness to recognize the sui generis claims of indigenous peoples. Tacho, a Zapatista leader who joined twenty-three others in an unarmed caravan from the jungle to the Mexican congress, said to the thousands of people waiting in Puebla that the accords demand "the recognition of our rights as indigenous peoples in the Constitution" (Mexico Solidarity Network, February 22–28, 2001). The Mayans, having endured a history of deception and obliteration, marched for memory again in 2006 from Chiapas throughout Mexico.

Among the main ratified claims of the accords is the recognition of indigenous rights and autonomy in ways that would amend the Mexican constitution, remunicipalize indigenous regions, allow for political and cultural self-determination of indigenous communities, permit indigenous people to use the natural resources on their lands, and grant indigenous women the right to hold positions of authority equal to men in shaping communities. Based on the accords, signed by the Zapatistas and the Mexican government, the congressional Commission on Concordance and Pacification (COCOPA) presented in 1996 a legislative proposal for changes in the Mexican constitution. In their proposal, the claim to indigenous autonomy was legally defined, among others, as the right of the indigenous to "choose their internal forms of social, economic, political, and cultural organization"; "apply their traditional [judicial] systems of regulation and solution for internal conflicts"; "elect their authorities and exercise their internal forms of governance"; "fortify their political participation and representation in accordance with their cultural specificities"; "collectively agree on the use and enjoyment of natural resources of their lands and territories"; "preserve and enrich their languages, knowledge, and all the elements which form part of their identity and culture"; and "acquire, operate, and administer their own means of communication." The Mexican government and the ruling parties, PRI and PAN, instead introduced counterproposals that would absorb indigenous claims to autonomy into existing political structures. With this legislative change of the 1996 accords, the indigenous would receive recognition on terms that, while assuming a degree of discursive symmetry and liberal reversibility of perspectives, were skewed in the direction set by the existing state.[2]

The signed San Andrés Accords aim to redeem the claim of destroyed peoples against oblivion. In this nuance the accords are as much political as cultural and spiritual acts. The accords confirm that the habitat for autonomous political and cultural self-organization of the indigenous is a singular and unique right. They do not ratify a procedure for mutual recognition whereby the indigenous would be brought into Mexico's mainstream culture. Nor are they a legislative or artistic monument to an injurious past to be paid for with liberal equality discursive reparation. Rather, *the accords present a legislative recovery of space and time in which a destroyed people's hope can be remembered and redeemed as an active form of life.* The government's offensive since 1996, whether by its political or counterinsurgent war against indigenous communities, misrecognized and silenced that recovery and claim. Given this misrecognition, from the end of 1999 until December 2, 2000, indigenous communities adopted complete silence. They withdrew from discursive debates with the powers that be. They insisted that the fulfillment accords, the release of political prisoners, and dismantling of 7 out of 259 federal military positions in Chiapas were preconditions for resuming dialogue between indigenous communities and the Mexican federal government.

The misrecognition of indigenous claims to be recognized as peoples likewise informed government promises to end the state of conflict in Chiapas. Whereas the accords recognize the differential "rights of the indigenous peoples," the Mexican ruling parties limited recognition to "indigenous communities." *Indigenous peoples* defines a notion of a distinct form of life, whereas the term *indigenous communities* absorbs any such uniqueness into the existing liberal imagery of the "indigenous" problem. The latter term *recognizes by misrecognizing* the specificity of indigenous "peoples" in their political and cultural self-organization, habitat, and natural resources. This deceptive scenario transpired under Mexican President Fox's watch. He campaigned on bringing full recognition and peace to the indigenous of Chiapas. On April 30, 2001, the Mexican congress, following on the heels of the Zapatista caravan and without asking or getting the indigenous consent, approved the altered text of the 1996 accords (Thompson, 2001). Under the conditions of misrecognition and destruction, between 1996 and 1998, autonomous municipal councils emerged in thirty-eight indigenous municipalities of Chiapas, all organized in ways that were stipulated in the rights of indigenous autonomy of the accords. In this act, the indigenous refused the federal conception of the indigenous problem—a conception that assumes an equality of symmetry and a discursive reversibility of perspectives between the Mexican state and the descendants of Mayans. It should not be surprising that in early 2006, a new voice emerged from various indigenous communities to bring the "other campaign" into official electoral politics. The Mayans from Chiapas have joined with the indigenous in Yucatán, Campeche, Quintana Roo, and elsewhere in Mexico to "awaken the other" memory. "The Mayan artisans who are resisting the seizure of memory made stone of their ancestors" (Marcos, 2006).

What does this brief meditation on the Chiapas reveal? Enough has been written about the struggle for recognition and redistribution, and I do not need to rehearse this here.[3] The politics of recognition gains its importance as a compelling democratic form of reparation for the politics of exclusion and destruction. The most advanced forms of the politics of recognition and redistribution are inscribed into the liberal-communitarian debates about how to resolve discursively the tension between individual and group claims. It appears that a procedural or discursive politics of recognition and redistribution should not only provide an adequate corrective for possible exclusivism in philosophical method, but they also should offer a fair reparation basis for undoing the material exclusion and destruction of peoples.

The Question Raised by Indigenous Struggles

If all perspectives are not symmetrical and reversible, then can the public discourses of recognition ultimately redress misrecognition and annihilation of peoples? Can the trauma and even silence of the descendants of destroyed peoples be restored to speech by raising and redeeming discursive validity claims? Limits of the path to recognition arise with the family of cases, such as the one in Chiapas, that are not addressed by this type of reparation. Such limits indicate a persistent memorial problem. The politics of recognition runs into limits when procedural symmetry and equality cannot assume reversible reciprocity with the perspectives of destroyed or forgotten peoples, when traumatic silence is not directly redeemable by discursive claims.

The clues to such limits are phenomenological as much as memorial. We get phenomenological clues from the irreversibility of perspectives or asymmetry between the claims of destroyed peoples (and their descendants who carry those claims) and other contemporaries (as witnesses, perpetrators, bystanders, later generations). We get memorial clues from silences accompanying, first, the trauma of destruction and, second, all attempts to redeem claims of destroyed peoples without actually paying attention to their silences and claims *as* such peoples.

Should any discursive redemption (e.g., an interpretation of the indigenous problem) require the indigenous to die their death of oblivion? If it did, then this redemption would become positively antiredemptory. Physical annihilation would be replaced with systematic obliteration (i.e., misrecognition that renders indigenous as the class of living dead). But then this substitution of spiritual for physical destruction allows the established power to insert annihilation into its very politics of recognition. Indigenous peoples are rendered invisible in a living act of oblivion even as they are ostensibly recognized and included in the public sphere.

The memorial problem from the Jewish Central Museum in Prague revisits us with vengeance. *Our* problem lies at the heart of the politics of recognition. This problem consists of the following poles of unacceptable choices: accept either a liberal or a calculated misrecognition of peoples! This acceptance is inscribed into the blind spots of the politics of recognition.

COUNTERMONUMENTS AND COUNTERMEMORIALS

The politics of museums, monuments, memorial sites, and the rituals of remembrance run into a twofold limit. On the one hand, the simulacra images *represent harmonious solidarity* with victims of history as if this solidarity were something always already real *for us*. On the other hand, the iconoclasts *prohibit representing disaster* as if radical evil occupied the utopian space and time of the sacred. The horror of kitsch (fake harmony) and the iconoclastic injunctions against representing annihilation are the two extreme limits, and as such both repeat *our* memorial problem. Both fail to connect with human suffering (Baudrillard, 1983; Felluga, 2000; Friedlander, 1984, 1992; La Capra, 1992).

To again rephrase Benjamin's sixth thesis (1968:255), even the dead are not safe from memorialization. Or as Baer (2000:178) puts the memorial problem:

> Even if a stone were lifted to reconstruct what had been destroyed, to be hurled against the perpetrators, or to relieve the dead of their anonymity, such actions deprive the dead of their final rest. The stark nakedness and horror of dying is repeated, and the effort to undo its oppressive weight finally amounts to an instrumentalization and usurpation of death for another purpose, which desacralizes the repose of the dead.

The remembrance of the end of World War II enacted by Helmut Kohl and Ronald Reagan in May 1985 at the Bitburg military cemetery illustrates the simulacrum of solidarity. The Bitburg ritual would cast the Holocaust victims, ordinary German soldiers, and the officers of the SS in the parallel dramatic roles of the dead to be honored. On the morning of May 5, Reagan and Kohl visited Bergen-Belsen and in the afternoon shook hands with the generals at Kolmeshöhe military cemetery at Bitburg. The concentration camp's Holocaust victims and Bitburg's thirty graves of soldiers from the Second SS Panzer Division are brought together in this handshake. In order to stage this kitsch of normalization, peace, and harmony, it suffices to append Reagan's words along with Kohl's and those uttered by the veterans of Waffen SS.

- Reagan (March 21): "I feel very strongly that . . . instead of reawakening the memories . . . we should observe this day as the day when, forty years ago, peace began."
- Kohl (April 25): "Reconciliation is when we are capable of grieving over people without caring what nationality they are."
- SS veterans (May 3): "We were soldiers, just like the others." (Hartman, 1986:xiii–xv)

The Limits of Memorialization

On November 14, 1993, the posthumous harmony of victims, soldiers, and perpetrators enacted at Bitburg in 1985 became enshrined in the memorial to *all* victims of World War II that Kohl fashioned at the historical site of Neue Wache in East Berlin. That this place, with Käthe Kollwitz's rendition of a Christian Pietà situated at the entrance, embodies *our* memorial problem can be demonstrated by two contravening tendencies. First, the post-Wall discourse that issued from the protests against the memorial politics of this site and lasted over ten years: Germans have been debating whether, where, how, and for whom to build the Berlin Holocaust memorial to the murdered Jews of Europe. Second, ironically at Neue Wache Germans could already in 1993 come to terms with the inability (prohibition) to mourn the loss of the leader. As one commentator asks, is not Neue Wache, as a simulacrum of peace and piety, "a disguised memorial to Hitler" (Wiedmer, 1999:120, 115–20; Mitscherlich, 1975)?

Such disguised memorials to the perpetrators grow in the absence of genuine coming to terms with the past. For example, in early 2006 the Czech National Party erected near Lety, the site of the former concentration camp for Czech Roma and Sinti, a stone dedicated to "Victims." In the 1950s the communist authorities built at the site a large pig farm. The nationalists deny that this was a Nazi-like concentration camp. The intent of their generic dedication is to diffuse the memory of the Czech participation in the Nazi persecution of Gypsies. The stone's sign is also a disguised memorial to those who suffered for making the Czech land free of racial minorities. When the Iranian president decided in 2006 to hold in Tehran a conference on the Holocaust, thinly disguised aim was to encouraged presentations denying the annihilation of European Jews.

Lanzmann's nine-hour film *Shoah* and his later criticisms of Spielberg's film *Schindler's List* exemplify the iconoclastic approach to memorialization. Lanzmann (1994:14) prohibits representing "a certain ultimate degree of horror." He makes horror unrepresentable in his own film composed entirely of witness testimonials by surviving victims, bystanders, and perpetrators of the Holocaust. He protests every transgression of his prohibition on representation, for example, by Spielberg's film narrative, which he derides as a "kitsch melodrama." Indeed, if anyone had made a secret film showing the gas chamber horror and would now produce it, Lanzmann vows to destroy it. Felluga (2000) names this sort of passionate attitude "Holocaust iconoclasm" (cf. Felman, 1992; Lanzmann, 1985).

Our memorial problem resurfaces with the iconoclastic prohibition on representing *the* disaster. The injunction draws its taboo strength from the Second Commandment, which prohibits pronouncing God's name or carving images of God (cf. Hansen, 1997). Lanzmann in film and Adorno in philosophy and aesthetic theory place the very same type of prohibitions on representing in image, poetry, narrative, even philosophy the unrepresentable or unspeakable horror of suffering. Famous is Adorno's (1967:34) claim that "to write poetry after Auschwitz is barbaric" (cf. Adorno, 1982:312). Although he later softens his claim, he only makes it for us existentially more difficult: "It may have been wrong to say that after Auschwitz you could no longer write poems. But it is not wrong to raise the less cultural question whether after Auschwitz you can go on living." And again: "After Auschwitz, our feelings resist any claim of the positivity of existence as sanctimonious, as wronging the victims" (1973:362f., 361). Lanzmann juxtaposes Auschwitz and the holy of holies in the way he practices his Holocaust iconoclasm. In saying what cannot and must not be represented, "a certain ultimate degree of horror," he invokes symbols of Orthodox Christian Easter icons of the resurrection, "the blindingly dark sun of the Holocaust" (1994:14). As I noted in the first introduction, Orthodox Christian icons show the risen Christ not only breaking the seal of death, and spending the first two days of eternity or of the new Genesis between God's death and resurrection in hell, but also shining more brightly than the sun, and so uncharacteristically for Plato's exit from the cave of ignorance into daylight, the noon sun rises behind the Redeemer in the black color of full eclipse.

But contrary to the memorial iconoclasts, the Holocaust, despite that word's sacred genealogy (burnt offering), cannot be governed by the same commandment as the relation to the holy. The structural and symbolic juxtaposition between the two prohibitions on representing the best and the worst, the holy and the evil, establishes a short circuit running from redemption to disaster. The Holocaust iconoclasm together with the simulacra or kitsch about harmonious solidarity constitute *our* aggravated memorial problem:

- The human self always already suffers posttraumatic anxiety. One's naive (Lacanian) desire for the really real can only be satisfied positively through cultural simulacra or negatively through prohibition. Can such a self exhibit anything but posttraumatic characteristics?
- We all are survivors suspended in a positive void. Redemption would seem to equal disaster.

Dangerous Countermemory

I return to my opening meditation situated in the project for the Jewish Central Museum in Prague. There the Nazis memorialized the anxiety structure of the posttraumatic self and its antiredemptory reality as humanity's positive void. From genocide of memory to genocidal memory, they erected the calculated resurrection of destroyed peoples.

Countermemorial Healing of Genocidal Memory

Post-Wall Germany is coming to terms with its disastrous past in countermonumental attempts to surmount the twin limits of the politics of memorialization. Countermonumental art or antimemorials reject the positive mirage of harmony. They likewise overcome the antirepresentational icon-oclasm that tends to enshrine radical evil in the aura of the holy. Daniel Libeskind's Jewish Museum Extension to the Berlin Museum (1997) pro-vides the most striking counterpoint to the Nazi design of the Jewish Cen-tral Museum in Prague. It too is the site of the best and the worst. How does it differ from its nemesis—the Jewish Central Museum in Prague, the twin failure of kitsch or simulacra harmony and the antirepresentational iconoclasm?

The space of the Berlin Jewish Museum Extension aspires to be coun-termonumental and countermemorial. The building architecture resists the fixed monumentality of a typical museum site. The building likewise vio-lates the linear narrative structures of completed and stored historical mem-ory. James Young (2000:163) explains how Libeskind architecturally strug-gled with the philosophical question of memorialization: how to create "a devastated site that would now enshrine its broken forms." Libeskind's mu-seum design poses the question of *our* memorial problem in sharply felt contours: "If architecture can be representative of historical meaning, can it also represent unmeaning and the search for meaning?" His design tested engineering ingenuity—walls with inclining angles where nothing could hang; blind walkways leading nowhere; architectural voids interrupting the linear narrative of corridors and rooms as well as of staircases; rooms either too small or too inhospitable to exhibit anything. Libeskind confronted memorialization's two limits: simulacra-kitsch and iconoclasm. Young brings home this challenge of architecturally conjuring yet not celebrating the void of annihilation (164):

> How to give voice to an absent Jewish culture without presuming to speak for it? How to house under a single roof a panoply of essential contradic-tions and oppositions? . . . How to give a void form without filling it in? How to give architectural form to the formless and to challenge the very attempt to house such memory?

Libeskind's museum is shot through with a straight void-line punctuat-ing visitors' "sense of continuous passage." The void is the only continuity one gains. Libeskind explains his design:

> I have introduced the idea of the void as a physical interference with chronology. It is the one element of continuity throughout the complex form of the building. It is 27 meters high and runs the entire length of the building over 150 meters. It is a straight line whose impenetrability forms the central axis. The void is traversed by bridges which connect the various parts of the museum to each other. (Libeskind, 1995:35, in Young, 2000:175)

The void-line fragments the building's narrative by two horizontal and four transverse voids. The first two voids are accessible from religious exhibits; the next two run diagonally across several floor levels and are only partially visible from different locations but remain inaccessible; the last two voids are vertical. The fifth void mirrors the external shape of the sixth void-space with no outer doors leading to it; sixth is "the Holocaust void, a negative space created by the Holocaust, an architectural model for absence" (Young, 2000:175).

Libeskind's design neither represents monumental harmony with the murdered Jews of Berlin, thereby somehow redeeming in museum form their felt absence, nor does it prohibit representing this disaster, as if it were a sacred image of transcendence rather than a mirror to *our* acts and history. Neither a kitsch of nor an iconoclastic distance from the radical evil of human destruction, the Berlin Jewish Museum Extension invites us, the visitors, to inhabit this living memorial without distancing the traumatic past from *our* experience. Young admits that this is "an aggressively anti-re-demptory design, built literally around an absence of meaning in history, an absence of the people who would have given meaning to their history" (179). Invoking Freud's (1955) work, Young (2000:154f.) explains the homeless, exilic quality of Libeskind's work:

> The memorial uncanny might be regarded as that which is necessarily an-tiredemptive. It is the memory of historical events which never domesti-cates such events, never makes us at home with them, never brings them into the reassuring house of redemptory meaning. It is to leave such events unredeemable yet still memorable, unjustifiable yet still graspable in their causes and effects.

Libeskind's museum is uncanny in Freud's secular sense because it visu-alizes a familiar yet repressed memory. Repressed memory of this sort can-not be redeemed directly by discursive claims or by reasons. The uncanny epiphany of the repressed and returned memory of void, without justifying its trauma, houses a site that is not at home with itself. As a countermonu-ment and countermemorial, the uncanny site becomes "a working through, a form of mourning" (171).

In a personal narrative about "Germany's Holocaust Memorial Prob-lem—and Mine," Young (184–223) recounts his involvement in a ten-year debate (from 1989 to June 1999) about the merits of building the Berlin Holocaust Memorial to the murdered Jews of Europe. I need not enter here into this intricate history (Wiedmer, 1999; Wise, 1999; Matuštík, 2001). For my purposes of sharpening the opening meditation on *our* memorial problem, it suffices to show that Young's initially unequivocal enthusiasm for countermonumental and antiredemptory memorializations gave way to a nuanced support for the now completed central Berlin Holocaust Memorial. Young's shifts reveal some of the core limits of memorializations:

- March 1995, after the failure of the first competition for the Berlin Memorial: "Better a thousand years of Holocaust memorial competitions and exhibitions in Germany than a single 'final solution' to Germany's memorial problem. . . . Instead of a fixed icon for Holocaust memory in Germany, the debate itself . . . might now be enshrined" (191).

- As a new member of Germany's Findungskommission for Berlin's Holocaust memorial (1998–99): "If the government insisted on a memorial in Berlin for 'Europe's murdered Jews,' then couldn't it, too, embody this same countermonumental critique?" (197).

- Public hearing in the Bundeshaus (March 3, 1999): "So, yes, I said. Gerhard Schröder's government should build the memorial and give the German public a choice, even an imperfect choice: let them choose to remember what Germany once did to the Jews of Europe by coming to the memorial, by staying at home, by remembering alone or in the company of others. Let the people decide whether to animate such a site with their visits, with their shame, their sorrow, or their contempt. Or let the people abandon this memorial altogether, if that is what they choose, and let the memorial itself now become the locus for further debate. Then let the public decide just how hollow or how substantial a gesture this memorial is, whether any memorial can ever be more than a ritual gesture to an unredeemable past. With these words I sat down" (221f.).

Redemptory Hope in an Antiredemptory Age?

The Nazi aim for the Jewish Central Museum in Prague raises the question of *our* memorial problem in an antiredemptory age. The indigenous struggle in Mexico revealed certain limits of the politics of recognition. The Holocaust memorials in Germany brought us to the limits of the politics of memorialization. As antiredemptory forms of reparation for misrecognition and annihilation, as reconciling and noncynical sites of the best and the worst, countermemorials dramatize the vanishing point of all these limits. These bold public and symbolic forms of memory work raise the initial problem most sharply; countermemorials show an obverse side of that same problem. They confront us with this question: *How hollow or substantial will be our recognition of and memorials to destroyed peoples?* Countermemorials compel us to question in the most uncompromising manner the voids and absences that those public acts, sites, and *we,* each in one's very self, house. Can any genuine hope, can our hope be more than a ritual gesture to an unredeemable past and still call itself hope? Must we accept how our antiredemptory age defines the possibility of what anyone may hope for?

I shudder at the Nazi answer from Prague that might return as an unwanted guest of the future saturated by aggravated scarcity of hope. How should we welcome the possibility of this visitation? The Nazis envisioned their antimuseum as a sinister countermemory and countermemorial. First, genocidal will understands that any future memorial or public act of recognition to a destroyed people *must embody and so resurrect a positive void.* Second, *genocide of memory* must represent the Final Solution, and hence *genocidal memory* can never allow itself more than a ritual gesture to an unredeemable past, present, and future. Finally, the will to radical evil fathoms quite clearly that any political misrecognition of peoples must be followed by an antiredemptory recognition and memorialization of their void. The physical annihilation of peoples must be *redeemed* affirmatively and perpetually as their disaster.

Must we not learn nowadays to resist these very answers and decisions? Must we not try to go beyond the received limits of political recognition and cultural memorialization? Whatever reparation, recognition, and memorials we decide to fashion, our efforts must return to the initial way of posing the question of the memorial problem. Kant's categorical imperative of reciprocal recognition (later enhanced by Hegel, Marx, Arendt, and Habermas) and Adorno's imperative to think and live in such a way as to remember and prevent another Auschwitz (1973, 365f.) call for a third kind of imperative, or better, for a commandment to pray even in hell:

- Prayer is redemptive or redemptory when one is moved by the suffering face of the other threatened by cruel death and unresponsive nothingness

- Prayer is redemptive or redemptory, whether wearing the *tallith* or uncovered, praying or praising, one names the impossible by its unnameable name for hope, when praying against the annihilating uncreation that wants cruel death and unresponsive nothingness to be stronger than love

- Redemptive or redemptory is any prayer for the ability to love even in hell and against the unresponsive, that is religiously tone-deaf and mute, nothingness of *khôra*

I envision an imperative or commandment to resist a positive void, such as the Nazi museum of destroyed peoples. This imperative or commandment goes against the antiredemptory spirit of the age, it means that recognition must become a form of witness against redemptory annihilation. The San Andrés Accords and the indigenous struggles against death by oblivion were one example of this witness. I envision an imperative or commandment of redemptory hope in our antiredemptory times. This imperative or commandment inscribes a witnessing posture against antiredemptory memorialization in order to resist equating redemption of peoples with their and our disaster. Our monuments and museums and rituals are powerless to redeem destroyed peoples. The discursively redeemed claims are as powerless as art is to deliver the dead to resurrection. But King Solomon's faith claim that "love is as strong as death" inscribes into our hearts a commandment to live with redemptory hope even in this antiredemptory age. For the sake of those without hope, if not for the sake of any other faith, we are commanded to pray even in hell and, with the biblical prophet Isaiah even in the absence of caring mother and father, that is, even in the awareness of unresponsive cosmic nothingness. The Holocaust survivor Emil Fackenheim (1994:213) advocated the "614th commandment" or "614th *mitzvah*"—one must never grant Hitler another posthumous victory—that in the Christian context and as a new categorical imperative becomes the "11th commandment." We are commanded to pray for the ability to love, and so resist within our terrified and cramped hearts the answer provided by those who would wish to resurrect any individuals or any peoples as always and already destroyed. Can the radical evil of cruel death prevail over love? Should we claim *khôra* as our true mother? "Can a mother forget her infant, be without tenderness for the child of her womb? Even should she forget, I will never forget you. See, upon the palms of my hands I have written your name; your walls are ever before me" (Isaiah, 49:15–16).

SIX

Radical Evil as a Saturated Phenomenon

In this series of meditations, I consider the second-order possibility of the impossible: radical evil as the negatively saturated phenomenon of the religious. The first-order possibility of impossible hope was defined from the secular dimension by paradoxical desire or intentionality that lacked any fulfilling intuition. The second-order of the impossible admits the possibility of the postsecular excess of intuition. Starting with the actuality of radical evil, rather than with any positively phenomenological or scriptural dimension of r/Revelation, we no longer need to worry about Janicaud's objection to Marion that the postsecular way of speaking makes an illegitimate theological turn in phenomenology. Nor do we have the problem of going directly to R/revelation, thus espousing the myth of the given or ignoring the hermeneutical circle of human situatedness or what some Christian thinkers call correlational theology and Jewish thinkers Midrash. To be sure, correlational thinking about the religious indicates the dependent if not founding relationship of revealability to every r/Revelation that passes on the way to us not only through many a burning bush but also through commentaries on commentaries. But this is not our question when it comes to radical evil.

In describing real existing radical evil in the world, we remain faithful to the phenomenal and hermeneutical field of immanence, and so we grasp and explain all phenomena of evil very much in terms they appear in themselves and of themselves and as they are given in the world as we know it. We are not flying to some other than this, our very messy world, for radical evil is suffered in our flesh, worldly events, ideas, and disclosures. Yet, and this thought distinguishes my postsecular mood and tonality, radical evil indubitably appearing in the world cannot be grasped otherwise than as a religious, saturated phenomenon.

Radical evil is the *negatively saturated phenomenon* that breaks the subject-object poles of possible experience and the bounds of rational categories. In all its intensities, from banal to morally radical to paradoxical to diabolical, practical evil exceeds what is intended by the common or ordinary phenomena of doing something wrong or bad, and hence it engenders counterexperience. Let me introduce this working definition: if radical evil can be described and yet is something that escapes purely rational explanation (it is neither visable nor bearable; it is singular and indirect), then we have come across a saturated phenomenon. It is the negatively saturated phenomenon because, unlike the sublime, loving, or faithful that break rational bounds in seeking receptive and accepting relation with the beautiful, self-giving, and the holy, radical evil breaches those bounds in defiance. Dialectically speaking, the negatively saturated phenomenon of defiance must be grasped as a resaturated position, full eclipse, rather than absence. Defiance performs from power; it does not suffer impotence or weakness of the will. Radical evil in its four intensities (banal, moral, paradoxical, and diabolical) is negatively saturated by the religious and positively asserted by the defiant will.

Learning from Schelling's as much as Kierkegaard's spiritual grasp of evil, I ask, first, if by translating the religious mode of sin into the moral language of radical evil, Kant muddles the issue. Second, with Kierkegaard's distinction between an aesthetic, ethical, and religious existence, I consider that there is nothing redemptive or holy in conducting a war on evil and that there is nothing wholly secular about violence. Third, I meditate on violence as a religious dimension of radical evil. Fourth, with Derrida, Kierkegaard, Lévinas, and Marion, I am prompted to ask whether or not the relation between religion and violence is intrinsic or accidental. Fifth, I resume the meditation on cruelty from chapter 4. I hold that unmasking cruelty not only delivers us to a genre of redemptive critical theory but also confronts the not so banal shadow of any human will wishing to do good and vanquish evil. The outcome of the foregoing meditations will lead to this combined figure of human evil: it should be regarded as at once banal, morally radical, ethico-religiously paradoxical, and spiritually diabolical. It is banal in the do-gooders who tranquilize themselves on the trivial pursuit of the good, radical in distorting human capacity to progress in freedom, paradoxical in its frustrated maximized intention of the impossible, and diabolical in its human-all-too-human religious cruelty. In part 3, I dwell on the unforgivable, unforgettable, unspeakable, and unexplainable features that saturate the arrival of radical evil and announce its possible overcoming in hope (*teshuvah, tikkun olam, chashmal,* and *berakhah/barakah*).

THE INNER POSSIBILITY OF
RADICAL EVIL AS A HUMAN POSSIBILITY:
SCHELLING'S BOLD SPECULATION

Can war on evil promise redemption without grasping what evil is? Waging a war on evil that one does not understand can be just as stupid as trying to destroy the ring of power in J. R. R. Tolkien's trilogy, *The Lord of the Rings*, by thinking that some good folks can safeguard the ring by attacking it with a hammer. Any naive externalization of evil proves to be dangerous in that it is attached to its own ignorance of the sources of evil. I question the very notion of *war on evil*, whether it is defined in political terms (evil empire, axis of evil, evil ruler) or sacral terms (jihad on Great Satan, evil people targeted by a suicide bomber). The significance of Kant's thinking about evil is that it exposes all externalizations of evil as *morally* deficient. If a discourse on evil fails to be moral in Kant's rational sense, it certainly cannot be genuinely religious either. This conclusion would be true regardless of whether or not we embarked on translating religious categories into secular ones. Those who externalize evil become doubly removed from religious categories even prior to any attempt at a possible translation. On the first remove, one fails to account for the origin of evil in human will, thereby falling behind the ethical and into the aesthetic sense of evil. On the second remove, since one is not trying to root out evil at the core of one's own self but is projecting it aesthetically outside of one's free will, one can only wage a war of annihilation on external caricatures of evil.

While Kant went beyond aestheticization of radical evil and defended its moral significance, Schelling and Kierkegaard help us rediscover its religious significance. The task of postsecular meditations on radical evil is to name what we already know about it intuitively—that it is saturated by invisable, unbearable, singular, and indirectly apprehensible excess which accompanies its ordinary aims and acts. Schelling's *Freiheitsschrift*, a groundbreaking treatise of about ninety pages, raises the metaphysical question of evil anew in a speculative way inspired by, among others, Jacob Böhme (1575–1642) and Jewish mysticism. I distill from Schelling's exposition three moves, thereby beginning to show why we ought to view radical evil as a saturated phenomenon (cf. Scholer, 1991; Rosenzweig, 2005).

- Correcting for one-sided idealism and realism, human freedom to do evil must derive its possibility in God, yet do so in such a way as not to identify its actuality with God.

- We must not think of evil as a privation of the good, nothing, or moral impotence of free will, but rather as a position, force, positively asserted power.
- Ability to commit moral evil attests to human freedom as a spiritual center of activity.

Ground and Existence

The first innovation thinks of God as the ground of living freedom; the inner capacity of humans to commit evil is the prime instance of such freedom. Schelling roots our freedom in God's ground. Yet our possibility to do evil must not identify actual evil acts one commits with the living God. God's ground and existence are thus distinguished. Classical thought allows two ways of justifying human freedom to do evil and God's status as the omnipotent and omniscient Lord. The option rejected by St. Augustine is Manichaeism with its eternal war between two equal powers or deities, one Good and the other Evil. The Augustinian solution, largely integrated into all variations defining the great medieval synthesis of monotheistic faith and Greek philosophy, explains moral evil as a privation of the good and thus ontological nothingness. Even Hick's (1987) sophisticated version of St. Irenaean developmental and harmony theodicy does not offer an alternative to this classical aspect of Augustine's view of evil as privation of the good. Schelling is most likely the first to part with either solution.

How are we to think of God's being? Schelling (1860) distinguishes between "being insofar as it exists and being insofar as it is a pure ground of its existence." Pertaining to God's ground and existence, these are not two gods, dark and light, mute nature and articulate love, but two modalities of eternally becoming unity of God. That "there is nothing outside of God" defines God's dark ground or primordial nature. Insofar as darkness desires light, and nature yields to love, God exists eternally as a living God. The ground of God's existence is a ground of a living God, and yet "God is the *prius* of the ground," for the primordial ground could not be what it is "if God did not exist in *actu*" (VII 357). The relation between ground and existence is neither a temporal nor vicious circle. Rather, it shows how the possibility of freedom originates in God's two modalities or principles. God eternally *becomes* one spirit insofar as God's existence integrates dark and light, desire and love.

Heidegger (1988) stresses that Schelling introduced "a *becoming* God!" (190), God's "eternal becoming" (213). Becoming of the absolute creation is eternal (234f.). How could anything else become insofar as God rests in the dark ground? The inner possibility of evil is coterminous with the possibility of human freedom, and both are rooted in our finite becoming. We become in what in God is ground and not existence (203, 206). Not our human finitude but our topsy-turvy, perverse spirit actualizes what appears as the possibility of evil (208f.).

The principles or modalities of ground and existence are never separable in God's becoming, as in God the ground is eternally coincident with existence, thereby subordinating desire to love. Yet these same modalities of being (ground and existence) are separable in human beings in whom they must be brought into coincidence by freedom's temporal becoming. This separability of ground and existence in human becoming is the root of human freedom granted to creation by God. The separability also brings out the possibility of good and evil (364). It is important to keep the distinction between possibility and actuality in view: God is the ground of finite human freedom, thus of the possibility of good and evil in humans, yet God is not the ground of actual evil. With the separability of ground and existence in human temporal becoming and their coincidence in God's eternal becoming, we grasp how human capacity for evil derives its possibility from God's ground—as God, so also humans exhibits ground and existence—yet it does not accuse God's existence of ever actualizing evil.

Permit me to amplify Schelling's speculation with an aside regarding the *khôra*. In Plato's *Timaeus,* the demiurge creates by shaping the practico-inert spacing of space, the cosmic or material surd of all that is. In Derrida's rendition, justice and gift are possible on the condition of the impossible as the nongiving and nonredemptory condition of the possible. In Derrida, *khôra* performs the role of resistance or defense by safeguarding a deconstructive deferral of all intentional desire for a meaning-fulfilling intuition (resisting any concept of totality). Only thus can a question arise whether the possibility of the impossible (either in thought or in prayer) names God or just this entropic spacing. But the spacing of space is sheer antiredemptory nothingness that is incapable of being motivated even by the moods of boredom or anxiety, not to speak by the ability to love or hate or hope and despair. What if we could see in Schelling's speculation about the dark ground of God another way of coming to terms with the surd of *khôra*? One can neither pray to God's ground nor to *khôra*. The God becoming in freedom and love from eternity shapes with meaning and care the dark ground, and this is the essence of God's existence as the creative demiurge, but *khôra* becomes a struggle for humans in whom ground and existence are separable. In asserting the ground over freedom and love, there arises the possibility of becoming overwhelmed rather than helped by the *khôra*. But is it then right to claim that one can ever pray to *khôra*, even if only by a structural default of undecidability, and is it then right to name it as one of the two sources of the religious (the other source being the messianic, cf. Derrida, FaK)? The religious marks a relationship of call and response to a vocative cosmic address, in God this is the call of love over the ground, in human freedom it is a response to overcome the possibility of radical evil with hope. While on my reading something like *khôra* is accounted for by Schelling in his metaphysics of God's ground, it is also clear that *khôra* cannot be a source of the religious as, unlike existence that shapes the ground, it is both mute (does not call anything or anyone) and unresponsive (responds neither lovingly nor defiantly). Whether or not love is as strong as death, *this* r/Revelation can never be given to us apart from our existence, by something without a face, and so it can never be mastered or even negatively conditioned by the *khôra*.

Radical Evil as Power, Not Moral Weakness

Yet what is moral evil? Heidegger (1988:184) derives a succinct definition from his penetrating study of Schelling's text by focusing on evil's "*inner* possibility." Moral evil harnesses the will of the ground against the essential will of existence. This would be possible in God only if Manichaeism were true, and in that case this reversal of ground against existence would beget a topsy-turvy God *(die Umgekehrte Gott)*. But morally evil human freedom embodies in a finite mode precisely such a reversal of ground and existence. The reversal of ground and existence is possible because of their separability in human freedom. I can become an inverse god in whom spirit is dominated by nature and love is subordinated to desire; I can exist separated from love and light (Schelling, 1860:VII 365). The possibility of good and evil arises because of the misrelation (this concept is crucial for Kierkegaard) or dysfunction between ground and existence (VII 372). The inner transmutation of dark into light, becoming self-realized harmony, is shared by all creatures (VII 362). Yet what lives eternally coincident in God's freedom is a task of finite becoming for creatures. Moral evil arises as inner misrelation or inversion in human freedom between its ground and existence. When the two principles, inseparable in God, diverge in the human self, then one's inverse ground made light desires to be God. Sartre rightly rejects any human claim to divinity as a useless passion.

Two consequences follow at once from this understanding of evil agency as inverse god: all forms of moral evil can be traced back to the radical evil of desiring to be God; and moral evil is never mere nothing, moral impotence, or privation of the good, it is always something positive. "The ground of evil must not only lie in something positive in general, but rather in the highest positive" (VII 368f.). Desiring to exist is what the ground of God realizes in God's love, creatures desiring to be God usurp divine existence. In this regard all moral evil is traceable by Schelling to its religious conditions of possibility—reversal *(Umkehrung)* or positive pervertedness (positive *Verkehrheit*) of the relation of ground to existence (VII 366). Going beyond Kant, Schelling grasps this usurpation of the divine by finite freedom as radical evil. The ground of evil lies in the inner inversion of the modes or principles of ground and existence. As their ordering and coincidence are the highest positive in the living God, so also their free human inversion is a position, rather than something absent, impotent, a mere nothing. Unlike what Kant thought, Schelling shows the evil will to draw its strength, force, and power from realizing its freedom against the moral law. Radical evil cannot be just a moral category set within the bounds of transcendental conditions of its possibility (respect for the moral law). Radical evil saturates this very possibility, it is a saturated phenomenon.

However, this phenomenon is perversely saturated, it is a *negatively saturated positive,* hence inverted god. The notion of position, force, positive assertion must be understood dialectically. Heidegger (1988:250) locates the ground of evil in the self-offering of the will of the first ground, whereby human self willfully places itself against the universal will as something positive and spiritual. "In this reversal of will the becoming of upside down God fulfills itself" (248). Because the individual will is spirit, it is capable of putting itself in place of the universal will (246). "Evil is actual as spirit" (257), "but spirit is the self-knowing unity of ground and existence. The possibility of evil is a spiritual possibility, hence possibility of such a self-knowing unity" (258).

To return to Schelling's text (1860), the "positive" excess of radical evil names "the inversion or the reversal of principles" (VII 366). The positive is an "expression of the inner selfhood" in its concrete assertion of free will and will to power (VII 370). Moral evil is never a mere privation of the good or absence of being; there is something positively asserted in it insofar as it reverses the principles of ground and existence and elevates itself onto its place (VII 368f.). The positive, albeit perverse, excess of radical evil must be grasped as something *religious*—in concrete terms discovered by existential thinkers after Schelling—as one's desire to be God. For this reason, radical evil exceeds Kantian transcendental conditions of possibility and shows itself as the negatively saturated phenomenon. Radical evil is negatively saturated by the religious longing to be God (the separation and inversion of principles of ground and existence). We must ponder its positively, that is spiritually, asserted will as an act of defiance.

Self Is Spirit; Therefore Radical Evil Is Possible

Schelling's first two moves explain speculatively how moral evil is possible in general but not how it can come about in human freedom. He explains the metaphysical possibility of moral evil: it is a positive albeit perverse power enabled by the separability and reversal of ground and existence in creatures. This metaphysical possibility—should we have Kant say here that this generalized evil possibility names the propensity (*Hang*) to weakness and wickedness?—consists in the relation of God's ground and existence that in God alone rests in harmony. The possibility of evil is not something wholly alien to God, as it arises from the dark longing of the ground that asserts its prius in perverted will. Yet God's being is not responsible for finite human freedom that can actualize this possibility. Schelling introduces an astonishing metaphysical thought, that if there were no possibility of radical evil, God would not be possible either (1860:VII 403). We will find something akin to this train of thought in Kierkegaard's analytically deductive path from forms of despair to faith. That God is a creator carries the price for God and creatures endowed with free will. For God the price is the mystery of eternal becoming and shared suffering, for freely acting creatures the price is their temporal becoming, suffering, and actualized evil agency.

So how is radical evil actually possible in human freedom? To explain this requires an agency able to commit moral evil. Since God is spirit (VII 364), if Manichaeism were true, then an evil god would be the spirit endowed with a reversal of chaos and love, wherein the ground of nature and its chaotic longing would be the dominating will of this god. The possibility of moral evil is given not only by the duality of basic principles, mute nature, and speaking, self-sacrificing love. It is not only given by the separability of these poles in free creatures. This possibility can be actualized only in human self *qua* spirit.

> The soul is spirit in that it is the living identity of both principles, and Spirit is in God. . . . The selfhood as such is spirit, or human is spirit as a particular selfhood separated from God. . . . Thus arises in human will a split of spiritually becoming selfhood . . . from light, that is the dissolution of the principles that are not dissolvable in God. (VII 364f.)

Schelling's essential insight into human self will have opened Kierkegaard's analysis of despair. It is in Schelling, rather than Hegel, that we must seek the protoexistential meaning of the category of spirit that we encounter in Kierkegaard. That self is spirit attests to human freedom as a creative center of activity. Evil agency emerges neither from blind necessity nor from God's self-sacrifice; rather, it arises in a particular will that separates from light and from its darkness asserts itself over the universal will, in this case over the coincidence of light and dark. The human self, however, exhibits "both centers" (VII 363), the highest heaven and the deepest abyss. Unlike God, who is the ground of God's existence, human self embodies the relative, temporally becoming principle of its natural ground. Free self houses an independent fount of creativity whereby one can become coincident with oneself by speaking and loving. The self that so coincides with itself in creative freedom radiates as spirit, as a center of light. Moral evil signals the reversal and positing of a false center for the *I* (VII 366f.). "The bond of the principles is never in humans something necessary but free" (VII 374).

Schelling thinks of radical moral evil as neither natural nor divine (whether ascribed to a good or evil genius), but as an essentially human creation. In this he parts with classical as well as contemporary analytical thinking about the problem of evil and joins Kant. Yet Schelling is not satisfied with Kant's moralization, even rationalization, of radical evil. He brings back the possibility of diabolical volition. Indeed, I find that all forms of moral evil can be traced back to radical evil and in that to defiance. Evil agency lies in the dominating assertion of the particular will (self-will, *Eigenwille*) in which the will of the ground (longing, *Sehnsucht*), that in God's universal will is subordinated to the living will of existence (love), asserts itself in defiance. To what degree does Schelling's treatise signal the final end of rational theodicy? Kant thought he had already accomplished this, but I concluded that Job's unmasking of idolatry destroys future attempts at theodicy more faithfully than Kant. Lévinas locates this end of theodicy after the Holocaust, and in that regard with Jonas and others he is thinking of God as otherwise than an omnipotent deity. Schelling gives us a new way of thinking about ongoing eternal creation that has been necessary insofar as it reveals God *(Offenbarung)*. He also gives us a new way of thinking about evil in relation to God and human freedom. He does not try to prove or exonerate God's existence; rather, he shows that without the possibility of evil, there would be no possibility of God or creation either. Schelling's mystical God-becoming out of dark hiddenness in order to create and radiate with light, word, and love offers us now something not wholly alien to Jonas's weak God after Auschwitz. Schelling separates two principles of being in order to make room for human freedom; he articulates moral evil as one's positive assertion of defiant will; and he boldly views evil agency as spirit. In all three ways his speculation paves the way for nonspeculative approaches to the problem of evil. One of these is found in Kierkegaard's existential encounter with despair; the other is the Lévinasian ethical response to the face of the other. Even more crucial for my thinking about evil is that Schelling prefigures the grasp of radical evil as a saturated phenomenon.

RADICAL EVIL AS DESPAIR: KIERKEGAARD'S BOLD EXISTENTIAL CONCRETIZATION

Kierkegaard agrees with Kant and Schelling that good and evil are categories imputable to free will alone. Good and evil arise for human beings for the first time with the question of their radical self-choice: What am I? What shall I become? If I pose these questions with absolute earnestness, I am delivered from aesthetic drift into ethical stage of existing. Only in the ethical, categories of good and evil begin to qualify the mode of my willing. This movement from one existential stage to another is not like a pledge of allegiance to this or that value domain or flag or cause; it requires inward self-transformation of my willing. The point of view of human freedom presupposes responsible individuals who would no longer flow with the immediacy of external identifications, but would become autonomous centers of value positing.

An aesthete might consider boredom to be the root of all evil, and he might embark on an elaborate method of self-evasion and external change. An external war on evil would be akin to crop rotation (Kierkegaard, EO I:291)—perhaps a regime change—but with no existential grasp of good and evil. The external, even though religiously dressed up, public discourse on evil fails to grasp not only Kierkegaard's view of religiousness but also the Kantian moral significance of radical evil. Wars on evil are but aesthetic rotation of likes and dislikes. But "an esthetic choice is no choice. . . . to choose is an intrinsic and stringent term for the ethical" (EO II:166). The aesthetic choice, by being purely external, gets lost in immediacy and multiplicity but with no inner "transfiguration" of willing (167). The external assault on evil shows certain "esthetic earnestness," and so we do get easily deceived and manipulated by public moralizers. And especially in public externalizations of the enemy, "evil is perhaps never as seductively effective as when it steps forth in esthetic categories." The ethical earnestness should preclude one from speaking of "evil in esthetic categories." Yet we only need to study the "predominantly esthetic culture of our day" that values such talk of evil. Consider a discourse on evil that produces in the speaker's eye a twinkle of excitement (the nether side of boredom that moves the speaker as well as pleases the crowd) when describing an execution of the criminal or destruction of the enemy. Mass culture provides a platform to "moralizers [who] rant against evil in such a way that we perceive that the speaker, although he praises the good, nevertheless relishes the satisfaction that he himself could very well be the most cunning and wily of men but has rejected it on the basis of a comparison with being a good man" (226).

Significantly, Judge William, the ethicist in Kierkegaard's *Either/Or*, does not "assume a radical evil" in his radical either/or choice between aesthetic and ethical ways of life. He confines himself to showing the difference between a life without any ethical axis and life that is self-governing (EO II:174f.; cf. Green, 1992). Any aesthetic discourse on evil, as it calls God's wrath down on evildoers and tries to root out moral evil externally, lacks the category of inwardness posited by ethical self-choice. The lack of inwardness leads to relations of "leveling reciprocity" (Kierkegaard, TA 63). The crowd is untruth regardless of whether it is secular or sacral. An aesthetic, crowd-pleasing notion of evil embodies social evil in its own right: "The distinction between good and evil is enervated by a loose, supercilious, theoretical acquaintance with evil" (TA 78; Matuštík, 1993, part 3).

Judge William, while he admits that one can repent oneself back into ethical life, stops short of considering Kant's late preoccupation with human weakness or incapacity to sustain freely goodwill. It is crucial, therefore, to note that the possibility of radical evil" comes onto the Kierkegaardian stage for the first time with the pseudonymous authors created by him for the ethico-religious and properly religious dramatizations of existence. These ethico-religious pseudonyma do for Kierkegaard what mature tragedies do for Shakespeare or literary characters struggling with faith do for Dostoyevsky: reveal the intensities of inwardness capable as much of demonic defiance as of spiritual self-transformation. If the problem of evil is understood under the category of despair, then we can understand better why it indirectly feeds on and thus posits the mode of religious existence. Kierkegaard agrees on this center discovery with Schelling—the possibility of radical moral evil requires a spiritual center of free activity.

There Is Nothing Redemptive or Holy in Conducting a War on Evil

This brings me back to the second-degree removal of the popular discourse on moral evil from religious categories. Let me recapitulate briefly what the study of the first removal did for us. That Kant concedes the radical perversity of the human heart while protecting the dignity of the human person, shows a definitive advance over many a contemporary discourse on moral evil. Kant resists every attempt to demonize evil that would either assign it a face or brand as evil some group, sect, or people and then rally others to annihilate the evil brand. Evil deeds also certify human dignity, yes, for Kant even a dignity of a terrorist or tyrant, precisely in qualifying their evil choice as an act "against the [moral] law." By committing even an inhuman, monstrous act, one does not thereby become a nonhuman species or vanquish the moral law within. Kant insists that radical evil is a rational phenomenon governable by the moral law. "The human being (even the worst) does not repudiate the moral law, whatever his maxims, in rebellious attitude (by revoking obedience to it)" (Kant, 1996, 6:36). The propensity to radical evil must be sought "in a free power of choice." "This evil is *radical,* since it corrupts the ground of all maxims. . . . Yet it must equally be possible to *overcome* this evil, for it is found in the human being as acting freely" (6:37). A political name for a Kantian way of overcoming sectarian violence is a procedurally enacted tolerance to disagreement and an institutionally anchored league of nations based on perpetual peace.

Kant saves humans from having to demonize the face of evil. He warns us that by externalizing our struggles against evil, we have not attended to its root in human freedom. It is in free will—hence in the security council of a league of nations—where all struggle must be waged while standing armies yield to the normative procedures of perpetual peace. Violence enacted against evil externally breeds more evil. Strictly speaking, there are no evil empires/empires of Satan, no axes of evil/jihads against evil, no brand names or faces of evil. There is only an evil will. The league of nations, not war, therefore, should allow us to cultivate the public meaning- and will-formation through political dialogue and just procedures of international law. Preemptive or unilateral (nondialogic) acts against the imagined faces of evil make it impossible to overcome at its root the international propensity to radical evil; for Kant this root lies in human willing.

Discourse on evil followed by war on evil cannot promise redemption without grasping the root of evil. Through externalizing evil in political and religious debates, one becomes removed not only from the moral point of view (a conclusion we draw from Kant) but likewise from religious categories (as we learn from Schelling's and Kierkegaard's innovations). By externalizing moral evil, one remains doubly ignorant of what one wants to overcome. First, one deceives by employing religious language about external evil; then the aesthetic chatter about evil is followed by a failure to act morally. External war is an aesthetic rotation of the same. Second, when war on evil targets the faces of evil, human beings are demonized as nonhuman. Wars purify by outward cleansing, if not annihilation, of all deemed nonhuman. We know that this is a fantasy projection because war that begins with aesthetically abstracted or unchanged human beings "nonetheless creates more evil men than it takes away" (Kant, 1996, 6:35).

Defiance as a Saturated Phenomenon

Can any self-assessment of radical evil that wants to stay within the boundaries of mere reason, apprehending evil as a rational phenomenon because it does not acknowledge its willfully bound free will, curb the existential roots of violence? Is violence a phenomenon that can be cured through enlightened forms of tolerance? Or must it be admitted that radical evil and accompanying violence are modes of a saturated phenomenon; said otherwise, that there is nothing wholly secular about violence?

A poster from a New York worldwide antiwar demonstration on February 16, 2003, proclaimed that if you want to be a cowboy, you've got to be smarter than the cows. Kierkegaard's religious pseudonym anti-Climacus says as much in his phenomenology of despair: "A cattleman who (if this were possible) is a self directly before his cattle is a very low self"; one gains "infinite reality" in the "self directly before God" (SUD 79). Ranting about evil and sin aesthetically is not to become a self even ethically, and one acts more stupidly than a cow.

If violence reveals at its core a spiritual significance, we need to determine what has been lost with the translation of the religious category of evil as sin into the moral significance of radical evil and into its rational overcoming. Can the discursive, moral, and political translation of religious contents—including Kant's translation of sin into a truce between unwavering enlightened respect for moral law and ongoing perversion of human willingness to obey it freely—arrest the *positive* impetus to violence that arises from radical evil?

Kant should not have equivocated the origins of evil choice by translating "sin" as "depravity" that can be overcome in time with our power of repentance into the light of reason and goodwill (1996, 6:39, 41–43). To await "a *revolution* in the disposition of the human being. . . . and so a 'new man' . . . a kind of rebirth, as it were a new creation . . . and a change of heart," this Kant cannot postulate even morally. He invokes a gratuitous cooperation of "reflective" faith with available grace, but does so without grasping how radical evil robs intellect and will of their natural light and willingness—how we become more confused by the very use of rational light, more bound by our free will (6:47, 52f.). Kant's human-all-too-human way of talking about the epistemic and moral effects of "sin" hides the *radical*—positive, spiritual—root of radical evil.

Perhaps our present age will shrug its shoulders at preserving religion, even within Kant's limits of human reason, as past its time at best and boring at worst. Nobody cares about *rational* religion any more, certainly not atheists, to be sure not fundamentalists. Kant (6:43) and Kierkegaard (CA 21, 50, 30, 112, 161; SUD 106f.; cf. Green, 1992:160–63, 64f.) agree that evil, like freedom, is a rationally inscrutable and self-propelling existential whole, a moment of leap. Yet the idea of a rationalized radical evil is metaphysically counterintuitive (Schelling), existentially self-contradictory (Kierkegaard), and historically falsified (post-Holocaust reflection on moral evil). Radical evil in the post-Kantian age has remained anywhere but within rational boundaries. If human evil as we know it in the past hundred years has been transgressing all rational frames, then is there anything wholly secular about violence? Is not violence a paramount case of a saturated phenomenon? The radicalness of radical evil must be clarified outside of the safe boundaries of mere reason. Kant fears to name as "diabolical" that moral evil which humans bring into the world. He aims to preserve the dignity of human self-legislative reason and goodwill as more originary than the actual free will to do evil. He keeps open the metaphysical access of even corrupted free will to moral repentance as if grace always and already sustained progress and transformation of the human race.[1]

Kierkegaard acknowledges sin as the beginning of religious life. Religiously speaking, when despair is grasped as sin, then it is essentially a category that cannot be translated into secular or even moral language without softening the issue of radical evil. The sin category discloses the radical limit of repenting oneself back to the ethical sphere of existence by the light of one's reason or by the moral reformation of free will. Yet the sin category by itself does not explain why radical evil (e.g., genocide or indiscriminate warfare) committed by humans could be achieving diabolical intensities.

By "diabolical" I mean a positive act of freedom that is saturated by perverse religiousness. The negatively saturated phenomenon is any positive act of freedom for the sole sake of defiance—wanton violence, cruelty, crimes against humanity. If we were to address Job and Kant, we would have to say that radically evil acts are perpetrated by a free agency that, albeit respecting the moral law as a rational condition of its general possibility, positively actualizes its spiritual possibility, draws its power to act, and realizes itself by defying the law of anti-idolatry.

Kant shuddered at the possibility of a "diabolically" free human act: if I am unable ever to choose evil freely as my maxim, then I can never act strictly speaking "diabolically." With Kant, humans are safely off the diabolical hook. Does this concession not fail to grasp human freedom in the depth that Schelling's speculation reveals and Kierkegaard's experiment with the self performs? If yes, then it is not Kant who in the end can save human dignity by confining radical evil within the boundaries of mere reason. It is Schelling's speculation that defined human freedom in spiritual terms, and it is Kierkegaard who discovered, in the dreaded possibility of humans to despair, the depth of human excellence (SUD 14f.).

In order to be smarter than cows and speak about evil more knowledgeably than a cowboy would, one needs to acknowledge that one's existence unfolds before the infinite spirit. Kierkegaard allows us to save human dignity not by downplaying the possibility of "diabolical" extremes of human freedom (Kant's solution to the problem of evil), but rather by looking this possibility squarely in the face. This "diabolical" possibility attests in the same measure to the spiritual intensity of human existence. By calling the most radical form of evil a defiance of unconditional love, Kierkegaard does not devalue the self to nonhuman status. Rather, he builds on the Kantian moral basis for human dignity and then goes beyond Kant. Kierkegaard shows the greatest expansion of human dignity to lie in the category of the "theological self" (SUD 79).

For Kierkegaard, the radicalness of radical evil inheres existentially in the possibilities of a human spirit who can say (take a free position) yes or no to the offer of unconditional love. To be diabolical, then, is to reject emphatically the gift of creation and forgiveness; this can be called "diabolical" because the act is saturated by defiance; because there is no rational explanation for a human person who wants to exist as an accusation of and against the loving cosmos. Such defiance reveals a fully human, positive expression of freedom, and yet human self-realization in defiance is no longer confined within the boundaries of mere reason, for it draws its positive strength negatively from the religious.

Defiance does not render a person nonhuman. To defy creation and forgiveness means to will to be oneself *despairingly;* in the deed one desires to exist by defying that the very ground of one's existence (as in Schelling's speculative grasp of divine existence wherein the will to chaos is subordinated to will to life) consists of unconditional love. Why is my willing to be myself in despair a saturated phenomenon? Why can this will be described and yet escape rationalization (neither visable nor bearable, it is singular and indirect)?

One of Kierkegaard's major discoveries is the insight into despairing will. How can I despair of wanting to be myself? By grafting Kierkegaard's analysis onto Marion's four characteristics of the saturated phenomenon, we discover:

- Despair has no foreseeable object at which I can aim (it is invisable), yet despair is something that fascinates and draws my will (cf. Marion, 2002:199–202).
- Willing to be myself in despair produces an intensity that "cannot be borne" (202). Despair, albeit I will to be myself through it, becomes unbearable, and so that which propels me also blinds and cripples my desire to be.
- Defiant willingness to exist "evades any analogy of experience" (206), and so I discover that it occurs without relation to my prior experience as my positive sui generis assertion of power. Despair is always a singular event and intensity of creative center, a desire to be a self.
- Despairing existence breaks the subject-object pole of horizon. It breaks the conditions of possible understanding, for the despairing self is given to me only indirectly, broken, as something "irregardable" (212)—as this myself willing to exist in despair.

"In saturation, the I undergoes the disagreement between an at least potential phenomenon and the subjective condition for its experience." Yet the despairing self does appear as something positive. It is not a mere negation or absence but a center of its willing to exist—it is a defiant spirit, a self negatively saturated by spirit. "Intuitive saturation, precisely insofar as it renders it *invisable,* intolerable, and absolute (unconditioned), is imposed in the type of phenomenon that is exceptional by excess, not by defect" (213). Radical evil, and here despair, is an instantiation, is exceptional by excess, not by absence, negation, or lack. Despair positively albeit perversely creates the self, or as noted in the previous chapter, my will to be myself despairingly uncreates the very self I want to be.

How can one freely draw strength to be oneself and in that power suffer despair? Kant depicts radical evil as moral weakness, yet despair of weakness is a less intense form of despair in which one wants to do away with oneself. Defiance is a positive act, position, will to power. Yet if the universe were only chaos and never cosmos, then one could have no *personal* relation to it, then defiance would make little metaphysical sense and it would be performatively without fuel to propel itself. Then there could only be the despair of weakness, never that of strength. What propels the defiant-despairing will to exist is likewise what despair forbids itself as its *telos,* and still what despairing will finds unbearable, what it cannot find in its field of experience, and yet what it cannot achieve by its own coincidence—to rest transparently in the unconditional love that creates and forgives it. Despair marks an excess of perverse intuition, and so despair does not suffer from intellectual doubt. Despair does not miss adequate concepts. To be negatively saturated by despair is to lack faith. Active, demonic, raging defiance makes no sense without a personal relationship of the rational and free self to the offer of unconditional love. It is precisely this rejection of creation and forgiveness, and both are paramount figures of unconditional love, that marks the "diabolical" extreme of human freedom.

Why Demons Are Not Atheists

I can draw a twofold consideration from the foregoing meditation on Schelling's metaphysics of freedom and Kierkegaard's experimental insight into despair. First, one cannot be defiantly related to an empty and meaningless cosmos whether or not the image of impassable nothingness is practico-inert and entropic matter, mythical *khôra,* or deconstructive spacings and deferrals of meaning. Defiance is addressed to a face, and so it means that one always and already knows in one's heart what is being rejected and yet rejects that very call and gift. In mythology, devils are never portrayed as intellectual atheists; they are spirit beings who insist on existing unloved and unloving. Hell is never an entropic *khôra* but rather a state of despair incapable of love, not an intellectual field of philosophy of religion or religious studies preoccupied with proofs regarding God's existence but a field of battles for human spirit and self-transformation. Dostoyevsky's Ivan Karamazov is not strictly speaking an atheist either; he is troubled by the demon of despair. Even if God existed and offered him love, he would reject it. The Grand Inquisitor defies creation and forgiveness by drawing on the power to uncreate and permit freedom to commit evil.

Paradoxically, the despair of defiance, the very "diabolical" possibility to usurp divinity, attests to the most human and spiritual core of selfhood. The redemptive overcoming of radical evil lies for Kierkegaard in accepting the gift of unconditional love. Because he considers the radical evil of my acts as no longer confined within the bounds of mere reason, because it is a phenomenon saturated by a topsy-turvy spirit, he can confront evil at its root—in despair. Far from externalizing evil (he rejects the aesthetic version of evil), and with Kant decidedly opposed to the dehumanization of evildoers (he accepts the moral argument against the cowboy approach to evil), Kierkegaard acknowledges the possibility of "diabolical" freedom. In that feat he experimentally witnesses the spirit reality of the self. The spirit self embodies the most dignified mode of humanity because therein one exists as a self directly before God.

In reverse, having now rejected the aesthetic theory of moral evil as only partially explanatory even of the banality of its saturation, common aesthetic discourses on evil must be judged as but masked forms of defiance that fall even behind Kant's rational hope in moral *metanoia*. Aesthetic discourses on evil (not to be confused with the aesthetic intensity or banality of evil) are always already forms of demonic usurpation. When theft of fire from heaven hides behind a religiously flavored external war on evil, it becomes an act of willed ignorance about its own despair. At its highest pitch the belligerent willingness to wage external war on evil is an act of defiance. The cowboys who wage external wars on evil, parading in religious costume and without grasping evil and yet bereft of minimal ethical capacity for repentance, disrespect even the cows that are God's creation. Willed stupidity even in aesthetic self-and-other relations is revealed as always already something harboring the diabolical excess.[2]

Radical Evil as Addiction, or There Is Nothing Wholly Secular about Evil

The second conclusion is that radical evil at its existential roots must be grasped as neither merely aesthetic (banal) nor morally radical (within the bounds of mere reason), nor paradoxical or aporetic (in the ethico-religious intention of and desire for the possibility of the impossible) but as spiritual disorder (defiance of the redemptive possibility of the second-order of impossible, e.g., forgiveness). We arrive at an integral figure of human evil as at once banal, morally radical, ethico-religiously paradoxical, and spiritually diabolical. Eichmann's case of evil is banal only insofar as he tranquilizes himself on a trivial pursuit of the perceived good as prescribed by the leader's will. Kant's descriptions of radical evil are morally superior only insofar as he detects distortions of the human capacity to progress in freedom. Derrida's aporias of paradoxical evil are superior only insofar as he can detect what Kant or Husserl could not, namely, the frustrated maximized intention always striving for and failing to reach the impossible. Yet radical evil is grasped in its full performance only as the site of the best and the worst, as the diabolical volition in its human-all-too-human religious cruelty.

Humans despair in the deepest recesses of the spirit self about accepting the unconditional gift of love—that I exist before infinite spiritual reality, that my life without anxiety and despair is possible, that unconditional love is my redemptive possibility. Spirit reality endows human free will with the metaphysical and, in despair, performative possibility of choosing to act defiantly. Even while practical reason is formally respecting the moral law, as spirit, I can existentially defy the anti-idolatry law. Yet even a defiant human agency retains its dignity. Kant did not consider the possibility of human defiance seriously enough and in his haste to protect us from the "diabolical" use of freedom, he diminished human dignity. The first step out of despair, as in any twelve-step program for liberation from negative saturation by addiction, must be my acknowledgment that enlightened reason and moral repentance must yield to a spiritual admission that I am powerfully binding myself by my defiantly despairing will.

In the second step out of despair, after owning my defiance and thus willing to be myself, I must let go of my despairing willing to be myself. Concepts such as violence, evil, and redemption are related yet distinct religious categories that cannot be translated into secular languages without watering down the radicalness of radical evil. Yet this untranslatability does not diminish the dignity of rational and moral beings. By refusing to set the fact of radical evil within the boundaries of mere reason, by grasping it as a negatively saturated phenomenon of religious despair, knowing now what it is we pray for when we want deliverance and purification, we are able to restore greater dignity to humans than in the confines of the cowboy wars on evil or in mere procedural tolerance of conflict.

VIOLENCE AS A RELIGIOUS DIMENSION OF RADICAL EVIL

Mindful of the aesthetic, moral, ethico-religious, and spiritual intensities of evil, we can meditate on violence and slowly overturn the bias regarding secularization and redemption:

- There is nothing redemptive or holy in external war on evil (*ad* Kant).
- There is nothing wholly secular about violence (*ad* Schelling and Kierkegaard).

I question next whether enlightened tolerance deters sectarian conflicts. Can modern translations of religious contents into moral procedures, that is, by secularizing sin consciousness, resolve the problem of invidious violence? Can perpetual peace be achieved by secular means alone? If both answers are no, then not only modern religious but also secular conflicts must be grasped as saturated phenomena. I suspect the claim that with the secularizing reflection on and tolerance of worldviews we have overcome the sectarian conflict of beliefs. This situation does not call for more secular translations of religious claims (cf. Habermas, FK, ID) but for a religious critique of discourses on violence, evil, and redemption. *A redemptive critical theory* facing this postsecular constellation is equipped to deliver a religious critique of religious claims.

The process of secularization has been gradually translating sacred or traditional beliefs into publicly redeemable validity claims, thus overcoming the problem of intolerance and violence. Yet if the outcome of this process is a degree of emptiness that renders human existence unlivable, can the vanishing point of secularization offer a true path to uprooting sectarian intolerance and violence? Another way of posing this question: Is secularized consciousness capable of living without redemptive hope? Can humans exist without wonder and mystery? Can humans flourish without inhering in the cosmos that receives them and in that embrace stimulates their freedom to find their vocation? What is the dimension of time and space that secular consciousness opens for us? While I take no issue with deflating the rational argument for tolerance, I ponder whether the possibility of uprooting invidious violence must go to the heart of intolerance, which arises even in secular existence from free will saturated by despair. The answer to the question, Is secularized consciousness capable of living without redemptive hope? is not whether or not modern mind wants to keep rooting out the most entrenched source of violence, but whether it can do it by its secularizing resources.

The twentieth century witnessed unparalleled violence inflicted by secular societies. Our fascination with retributive death dealing and war, our desire to purify the world of all evil—these are hardly secular ambitions. They are always and already *spiritually* saturated desires. If modern violence inflicts wounds to the interiority of a fully secularized consciousness, if it thus behaves as the negatively saturated phenomenon par excellence, how can the argument for a rationally achieved tolerance carry the day? How can secularization be an answer to invidious violence emerging from the heart of secularized consciousness? The argument for tolerance addresses one side of the issue, but it fails to reach the core of wanton violence in secularized consciousness. The side that the argument does address well is how to resolve the clash of belief systems or of civilizational values. The process of secularization is a self-correcting process of learning, whereby we come to view our differences without the need to annihilate or assimilate them. Secular consciousness can learn to live next to the religious one; in reverse, tolerance can flourish in postsecular societies where different religious beliefs learn to coexist with a fully secularized consciousness. Believers learn from this process of secularization to value tolerance, as they too must vie for their autonomy on the procedural grounds of secular society.

But why does wanton violence arise at the heart of a fully secularized consciousness? Violence arises in postsecular societies that have their share of sectarian hatred. Does it not mean, then, that there are saturated dimensions of violence not curable on the path of secularization? If that is so, what can secular translation alone do to cure violence, especially the ongoing need for retribution, revenge, and war? If an impetus to invidious violence comes from the newly sacralized rage against human finitude, disease, fallibility, death, how can secularization alone enlighten us with sobriety?[3] If violence has to do with the need to purify oneself and the world of evil—if evil is defined as human finitude and mortality—there is nothing entirely secular about such violent flight from evil (Becker, 1975). The secular is negatively saturated by the religious. By calling wanton violence a spiritually sacralized, albeit negatively saturated, rage against the evil of finitude and death, I do not mean that all religions are motivated by hate. I am making a distinction within the religious intensity of existence that secular integrations are not sober about the negatively saturated, religious aim of their violence.

This distinction implies that in all religious traditions there can be found a spiritual route to sobriety that deters the religious motivation to violence: admit my finitude and death. Face my own inability to sustain free existence. Hope for redemption but first give up my heroic rage against the cosmos for inflicting on me the evil of my finitude and death. Therein lies the nonviolent core of great spiritual traditions. It leads by way of divestment, detachment, openness to the cosmos, acceptance of one's vocational place in the larger unknown of the mysterious universe, self-forgiveness of one's finitude and mortality, yielding to the sources of unconditional love, and embracing the works of such love as a way to healing all that suffers.

To curb our propensity for violence on the other side of secularization—whether or not we actually coexist in postsecular societies with a mix of religious and secular attitudes or live already in postmodern fundamentalist revivals—requires a spiritual corrective to both religious and secular validity domains alike. Such corrective would fund the core motive and intuition behind what I call redemptive critical theory or redemptive criticism. Any postsecular redemptive reality must come to terms with human finitude and death—without inflicting pain and violence on others in the process of escaping mortality and without needing to purify the world of such projected and feared evil. This redemptive reality is postsecular because it affects both secularized and religious consciousness; still, it is a redemptive reality (it is faith rather than a belief system) because no present validity domain knows how to secure redemption without reproducing the attraction and terror of violence that deals death.

Intolerance at root is a claim of the morally goodwill that my or our way is the ultimate path to redemption for others to follow. This arrogant blind spot does not bypass secular consciousness. Redemptive reality cannot be a validity claim—whether one means a belief proposition about redemption or raises claims to be "redeemed" in public discourse. Our waiting and working to hasten the realization of the not yet cannot depend on any validity domain, even the messianic one. The redeemed reality is not won by redeeming an unconditioned claim. We do not own the shape of redeemed reality; we can only come to exist in it. Such reality is after all a matter of gift, grace, faith, hope, and love. In redemptive criticism, we are not resting in some quietist paralysis. On the contrary, we must faithfully challenge all beliefs (religious or secular) in possessing the ultimate shape of the gift, all translations of such beliefs, and any secular belief that hopes to redeem hope in the form of public discourse on the criticizable validity claims.

There is a double acoustical illusion (Kierkegaard, PF 49–54) that issues first from religious belief claims (and these must be distinguished from the autopsy of faith) about redemption. Second, it arises from the secular translations of religious beliefs (this is the illusion of someone who secularizes beliefs without ever grasping the dimension of faith). The distinction within the religious sphere is the following: belief is to faith, as sectarian violence is to nonviolent receptivity. Redemptive criticism deters the violence of these twin illusions, a violence they inevitably inflict on religions in forms of fundamentalism and on secular societies in forms of spiritlessness. This would be a deterrent free of that negative saturation by wanton violence because it would be a deterrent without calling for retributive death or holy war.[4]

VIOLENCE AND RELIGION:
MEDITATING WITH DERRIDA,
KIERKEGAARD, LÉVINAS, AND MARION

In his rereading of Kant's (1996) fourth critique, Derrida offers the following concise definition of the religious: "The possibility of *radical evil* both destroys and institutes the religious" (FaK 100, par. 51). Vries (2002:162, cf.105, 108f., 170f.) perceptively describes this at once Kierkegaardian and

Derridean-Lévinasian differentiation from Kant's view: "The 'spiritual' [the best] and the 'demonic' [the worst] occupy [structurally] the same 'space.'" Lévinas's classic definition of religion as the "bond that is established between the same and the other without constituting a totality" (1969:40) gives us a pretty good idea why, for him, violence of "the same" lodges at the heart of any attempt at conceptual or practical closure. Religion eschews violence. By holding out for the impossibility of pure nonviolence, Derrida accentuates the obverse side of Lévinas's definition of religion. In Derrida's view all human history and articulations must pass through the violence of determination, and in his Hegelian parlance this means that they must go "through the violence of the concept." On his view, "within history," there is never a "nonviolent" articulation of justice. There is one or another "economy of violence" within the "circulation of Being."

Lévinas's ethics of responsibility builds on the face-to-face encounters whereby it aims to resist all conceptual as well as practical closure. The ethical exercises priority over ontology—hence it is called meontology. This ethics always already satisfies Lévinas's definition of the religious whose infinity resists and escapes *all* economy of violence. The religious opens onto the infinite whose excess always and already breaks all attempts at achieving totality.

Derrida's Square Circle around Kant and Job

Unlike Lévinas and more like the memory site of Prague's Jewish Central Museum during the Nazi period discussed in the previous chapter, Derrida captures the religious as the saturated site with mixed possibilities of the best and the worst. Derrida's (WD 136, 218f.) reply to Lévinas's ideal view of the religious as infinite excess is that the human face can halt the economy of violence only because it either provokes or receives violence in the first place.

I wish to dwell on Derrida's emphatically religious rendition of Kant's moralized evil:

- The religious opens up the site for both the best and the worst.
- Radical evil institutes and destroys the possibility of the religious.

Derrida follows here in the footsteps we have traced from Kant to Schelling to Kierkegaard. Yet must our grasp of radical evil as the spiritual, albeit negatively saturated phenomenon mean that invidious violence (e.g., totalitarian closure) is always *intrinsically* related to religion? If this were so, then theoretically there could be no religious critique of religion and no redemptive critical theory or critical theory of redemption to boot. Practically, not only religious terrorism but every form of the religious would be incurable of wanton violence. Derrida's essential or structural, aporetic, paradoxical impossibility of pure nonviolence, even as a *khôra*-condition of impossibility that like a cosmic invisible hand safeguards our resistance to any and all totalitarian closure, situates us between hope and terror—with no exit. We must return to themes left in part 1 regarding the first-order of impossible hope and Solomon's hope that love is as strong as death, indeed, stronger than the *khôra*.

I am brought to the following conundrum: if violence results from either conceptual or practical totalizations (in Lévinas's definition religion resists them), if violence reveals the proximity of human history and every articulation to the *horror religiosus* (in Derrida's definition of the religious in FaK pure nonviolence is impossible because he locates the second, antiredemptory and entropically blind and ethically inert source of the "religious" in the *khôra*), does it inevitably follow that there is "no religion without (some) violence"? Granted that the religious is the site of both the best and the worst, must the redemptive Other of violence be "violence or violent still, in yet another meaning of the word" (Vries, 2002:1; cf.135f.)? Are we stuck in the aporetic autoimmune loops of bad infinity of self-destruction for the sake of survival? Even when not choosing, must we choose at best "a lesser violence" (Derrida, WD 136; A)? Is a form of greater or lesser violence what the religious—the *khôra* which is undoing and overwhelming even the redemptive-saving Other of violence—incarnates at the end of the day?

Meditating on religion and violence, I am in no hurry to flee Derrida's grasp of the religious as instituted and destroyed by the "possibility of *radical evil*" (FaK 100). I dwell on this consideration: Derrida is right on target in his Abrahamic phenomenology of the religious as messianic without messianicity, religious without religion, the site of the possibility of radical evil and hope for its overcoming, but he is off the mark in his ontologizing of violence on account of the second, *khôra*-source of the religious. I turn the Derridean aporia of the link between religion and violence into a koan of the religious: I move from Derrida's conceptual (aporetic, antinomical) into self-transformative (inward, existential) mode of thinking about religion and violence. I return to Kierkegaard's grasp of the demonic and diabolical and complement it with Lévinas's view of radical evil as the excess which *also* breaks every totality.

Delving deeper into Derrida's phenomenology of the religious, we find him learning from what I described in previous chapters as Job's corrective to Kant. Unlike Job, Kant would run into an insurmountable difficulty at Auschwitz trying to account for the "rational origin of an evil that remains inconceivable to reason" (Derrida, FaK 49). Derrida hides his perceptive amplification of the Judeo-Christian phenomenology of the religious in a long footnote (GT 165f. n. 31). Kant concedes that the possibility of radical evil may corrupt our maxims for action, but only to explain it away as a perverse tendency of an otherwise rational human agency. Evil acts may never convert humans into diabolical beings. "Kant thinks and asserts," Derrida writes with great clarity, "it is *a fact* that . . . [human being] is not such a [diabolical] being. Kant's whole argumentation seems to proceed from the *credit* granted this supposed *fact*." Human freedom is neither attributable to a beastly sensibility nor essentially destructible by a devilish perversion, Kant holds. The only evil that Kant recognizes as radical would be acts morally forgivable or repairable by human progress. He does not conceive that humans are capable of anything unforgivable. "In the species of a diabolical 'bêtise' [stupidity], in other words, that satanic *cruelty* that Kant does not want to acknowledge."

At this juncture Derrida's insight into the religious achieves its deconstructive crispness. Diabolical stupidity is capable of inventing that mode of evil which calls for forgiveness—and this mode bears the name of the unforgivable. Derrida obviously learned from Kierkegaard's distinction between the ethical and religious spheres of existence. This distinction of two spheres is often placed in opposition to Lévinas's single sphere of ethico-religious Judaism. Yet Lévinas's religious matches quite neatly Kierkegaard's existential ethics (his ethico-religious sphere) and even better his second, religious ethics of unconditional love. Johannes Climacus's ethical sphere embodies a more intense inwardness than the conventional communitarian ethics of Judge William, and so it is already meontological (otherwise than grounded in ontology of being). Kierkegaard's religious ethics is rooted in the second commandment of the face-to-face neighborly love, and so it surpasses even his pseudonyma, William as well as Climacus. Kierkegaard's second ethics thus corresponds to Lévinas ethico-religious life. This ethics is religiously anchored in the gift or works of love.

Why do we need Kierkegaard's distinction among existential spheres, a Buber or Lévinas might ask? For Kierkegaard—and Job would defend his reasons—the distinction is needed because of Kant and Hegel who each translate religious self-transformation into a rational religion. In this translation they move away from Job. Their move was undone also thanks to Schelling. The possibility of radical evil that for Derrida both institutes and destroys the religious is not thinkable without the distinction between the ethical and the religious. Derrida's religious, like that of Kierkegaard, must be read against Kant's religion that remains of a moral kind. Lévinas spars in this regard with Kant and Hegel, and so his ethical is never equal to Kant's morality or Hegel's communitarian ethics. Unlike the religious within the bounds of mere reason (Kant) or in civic religion of the social whole (Hegel), the saturated religious phenomenon instituted by the possibility of radical evil emerges beyond the experience of the forgivable moral fault. Moral or existential guilt (e.g., finitude or temporality) is something I can repent and so lift off my shoulders by my goodwill. So I can return with my own rational resources intact into the ethical; I just need to repent and accept my finite human condition. But the religious whose view I share with Derrida, Kierkegaard, and Lévinas is beyond the dimension of moral guilt my will can repent on its own. The religious arrives on the dramatic scene with the phenomenon of something unforgivable, cruel, diabolical, or what Kierkegaard calls the demonic.

Moral guilt can be repented and so may be repaid by just punishment (Kant and Hegel cite the death penalty as an extreme example of such moral repair available to the one who is being executed). Yet radical evil as we have been discussing it is never the same as ordinary moral guilt. The requisite distinction must be established between repentable and punishable moral failures and diabolical perversity that raises the question of forgiveness as something that cannot be achieved by ordinary penance or punishment. The radicalness of evil under consideration is a form of hubris or addiction that breaks one's capacity for sustained development and nondestructive agency. Great religions address the evil mode of this intensity when they insist that it must be atoned for and forgiven in order to restore the human capacity for moral freedom.

If radical evil amounted to moral guilt (Hegel shares this Enlightenment hope with Kant and Habermas shares it with both), then ethical community, democratic procedures, and just courts could replace Yom Kippur as well as the Kyrie eleison or Buddhist meditations on nothingness. After Auschwitz, the gulag, or Rwanda we definitely *know* that there exists the negatively saturated phenomenon—an excess—of something beyond ordinary moral harm and repair. This phenomenon exceeds even the horrific emptiness of the *khôra:* Could I ever despair of *khôra*? Would I ever find the need to defy *khôra*? Would radical evil and its cruelty arise in an empty, faceless universe in which the possibility of love being as strong as death could not even arise as a question? And so how could *khôra* ever be a genuine source of *any* resistance, indeed of a *religious* response, be it religious in loving or hateful ways, rather than be a musically tone-deaf and mute ground never in itself called to being, love, and freedom of existing?

The possibility of radical evil institutes the worst and the best *as* religious phenomena because of its vocative dimension in the doer and the receiver. This is the willed stupidity of the diabolical that Kierkegaard calls despair. With Schelling we witness the diabolical as a category of human freedom, and so its actuality cannot be attributed to conceptual paradox of intentionality desiring the impossible, or to an ontological aporia, or to structural and intertextual violence of deferred meanings or to the inertia and empty spacings of the *khôra*. And as a category of freedom, radical evil's actuality is not granted in God's ground, even as it allows for evil's free play of possibility. The positive epiphany of the negatively saturated phenomenon arrives as something spiritual, albeit the secular age is unable to name evil with religious names as "sin," and so it is equally unprepared to discover the sources of redemptive forgiveness as "spiritual" realities.

Lévinas and Marion: Evil as Excess

Not unlike Arendt noting in her early writing and before revising the notion of radical evil by attending to its banality, Lévinas stresses the "diabolical horror" of "gratuitous human suffering." Speaking of the Holocaust victims he was nonetheless concerned for all victims of the regimes of "totalitarianism of right and left" (1988:162). Auschwitz has provided him, as it does in these meditations, with a focal name for forms of radical evil (167). The most important support for my treatment of radical evil as the negatively saturated phenomenon is found in Lévinas's thought that not only religious infinity but also evil is marked by excess. The religious as well as radical evil break the totality. Moreover, as if at times thinking along the same track, Marion depicts among saturated phenomena also the suffering and evil of the extermination camps.

Marion (2002:317f.) shows how the "phenomenon that had saturated them [victims] in their flesh—evil and suffering—could not be said, understood, or therefore appear in the world." That extreme evil could not be said, grasped, revealed, "we could not phenomenalize what is nevertheless given to the survivor." The gratuitous suffering of the victims of history is marked by "the unsayable." One (survivors as much as guilty bystanders) cannot hear it spoken; one is too traumatized to speak it. It is likewise rendered "invisible." Its sight is unbearable, and so it cannot be revealed for what it is even if it is presented and seen. This is why Marion often describes various saturated phenomena as paradox. And this is much more a Kierkegaardian, intuitive way of speaking than if he described them in conceptual terms as Kantian antinomies or Derridean aporias. Lévinas's paradoxical language of radical evil as excess breaking conceptual totalities plays the very same role as found in this regard in Marion.

I wish to identify here yet another confirmation of why we need to view radical evil as the negatively saturated phenomenon. First, there are striking phenomenological overlaps between Marion and Lévinas in their descriptions of our inability to "synthesize" or integrate what we nonetheless suffer as monstrous evil. Lévinas considers evil as excess, and by this he means a mode of transcendence that structurally parallels the infinite transcendence of the religious. The religious breaks the conceptual and historical totality in ways that establish the ethical relation between what could not be synthesized and integrated—the face, the otherness of the Other. Monstrous evil breaks the totality in ways that violate the ethical relation with the Other. Unlike Derrida, Lévinas distinguishes between these two ways of destruction or deconstruction of totality. Derrida, Lévinas, and Kierkegaard place the possibility of the best and worst, the religious and radical evil, at the same level structurally. Two sides stand in tension:

- The best and the worst undecidably define the religious (Derrida).
- Infinite transcendence of the evil deed destroys the infinite transcendence of the face (Lévinas).
- Despair is negated by faith (Kierkegaard).

How should these oppositions be viewed? Are they aporetical (conceptual, structural, or ontological problems) or performative (meontological—ethical-existential) tasks? For Derrida, following Heidegger, the relation between religion and violence, with his post-Kantian angle on radical evil at its center, presents an ontological limit. For Kierkegaard and Lévinas this issue poses the tasks of self-transformation and commanded works of love. The former two stress aporia, the latter two responsibility.

Second, Marion (2002:219ff.) discusses the Cartesian idea of the infinite, the Kantian experience of the sublime, and the Husserlian internal time consciousness as examples of the saturated phenomenon. The infinite cannot be synthesized; it surprises, it exceeds all measure of experience, and it overwhelms the ego that cannot comprehend it. The sublime is incomparable. It appears as something dissonant and even monstrous, it breaks our finite horizon, and it contradicts all ego expectations. The flux of time cannot be integrated. I said at the outset in part 1 and will conclude in the final chapter that we interpret time's passage nostalgically unhappy remembering and longingly unhappy hoping as our existential scarcity. That abstracted time without duration, the dead or dearly departed time makes its actual passage unbearable in every now. Secular time consciousness apprehends no possibility of the redemptive now-time, its hope is always already scarce, it is emphatically saturated by the impossible. Contra Kant, Marion, following Husserl, holds that time has no analogy in experience: "It shows itself in itself and by itself without relation to or among objects, in short, absolutely." Time cannot be seen by the I; it constitutes the I's experience that is "transcendentally taken witness" (221).

I already stressed the double role of the infinite in Lévinas. Both the divine trace and radical evil cannot be phenomenally synthesized. The ego can be taken hostage either by the monstrous, when it does not respond to the face, or by the otherness of the other when one heeds the ethical task of responsibility. Lévinas (1983:158) depicts the sublime and radical evil as if both were exceeding in our awareness of them the categories of understanding as well as the immanent horizon of experience. In sum, Lévinas identifies what I call, inspired by Marion, the negatively saturated phenomenon that can be neither comprehended nor integrated.

I excavated this phenomenon already in Schelling's perversely sublime. Perversion of freedom is formed by a topsy-turvy center of creation that gets dizzy by the monstrous, or as Bernstein (2002:175, 182) suggests, by "a malignant sublime," by "an immanent transcendence." This immanence is likewise bereft of conceptual closure or rational theodicy. Structurally it appears like the religious. In this vein, radical evil's peculiar resistance to conceptual closure itself offers a Job-like, albeit negatively saturated, clue to the law of anti-idolatry. Otherwise the negatively saturated phenomenon would not be able to reveal in its defiant will its particular mode of existence as despair.

The Religious as the Site of the Best and the Worst

To intensify my meditation on the religious, I must face squarely Derrida's ontology of violence. Our present age knows the faces of radical evil in ways Kant dared not to imagine. Does it follow that every prayer of forgiveness must proceed by way of some violence, however otherwise "lesser" than the mode of radical evil to be atoned? Do all conceptual and practical totalizations and all attempts to mount a nonviolent resistance to closure—what has been defined as the religious site of the best and the worst—produce a form of violence? Lacking polite words, I label this view of the religious as a secular postmodern sin consciousness without redemption. Would not Kierkegaard call ontologizing of violence but a "desperate presupposition of predestination" (CUP 513) Are we predestined to pray in vein because praying to *khôra*?

Why do I think that Derrida's phenomenology of the religious is right while his ontology of violence is wrong? I will meditate afresh on his insightful yet misunderstood aporia by turning it into a koan: "The possibility of *radical evil* both destroys and institutes the religious."

Let me sum up our journey so far. Kant saves the dignity of evildoers from demonizing their human face. Even the terrorist is a human being, even countries on the axis of evil are human communities. He moralizes rational freedom's perversions for the sake of the dignity of the enemy. Many a contemporary politician or religious leader has a lesson to learn from Kant's *morally* bounded religion. Invoking holy wars on subhuman infidels is not *religious* even in Kant's rational, moral sense of religion! Kierkegaard rejects the aesthetic religiousness of those who have forgotten what it means to become a self; here he stands guard with Kant. In Schelling's footsteps, he found in human capacity for the demonic-worst also the springboard for the redemptive-best, thereby granting humans an even greater dignity than Kant, that of becoming a theological self.

Is saying that *the religious is the site of both the best and the worst* the same as saying that *radical evil institutes the possibility of the best and the worst?* Does the actual violence of human history and the aporetic, paradoxically structural violence of the concept per se define all articulations of human possibility? Even if we interminably postpone the mystical founding of authority and human projects to a nondeconstructible realm of the event-to-come that is neither articulable nor historical, must our suspension of the heroic inscribe all religiousness into the antinomial economies of violence? Or what does the talk of "lesser" violence mean when we hope to find forgiveness for the unforgivable?

Kierkegaard describes the demonic as one's proactive self-destruction, an act that arises after one has encountered one's own potential for nihility. The diabolical lies in the attitude whereby I will to be myself in despair and so unforgiven; indeed, I am despairing of forgiveness altogether. Derrida's thesis of the conceptual and practical ubiquity of violence sounds awfully close to this despairing attitude. What institutes and destroys the religious is not the *actuality* of radical evil (a common error of many a reader of Kierkegaard is to conflate knowledge that I can despair with its actually doing so) but its *possibility*. Already Schelling carefully drew a distinction between the possibility of radical evil (this lies in God's eternal becoming insofar as humans are created in God's image, having in them their separable ground and existence) and its actuality (this requires a perverted god to emerge in our deliberate reversal of ground and existence). The difference between an intellectual aporia of the impossible (paradox or antinomy) and its lived koan (self-transformative task) runs parallel to this distinction between possibility and actuality. Derrida's corrective to Kant agrees in part with Kierkegaard. Is it not, however, existentially comic to project as my future possibility but one single actuality, a paradoxical intention of the impossible, that I cannot live without despair, that violence must always saturate the religious, that faith response to despair must defer true gift or forgiveness?

It is not clear that Derrida holds this view consistently when he envisions hospitality, a new international community, or democracy-to-come. At the end of the day he recognizes a difference between Kierkegaard's knights of resignation and those of faith, whose possibility he locates with Lévinas in every genuine face-to-face encounter. The resigned knights, like those readers of Derrida on violence who conflate possibility with actuality, would ontologize the Abrahamic violence. Like the false doctrinal portraits of the religious, the out-of-tune sketches of the sacrifice of Isaac introduced by de Silentio in *Fear and Trembling,* they would repeatedly despair of forgiveness or of their faithful return from the Mt. Moriah back into their ethical community. Yet the true Abrahamic knights of faith would not speak directly of their ordeals or returns. Embracing hope filled silence, they would never have to pass through the violence of the concept. Without cocksure certainty about the religious as a concept, they would eschew any terrorist highway to heaven. But then they would express faith, spiritual awareness, and enlightenment (albeit these would go often doctrinally unrecognized as one of the articulated beliefs) in their concrete material and historical existence.

The distinction between belief and faith operative throughout my meditations is not necessarily bound to Martin Luther. We find analogically that all great religions draw some difference between received traditions (ordinary phenomena that can be directly expressed and passed on) and revelation (the saturated phenomenon that exceeds ordinary experience and known articulations). Ritual and liturgical practices draw distinctions between the right form or articulated content (orthodoxy) and mystery (sacrament). Institutional religion, like culture, cannot but rely on core beliefs or teachings that are necessary for the transmission of meaning and values. Yet spiritual awakening, awareness, and faith, which occur in the world, are not of the world. For this reason conflating revelation with tradition, mystery with doctrinal orthodoxy, or faith with received beliefs generally proves devastating for genuine religious life.

Kierkegaard distinguishes between two modes of communication. The direct mode uses concepts and raises validity claims. It is this mode that worries Derrida and Lévinas, as it progresses through conceptual and historical articulations. The indirect mode of communication responds to Hegel's totalizations as much as to the above worries: it leads through singular self-transformation. The latter mode affords Kierkegaard a nontotalizing medium of existential communication. In place of the aporetic economy of violence, stuck in the loops of direct communication, there is the uncanny economy of works of love, growing out of silence of love's ground into silence of edifying existence. Life without despair requires ongoing faith that negates despair's actualization. Loving without despair, hence any genuine consideration of the economy of the gift, is possible because despair or radical evil are never necessary but only possible. One despairs by freedom, never by nature; radical evil is possible because of our nature but is not actual by nature. If that nuance between possibility and actuality of despair is true, then the economy of violence cannot be inscribed into human nature but only ascribed to freedom. Then justice and love must be actualized in concrete existence or they are nothing to write home about.

CRUELTY AS A SATURATED PHENOMENON

In part 2 (p. 99 above), we noticed how Adorno disparages false reverence for evil. But what about the false reverence for progress? Is not immediate faith in my own goodness not only banal (and on this we can agree with Arendt) but also dangerously naive and so bordering on the diabolical? When I project this naive faith as an idea of or belief in progress, I embark on a grand plan for the regime change of the world. I shall uncreate what has been badly done. Not only must I now correct the world that offends me, but my good intensions pave the way to hell, and I begin to serve tyranny instead of curing it. Inwardly I become a retributive judge of creation and outwardly rally others to my last judgment. This judgment becomes the negatively saturated, hence no longer rational, apotheosis and theodicy of the cruel will. Because the Grand Inquisitor presumes to work in God's service, he is all along fortified by his offense at evil and by his belief in his own goodness. Lest we are permitted to draw religious cartoons of the sacrilege when it becomes enthroned at the highest altars, when we draw them without others calling God's wrath on us as the infidels, the law of anti-idolatry somehow cannot apply to the religious zealot who parades as a warrior at God's side. We are treading on very dangerous ground when we expose fake religiousness.

Therein dwells the banality of evil deeds carried out in the name of the good. The evildoer is not offended by the philosopher's evidence from evil against the goodness of the world, as one now usurps God, one measures goodness by one's own ideal of progress. Therein lies one's radical moral evil done to promote progress. Are not humans who name good and evil by their own name the most cruel? Therein is defined the paradoxical intention of evil as the structural, inescapability of violence. From the ethico-religious perspective one is always in an Abrahamic pickle of the undecidable, sacrificing one for another. Yet only a postsecular, redemptive critical theory is able to ask an even sharper question, the question that must be posed to all religious establishments: Are not the Grand Inquisitor's prayers and public invocations of God also the most spiritless cruelty, the horror that even a religiously tone-deaf (*religiös Unmusikalisch,* Habermas, FHN:114) atheist faintly intuits as the once recognized diabolical sense of evil?

Students always find it shocking to read that Frederick Douglass (1968) described his religious masters as more passionately dedicated in their cruelty to slaves than those who "made no pretensions to, or profession of, religion" (86). The reader must hold no doubt about this:

I assert most unhesitatingly, that the religion of the south is a mere covering for the most horrid crime—justifier of the most appalling barbarity,—
a sanctifier of the most hateful frauds,—a dark shelter under, which the
darkest, foulest, grossest, and most infernal deeds of slaveholders find the
strongest protection. . . . I should regard being a slave of a religious master
the greatest calamity that could befall me. For all slaveholders with whom
I have ever met, religious slaveholders are the worst. I have ever found them
the meanest and basest, *the most cruel and cowardly*, of all others. (86f.; emphasis mine)

In the appendix to his autobiography, Douglass attacks the "*slaveholding religion* of this land"—all along distinguishing it from the "Christianity of
Christ" (120) that he embraced—with force that is equal to the attack on
Christendom delivered only ten years later by Kierkegaard. Their dual attack on existing Christianity allows us to note that even if God can be
viewed as not neutral between justice and cruelty, that someone who invokes divine judgment on humanity, and who believes in the goodness of
such acts and prayers, could be a practitioner of the religion of fear and cruelty. Enter radical evil as a species of the false reverence for progress.[5]

What Is Cruelty?

When guilt consciousness over one's finitude or inability to deliver good becomes one's masked despair; when this despairing self latches onto the negativity of its weak will; when this weak self willing nothing stands in its own
shadow all along masking itself as willing to do good in the world and thus
to purify itself of its hidden worm of quiet desperation; then cruelty becomes the master of this self willing to be itself in despair. Cruelty to others
reaches its most intense modality in the pursuit of high moral and religious
ideals of humanity and progress. Indeed, human evil is at once banal or
trivial, radical or morally perverse, and diabolical or religiously cruel.

Why Does Cruelty Have Anything
to Do with Goodwill or Religion?

Why is moral and religious zeal the most cruel? The addiction to self that is
weak in its willing, yet wills its nothingness (its shadow existence) rather
than nothing at all, this addiction in moral and religious crusades becomes
the despair of cruelty.[6] This is the self that pontificates about God who is
not neutral between justice and cruelty. When this despairing self pledges
itself collectively, it will call evil by its fear name and become cruel to those
it wants others to fear. In cruelty one seeks to sever another from the ideal
of humanity in the name of progress. This despairing self hides from itself
by promoting moral good and God's will. Douglass took no prisoners when

he described the religious sanction of racism and slavery, and he was not afraid to call such human acts for the ideal of humanity diabolical. "Never was there a clearer case of 'stealing the livery of the court of heaven to serve the devil in.' . . . Here we have religion and robbery the allies of each other—devils dressed in angels' robes, and hell presenting the semblance of paradise" (1968:120–21).

How Does a Spiritless albeit Religiously Inflected Cruelty of the Do-Gooder Originate?

Religious cruelty begins in my offense that any evil exists. It grows in despair about the failure of God who allows evil to exist and the powerlessness of the human race to do good. Finally, offended despair matures in smugness whereby I embark on the heroic project of vanquishing evil with my own will.

How Do We Resist Cruelty Infecting the Very Ideals of Humanity and Progress?

Adorno's negative notion of progress as resistance, with which one may inhabit the imaginary domain of open and critical ideals of humanity, can help us only part of the way. We can learn to resist false reverence for evil and idols of progress. But by secularizing the spiritual dimension of existence, including banalizing and moralizing evil (and we know now why radical evil is more than a banal and moral phenomenon; it is diabolical because of its spiritless religious cruelty), we rob ourselves of any resistance to a false reverence for the Grand Inquisitor at the political pulpit. *Cruelty must be grasped as a religious phenomenon:* I hold dear my naive innocence (this is evil's banality). Once offended, I elevate immediate faith in my goodness into a moral idea (belief) of progress (this is radical moral evil that wants the regime change for the world). At its most intense, in my despairing offense at the state of creation, I become a heroic yet cruel master praying to myself (this is radical evil's spiritless religiosity, namely, the diabolical, or deeds negatively saturated by spirit).

Yet Who Can Truly Name the "Religious"?

Who can name the religious in this predicament when God, country, and evil are all invoked in the same breath? When I confront the spiritless religious cruelty of my will, then my false reverence of progress becomes unmasked as itself a species of radical evil. I cannot vanquish any evil before giving up my offense with which I embarked on the regime change, uncreation of the universe. I must divest myself of false reverence for my goodwill, shed my banally naive belief that I can do good or vanquish evil or remake the world in my own heroic image. Free of offended despair and free of cruelly spiritless religious will that masks it, I could one day become a finite source of compassion and even change for the good.

How Do We Face the Limits of Humanity?

How do we inhabit finitude freed from an aesthetic self-relation to our becoming human? For Kierkegaard (SuD 45), "the esthetic conception of spiritlessness by no means provides the criterion for judging what is despair and what is not." "Spirit cannot be defined esthetically." We must distinguish between aesthetic and religious existence in order to resist reverence that is falsely religious and reverence for false religious. We must resist cruelty masked as moral and religious righteousness. Cruelty is an aesthetic self-relation to oneself and God that has become aggravated by one's moral as well as religiously empowered despair. Only thus can Kierkegaard write about the despair of religious Christians; only with this nuance can also Douglass warn about the Christian religious cruelty.

How Can One Exist without Despair?

How can one live in a self-relation free of cruelty? How do we progress (or better: become human) in concrete existence? Insofar as we try to resist the false (aesthetic) reverence for the religious within the ideals of humanity, and we must resist in existence, we raise questions about spiritual transformation as the basis of human ideals and progress. By this questioning, we are instantly delivered to a genre of redemptive critical theory. Our discovery of cruelty at the heart of moral and religious zeal secures the ultimate reason why ideals of humanity and progress, why radical evil, must be studied from a postsecular vantage point. The secular take on religion cannot accomplish what Douglass, Dostoyevsky, and Kierkegaard, among others, can do from within their articulations of what it means to become human in actual existence. The secular mind-set cannot confront despairing offense at its most radical core—as spiritless religious cruelty.[7]

Cruelty that is "altogether secure in the power of despair" (Kierkegaard, SuD 44), because it is either unaware or ignorant or repressed, can parade itself as the will to good. This will can in despair take joy from capital punishment or holy war on evildoers. The more unconscious one's despair, the greater the outward moral and religious zeal, and the greater the cruelty inflicted on those one has labeled evil in the name of the good. When the cruel will becomes internally consistent, it acquires "certain strength" (106f.). And we get what Kant calls but rejects as the "diabolical" dimension of human willing and what Kierkegaard contra Kant describes as the "demonic person" (108).

Kant and most philosophers who follow him in this regard, from Arendt to Habermas to Adorno and Cornell, do not grasp the demonic, or perhaps do not want to because they place religion within the bounds of reason alone. In Habermas this strategy calls for the translation of religious language of faith, evil, and atonement into the discursive validity claims of truth, rightness, and sincerity. My postsecular meditations are concerned with what is lost in such a translation, or with the price one must pay for perpetual peace and rational tolerance that evades the real problem of radical evil found in terror and external wars on terror. One can rationalize the beliefs and practices of religion, but one fails to rationalize the modern discontents of evil that burst those rational bounds. Cruelty is marked both by aesthetic self-relation (the banality of abstract humanity) and a false reverence for the religious (the idolatry of progress). Ultimately the manifestly *cruel* is precisely what Kant fancies yet exorcises as the diabolical will. Thinkers from Dostoyevsky to Douglass to Kierkegaard call attention to the diabolical or, *avant* Sartre, they unmask the religious root of one's demonic rage as the desire to be God. This idolatrous desire is at once the most hidden and the most blatantly displayed in the do-gooders who pray God's wrath onto evildoers. Its figures are the Grand Inquisitor's or slave owner's holy zeal for the good, it is likewise the suicidal despair of a religious adherent.

To resist the intensity of despair found in idolatrous defiance, and this is precisely the problem of the book of Job as well as the more heady task of redemptive critical theory, one would have to acknowledge the possibility that one can be cruel and yet not thereby lose one's humanity or even morality and "religion." I can be cruel precisely in my banally goodwill and even with my heroic moral struggle against evil. That is why false reverence for progress is in its despairing offense itself a species of radical evil.

Another way of resisting the desire to be God or the imperial idolatry of the nation would be to admit that in the pursuit of the ideals of humanity and progress, I exist before something wholly other than I ever imagined possible in my imaginary domain. I must become aware that there is a cosmos or spiritual reality that measures my human self and my progress. It measures every established secular and religious order. For this reason, once again, respect for the law of anti-idolatry must correct respect for the moral law. But then I would know that even in my moral and holy pursuit of the ideals of humanity and progress, I could utterly fail to inhabit that spiritual reality even in my goodwill that respects the moral law. Indeed, this is how good and religious people and nations in the process of heroic enthusiasm do inflict cruelty on others—from holy whipping of slaves to the even more holy shock and awe bombing to the still more holy calls for holy wars on the cartoonists who unmask idolatry of the holy. To confess singularly and as a league of nations the double idolatry of moral and religious heroism in human ideals and progress, and thereby to expose from within our lived spiritual horizons the shared, ecumenical dangers of religious aestheticism, that alone could be a beginning step out of the negatively saturated phenomenon of cruelty.

Part 3

●

THE UNCANNY

In hope Abraham believed against hope
—St. Paul to the Romans 4:18

It is for the sake of those without hope that
hope is given to us
—Herbert Marcuse,
citing Walter Benjamin

In parts 1–2, I showed that intransitive hope can be impossible in at least two ways. Meditations on the "death of God" in part 1 confronted us with the paradoxical, aporetic dimension of *impossible hope.* This first-order impossibility maximizes the intention of hope whose satisfaction is permanently deferred. The honestly secular (a/theistic) and the deconstructively ir/religious (religious without religion) mind hopes by straining against its immanent horizon of unfulfilled desire for the gift, for the wholly other, all along fueling expectations of desert faith. In a thoroughly secular age, by what resources should we invoke hope when all hope is lost? We should be incapable of Abrahamic or Pauline hope against hope, and even the Benjaminian-Marcusean hope for the sake of ourselves who are without hope might be too much to ask of a thoroughly secular social theorist. Derrida overwhelmed by the mute prayers to the unresponsive *khôra* no less than disconsolate Habermas is tone-deaf to the messianic promise of the eschatological now-time. Theirs is the fallible messianicity not only without messianism and in that without the unveilings of the holy of holies but also resistance bereft of any possibility of the redemptory:

- In place of radical evil, there should be only correctable errors.
- Hope should arise from progress.
- Morality and law should dissolve historical guilt.
- Human projects and solidarity should heal all wounds of history.

Part 2 revealed the second-order impossibility in the postsecular counterexperience of lost hope. This dimension of the impossible shows the saturated phenomenon returning from the Lutheran dark hiddenness and the Pseudo-Dionysian mystical incomprehensibility of God. The negatively saturated, the repressed returning *after* Nietzsche's "death of God" appears in part 3 in the faces of the uncanny. Our journey brings us to an astonishing discovery of the uncanny at the heart of the impossible in both its aporetic and saturated dimensions. Freud (1955) means by the uncanny a dimension of feeling that arises from the duality in the nature of objects we find at once familiar and foreign. The uncanny as I speak of it in these mediations is revealed within the scarcity of hope. The two dimensions of impossibility, two paths revealing the scarcity of hope and its possible overcoming, are paradoxical faith and saturated givenness. It is from this integral perspective and from the vantage point of intensified secularization in the West with its global impact that we must ask anew, *What is the category that institutes the religious?* The classical views of the religious, from revelation to holy texts, acts of religion, public prayers, communal religious practices, or the monuments of religious culture leave many nowadays unsatisfied. I have been seeking a glimpse of the religious at the excess of the "death of God" as its postsecular remnant. The aggravated scarcity of hope in radical evil has brought us to the excess of the uncanny.

In part 3, I limit myself to four areas of the postsecular excess in which the uncanny appears: *the unforgivable, the unforgettable, the unspeakable, and the unconditional.* Entering these four gates of the uncanny-impossible, I undertake four series of meditations, playing each series in two sets of double modal keys—in the negative and positive modal keys, and the (inter)personal and impersonal ones. The negative modality expresses what binds, the positive modality what releases. The distinction between "personal" and "impersonal" is drawn primarily with a view to personal and impersonal faces of spirit (sometimes called the "I" and "It" aspects of or perspectives on God). In the first introduction, I questioned whether or not the personal dimension of God requires a formulation of *theism,* where classical *theism* is often identified with *personal* in God. Many religions (e.g., Taoism or certain forms of Buddhism and Hinduism) and various mystical traditions emphasize the impersonal dimensions of God. Some Buddhist traditions, not just monotheistic religions, emphasize the personal face of God. Some thinkers would not consider religions that lack the personal face of God to be *theistic* in the sense revealed in Christianity or Judaism. I have been arguing two things: *personal* does not necessarily imply *theistic* (though the latter implies the former, e.g., in Christian theism), and the saturated phenomena in *our* postsecular age reveal both personal and impersonal dimensions of spiritual life. There is yet a third face of God, the "We" or *sangha* or the people of God perspective. This perspective is also intransitive and so not to be identified with social ontology, phenomenology of intersubjectivity, or social theory as these add nothing to the "personal" face of God who is not "social" or interpersonal (even in the Christian Trinity) in ways humans are described in social ontologies or moral theories. I do, however, agree with thinkers like Wilber (2006:20–25, 219, 264) that we need to speak about all three faces of God as revealed to us: I, It, and We. I am using im/personal categories to describe "religious phenomena" in their self-and-other transformative reality, and in that sense I speak as much about single persons as about human social reality. The locution "inter(personal)" indicates that even the existential primacy of self-transformation is always already rooted in some social ontology. As I have articulated elsewhere (1993) about the relations between social-existential or singular-communicative, everything said about human singularity, despair, solitude, evil, or healing applies to individuals who are never some Robinson Crusoes but rather always already socially formed and historically situated.

The first two modal keys, the (inter)personal and impersonal dimensions of the human-divine relationship, translate any r/Revelation into our postsecular hermeneutical situations. The second double of modal keys, the negative and positive field of forces, describes how the free agency either binds itself or becomes released. These two sets of double modal keys raise further implications for the question whether the religious should be an emphatically theistic or nontheistic category (not to be confused with the atheistic or even passing for one). Suffice it to add to what I have already said that there is no good reason to hold the (inter)personally revealed God to be contradictory to the impersonal ground of God. As all great religions manifest the I, We, and It intransitive dimensions of spirit or hope—the personal (I), the interpersonal (We), and the impersonal (It) faces of the divine or God—it would be misleading to view some religions as impersonal and others as personal or merely ethical (social we). For example, Christianity is distinct in ways that the personal face of God is revealed but its uniqueness does not consist in the personal face being revealed there for the first or the last time. Parallels exist in Judaism as well as Buddhism. By the same token, Islam or Taoism cannot be viewed as revealing all but the impersonal face of God. This nuance between the impersonal ground and personal existence of God informed Schelling's speculation that itself drew on the rich mystical tradition. The personal face of God or of cosmos need not be painted with anthropomorphic brush strokes either as if the revelation of God in the burning bush or the cloud of unknowing or even human form delivered one automatically to the saturated phenomenon of transfigured faith.

The uncanny is saturated and so revealed by the negative impersonal and (inter)personal modalities of bondage:

- The *unforgivable* deed is exceeded by one's *despair*.
- The *unforgettable* event is exceeded by one's *suffering*.

- The *unspeakable* trauma is exceeded by one's *loneliness.*
- The *unconditional* annihilation is exceeded by one's *cruelty.*

The uncanny is saturated and so revealed by the positive (inter)personal and impersonal modalities of releasement:

- The unforgivable wound is released by one's *healing* through the granting of hope in *forgiveness* (*teshuvah*).
- The unforgettable suffering is mended by *blessing* that intimates hope in *tragic beauty* (*tikkun olam*).
- The unspeakable trauma of loneliness yields to the *soundings* of hope in the silence of *solitude* (*chashmal*).
- The annihilating cruelty is overcome in the *gift* of hope by *unconditional love* (*berakhah/barakah*).

The bondage is *my* despair which I freely adopt; the releasement grants *my* healing which I freely receive. Despair and healing even for the community pass through the self-transformative refractory medium of the singular person. The impersonal dimension of the religious describes what binds my agency or what releases me from bondage. In bondage something or someone becomes unforgivable; in releasement forgiveness is granted. The religious—by this I mean spirit or what all great faiths call the living God—is thus not necessarily limited to what theoreticians mean by religion or theism. The religious is revealed in (inter)personal and impersonal dimensions of faithful awakening or awareness as well as by saturating my ordinary experience with the counterexperience of impossible hope.

"The uncanny phenomenon" is a variation of the saturated phenomenon that exceeds ordinary experience; it is a counterexperience. *After* the "death of God," neither the negative modalities of the uncanny nor its positive modalities (we speak of the Janus-faced uncanny) may be grounded in a theodicy or with recourse to philosophical argument, postulates, or theological doctrines. In this learning, one integrates the hidden or dark and incomprehensible or mystical faces of God. For the same reason, I have resisted the temptation to fashion a negative theodicy of scarcity hinted at by Kant in his reception of Job, by Jonas in his self-limited and suffering God, or by Schelling in his speculation on God's infinite becoming.

I express my reservations by a reverse thought, by speaking counterfactually (contrary to fact): no modal or saturated excess, whether positive or negative, should exist if the "death of God" delivered us to a truly secular age; ergo, all existing modal excess manifests in the postsecular context of the uncanny. The *khôra* knows, reveals, hears no melodies of the uncanny. When religious forms of life fail to be supported by classical and neoclassical-analytic philosophical arguments for God's existence or by doctrinal beliefs of great religious integrations (keeping in mind Kierkegaard's lesson that faith is not the same as belief, God is not revealed by a doctrine, and so "the religious" is not synonymous with the sense of "theistic"), when the religious fails to reconcile evil and God by a theodicy (and these failures have intensified in the West from Kant to Nietzsche), then the uncanny phenomenon is instituted as the saturated excess *after* the "death of God."

Phenomenologically, the (inter)personal dimensions of the religious bespeak the vocative modality of the uncanny, namely, that it can be revealed to me and the human community, that it can address me and us, and that I and the community can respond to its call.

An entropic, practico-inert universe turns to me with neither a vocative voice nor an iconic face. A cold universe allows for no redemptive hope even for the sake of those without hope. Beyond my engagement with Sartre via Marcuse (part 1 was devoted to secular as well as deconstructive reflections on impossible hope), I do not intend to take on Sartre's social and existential theory in this work. Sartre's material universe *hopes* to be humanized by social and free praxis alone. There are no saturated phenomena aiding this freedom, and so none could relieve the nausea, forlornness, or anguish of individuals or social practico-inert institutions. Even bad faith is not that *evil* that it could not be healed by social praxis alone. On this Sartre's practico-inert, Derrida's *khôra*, and Habermas's disconsolate reason agree, and I do not lie about my suspicion that all three rely in their respective appeals to freedom on a degree of intransitive hope for which they are unable to account. My point is that even the secular social theorists and activists cannot do without intransitive hope. Do not Sartre (1990) and before him Marcuse anticipate Derridean messianicity without messianism, conceding to Benjamin's "theological" (anamnestic) reversal of anomie and meaninglessness? I intimated all these connections in part 1 and brought them into the foreground on their own terms in parts 2–3. I politely disrespected restricting hope to overcoming material scarcity alone. I intensified the first-order impossible of Derrida's religion without religion into the second-order impossible of Marion's saturated phenomenon. Radical evil challenges the unsaturable view of the universe as reducible to the empty *khôra*, for the facticity of radical evil witnesses to the instantiation of the religious, albeit negatively. Even if one is religiously tone-deaf, unlike the song of the Sirens that Odysseus must not hear if he wants to return to himself, what unplugs one's ears and heart to the vocative call of the uncanny is human cruelty. This call wakes up hope against the claims of cruelly annihilating death for the sake of those without hope.

But could any face of God be r/Revealed to humans who are not only finite but also shaped by language? Could God bypass the hermeneutical overcoming of the myth of the given? To see God is to die; this too is a biblical revelation. Neither compelling God to appear on terms of the saturated phenomenon described by a new hyperphenomenology nor streamlining the biblical revelation to match it in a literal way with terms of counterexperience, I hold nonetheless intransitive space for I-Thou relationship with the divine whether in prayer or otherwise. Admitting the hermeneutical turn through which every phenomenon must pass in revealing itself to me, prayer needs to be no more hostage to the entropic view of the universe than it needs to be lost in signifiers. Whether or not the universe is empty and cold or vocative and with an iconic face, on this even a hermeneutically savvy thinker bathed in the dark night of the hidden and incomprehensible God can no longer easily pass as a certain believing atheist. One either prays, and so relates to a living intelligence, call it God or Spirit, and does so through texts, signs, and an infinite Midrash of readings; or one faces an entropic, practico-inert universe in which one's hope is always already an orphan. The rabbinical tradition attests that one can never properly name God, even on Yom Kippur when all become high priests and like Moses ascend Mt. Sinai and descend to the depth of oneself to undergo *teshuvah* (turning). Yet God is revealed in uncanny ways and in many a lived story of creation, atonement, and resurrection, and this alone is how the religious is instantiated, or it is just that unresponsive nothing to which one cries out at the Wailing Wall, from the Mosque or in the song of the Church bells, and then one cries out in vain.

SEVEN

The Unforgivable

●

There are unforgivable deeds.

Chapters 7–10 will be devoted to the uncanny that arrives in four epiphanies—through the *grantings, intimations, soundings, and unconditionality of hope*. I begin with the epiphany concerning the possibility of forgiving the unforgivable. If there is the *unforgivable* (impersonal modality of bondage) and so human *despair* (interpersonal modality of bondage), then how is the possibility of *healing* (interpersonal modality of releasement) *granted* in forgiveness (impersonal modality of releasement)?

The unforgivable exists. Much has been written on the gift, yet the unforgivable remains rather hazy. I may be forgiven even while remaining ignorant of my deeds. That would be a gift. Can I know what there is to forgive without grasping the unforgivable? We meditated on Kant's radical evil and found his depiction of unqualified self-interest not to be among the most radical of evils. The unforgivable negatively saturates the bounds of mere reason. We must meditate on the unforgivable in order to raise stakes for the second-order impossible hope.

I move my meditating pillow to the moment just before philosopher's mantra, "If there is such a thing," is intoned about the "impossibilizing" of forgiveness (Derrida, 2001a:48). That mantra skeptically glances back at forgiveness. Let us hear it, let us not hurry beyond the unforgivable, as *this* meditating event is not impossible *for us* and so requires no skeptical self-limitation. Behold the unforgivable! Witness how it chokes our welcoming of possibility, just as fateful tragedy dulls our intimations of sublime beauty, cruelty smothers speech, and annihilating hatred shatters all capacity for love!

There is nothing secular about how the unforgivable saturates the bounds of reason. Impossible forgiveness already grants its very possibility to (albeit it is not responsible for the actuality of) the unforgivable. The uncanny forgiveness arrives at the apposite of the negatively saturated excess of the unforgivable.

THE UNFORGIVABLE AS IMPRESCRIPTIBLE

There is a shared normative intuition that only transgressions that admit punishment can be repaired. The twentieth-century set-aside from this accepted notion a special category of misdeeds we call the crimes against humanity. These crimes are in legal terms imprescriptible, which means that there is no time limit on punishing the perpetrators of genocide, lest they expire in jail, like Slobodan Milosevic, before the court delivers its verdict. In the legal context the notion of crimes against humanity appeared after World War II at Nuremberg in 1945 and Tokyo in 1946. The United Nations issued the Convention on Genocide in 1948 and the Convention on Imprescriptibility in 1968. It passed the resolution on international cooperation in hunting down war criminals in 1973. The French discussion of the excess of penal logic that all such crimes contain comes into view with the 1964 law on their imprescriptibility.

Imprescriptibility carries two immediate outcomes. First, there is no time limit on punishment as long as perpetrators live. Infinity of time immigrates into imprescriptibility. A suprahuman temporal weight is placed on crimes against what it means to be human. We can discern this postsecular dimension of law in Derrida's (2001b:70f.) perceptive remark that there is nothing secular in the international law that integrates the notion of infinity into the imprescriptibility of certain deeds. However, the expanded time limit exceeds only the passing away of finite time; it does not inscribe law into the messianic now-time of redemption. The imprescriptible is only imperfectly saturated by the unforgivable. Dead, Milosevic can neither be forgiven by the courts (only by the nationalist stealth of erased memory) nor punished in order to repair the historical impact of his deeds. The revision of memory is the great temptation of a nation whose imprescriptible war crimes died with an unpunished criminal.

There is a second outcome that shows why there is nothing secular about international laws against such crimes. Even if Milosevic or Saddam Hussein lived forever, and we the people replayed the guilty sentence in the Nietzschean-Kafkaesque eternal recurrence of the verdict, there is no possible punishment humans could come up with that would be a just retribution for crimes against humanity. Hell's tortures are imagined to be filling this very gap. The notion of imprescriptible crimes replaces the classical proscription on sacrilege. Such crimes exceed legal boundaries not only in time (the punishment is guaranteed by no limit placed on lived time), but also in kind. The state or courts can decree that certain human acts (e.g., indiscriminate violence of protracted civil or religious war) be erased from national memory or cleared by the blank check of amnesty. Victims of history can be memorialized in the great public dramatizations of reconciliation, healing, and coming to terms with the tragic past. Yet we know that even legally punished misdeeds do not restore shattered human solidarity. There is no human-type contrition that could by itself expiate evil deeds even if punished and perhaps morally repented.

It is counterintuitive that amnesty, royal pardon, or clemency could ever grant hope.

Can the state or truth commission forgive what cannot be legally repaired and morally expiated? Can the public for the good of social peace command that victims forgive their torturers? Is this not at best an political injunction to selective forgetting or remembering? Even when duly punished in time, monstrous misdeeds linger as what is morally inexpiable. And every instance of amnesty, pardon, or clemency must strike the victims and their descendants as gravely unjust. Forgiveness of the unforgivable cannot be legislated, commanded, expected.

Does This Mean That the Legally Imprescriptible and Morally Inexpiable Equal the Unforgivable?

Is calling some crime imprescriptible the same as calling it unforgivable? Jankélévitch (1986, 1996) in some of his formulations thinks as much. For him "the unforgivable" means exactly "not to be forgiven" or "impossible to forgive." Before him, Arendt (1958:214) established that a symmetry exists between punishment and forgiveness, as "both have in common that they attempt to put an end to something that without interference could go on endlessly." She considered punishment to be just as much a human act as forgiveness is. The dimension of something "endless" at best betrays the cognitive and motivational weakness of the law, but not something that exceeds its capacity. Once the symmetry is broken by introducing the morally inexpiable and legally irreparable crimes, the unforgivable complement of the punishable immigrates into the same spot with the imprescriptible (cf. Derrida, 2001a:30f.).

I think that two postsecular dimensions projected into the notion of imprescriptibility—the fragile infinity of time allotted for possible punishment and the abysmal asymmetry between the dastardly deeds and any possible punishment or repentance—lead to a conflation of the normative (legal, moral) and existential (self-transformative) orders. Whether or not punishing crimes against humanity clears the way for forgiveness or the other way around, we must put in question the relation of the normative and existential dimensions of human acts. If we separate legal punishment, political dramas of reconciliation, and moral scenes of repentance from the existential dimension of the unforgivable that saturates the law, politics, and normative ethics, then the unforgivable can no longer be simply subsumed under the imprescriptible.

THE UN/FORGIVABLE AS
IMPOSSIBLE AND DIFFICULT

There is a newly shared spiritual intuition of the uncanny in the acts of forgiveness. These saturated acts are distinct from legal punishment, moral repentance, supralegal and extramoral amnesty, pardon, and clemency. Forgiving exceeds equally the borders of just procedures and moral norms. The uncanny saturates by the granting of hope to all acts of forgiveness.

After trying to balance the strength of evil with that of forgiveness in *Forgiveness* (2005), Jankélévitch came to believe that forgiveness "died in the death camps" (1996:567). He says so explicitly in the foreword to his article "Should We Pardon Them?"

> Between the absolute of the law of love and the absolute of vicious liberty there is a tear that cannot be entirely sundered. I have not attempted to reconcile the irrationality of evil with the omnipotence of love. Forgiveness is as strong as evil, but evil is as strong as forgiveness. (1996:553)

Echoing Jankélévitch's late conclusions, Gibbs in a conversation with Derrida suggested that we live not so much in a postmodern but in a "postforgiveness" condition. "Nietzsche has his reasons for saying that God is dead, and Jankélévitch obviously links his claim to the Shoah" (in Derrida, 2001b: 54). Derrida reverses this prophecy of decaying forgiveness:

> Jankélévitch says that forgiveness has come to an end, has died in the death camps. I oppose this. It is exactly the opposite. It is because forgiveness seems to become impossible that forgiveness finds a starting point, a new starting point. So I would not say that we are entering a post-forgiveness era at all. (Derrida, 2001b:55)

Derrida (2001a:25) and Ricoeur (2004:596–98 n. 17–18, 598 n. 19) disagree with Jankélévitch. Both insist that it is the unforgivable that calls for forgiveness—whether or not anyone asks for it in the first place. Forgiveness is neither a political nor a public category that can be translated into acts of amnesty, pardon, or clemency. Neither the state nor the church nor a truth commission may forgive en masse or on behalf of victims who suffer the unforgivable. Forgiveness is a singular and in that sense mysterious act that exceeds as much the practical normative frameworks of morality and law as the history of crime, punishment, and expiation. Derrida welcomes forgiveness arriving at the end of the history of crime and punishment (2001a:27f.). Derrida and Ricoeur in essence each want to cut through Jankélévitch's short circuit suffered between the imprescriptible and the unforgivable nature of the crimes against humanity. Jankélévitch presses the imperative of their unforgivable character in order to sustain them against any exhaustive settling of moral accounts. No punishment is "good" enough for a crime against humanity, and there can be no repentance that could morally undo the irreparable. Acts that are imprescriptible are strictly speaking unpunishable and thus unforgivable, as no punishment fits the deed. One implication of Arendt's insistence on symmetry between punishment and forgiveness appears in Jankélévitch's admission of law's failure to forgive. The law can punish the crimes against humanity, but it cannot forgive them. Derrida and Ricoeur harness that very implication, but unlike Jankélévitch, in order to set aside forgiveness as an extramoral and extralegal category. This admission of the uncanny renders forgiveness *impossible* for Derrida and *difficult* for Ricoeur.

Impossible Forgiveness

Derrida's distinction between conditional (heterogeneous) and unconditional (pure) forgiveness sets apart the normative economy of law and morality from the uncanny sphere of the gift (2001a:45). Forgiveness is a Janus-faced event, with one face turned toward the traumatic past and the other facing the future promise. The economy of the gift reaches beyond the normative sphere of exchange (crime and punishment, guilt and repentance) to the "hyperbolical ethics" (29). The classical lineage of forgiveness as exchange and reciprocity (Derrida indexes here all meaning-giving such as reconciliation, healing, salvation, redemption, sacrifice, and expiation) comes to an end. After Auschwitz the origin of forgiveness invokes its impossibility: Could there be such a gift (30f.)? With this at once historical and existential learning, we separate the juridical reparation for past injuries and the functional construction of the future, on the one hand, and the inexpiable as what is impossible to forgive on the other (34). Forgiveness cannot be achieved by means of reparation. For Jankélévitch this learning bears out a somber truth; for Derrida it delivers a promise of another beginning.

Two levels of work arise from this cleavage, one being the history of mourning, reconciliation, therapy, forgetting as well as remembering. The other arrives when radical evil interrupts the history of forgiveness, "the work of mourning forgiveness itself." Whereas Habermas, echoing Hegel, holds out for hope that communicative reason could heal all wounds of history, Derrida's second-degree task enters the paradox, aporia, or hyperbole of "an infinite . . . and . . . unsuturable wound" within history and human existence (42; cf. 2001b:56). Both forgiveness and its two levels of work are mutually contaminated. Historical victims who are dead cannot receive the petition for forgiveness, even if asked for it, and the history of unrequited innocent suffering continues to haunt new generations long after criminals are either punished, die of old age, or vanish into the abyss of amnesia. Benjamin's materialist theology of hope—that new generations would carry out the messianic expectations of the past ones—is only faintly echoed by Jankélévitch: "In the universal moral amnesty long accorded to the assassins, the massacred have only us to think about them" (1994:225; 1996: 547). As noted in chapter 2, Horkheimer rejects Benjamin's weak messianic hope held out for the victims of history. Horkheimer strikes down the latter's notion that history of suffering could be rendered open and perhaps worked on by messianic remembrance. The victims' history is closed; the dead are dead, he insists against Benjamin. Habermas comes up with a more secular rendition of Benjaminian messianic now-time: by deploying procedural and communicative reason, the living community exercises anamnestic solidarity vis-à-vis those inherited living traditions that must be preserved and those bankrupt ones to be jettisoned. Habermas's anamnestic solidarity replaces Benjamin's messianic remembrance. Yet ironically, in his Hegelian translation of messianic hope into a project of historical reconciliation, Habermas becomes even more optimistic than Benjamin's and Jankélévitch's materialist hope. Habermas's Kantian delimitation of Hegel's project of reconciliation is finite, yet it promises to heal wounds of history. Derrida resurrects Benjamin's hope against Horkheimer's skepsis, thereby consoling Jankélévitch. Derrida's hope is emphatically impossible, and so it never rationally heals all wounds of history.

Difficult Forgiveness

The uncanny of forgiving does not lie in the erasure of painful memory through punishment or amnesty. Ricoeur (2004) sharply demarcates between "commanded forgetting," such as pardon, and forgiveness. There is a subaltern link between amnesia and amnesty: both make "a secret pact with the denial of memory" for the sake of national unity and civil harmony (453). Yet forgiveness does not obliterate the unforgivable—this is not its *ars oblivionis* or "optative mood of happy memory" (505). The real difficulty is how to transform the memory once it has been wounded by the unforgivable.

Against amnesia or amnesty of commanded forgetting, something from which even dead victims are not safe, Benjamin stresses the need to preserve dangerous memory. Genuine forgiveness allows us to mourn and come to terms with crimes and woundings, yet we retain the public memory of them as resources for dissent. Forgiveness and dissent draw upon rather than push to abjected recesses of the forbidden, the dangerous memory of victims. Amnesty facilitates needed social therapy that cites existing evils without manipulation and anger, yet the extent of its public utility relies on its ability to retain open access equally to forgiving and dissent. Amnesty's desire for the harmonious state of our union must not silence memory's duty to speak truth to power (cf. Ricoeur, 2004:455f.).

Why is forgiveness not only paradoxically impossible (conceptually aporetic) but also exceedingly difficult (self-transformative, or impossible in the second order of difficulty)? First, this difficulty lies in a "vertical disparity" or asymmetry between the depth of the wounding and the height of forgiving required for its healing. Forgiveness can neither be commanded politically nor translated into publicly accessible procedural language (457f., 479). There is no economy of exchange between crime and forgiveness, albeit there is one between crime and punishment, the nuance around which Dostoyevsky's novel by that name is built. Ricoeur drives home this same nuance when he shows that while punishment, even of imprescriptible crimes, balances the scales of the criminal deeds and their repayment, it can never address moral evil on the level of its "attestation" about the self. The law is impersonal.

Enter the second difficulty—the uncanny of forgiveness unbinds the agent from the evil act of which neither punishment nor political pardon is capable. Punishment repays for the dastardly deed; forgiveness is vocative, for it personally addresses the criminal self. Radical evil's excess, "unjustifiable" saturation, has its darkest work within the self. The irreparable or imprescriptible pertains to the deeds, the unforgivable to the person. The fault, its bearing and admission as well as absolution, speaks to the unforgivable within the self (463–67).

Ricoeur agrees with Derrida, Dostoyevsky, and Kierkegaard that "if love excuses everything, this everything includes the unforgivable. If not it would be annihilated . . . forgiveness is directed to the unforgivable or it does not exist" (468). Dostoyevsky (2003:72) articulates this view through Elder Zossima, a saintly monk in *The Brothers Karamazov* who consoles a woman after she kills her husband; she now lives in fear of herself and her own act: "I am afraid of my sin," she confesses. The Elder absolves her self:

> Just as long as repentance does not grow scarce within you—then God will forgive anything. And indeed there is and can be no sin upon all the earth that the Lord will not forgive the truly repentant. And there is no sin that man could commit so great as would ever exhaust God's infinite love.

And yet, as in the entire novel, Dostoyevsky addresses his own doubts by posing a question:

For could there ever be a sin that could exceed God's love? . . . With love
all things may be redeemed, all things may be rescued.

War criminals and terrorists, as they have not been excluded from the
human race in the very status of their imprescriptible and inexpiable deeds
(and I praise Kant's moral view of radical evil on this account), become the
quintessential addressees of difficult forgiveness. "The fact that the horror
of immense crimes prevents extending this consideration to their authors is
the mark of our inability to love absolutely" (Ricoeur, 2004:474). Forgiveness is always and already an existential (self-transformative) and not a conceptual (aporetic) issue. Forgiving the unforgivable is impossible for humans. But is it impossible from the side of hope invoked by the hopeless
—that there be possibility? We find here no easy symmetry either. Forgiveness alone allows me to return to myself, but no longer identifying myself
with my evil deed (486f.).

While there can be no political sacrament or new orthodoxy of forgiveness, the unconditionality of forgiving has its public impact, as Ricoeur
(488) glimpses from Dostoyevsky's (2003:322–44) critical sketch of the
Grand Inquisitor. Forgiving love can at best involve antipolitical politics or
the politics of truth commissions; they would not legislate but facilitate the
impossible and difficult birth of forgiveness. Such stages of possible forgiveness would serve as public correctives to a commanded politics of forgiveness. Political pardon is incapable of releasing the agent from the action; it
can condemn the action but leaves the actor fractured. Only forgiveness
renders the agent "capable of beginning again." Political theory and democratic procedures all presuppose innocent beginnings, something they fail to
deliver by their own means. Without hope, political theory and procedural
justice equally fail us in the hell holes of the world where the impossible becomes our difficult task. The "ultimate act of trust" is that the repentant
guilty person is seen again as capable of some other life than accomplished
evil deeds. Forgiveness restores that agent's capacity for communicative action. The impossible difficulty of forgiveness lies in its uncanny act of releasement, as if saying to the evildoer, "You are better than your actions"
(Ricoeur, 2004:490, 493).

The difficulty of forgiveness is its achievement of a "happy forgetting,"
that new innocence or beginning that would not require a "censure of
memory," a positing of the myth denial of "founding violence" (500f.). This
is the paradox of becoming a forgiven debtor who knows oneself as always
insolvent, who is in "debt without fault" (503). There remains another
asymmetry between forgetting and memory, and that is their relation to
forgiveness. Forgiveness is not *simply* forgetting, a careless memory that
magically brings me back to the state prior to forgiveness. In forgiveness I

am freed to care for myself without fear of myself as I am. I am restored to second innocence, "carefree memory on the horizon of concerned memory, the soul common to memory that forgets and does not forget" (505).

TO WHOM SHALL I FORGIVE THE UNFORGIVABLE?

Marc Chagall's painting *White Crucifixion* joins two religious fields of experience into one symbol: the Jew crucified by anti-Semitism. In the age when cartoons of the idolatrous-religious are dangerous business, Chagall's religiously syncretic symbolism of religious hatred still makes a bold statement. By globalizing the notion of the crimes against humanity, have we perhaps universalized the Judeo-Christian discovery of the unforgivable (Derrida, 2001b:70)?

Jankélévitch (1996:555) contends that because the Nazis found the very existence of the Jew unforgivable and inexpiable, they had to act against Jews beyond all forgiveness. The Jew has become historically and singularly the key instantiation of the unforgivable. Chrétien (2002:xxii) finds the heart of the unforgivable in its relation to hope. "The Jews are a people of memory only because they are, and only if they are, a people of hope: hope is memory of the promise, conjoining future and past." The unforgivable arises with the annihilation of hope. One shall not forgive the one who *is* unforgivable, who is beyond all hope. Acts against "the Jew" as a placeholder of immemorial memory and unhoped-for promise propelled my meditation in part 2 on Prague's Jewish Central Museum intended by the Nazis, against its curators, to celebrate the extermination of the Jewish race. Nazis were constructing a site of the worst memory, antihope, a museum of radical evil, a radically evil museum. Had they prevailed, their act would repeatedly embody the unforgivable. To whom can one perpetually refuse to forgive? The unforgivable must be resurrected in order to sustain impossible forgiveness.

The Unforgivable and the Antiredemptory

The voids of Libeskind's Berlin Jewish Museum do not pretend to heal the unforgivable or redeem the dead. They are silent on forgiveness, yet these silences do not annihilate hope. The museum of radical evil would be in the business of rendering it impossible to forgive. This latter impossibility is fueled by a positively defiant, negatively saturated will. Is perpetual resurrection of hopelessness the final word on the human journey? We return to the acts that uncreate hope and create the antiredemptory void. The unforgivable becomes emphatically unredeemable. If victims are dead, if history is closed, if the unforgivable thereby closes the path to redemption and healing, then who will forgive, who is forgiven, to whom could one ever forgive the unforgivable?

Derrida's (2001a:48) invocation of impossible or unconditional forgiveness does not represent a dialectical or apophatic negativity, that is, an impossibility representing a lack that could be overcome by reconciliation. Unconditional forgiveness is not pragmatically impossible, even as it is sought, but rather, to echo Lévinas's turn of the phrase, it is otherwise than conditionally possible. The unforgivable marks an incalculable tear or abyss, and so pure forgiveness eschews all hope for the economy of exchange. Derrida clearly identified all senses of healing and redemption with some form of reconciling exchange and for this singular reason he dropped all language of redemption. I want to guard against conflating his iconoclastic purism with the intent to link impossible unforgiveness emphatically to the unredeemable. My reservation is distilled from the meditation on the Nazi plan for the antiredemptory museum. The link between the unforgivable and the antiredemptory must be examined with great vigilance. Does the notion of impossible forgiveness on its own merits foreclose antiredemptory possibilities of celebrating the positive, uncreative void of annihilation? Have we meditated deeply enough on the unforgivable and its relation to the antiredemptory to grasp this danger?

Jankélévitch thinks that forgiving the Nazis would be a bad idea. Derrida and Ricoeur agree with him that the state or courts might punish all crimes but could never order others to forgive those who wounded the core of humanity. Both insisted, against Jankélévitch, that paradoxically it is the unforgivable that calls for forgiveness—if there is such a thing. That Derridean aporetic mantra about *the first-order possibility of the impossible* occurs each time in tandem with the invocation of the second-order impossibility, the uncanny of unconditional forgiveness: "There is only forgiveness, if there is such a thing, of the un-forgivable" (Derrida, 2001a:48). Yet there *is* the unforgivable, and even devils know as much. As duly noted, they are not philosophers of religion who suffer from intellectual a/theism; perhaps they are not even trying to pass for human feats of undecidability; and their judgment from hell about the unforgivable is neither overwhelmed (in despair) nor helped (in seeking sources for resistance) by the *khôra* that knows of no such wonders. And so, in order to be able to resist dangers of a totalitarian closure, we do not have to add doubting mantras to the facticity of evil. This has been my starting point.

After the "death of God," we still recognize the unforgivable. No doubts here: *Es gibt, il y a* . . . the unforgivable. Should we pardon its perpetrators? Two postmodern conditions—that God is dead and that there is the unforgivable—would be the same claim only and only if the latter condition, just as in my meditation on cruelty, disclosed a pure secular phenomenon. Not the rational penchant for the aporias of the im-possible, but resurgence of hope when none should be expected at the heart of the unforgivable; this uncanny epiphany prompts me to postsecular meditations. If there *is* the unforgivable, then even after God's secular death hope is not dead. Hope is invoked by the very lips that find themselves without hope to forgive.

Why or How Is Something Unforgivable?

With the international law of crimes against humanity the unforgivable exceeds the bounds of mere reason. How does the unforgivable itself exceeds those bounds? And to whom does one refuse to forgive the unforgivable? Unexpectedly from Derrida's pen, we learn that God as "absolute witness" of the victims of history appears to be the only singularity that can receive and grant forgiveness (2001a:46). Neither the unforgivable of the crimes against humanity, nor impossible forgiveness can be merely "a human thing" (30). Does not impossible forgiveness already grant possibility to the unforgivable?

One fails to recognize this uncanny granting of hope at the heart of the worst because one takes the unforgivable gratuitously. There is the unforgivable! What an uncanny actuality! The unforgivable for us already arrives saturated. What saturates this phenomenon remains for us invisable, without relation to prior experience, singular, and something irregardable. My ego cannot constitute what saturates it, as I am addressed by it in turn. The unforgivable is saturated, for it never appears apart from its negative excess, without that overflowing intuition of forgiveness. Must we speak of impossible forgiveness in hypotheticals—if there is such a thing—or should we better assign it its rightful place at the heart of radical evil? Would we be able to perceive any abysmal breach, would we not grow entirely mute and unable to begin or relate to one another in the world, if the unforgivable were not already empowered and yet negatively saturated, thereby blinded and bedazzled, by its reversal—impossible forgiveness? Enter the uncanny epiphany of hope: that there is the unforgivable, that we apprehend it as if it always and already annihilated all our possibility, beauty, speech, and capacity to love!

Impossible forgiveness dwells at the heart of the unforgivable not as something hypothetical but rather as empowering our apprehension of itself. I take another step back. How do I perceive hope's impossible forgiveness and yet yield to its annihilation by the same unforgivable? Whom do I ask to forgive me, whom do I forgive, who forgives?

Derrida severs unconditional forgiveness from all figures of redemption or healing: "I am trying—and I know how violent this is—to disassociate true forgiveness from all these finalities—of reconciliation, salvation, redemption, and so on." He identifies those finalities with Hegel's historical metaphysics of reconciliation and with the political economies of exchange that heal all wounds of history. "So forgiveness, if there is such a thing, should be devoid of any attempt to heal or reconcile, or even to save or redeem" (2001b:56f.). Yet if unconditional forgiveness is to be an even match for the unforgivable, then, as in Solomon's song of love—this is what Derrida's delimitation does not heed—must it not be able to reverse every positively enacted antiredemptory void?

I am brought one more time to the Nazis' antiredemptory intent. Their memorialization of annihilation performed an inversion of unconditional forgiveness. The Nazis enacted positively the unforgivable. That is why the absolutely unforgivable had to be manifested always and already as antiredemptory. Like the demons we meet in myths, the human evildoers grasped the ideality of redemption in its spiritual core and did not confuse it with some economy of exchange or the practico-inert emptiness of the *khôra* to whose apathetic oblivion they could have easily relegated all their victims. Their ashes offered to the *khôra,* why desire any excess of this forgetting space? A redemptory scheme that comprised part of any such economy would not pose a real threat to the unforgivable. In the economy of exchange, secular redemption inhabits a practico-inert of institutions, it depends on one's adherence to beliefs or a creed, it promises a risk-free deliverance, or it is a religious equivalent of retirement benefits. But it is spiritual redemption that is at stake in any genuine sense of unconditional forgiveness.

How Does the Usurpation of the Site of Memory Reveal the Unforgivable as Antiredemptory?

Crimes against humanity exceed the secular sphere; they commit sacrilege against the goodness of creation. This is why Jews, whose ancient task it is to bear witness to the Creator, become subjects of the ultimate crime whose antiredemptory intent is lodged within the unforgivable. That crime is to usurp creative powers. If one cannot forgive the people of God their very existence, then one must act against the possibility of their creation as well as redemption. The unforgivable is revealed as the antiredemptory, for no ancient or modern witnesses to the law of anti-idolatry can be forgiven. Witnesses must be memorialized as unredeemable. The perversion of immemorial memory enacts antiredemptory creation (uncreation) because unconditional forgiveness would redeem existence as worthy of creation. Spiritual redemption has nothing to do with economies of exchange; it has everything to do with a new creation.

Derrida twice came very near to this core issue of the unforgivable. In his interview with Michael Wieviorka, Derrida (1999) hits upon the mortal wound inflicted by the unforgivable: "All is pardonable except the crime

against the spirit, meaning against the reconciliating power of the pardon."
Curiously, he invokes Hegel's metaphysics as if it provided the best source
of knowledge about the sin against the Holy Spirit: "As in the Hegelian
logic . . . the only unpardonable crime is against what gives the power to
forgive, the crime against the pardon, in sum—the spirit according to
Hegel, and what he calls the spirit of Christianity." Crime "against what
makes the man a man—meaning against the ability to pardon, itself," Derrida says, is the cardinal sin that Jankélévitch finds impossible to pardon.

In another interview, Derrida (2001b) opens a new angle onto my
question, Whom do I ask to forgive me, whom do I forgive, who forgives
the unforgivable? In finite time I repeatedly struggle to forgive myself, and
I infinitely strive to forgive God. The key question posed to Job in his trial
of suffering was, Who can judge or ethically evaluate God? Derrida charac-
terizes persons of genuine religious faith as "those who think that they do
not have the right to judge, that a priori they forgive God for whatever God
does." Again, curiously, he acknowledges this impossible possibility,
namely, that there can be genuine religious faith, whereas he denies the
same possibility to spiritual redemption because he views it as part of the
economy of exchange. In my meditation on the unforgivable, it is precisely
Derrida's own description of faith that also satisfies Job's forgiveness of God
and moreover shows what is redemptive in all acts of impossible forgiveness: "The people who have faith in God—since faith is not certainty and
since faith is a risk—are also the people who are constantly tempted not to
forgive God, tempted to accuse or to denounce God. That is part of the risk
of faith" (61).

What Is the Depth of the Unforgivable?

How can one make oneself or another unable to pardon a sin against the
Holy Spirit? How is this Spirit the addressee of all acts of the unforgivable?
If the memorialization of annihilation were to celebrate and thus render itself forever unpardonable, then to whom would such a project be addressed
but to one's own despair of pardon? Since unforgivable acts lie in one's positive use of freedom to undo creation—to uncreate—and to make flawed
what has been deemed worthy of existence—to unredeem—then the unforgiving act is addressed to oneself and to the cosmos. But now the question turns on forgiving the unforgivable to oneself and in that fashion to
the Creator.

If faith is not belief, if sin is not sins, if hope is not hopes, if hope is not
optimism and if redemption is not equal to progress, then there is but one
cardinal mode of sin and one of hope. My sin is to become offended at
being taught that my sin is hopelessness (cf. Kierkegaard, SUD 113–24). I
am offended not only by the epiphany of how I willingly dwell in my de-

spair; I am also struck by learning that what unbinds me from anguish is impossible forgiveness. I can become offended by the offer of forgiveness. Loved and forgiven, I bolt against all possibility to live otherwise than in despair. Creation already grants forgiveness to the unforgivable, since it allows it to exist. Each moment the unforgivable can do its despairing work—this allowance of freedom to uncreate lies in the ground of forgiveness—it also partakes of a new possibility of things becoming different. Hope smuggles possibility within the unforgivable: the unforgivable can exist only if creation does not prevent its possibility. In its actuality, as the negatively saturated excess, the unforgivable can be undone by redemption that creates anew. We witness both dimensions of this negative utopian sobriety in an addict who forgives herself even while unable to command power over herself.

How Can Forgiveness Dwell at the Heart of the Unforgivable in Such a Way as to Offend Me?

How else can forgiveness, hence hope's possibility, dwell within the unforgivable than by its continuing creation, that is, also by redemptive work? How else can I be offended by forgiveness than by my repeated fear of myself as unforgiven and unforgivable? How else can my offense intensify than by my aggravated scarcity of hope whereby I refuse forgiving myself and life—I uncreate myself ever anew in desperation? I refuse to forgive the cosmos for the Job-like setup, I reject the task of living a life that has the unforgivable in it, and to prove it, I will myself into existence as an unforgivable self. I seek in despair my sole meaning; if I continue to exist as unforgiven, then continue to exist offended by forgiveness, and finally continue to exist with bolted lock to my heart as unforgivable existence, how can I receive the grantings of hope? Nobody and nothing can get to me. This is the closest phenomenological description of the existential state of hell. It is not the Jew, black, Roma, or another object of hated otherness whose existence must be posited as unforgivable or abject in order to grant me an illusion of vicarious joy and deliverance. Rather, I must confront my own strange willingness to exist as unforgiven, offended, and unforgivable. That uncanny forgiveness—and there is always and already such a possibility—lies in releasing my despairing will from binding itself in hopelessness.

But What If Forgiveness Is Always and Already Commanded?

Unlike the forgetting declared by amnesty for the sake of civil peace, forgiveness cannot be commanded politically. Why should any commandment apply to the unforgivable? Kant tries to rationalize radical evil, though he finds its grounds inscrutable. Schelling discovers something positive and spiritual in the possibility of human agency to commit evil, yet can assign no "why" for the actual free reversal of ground and existence. And so it stands also with forgiving the unforgivable. Why are unforgivable acts committed when cruelty and monstrous annihilation yield the doer nothing tangible? The unforgivable reveals no reasons for its being apart from itself. *The unforgivable is without a why.* If I cannot create like God, I can destroy as one. Defiance has no why except to uncreate, to fashion itself into the unforgivable, and—this is crucial—to refuse forgiveness to oneself as well as to another.

I will meditate on the uncanny unconditionality of "without a why" in the final chapter. Suffice it to pause here and ponder certain astonishing parallels. Refusing forgiveness to oneself and vicariously to the unforgivable deeds of others is always and already without a why. Jankélévitch reveals as much in saying that he would not forgive the Nazis, but he never explains why he would not. *Forgiveness too remains without a why.* Derrida and Ricoeur's insistence that forgiveness cannot be commanded politically further raises its Janus-faced impossibility and difficulty.

I can gather now three parallel impersonal structures of this uncanny "without a why":

- The unforgivable acts (defiance)
- The refusal of forgiveness (offense)
- Forgiving the unforgivable (unconditional love)

The three structures are asymmetrical: only the third dimension of acts enables creating and forgiving (creation anew, healing, redeeming). The first two dimensions of acts reverse the principles of ground and existence. They are actualized in acts from despair—employing freedom to create positive nothing (defiant annihilation) and uncreating (antiredemptory offense).

Another name for the saturated phenomenon would be "without a why." If there is no why, then why should *I* forgive? But why shouldn't *I* forgive? Why should *I* be forgiven? There is no more intuitively satisfying conceptual answer to these questions than if we asked why *after* the "death of God" one continues to commit unforgivable deeds. Such deeds negatively exceed the secular. There is no "why" answer to our existing in the first place. No less than the offer of forgiveness, our creation carries no "why" flags on creation except that it is either found good (forgivable) or despairing (defiant, offended, unforgivable). Human acts of annihilation and uncreation remain equally without a "why" as the acts of unconditional love.

Lévinas and Kierkegaard invoke the Second Commandment to love one's neighbor as oneself as their lived, *personal* answer to the "why" question. They respond like Job, rather than like Kant or those philosophers of religion who seek propositional beliefs to settle the issue. Love and forgiveness are commanded not politically but singularly in every face-to-face encounter. What commands me to do works of love is the infinite trace of love in the face of my neighbor. Jankélévitch and Dostoyevsky are right that radical evil and forgiveness play an even match for the human heart. Yet we should not view the unforgivable and forgiveness as Manichaean gods. Dostoyevsky has Ivan Karamazov think that if God did not exist, everything would be possible; Žižek (2006) thinks that "if God exists, then everything, including blowing up thousands of innocent bystanders, is permitted" in God's name. Yet Schelling, who supplies the epigraph for part 2, produces the best triangulation between the possibility of evil, God, and freedom: "Damit also das Böse nicht wäre, müsste Gott selbst nicht sein" (1860, VII:403). As Heidegger (1988:276f.) comments on this passage, Schelling's notion of a becoming and suffering God requires the divine choice to will love as the essence of all existence, and for the sake of love God cannot forbid the possibility of evil. Even with this allowance, God's will to love and forgive is superior to the will of the ground. The eternal decision to love forms the essence of absolute freedom; it would thus form likewise the core of the commanded love of forgiveness. The possibility, though not actuality, of evil is metaphysically necessary out of the ground of absolute freedom. Evil could cease to exist as a possibility only under the strict metaphysical conditions that God's absolute freedom and will to love did not exist in the first place.

Unconditional love cannot but create and forgive out of its ground. Creaturely offense at such *impersonal* (nonpreferential) loving is that in creating it would allow the possibility of the unforgivable, and in that allowance from the start it would not will to annihilate or uncreate the actualized unforgivable. No. It would rather *(inter)personally* will to forgive and redeem the actual evildoer. On either scenario, Dostoyevsky's Karamazovian religious worry about the world without God or Žižek's atheistic worry about the world with the terrorist's God, even if everything were possible (and our times have taught us that in evil matters everything *is* possible), the unforgivable would point us back not to God but rather to human defiance of and offense at unconditional love. In human defiance and offense, the unforgivable is at heart underwritten by the idolatry of the human will.

EIGHT

Tragic Beauty

●

There is suffering.

I could have entitled this chapter "The Unforgettable," for, like the preceding meditation on the unforgivable and the following one on the unspeakable, the epiphany of blessing captures the tragic and sublime faces of beauty. The second epiphany of the uncanny intimates in the tragic beauty that blessing which allows for the mending of the world (*tikkun olam*) and so allows one to bear (live with joy again) the unforgettable suffering. If there is the *unforgettable* (impersonal modality of bondage) and so human *suffering* or wounding (interpersonal modality of bondage), then how is the possibility of *blessing* (interpersonal modality of releasement) *intimated* in tragic beauty (impersonal modality of releasement)?

Chrétien (2002:78–98) lists suffering among the "unforgettable" phenomena. Can we untie the knot that binds suffering and hope to the unforgettable? There is nothing beautiful in gratuitous pain. Innocent suffering is "useless" because even as substitutive, that is redemptive, its arrival and bearing cannot be justified rationally, morally, aesthetically, or even in a theodicy (Lévinas, 1988, 1981). If ugliness clothes the suffering face with grimaces of pain, can beauty bless us and so redeem pain? Beauty, just like ugliness, can suffer. The suffering beauty appears as tragic beauty. Tragic beauty does not justify the tragic, yet bears it, substitutes itself for it, and in that blesses and so redeems, makes whole again. The epiphany of tragic beauty is *tikkun olam,* making whole, and it intimates *berakhah/barakah,* the blessing of creation and unconditional love. Tragedy accentuates and so exceeds ordinary pain. There is the weight of fate in the tragic, and fate saturates suffering with wounding. The excess of wounding overflows into the unforgettable.

We often speak about the epiphany of hope in the mythical words of beauty. Two films, *Life Is Beautiful* and *American Beauty,* capture some of this response. In the first film we witness the human ability to invent life-giving stories to help us survive and live after the disasters wrought by radical evil. In the second, a dancing trash bag becomes a still point fixed against modern suburban emptiness. In the meditation on forgiving the unforgivable, we became aware of the integral phenomenon of the beautiful and the sublime—tragic beauty. Hope's upsurge opens us up as a flower blooms in the wasteland. Harmonious purposefulness without purpose of beauty lives in a sublime tension with tragic dissonance. Fateful tragedy dulls hope; tragic beauty reveals hope as destiny. Fate and destiny open two paths for undergoing time.

Expressions like "I suffer my fate" or "my life is fated" convey the sense of a life journey that has become inescapably unbearable. Fate, such as Sisyphus's stone rolled over and over up the hill, seems to lie beyond redemption. Sisyphus talks himself into contentment, but is his ordeal, even as accepted by him in finitude, a blessing of destiny or an aggravated suffering of fate? The keen sense of tragic fate is underwritten by nostalgia and a longing for new beginnings. And so the fated life imagines itself to be happy. In this margin between living without hope of redemption (life's undergoing or suffering is identified with the necessity of the *khôra*) and the immemorial memory of beginnings (life signifies a journey that is always already marked by possibility's possibility) lies the difference whether one experiences life as (ill) fated or (blessed) destined. In undergoing nostalgia and longing, I suffer from transitive hopes, I am Kierkegaard's (EO 1) unhappiest of all human beings, unhappy in the memory work of mourning, unhappy in hopes that never bring me into coincidence with myself, remembering what I long for in the future, desiring what lies in regrets of the past. As a Sisyphus, do I hope? Fate is about hopes dashed to pieces. Fates like furies crash us by the tragic weight of life. Destiny reveals hope when within the tragic sense of life, beauty dawns like rainbow, blessing the stormy skies.

Unforgettable suffering binds the innermost self in hopelessness. Does hope release me from wounding? Hope is not a justification, it is not a false idol of theodicy. When I suffer from hopes—nostalgia and longing of the passing away of time—I do not hope against hope; I do not hope for the sake of those for whom hope has become scarce. Hopes bind in idols, hope releases into possibility. Beyond the blind loops of nostalgia and longing, in my saturated albeit useless-cum-redemptive suffering—wounding—I negatively intimate hope. I suffer in that I am impressed by an unforgettable wound, and I bind myself in nostalgic and longing hopes. Intimating hope, my unforgettable (useless in justification and yet redemptive in substitutions of bearing and in intimations of tragic beauty) suffering is transformed in the epiphany that releases me from interminable wounding. I suffer fate, I yield to destiny. But *how* does hope accomplish such uncanny feats of transforming unforgettable and yet useless into redemptive?

Beauty shines through suffering, but beauty can share my tragic destiny. Beauty is not lost to itself within the tragic. Beauty transforms suffering fate—wounding—into the destiny which one can accept as one's way. Is Oedipus at Colonus beautiful even in his tragic condition of blindness? Is King Lear more beautiful when he is blind to the true love of his daughters, or when he becomes utterly mad in his new awareness of fatherly folly? The beautiful blesses us within the ugly; the sublime blesses us within the fated. Intimations of hope within tragic beauty transform our suffering and nostalgic longings. Hope intimated in tragic beauty promises new beginnings. I want to ponder these uncanny blessings of hope showered on us in the midst of the tragic and the unforgettable fates. The first meditation asks, How is hope granted? The second considers hope's difficult beginnings. The third wonders, How do hope's blessings disclose to us that tragic beauty can be something good?

THE HOW OF HOPE

Even if granted, how is hope given to those with eyes shut by ugliness and hearts locked by suffering? What can free one from the unforgiven and unforgiving self-and-other relations? What releases one from the unforgivable? Is not ugliness what revolts all my senses, are not tragedies and suffering precisely what I cannot forget and will not forgive? Is not life that has grown too difficult deliver me to that tragic fate which I suffer without forgiving and forgetting? Even if hope were granted in the midst of pain, how would it be apprehended by the one who has been wounded in time by painful memory, unjust history, anxious anticipation of the future?

Hope reveals that a sense of abundance and gratitude may overflow even the desolate space and time of disenchantment. The unforgivable makes beginnings impossible; intimations of hope in disguises of nostalgia and longing are already saturated by the chips of the uncanny.

How Does Beauty Intimate Hope?

Hope is intimated as beauty that manifests itself in the midst of the tragic. Hope arrives out of the dimension of time discussed at the end of chapter 1, which is neither marked by our melancholy past nor by nostalgia and longing for an anticipated future. If hope were something determined by the phenomenological field of experience, then it would not signify a radically new beginning. Any such novelty would be of the passage of time, it would lie in my agency, it would not be a dimension that affects my relation to time. Beauty transforms my relation to lived time. I apprehend my fate as my destiny. I begin to view the ugly, the chaotic, and the tragic as beautiful, cosmic, and sublime. My relation to lived time and space becomes transformed. If intimations of hope in beauty could not lift the veils of my pain, then granting of hope in forgiveness would never reach and unlock my heart.

Beauty must not be viewed as a "what," a criterion of rank. When beauty becomes a rank ordering of things, then it is applied in order to arrest the flow of time, then melancholy and nostalgic self-and-other relations aggravate hopelessness. The self-proclaimed beautiful group of Aryan whites or Rwandan blacks could exterminate those deemed to be the inferior/ugly group, Semitic whites or "other" blacks. We must not speak of beauty as an aesthetic preference of rank. Why can one call an ordinary trash bag—the ugly and boring North American suburb—equally as beautiful as Socrates's nose or Sartre's face? At the same time why can relations in beauty salons or self-relations of top fashion models become ugly? A beautiful ugly duckling tells the self-transformative fairy tale of hope. The intimations of hope in beauty are never to be conflated with the aesthetic categories of preference. Beauty's hope marks the lived dimension of time but is not of time's flow. Otherwise old age could never be seen as beautiful or its end time intimate hope's beginnings. Otherwise death could never be called beautiful and youth would always be.

How could one intimate hope face-to-face with death? Many an artist struggles to reach the depth of suffering, wounding, and decay, thereby reaping the harvest that the reaper of death did not sow. The mortal wound hides its secret behind the veil of Ezekiel's prophecy that our dry bones will rise. An artist's resurrection of tragic beauty in the face of death is no less uncanny in its intimation of hope than is St. John's vision of love in which he apprehended his suffering master on the cross. Speaking of tragic beauty, we intimate hope against hope in the midst of loss. Tragic beauty lifts us from hopelessness without thereby forgetting the catastrophe of time.

Yet even tragic beauty cannot explain *why* hope is given at all or *why* it is given to us here and now. I meditated on the why of hope in chapter 7. We must not explain the intimations or language of the granting of hope argumentatively. Meditations on granting, intimations, soundings, and the unconditionality of hope assume the role of a witness. Tragic beauty explains *how* hope is given when only hopeless tears should flow, not *why* it is given.

There is a poetic dimension in tragic beauty that includes humor and laughter along with tragic tears. Certain seemingly senseless acts of futile struggle, parody, and irony represent the most important vehicles for the renewal of human flourishing in hope. In "Ski Masks and Velvet Faces," a chapter of my book on the possibilities of liberation (1998), I recorded some act-up scenes from Prague Spring in 1968, the Velvet Revolution of 1989, and the rebellion in Chiapas of 1994. Nowadays, in the world of seriousness and dedication to ugliness, with the fear that cartoons ridiculing idolatry could even desecrate the holy, we must create new forms of humor that restore our capacity to receive the promise of hope.

DIFFICULT BEGINNINGS

None of the beginnings in innocence can be taken for granted, whether in our lives or in doing philosophy. Nietzsche spoke of winning back our ability to embrace this earth, Adorno taught us to come to terms with our past, and Benjamin envisioned in the image of *Angelus Novus* how historical progress turns into disaster. History's disaster is rescued, if hope is granted, by the chips of messianic now-time. The time of promise marks that uncanny dimension of time. In part 1, I insisted that this is not another kind of time but its saturated dimension. I ascribed its uncanniness to hope's upsurge. Hope intimates a promise granted within our nonanxious relation to the passing of time. Yet neither individuals nor our traditions and cultures can be said to begin innocently. We begin with the wounding of the lost Eden. Our beginnings are difficult because they have never been innocent. The saving power of beauty is that it intimates hope even within the ugly and painful.

In the first series of meditations on the uncanny, I pondered how the unforgivable stole its strength from hope's granting of forgiveness. The unforgivable robs heaven's manna, and so it exists in its core as a defiantly willed refusal to forgive. The unforgettable suffering intimates in wounding its own transformative possibility. Unforgettable wounding binds me in hopelessness through its nostalgic longing. Hope releases me through nonanxious self-and-other relation to time. The strings tied to hopes are my bondage, intimations of hope are my releasement.

How Does Hope Begin to Begin?

If I suffer wounds in ways that cannot be forgotten, how can I ever begin anew? Is not a new beginning akin to becoming innocent—a newborn. Is not innocent beginning like forgetting? Are not those attempts at beginnings that are lost to hope—that I cannot forget the wounding—always and already lost, and so lost absolutely? To be lost absolutely is to lose my path to the infinite. I lose the infinite here and now within the passage of time. I must rediscover that path to the infinite in every now in order to begin my beginnings. To hope is to be able to begin. To hope is to find my path to the infinite in time.

How Does Hope Forget the Unforgettable Wounding
in Ways That Do Not Forget with the Sleep of Oblivion?

Genuine beginnings are still points of the infinite inserted in the ordinary flow of time. That is why hope's beginnings grant and intimate the uncanny. Asking with Adorno, what would it mean to write, sing, and dance after Auschwitz—after all forms of radical evil?

With this questioning, I return to the third dimension of time, not another kind of time but a change of one's self-and-other relation in time: hope's time passes, creatively bypasses the inert timelessness of the *khôra,* from an absolute past to its radical future. The passage from unbearably unforgettable to unforgettably new beginnings renews us and mends the world in innocence. This dimension of time transpires through supratemporal polarities with mythical wings. Hope promises, but promises here and now in responsibility of bearing its suffering existence and in responding to the suffering of another. Hope promises in responsibility-responding as a new beginning what temporally lies in a mythical—historically nonlinear—dimension of time. Myth is time before all time, a time of the immemorial promise. Hope raises an existential promise in one's response-responsibility to the undergoing (read: suffering) of the present. Even though the religions of the Book accentuate the historical-salvation time, the linear over cyclical time, the faith of the Covenant People operates in the transformative, liturgical dimension of time's hope. Abrahamic beginnings lie in history yet are not of it. Abraham moved by the force of paradox, Moses learned commandments as *docta ignoratia*—in the cloud of unknowing—and historical Jesus required faith but, just as Socratic philosophy and Jewish Midrash, refused to offer positive data for acquiring it.

Myth narrates creation and promise. These mark out the outer frames of time. Existential time is lived always already late with regard to creation and yet it is transforming the mythical in its response-responsibility for the promise. History contains neither its radical beginnings nor its end, though philosophers of history have tried to reinvent both. Even if we invented the myth of beginnings or the future promise, we could not create *ex nihilo,* out of nothing. Our creations are burdened by unforgettable pain and longing. This is the burden of history. Radical beginnings do not and must not simply erase the memory of suffering, but they are allowed to transform us in relation to its wounding. This is what transforming useless, unjustified, suffering into redemptive, still unjustified, suffering of substitution means in concrete questioning: How can we resume our lives in the village that witnesses rape and murder among its neighbors? To simply forget is a sacrilege, as to forget is neither to honor nor to forgive. That is why woundings bear the stamp of the infinite, and so they portend the unforgettable. Yet to sink into the historical memory of pain means never to begin anew in joy.

The victims of history, whose unforgettable woundings are carried by future generations, cannot in truth place their messianic expectations on posterity in any real historical sense. Victims and their posterity can neither attain innocence by forgetting the wounding received by them or their ancestors, nor can they fulfill the messianic promise through historical memory, memorials, and monuments. The beginnings of the dead and the living are indeed more difficult than what for all their differences both Horkheimer and Benjamin thought; they are pregnant with an aggravated scarcity of hope.

Artists create out of suffering in order to conquer the tragic of their wounding; they borrow in inwardness from the uncreated well of nothingness. Through the artist's intimation of hope, the sublime joins in with the beautiful. Within tragic beauty, the unforgettable suffering is allowed to accept blessing. In so apprehending my tragic destiny, I may forget myself without oblivion of wounding or of its victims. Not by committing sacrilege, tragic beauty remembers; not by oblivion, tragic beauty releases me from the unforgettable wound. *Blessed by tragic beauty,* I am not burdened by the weight of history, or by its longing and nostalgia. Art gifted by tragic beauty gifts us in turn with the mended worlds of beginnings and promise.

Why Are Beginnings Difficult?

Our beginnings are mythical, as none of us stood at the beginning. We are always and already late. Kafka's antiheroes suffer the existential guilt of tardiness before they do anything. Myths are among the most ancient reservoirs of human creativity as they are at the beginning. They provide narratives of time immemorial and time beyond our time.

When our stories suffer exhaustion, as they do in Western modernity, then identities fashioned on our religious and secular myths stand at a crossroad. We find ourselves between the abyss of nothingness and reaching over ourselves. Two extreme possibilities open before us: fear from the emptiness of exhausted myths or exodus from that exhaustion. New myths can replace the decadent ones, and thus Christendom arose in the West on the ruins of the Roman world. But is there anything beyond the horizon of exhausted myths when the difficulty of beginnings becomes an aggravated scarcity of hope? This question goes to the core of today's global unease within religious and secular cultures that no longer find an unproblematic access to their myths of origins. Holy wars of religions that feed terror by promising heaven to suicide bombers have no other civilizational impulse but the destruction of the infidel. The zeal of the nation-states, that caricature of the medieval crusaders and their holy wars, lives off a democratic myth. These decadent religious and national myths pale in contrast with the creation myths of the ancients. Myth is not the opposite of truth; rather, it is a truth about beginnings that cannot be provided by arguments or direct evidence. Myth creates narratives about the horizon beyond the known and knowable. Beyond such horizons lie the beginnings, our absolute past, and the future promise. Mythical traditions, religious intuition, and creative art are the main vehicles for the encounter with the directly unknowable. As artful creation, myths about human beginnings and future promise carry in them much more truth about reality than we would get from a blind fear about nothing.

Fear makes beginnings difficult. Fear arises from the exhaustion of myth, from the deepening of the abyss carved out by the fallen myths, and from the ensuing crisis of identity that was fashioned by them. Fear can penetrate the core of once-creative religious and secular cultures. In itself fear has no positive creative value. As a defensive, reactive attitude, it lacks the wisdom of negative intuition. That is why we call fear blind; running from its past, shielding itself from the unknown, fear cannot but fail to hope. Unlike myth, whose illusions positive science wishes to cure, fear produces illusions about beginnings and ends. Science, even as it again and again opens itself to the unknown, is helpless in dealing with blind fear. Fear is a nightmare deepening our dreamless and unrefreshing sleep. Fear aggravates hopelessness. Whereas fear embraces the entropy of meaning, creativity blesses us with innocent wonder. Fear and creativity stand against each other as sleep and awakening. The culture of fear, whether clothed in the holy or worshiped in the icons of political power, produces not only a decadence of creation myths but also of political constitutions. Fear infects our care for the psyche and polis. Fear commits individuals and society to the sleep of spiritual death.

Every polis has myths about beginnings, and they likewise promise a future. The polis cherishes in its myths its untimely dimension. Civilizations are born and die with the vitality of their immemorial myths. That is why myths beget civilizational hope. Political constitutions translate in secular vernaculars the language of myths. Cultures, civilizations, nations are born from their narrations of beginnings and promises. Myths intimate beauty, foreshadow tragedy, and prophesy destiny. Living myths are realistic, tragically beautiful, telling stories of difficult beginnings. Such stories contain the dimension of the absolute past, the immemorial, that impossible hope against hope that Chrétien (2002:99–118) calls "the unhoped for."

What Is the Birth Cord of Hope?

The impossible and the unexpected are the Janus faces of hope.

> The *unhoped for* is what transcends all our expectations, and the inaccessible is that to which no path takes us, whether it is one that is already

traced or one that we project in thought. . . . No radical philosophy could ever make an economy of suddenness, of discontinuity, and thus could ever dispense with hoping for the unhoped for. (Chrétien, 2002:105, 107)

Myth that has not suffered its decadence holds an umbilical cord to hope. We intimate hope in supratemporal dimensions of our immemorial origins when we no longer wish to be our own creators. We intimate hope even within the unforgettable wounding when we shed hopes of longing and nostalgia about the passing away of time. We intimate hope in releasement when we grasp that hope is as impossible for free agency to secure as its granting to us is sudden and unexpected, "the unhoped for." Mythical time renews hope in the beginnings, and thus hope becomes saturated by the promise of transformation. Hope, that twin of a living myth, speaks through excess, hence not directly by analogy with experience or in the ordinary flow of time.

The origins of hope, its *why,* remain shrouded in myth and mystery. As granted, hope blesses with forgiveness what has been condemned as the unforgivable. Hope strains against despair's willed and thereby negatively saturated refusal of forgiveness. As intimated, hope enters the tragic as what sublimely exceeds the beautiful. Hope positively saturates tragic fate with destiny.

Why Is Forgiving Not Forgetting?

Tragic beauty does not forget the wounding, just as what was fated is not forgotten when one grasps one's destiny. Forgiveness remembers without regret; hope remembers with joy. The unhoped for in releasement, that mysterious dimension of the unforgettable, does not erase the memory of innocent suffering. Transformed in suffering by the granting of beauty, I intimate how within my life are conjoined tragic memory and sublime hope. The tragic is remembered in hope as the promise of the beautiful. In beauty my memory returns from the future. The unforgettable wounding refracts beauty's rays in the dissonance of the sublime. This tension of fate and destiny, tragedy and beauty, necessity and freedom, elevates the painful sweetness of hope to the joyous tears of the sublime. Wounding forgiven is recalled in the blessing of sublime tears.

Chrétien (2002) graces us with an insight into the link between memory and hope. He offers a more emphatically theological twist than I allowed myself in meditating on the saturated excess of tragic beauty. He retraces the promise that unites the immemorial, unforgettable, and unhoped for to God's creation, word, and redemption.

The genesis is immemorial, for we were not there. . . . Through the word of God, this immemorial becomes unforgettable, for the sacred history that we must always remember begins with creation itself. This remembrance of the impossible is anticipation and this memory is hope. . . . Recalling the origin belongs properly to hope tending toward its end. (117)

Chrétien accentuates God's hiddenness as well as incomprehensibility. God's secret manifestation in the unhoped for and sudden becomes disclosed by what exceeds, flows "over our speech and our thought" (117; cf. 113, 125f.). I have been proceeding from the opposite direction than Chrétien, all along accentuating the negative saturation of the hopeless in the willfully or radically evil, cruel, unforgivable, and unforgettable. These two approaches, theological and phenomenological, meet each other at this intersection of memory and hope. Yet only the negatively saturated excess can be grasped also nontheologically, that is, as the uncanny revealed even to a secular witness of the postsecular saturated phenomenon *after* the "death of God."

BLESSINGS OF TRAGIC BEAUTY

I opened part 1 with phenomenological considerations of hope lost and with Kofman's transformation of smothered words. Taking her starting point in human suffering, she witnesses to the unity of the human race, "the irreducibility of man reduced to the irreducible" and "the indestructibility of alterity." She discovers hope for a new kind of "we," "a new ethics," and "a new 'humanism'" (1998:73). Her uncanny vision of the passing away of time at the latrines in Auschwitz testifies to tragic beauty: when endowed with humor, it can resurrect speech. How astonishing that one could be so blessed on the pile of shit and at the most horror-filled place and time on the planet! Her bold secular hope pointed my Sartrean-Marcusean meditations to the first-order of impossible hope at the limits of ordinary experience and within the critical theory of liberation. In the next chapter, I will ponder how hope transforms the unsayable and mute loneliness by its soundings of silence and solitude. In the concluding meditation of this chapter, I stay with the difficult blessings of tragic beauty. Why do they intimate hope and mend our worlds? Why are grantings and intimations of hope, sequestered in the aggravated scarcity of radical evil, not just tragically beautiful but also *good*? How do they render our beginnings new, indeed, innocent?

How Does Hope Allow Us to Apprehend within the Tragic Not Only the Beautiful but Also the Good?

Is this question touching on the timeworn adage about God's visitations of love through suffering? Why should tragic fate ever be a blessing?

Blessings do not descend from acts saturated by the scarcity of hope, as if good came out of evil, as if we should consider ourselves visited by a perverse God in a wanton play of divine cruelty. Yet this is how fate and inscrutable decrees by gods, often testing human beings, are narrated in myths. The story of Job, in friendly suggestions provided by his "good" neighbors to explain his suffering, echoes those mythical narratives of tragic fate decreed by gods at play in divine comedy. We have long ceased to find such stories impressive, unlike the innocent suffering of Job. Blessings of tragic beauty must testify to what, even in the latrines of a death camp, cannot be reduced in humans to shit. What we encounter again and again is Kofman's figure of "the irreducibility of man reduced to the irreducible." The blessings of tragic humor grant and intimate beginnings of another humanity. Their difficult and tragic innocence reveals an irreducible spirit of the holy of holies living within human beings. This spirit's tragic hope is beyond radical evil—and it is good. Its uncanny blessing emerges from the depth of suffering.

It bears repeating: the sacrilegious is not the sight that witnesses hope mired in unforgettable suffering, but rather it is the voice that denies memory to hope. The suddenness of the unhoped for bursts with the laughter of tragic beauty from the Auschwitz latrines. Hope is the good that breaks the hijacked site of memory (e.g., the Nazi design for the museum of an exterminated people) with its undeferred, lived promise of bearing, responsiveness, responsibility.

The uncanny blessings of impossible beginnings mark our human praxis with saturated sensibility. Hope becomes the saturated phenomenon insofar as one should not be capable of laughing with innocence or of calling life beautiful in the factory of violent and anomic death. There should be nothing good in us discoverable within such total degradation. All should be reducible in humans to ashes of oblivion, as if beauty could not bless us and goodness could not save us even in hell. *Khôra* knows no beauty, no tragedy, no tragic beauty, and so never endowed with a face and never witnessing the Other, how can it ever help humans to resist despair? Tragic beauty is a category that does not explain *why* hope is granted (and this was not my question) but rather *how* hope is possible when it is all but destroyed. The how of hope we call beauty, and its difficult beginnings tragic beauty. Sublime beauty endows hope with wonder. Because beauty is not free from tears, hope is never cheap. Tears and laughter are as mysterious as solitude and love are, and I would not wish to take the ability to stand alone in love, loving and being loved, for granted either. What I said of the scarcity of hope applies in an even measure to the scarcity of silence, solitude, and love.

Fear of Decadent Myths, Blessings of Creative Myths

In dreams one is motivated by collective myths, and those give rise to religious integrations, cultures, and traditions. Archaic myths and their expression in religious and secular cultures motivate all individuals. All our actions even in the modern period are tied to the archaic center of our beginnings, to the mythical in us. Apparently neither polis nor psyche can act free of myths. Yet apart from myth, in modernity the law comes to motivate many of our actions. When that motivation grows weary, the individual stands before the law with uncertain guilt for an unknown crime; and when culture and politicians designate this unknown with the name of that or those whom we must fear, then we have turned primordial anxiety of nothing into a feared enemy—the greatest of all political motivators of souls.

Motivation by fear is a danger facing not only fundamentalist religious regimes but also secular Europe and the cultural hybrid of North America. How should we hope for a nonsectarian space and time of beginnings and promise? Are there social blessings of tragic beauty?

Echoing Plato's skepsis about political reforms, we suffer nowadays as much from the motivational weakness of law and the disconsolation of procedural justice as from exhaustion of vital myths. Even with Derrida and Habermas's secular hope for the European Union, discussed in chapter 3, we seem unable to constitute ourselves in a polis without fear. Every constitution sets an arbitrary start and many do so with acts of violence. To forget the violent founding, national myths grant us blank amnesty for the history of genocide and narrate glorious beginnings. Without mythical origins of polis, how could we celebrate state holidays and sing national anthems? Imagine Germans recalling their foundings and refoundings in the twentieth century, imagine Americans and Christendom remembering original inhabitants and slaves in the colonies, imagine small nations like Czechs recalling how their royal dynasty rose from murder and their postwar state cleansed the nation not only of the collaborating Germans but also many innocents. Imagine the assembly that would memorialize founding guilt as its state holiday! This is why innocent myths cannot be easily replaced by the law, even as all states narrate innocent origins. The rise and fall of civilizations and nations are bound with the vitality of their myths (e.g., the U.S. myth of freedom) more than with the price of oil or the strength of hurricanes. Vital myths already mend our worlds.

Religious terror and the politics of fear are two forms of decadent mythologizing. Narrations of the beginning and end of times suffer decadence when they become an ideology, belief system, doctrine, group adherence. Vital myths open space and time to the unknown and unknowable.

Ideologies depend on the human, to be sure, despairing will. Living myths escape human possessiveness. Beliefs aim at absolute certainty and thereby promote fanaticism. Genuine myths open up to the absolute as something beyond our grasp and will. Myth tells a depth story about us, such as we receive in a lively dream. It makes no difference if ideology or decadent myth is secular or religious. The God of faith, unlike the idea of a belief, cannot be crafted by the logic of human fear. Faith or awakening is to belief as living myth is to ideology. Ideology is never genuinely beautiful, and in the aesthetic domain it produces kitsch. The danger of every ideology, whether the Soviet mythology of revolution or the American dream of freedom, is that it parasitically draws on the human need for the mythical dimension of life. Religious terror and the politics of fear parasitically receive demonic strength from that very same dimension.

Yet it is impossible to feed terror with creative myths. It is likewise difficult to die as a suicide bomber or to march into a holy war while invoking the blessings of tragic beauty. Myth opens us to uncertainty of the unknown and unknowable, yet fanatics *have* certainty of belief. Myth is to absolute certainty as the risk of faith is to a conviction of belief, and as beauty is to kitsch. The decadence of creative myths propels the decadence of religious and secular cultures. The crisis of creative myths intensifies the original anxiety before the unknown. Mythical creation, beginnings that we do not own, comes *ex nihilo,* out of nothing. Ideology—and fanatical forms of religious and political kitsch—wants to possess its immemorial origins and the unhoped-for promise of deliverance. Fear arises with the manipulation of this primordial space and time of myth, manipulation to which both psyche and polis are prone in the postsecular age.

What Is Fear That Kills Hope?

We fear that the beginnings or the uncreated origins and unhoped-for promise, that sudden source of creativity in us and in the cosmos, never belonged to us. Creative myth always and already enables the story about beginnings and the future promise. The memory of hope is never ours to have.

Anxiety of nothing is what Kierkegaard perceptively calls the dizziness of freedom, yet fear is not anxiety. Nothingness of anxiety does not produce fear, even if it forms a horizon of all creating from freedom—out of nothing. Kierkegaard insists that anxiety and fear are not our destiny, but genuine faith is. If faith were anxious, that would require us to conflate anxiety with the Abrahamic fear and trembling while standing before God. Creation does not know boredom or uneasiness of fear either. Fear embodies the decadence of the primordial anxiety. Not fear of enemies but anxiety marks our vulnerable openness to the unknown and to the mystery of the unknowable. But faith moves out of nothing without despair or anxiety, so it moves against fear. Tragic beauty blesses us in sublime ways by always transforming fate into destiny and suffering into creative hope. In reverse, the politics of fear embodies the decadence of people's constitution.

After the cataclysms of modern era, nation-states and great religions alike suffer from the exhaustion of their myths. No wonder the European Union showed itself initially too weak to motivate many of its citizens to vote for a new European constitution, no wonder the many former captive nations of Eastern Europe live in fear of the European project. No wonder that religious terror and fundamentalist reaction to terror are two ascending forms of religiosity after the globalization of the "death of God." The exhaustion of myths, prophesied by Nietzsche, presses an urgent question how or with what narrative can we constitute ourselves (as psyche and polis) in creative ways today? Should we do it with fear? Bereft of creative beginnings adopted in faith and wonder of revealed beauty, we fall into boredom and unease. Terror arises from this crisis. The flight into boredom feeds unease, and from this unease every fanatical search for absolutes feeds terror, and terror feeds fear. That is why the politics of fear does not differ from religious fanaticism. This is increasingly the danger facing not only the fundamentalist religious regimes but also secular Europe and culturally diverse North America. How should we mythologize, how should we hope for a nonsectarian space and time of our immemorial beginnings and the unhoped-for promise of response and responsibility?

Nietzsche's prophecy of the "death of God" can mean two things: either God does not exist or the living God is dead. The former depicts the loss of belief, the latter the loss of faith. The former means that God never rose from the dead (the tomb is empty but not because the crucified one left it on Easter Vigil or, at any other time, in accord with Ezekiel's promise of the rising dry bones, that ancient Judaic promise of responsiveness and responsibility to the dead, that love is as strong as death, indeed stronger than the *khôra*). The latter means that even if believers celebrate the Paschal mystery of the risen God, and usually in the same week the Jews celebrate God's Passover that ushered in their exodus from slavery, what are their churches and synagogues if not empty tombs of dead believers, the sepulchers of buried religious faith? If the prophecy is about the latter meaning, then we do not receive a cognitive atheistic prognosis, but rather insight into the crisis of Euro-American mythologizing. The crises of religious and secular cultures alike are the crises of myth. We suffer unforgettably the exhaustion of our beginnings and of the future promise—of our radical memory of hope, of our ability to hear, respond, become responsible.

Nihilism and Cynicism

What are the blessings that tragic beauty can deliver beyond the horizon of decadent mythologizing? Are not nihilism and cynicism the twin faces of this exhaustion, and are not religious terror and politics of fear born as their sinister offspring? This question is answered affirmatively by Glucksmann (2002) in his discussion of the 9/11 terrorist attacks. If faith and beauty find their source in creative mythologizing—the time of the immemorial and the sudden—then one of the faces is turned to the nothingness of creating. As Moses in the cloud of unknowing, faith and beauty count their blessings in the dark. The other face apprehends the perpetual crisis of human efforts, overcoming our fatigue from freedom. That second face is all about risk and leap. Conviction and fanaticism propel their movement through tragic fate with the twin dangers of nihilism and cynicism; faith and beauty energize their movement by sublime destiny with the twin motives of creation and venture.

Every religious conviction carries in itself a secular dimension of its care for the purity of teaching or rituals. Yet every secular story that divinizes its historical role in myths such as those of individual freedom, free market, or egalitarian revolution only colonizes the religious dimensions and sucks dry its creativity. Thus most of what we consider to be "religious" pertains to culture and conviction, and many a secular and atheistic conviction fills the emptiness of decadent religions that have lost faith. One belief exchanged hands with another. The postsecular decadence of myths delivers us to the postmodern crisis of religious and secular cultures. Fanaticism and religious fundamentalism, like the politics of fear, suffers the decadence of their myths, thus of their cultures and convictions. Those inflexible thought formations are incapable of motivating psyche and polis otherwise than though violence. Only if we grasp the crises of religious and secular cultures as crises of their myths about immemorial hope and the future promise of hope, will it become apparent that every collapse of belief architectonic is preceded by the crisis of faith and wakefulness. The crisis of faith is nothing but one's inability to wonder at creation and to apprehend even the tragic world of suffering in the innocence of sublime beauty. Secularization cannot cause the crisis of faith any more than genuine religion can motivate all ascendancy of fear, fanaticism, and terror.

Myth about the End of Myths

I have been pondering how hope is given and how it is intimated. I found in forgiving the unforgivable the answer for the former and in beauty that can forget without oblivion an answer for the latter. Forgiveness of the unforgivable reveals a granting of hope; tragic beauty answers "how" hope is intimated when it seems impossible to begin in innocence. Yet beauty too can suffer. It is the sublime beauty that suffers. Myths mark the difficult immemorial beginnings and sudden, unexpected future of hope. Blessings of beauty are both innocent and tragic. The unforgettable wounding is not erased by the beautiful nor does the tragic smother all speech by the weight of history. This impossibility is, minimally, what all truth commissions presuppose in letting the victims of suffering and perpetrators of war crimes face each other. We tell, we listen, we sit in silence, we forgive, we refuse to forgive or forget, we remember, we want to forget—and doing all that each person intimates hope against hope.

At the end of this meditation we are not any further from grasping why the blessings of tragic beauty are given beyond the horizon of decadent mythologizing. The message that "God is dead" tells us that we lack a myth that could replace its predecessor as a creative civilizational value. This state of culture is the meaning of the devaluation of all values; it also motivates terror and fear. The crusades and the colonization wars of Christendom once carried a civilizational value, but only insofar as they reeducated their holy zeal by turning religious zealots and nationalists into citizens of lawful states. Today's religious terror and its convex mirror in the politics of fear carry no such civilizational value, since nihilism and cynicism do not aim at anything creative. Neither nihilism nor fear can be reeducated into civilizational values. If we are not to collapse from the exhaustion of myths, we must seek beyond the "death of God" a paradoxical beginning—a myth about the end of myths. What would be the blessing of its tragic beauty? How would it mend our worlds?

There are three timely dimensions and one untimely dimension of the myth about the end of myths:

1. When we, like ordinary drug addicts, cease to get ecstatic with the heaven of fanatics, when we cease to fear and tremble at the beckoning of politicians, then we will be able to ask, What should we fear? The ancients used to call this courage.

2. In the motivational weakness of law, such as the European Constitution faced at the exhaustion of the European myths and the United States faces in its myth of freedom, we come to face anew the question of how to constitute oneself and polis. This is the dimension of justice.

3. In the midst of exhausted myths we face from one side emptiness and from the other the question, How should we wonder, what should we adore, what should we invoke in prayer? This dimension of unknown and, in every primordial wonder, unknowable can be called wisdom.

4. The untimely dimension of all narrations about beginnings and ends is nothingness, *ex nihilo,* from which every free creativity takes its start. Here we can ask, What is narrated by the myth about the end of myths? I call this untimely dimension, in contrast to religions as cultural expression of myths and in contrast to their deaths of gods, spirituality.

I am courageous in my self-and-other relations when I am neither a coward nor a terrorist. I am a coward when in fear of the nothingness of human efforts I die for the idols of religious fanaticism. I am a coward when in need of power and self-assurance I feed on the political phobias of others. I am just when I reject being lukewarm to human misery or seeking a solution to injustice through revolutionary terror. I am wise when I resist all forms of ideological mythologizing. The wise one seeks the unknown and unknowable from which free creativity takes its source. I am spiritual when I neither engage in fear nor suffer from boredom. Spiritual is the one who is no longer motivated by religiosity or its secular translations as forms of ethnic-national myths. Genuine spirituality can be born quite handsomely *after* the "death of God." In the present global historical constellation of dominant yet exhausted Western myths, that ecumenical spirituality might even presuppose this salutary death. With the twilight of idols, the motivation of modern media, terrorists, and politicians to produce fear vanishes. We no longer need to flee from our own nothingness or evoke in others stupidity with false reality shows, lulling them and ourselves into sleep.

Courage, justice, wisdom, and spirituality are dimensions of faith understood as awakening or awareness. This is how the blessings of tragic beauty may be given to us beyond the horizon of decadent mythologizing. It is easier to let people sleep: to provoke in them cowardice and call it courage. It is easier to ignore misery or invoke the myth of revolution, the other face of the gods of terror. It is easier to put everyone to sleep by ideologies, but wisdom begins with the crisis of such mythologizing. The greatest conflicts between religions and secularization are just so many fearful contests about the beliefs narrating our beginnings and promise. Spiritual life has nothing in common with religious and cultural sleep.

Uncanny Praying, Prayer of the Uncanny

Let us mythologize about and at the end of myths, thus expanding the uncanny prayer sounded as a promise at the end of chapter 3. Let us imagine how the untimely life of spirit and the timely life of courage, justice, and wisdom would awake in us wonder. What would be the blessings of tragic beauty in the myth about the end of myths?

Let us imagine that from the mosques and synagogues, cathedrals and temples, from all congregations that invoke religious names but also from the United Nations, one can hear the morning and evening call to prayer. Yet this call has an inverse effect of the myth about the Babylonian tower. In that biblical story we learn about the human race building a tower that would reach to the sky, thereby elevating humans to the status of gods. Our feat accomplished became our world as we know it, the infamous Tower of Babel. The human race has suffered division and mutual misrelation ever since the failed apotheosis. Why does the call to prayer we imagine in our myth about the end of myths carry an inverse effect to that of the confused tongues—our Babel or babble? In contrast to sectarian and ethnic disputes in many tongues or under various flags and symbols of divine names, the language of our mysterious call is without clear attribution. One hears it, one may even discern in it the messengers and prophets of one's beloved religion, the annunciation of the incarnation of the God among us, yet one is unable to assign it a definitive national or religious label. One must grasp the call within oneself, and so must awake. Otherwise the prayer is incomprehensible, untranslatable, and incommunicable to a third party. Unlike in catechisms or in the loudspeakers posted at the communist village where they gather us to a political meeting or brigade, this call to prayer is more like the tolling of bells.

When we begin to hear within ourselves to what or whom the bells toll, waking up from our dream, then we are still unable to translate this call into religious or national languages or to one or another symbol of adoration. We are thus unable to rank-order or compare it with other prayers, except that they are assignable to a group adherence and this call requires inherence in wakefulness. One hears from mosques that God is great, but God is so great that God remains unnameable in any one holy tongue; God fits neither within the confines of one holy book nor behind one Wailing Wall or tabernacle or sacrament. And we all saw that this prayer was good.

There is only one thing that everyone understands in his or her native language. It is a warning that spiritual sleep is mortally dangerous to our existence, a sickness unto death, a death from which one cannot die physically but would live through one's death, because spiritual death is a life of despair. Then one can hear clearly a global anthem of tragic beauty:

The God of idols is dead. Neither God nor God's peoples need heroes to die in the name of ideals. Atheism that placed itself on their throne is revealed to be itself an idol. The God of fear is dead. God does not name by one name with which one could vote theistically for or atheistically against God, and thereby could threaten hell and holy wars against infidels on either side of the human a-theistic equation. The God of hopes is dead. Infinity is the name of the un-

canny prayer, and sublime beauty teaches ways of hope. The God of terror is dead. Only a coward exchanges faith for belief, spiritual beauty for religious kitsch. The God of one exclusive path to God is dead. Faith and awakening are not obtainable by an ideology, party, orthodoxy, or risk-free certainty. Hell is idolatry and lovelessness among people. Religious fanatics and politicians of fear meet at the end of their efforts boredom and more fear; neither paradise on earth nor paradise after death nor God of life await them anywhere or anytime soon. The God of religious cruelty is dead.

NINE

The Unspeakable

●

There is loneliness.

The third epiphany of the uncanny reveals how the unspeakable trauma of loneliness can be transformed through the soundings of silence (*chashmal*) in solitude. If there is the *unspeakable* (impersonal modality of bondage) and so human *loneliness* or trauma (interpersonal modality of bondage), then how is the possibility of *solitude* (interpersonal modality of releasement) *sounded* in silence (impersonal modality of releasement)?

Traumatic events—abandonment, refusal of care, violence—enclose inwardness in an unspeakable muteness. The traumatized heart is like a jammed cavern, and locked within itself it grows lonely. Loneliness renders one mute when its negatively saturated silence becomes unspeakable. The unspeakable is not brought about by concepts that one does not know how to express (aporias, paradoxes, antinomies)—by things left unsaid or even unsayable because of the limitations in language or resources of hermeneutics. The unsaid and unsayable detect the first order of paradoxical impossibility. Paradoxical meanings are intended or desired and yet perpetually deferred in fulfillment. The unspeakable reveals the second order of saturated impossibility. The unspeakable traumas exceed all concepts, intentions, desires, and their possible fulfillment with excess of negative intuition. The unspeakable smothers words (even the sayable ones) within. One bolts, shuts one's mouth, will not open up.

This excess in the unspeakable reveals loneliness as something that one has always and already said and willed. Lonely silence has been exceeded by words that are buried within; hence unspeakable silence is negatively saturated by smothered words. No such negative excess overflows the unsaid or the unsayable silence. Intellectual aporias or paradoxes are not unspeakable but deferred meanings. The unsayable, unsaid, aporetic all hit conceptual limits of maximized intention or desire; trauma arises in conflicted agency.

The unspeakable traumas are occasioned by unforgivable deeds, unforgettable suffering, mute loneliness, annihilating cruelty.

Too much is always said and already deliberately willed within the unspeakable time and space of inwardness. Trauma saturates muteness by what it loudly protests and obstinately wills. The unspeakable muteness, unlike the indifferent and unaffected muteness of inert space, the *khôra*, fills the confines of the empty heart and submerges it in loneliness. Lived and unresolved traumatic events can arrest one in loneliness. The primordial trauma that antecedes all other traumatic events is the cosmic setup of human birth, life, and death. The immemorial stumbling block of all loneliness thus lies in our coming to terms with the passage of time. One can become mute simply by refusing that original setup, refusing the birth ticket.

Just as traumatized muteness is never unspoken and unvocative, hollowed out silence, so also loneliness is not solitude. *Khôra* knows no trauma, no unspeakable silence, no soundings of silence because it neither calls with a face, nor hears the Other. Unspeakable muteness is to loneliness, as the soundings of silence are to solitude. In solitude one is becoming empty for speech. Ceasing to think and speak words smothered by trauma, one must cease speaking oneself to muteness. In solitude one yields to the soundings of silence. Uncanny hope that is granted in forgiving the unforgivable and intimated in tragic beauty now speaks in the soundings of silence.

How can silence speak if my unspeakable muteness cannot or will not? Why would I seek silence to have anything to say? Loneliness, unspeakably traumatized, is too loud to be capable of solitude. Silence resounds in solitude. The soundings of silence neither grow mute nor become traumatic. Not to speak, to refuse speaking, is not the same as being silent. Both the soundings of silence and the unspeakable might be at the threshold of words, yet only the silence of solitude addresses one's unspeakable loneliness. Sorrowing loneliness is deafeningly loud, and in its inner noise grows mute. Deliberately shutting oneself down, one renders the singularity of aloneness traumatic and unspeakable—lonely. Aloneness is not the same as loneliness.

What makes one's mute, traumatized, unspeakable, willed loneliness speak? When the soundings of solitude speak in silence, their language spells its words from hope. The two grammars of hope are joy and prayer. To think of joy on the scale of fun and entertainment is to miss how, when granted in forgiving the unforgivable and intimated by sublime beauty within the tragic, joy bursts through sorrow. Praying with joy, I become capable of intimacy with myself and another. Intimacy is possible when loneliness gives way to solitude.

As loneliness is to solitude, so sorrow is to joy, and despair is to prayer. These six attitudes author the human self. The first member of each analogy is infinitely distant from the second member of each analogy. Loneliness wallows in sorrow and despair like a city clothed in melancholy mist; solitude overflows with joy and prayer like the rising incense and trembling of intimate embrace. Acts of intimacy—from lovemaking to adoration of the holy—are genuine prayers. Intimate lovers who dwell in the silence of their solitude are just as hopeful as the monks standing alone before the holy. Because intimacy intensifies solitude, without its silent language of hope the human touch becomes for us, finite creatures, unbearably lonely. Sex without intimacy among humans and religiousness without intimacy with the holy inflict traumatic wounds, and human hearts wilt in loneliness. Joy and prayer author the human self in hope; sorrow and loneliness author it in despair. Joy does not forget sorrow over what was lost or suffered, sorrow converts into joy by hope, loneliness converts into solitude by prayer, and the soundings of silence embrace the mutual intimacy of prayer and hope.

In chapters 9–10, I will meditatively walk thirteen steps into the crushing sorrow and despair of loneliness, thirteen steps into the ecstatic joy and prayer of intimate solitude. The thirteenth step and the fourth epiphany of the uncanny concerning annihilating cruelty and unconditional love will comprise the concluding chapter of the book.

The (inter)personal scales of sorrow and joy, despair and prayer pertain to the same human self. It is *I* who is lonely or sorrowing, *I* who despairs or dwells in intimacy, *I* who is joyful in forgiving solitude. Yet my *I* is not a self-possessed subject but rather always already response to the creative call of love, and in that sense also a commanded love to love myself *as* my neighbor. Created *ex nihilo,* I do not come to myself out of the nothingness of the *khôra.* There would never be an I-Thou possibility, there would be neither a phenomenological and communicative symmetry of the self-alter relationship, nor an ethico-religious asymmetry of *I* responding in redemptive substitution to the useless suffering of the other. There would be none of this without the first possibility of responding to the creative call of the Other. *Khôra* does not call me, but *I am here* always already responding to someone; hence deaf silence cannot be the first word (and can it be the last one?), nor can the hollow silence speak words I may defy in anguish. It is that love is as strong as death that *I* defy, it is over love's ability to love myself *as* another and *as* God in me that *I* anguish.

Converting sorrow into ecstatic joy, despair into love, I become a different self. Only by undergoing such a metamorphosis from loneliness to solitude, in what I have called the existential or self-transformative relation to despair and hope, do I make myself capable for the first time of responsible face-to-face relations. This becomes then my ethico-religious existence commanded as much by the Judeo-Christian, Lévinasian-Kierkegaardian neighbor love as by the Buddhist compassion for all life.

In loneliness and solitude, I am the same and yet different self. I scale the bottomless depths of sorrow and despair whenever I flee loneliness through another's embrace or through the sheltering multitude. I traverse the infinity of joy in myself and intimacy with another to the degree that I abide in my solitude. Seeking or finding another, as if two sorrows could drown each other's lonely depths, may never of itself cure loneliness. A city entire may be asleep in sorrow, begetting melancholy poets of sorrowing loneliness. Joy and prayer are awakening. The alter who abides in solitude is for the self singularly a wholly other, the two meet each other in solitude. Intimacy with another mortal and with the holy grows out of and abides in solitude; then joy *is* prayer, then prayer *is* intimacy.

MEDITATION ONE:
THE PASSING AWAY OF TIME,
THE FESTIVAL

In the opening phenomenological considerations of hopelessness at the end of chapter 1, I realized that when seconds pass by me without any measure of granting time's passage meaning, then my ordinary lived time suffers from a runaway infinity or false eternity of empty nows. My sorrow appears infinite and eternal in every now. Possibilities for relationship pass me by with the same sense of futility I undergo in the unrequited yearning for vocation. I am unable to find an axis of motion that connects the time of my passage. What would grant me an inner history that would rescue my time from this flux? In chapter 1 we discovered the intransitive dimension that is in time but not of it. Hope is not granted by the passage of time (the field of phenomenological experience offers by hopes and fears) but rather in the now-time of new beginnings (intransitive hope is always already the counterexperience of creation and redemption).

The sorrowing infinity of time's passage dupes me, for mine is an infinity reaching for its depth. Still, the bottomless sorrow brings me no solace. Out of bottomless depth, I drown in my sorrow. For all imaginative freedom to flee and even fly, this sorrowful infinity paralyzes me by its appearance as fate. I am *fatally* free, and to suffer fate means that I cannot move even when I flee. My spuriously infinite motion—be it realized in a multiplicity of lovers, in jobs without vocational moorings, in finding and losing homes or cultures, yet never being in earnest anywhere—has its obverse comic effect. My motion is "on the way to nowhere," as the Talking Heads sing in one of their songs. My nowhere names one of the faces of loneliness: I am disconnected from encounters with others, I regret life projects I have not taken and feel melancholy about those I have, I drift as a victim of history in which all relationships and self-discovery are frustrated before they begin. Time is passing away, time passes me by (if I am there); in motion I do not move; if I move, I go nowhere. My loneliness grows weary. Fatigue mainlines me into bad infinity that does not rescue but drowns me in sorrow. Boredom knows no motion of converting sorrow into joy; it cannot transform the desperation of an anonymous embrace into prayers of intimacy.

If I were at Rio de Janeiro's Mardi Gras carnival, perhaps I could enjoy myself. But would I grasp the meaning of the festival? I might be ecstatic, but would my vicarious ecstasy give me joy, would it sound the songs of loving? Could I shed loneliness in a festive multitude? Could I become intimate en masse? The festival is quintessentially repentance; then joy and prayer *are.*

The festival ushers me into the time apart from ordinary time, moving from *chronos,* the road of clock time, to *kairos,* the timely time or time out of ordinary time—an untimely time. The festival rejoices in an untimely meditation. The festive timeliness is lost to the sorrowing melancholy of time's passage. The festival does not mark a date on my calendar's monthly planning, but as a liturgical calendar of infinite advents and returns to depth, paschal deaths and births, it interrupts ordinary time. In the potlatch festival, an overabundance of goods is destroyed or given away; in the ancient Judaic sabbatical year (unlike its poor academic replica) all debts were cancelled. Even in modern times, the festival promises that time be rescued from time. It is a deceptive "ecstasy" that abounds in festive promises coming in the clothing of the rave, for sorrow—seemingly lost in ravenous exuberance—arrives after the rave. I cannot get to the Pure Land of the Festival along a mapped route, reaching through progress an end of history. Someone or something cannot make me festive. Beware of a melancholy-activist colloquialism: "Making an occasion festive!" There are no how-to manuals for joy and intimacy, anymore than there are rote methods of prayer.

To enter festival truly, I must convert my loneliness into solitude. In a timely time of rescue, my loneliness yields to festive joy. I might never attend my true Mardi Gras if the surface joy of my Fat Tuesday arrives before prayers of repentance on Ash Wednesday. The separation of the two—joy and repentance—is modern paganism and its bacchanalian confusion. Ordinary time means that all human instants turn to ashes. Religions—whether on the Jewish Day of Atonement, Yom Kippur, or in the Buddhist ever-present sense of transitoriness—do not deceive about finitude and death. I might never go to Rio to solve my difficulty. I either remain a dupe of my sorrowing passage of ordinary time—my passive suffering of unspeakable loneliness—or I must come out of the time of the ordinary.

The festival transforms the instants of a runaway infinity, granting them the cosmic meaning of the infinite. Milan Kundera discovered this infinitely intensified, second-order infinite (thus the second-order impossibility) in Beethoven's sonata variations. In true sorrow, I repent without trauma sinking my soul into loneliness, I rejoice anew without the weight of history rendering me mute, I inhabit a decisive moment of the intransitive, nonlinear, indivisible now. I begin to unlock my heart, begin to hear the soundings of silence. The unspeakable is broken and so spoken in silence (*chashmal*) by the language of hope. The speech that was once negatively saturated by an unspeakable trauma is interrupted by the second-order infinity, an intuitive excess of possibility that new beginnings may be sounded, by the impossible language of hope:

- That debts be cancelled (not repaid) as a gift!
- That time be rescued (not erased) by timeliness!
- That sorrow be repented (not forgotten) free of nostalgia and longing!

Then time's joy *is*. In that uncanny moment when intimacy becomes possible, prayer *is*.

MEDITATION TWO:
NOSTALGIA'S LONGING,
LAUGHTER'S SUBLIME BEAUTY

One way that lonely sorrow tries to rescue itself from drift is by a two-edged bow of longing for the future and nostalgia over the past. Longing and nostalgia infinitize themselves through endless time bridges of sadness. Neither a vanishing historical point nor an imaginative futural horizon can limit desperate grasps for what had passed, what could have been, what might be. Time bolts in the vanishing horizon of longing. The negative modality of time's bondage has an impersonal dimension of the unspeakable fate and personal dimension of suffered loneliness.

Longing infinitizes the teenage search for intimacy, friendship, and vocation. Who does not recall those high school weekends clothed in aloneness made weary by an anguished longing for embrace, by nostalgia for the losses of what one never owned in the first place? Young people are so approachable and yet so awkward in trying to meet one another. I used to attribute my pain to the girls who were unattainable to me. Many an adult, straight or gay, suffers from this affliction throughout life. The secretive life of pornography and vicarious sex encounters only resembles rescued loneliness. The emergency rooms of desperately consumed sex, those purchased indulgences and absolutions given for unrepentant sorrow are filled with more anguish than church pews and confessionals can bear. Is the anguish of brothels and dark alleys a form of prayer? Seduction cannot teach intimacy anymore than proselytism can teach about faith; but in yielding to seductiveness or bigotry, one heightens nostalgia. Successful seduction comes away empty-handed even if we fill church halls and party coffers with collections. Yielding to seduction resumes lonely longing. The night of anonymous flights into a quick release from loneliness prolongs one's own sorrow. Neither free sex practiced with the zeal of political dissent against the oppressive regime, nor Eastern Europe emerging from totalitarianism to a delayed sexual revolution, nor sorrowing loneliness prepared me in my youth to love another in intimacy. The cultivated incapacity for intimacy and the failure to pray (rather than statistics about waning theism or church membership) produce joylessness and the spiritlessness of the age.

Kierkegaard (EO I:19) writes of the poet as "an unhappy person who conceals profound anguish in his heart but whose lips are so formed that as sighs and cries pass over them they sound like beautiful music." In a journal entry from 1846 he notes that, if we remove all anguished conscience, we may just as well close the churches and turn them into dance halls (JP III:2461). This pairing of praying and dancing is truly comic. But as Kierkegaard's (CUP) Johannes Climacus observes, it is my temporal striving for the infinite that renders me comic. To live earnestly, I need not enter a monastery, he says; I may just as well sit in a café. Before I can approach another, God or human, in intimacy, I must convert my loneliness into solitude (whether I dance in a disco or dance before God). Solitude is an essential condition for genuine prayer as much as for dancing and loving.

Longing and nostalgia bloom into poetry in many a youth. Aesthetically elevated poetry longs with and for lovers. On spring or autumn evenings cities like Prague become poetic vessels hiding lovers on bridges, under the wings of baroque angels, in the nooks and crannies of alleys and parks. That city cloaks itself in longing and nostalgia, at once sweet and painful; poets lift their pens, painters stroke their brushes, and musicians sound their instruments. The city of lovers infinitely hurts and pleases at once, and the secret of its magic is highly cultivated melancholy. In painfully beautiful Prague one never need give up sorrowing loneliness; it almost reaches to the stars. They call this city Praha—a doorstep—a door or window to heaven. The sorrow of our age produces many bad poets and a crop of mediocre poetry readings aspiring to an open microphone. Heightened anguish sows not only loneliness within but also destruction around. Kundera's (2000) Jaromil is a sorrowing, bombastic young communist poet whose anguish terrorizes lovers and Czech citizens. Kundera portrays the poet of kitsch and the Stalinist hangman working out their romantic-revolutionary melancholy on others. Kitsch is just as ugly as lovers without pathos are pathetic.

A few transmute anguish into the melancholy fruit of sorrowful beauty. Kant in his third *Critique* distinguishes harmonious purposefulness without purpose of the beautiful from the dissonant or negative pleasure of the sublime. Adorno grasps that in time (and for him after Auschwitz one cannot enjoy ordinary poetic beauty without the negative) we must bear the dissonant dimension along with the beautiful. In his thinking the negative is inspired by Schoenberg's atonal scales, if not by Kierkegaard's passion for paradox, rather than by Hegel's harmonious holism. Must not nostalgia, when lonely sadness converts into solitude's joy and when its desperate grasping for another transforms into intimacy's prayer, yield to *sublime beauty*? What Kant aporetically separates or what Hegel harmoniously mediates—the beautiful and the sublime—belongs to one's existence in its finite time lived with infinite pathos. In existing I suffer time as my loneliness; in pathos I inhabit singular solitude. Shedding nostalgia and longing, I exist by rescuing the sorrow of time's ordinary passage with love's moment in infinite pathos. The sublime and beautiful meet in my repentant laughter; then joy *is*. The sublime and beautiful release me from infinite longing into intimacy's infinite; then prayer *is*.

MEDITATION THREE:
THE PAIN FOR THE WORLD,
TEARS OF TRAGIC BEAUTY

Earnest laughter converts nostalgia about the passing of time into sublime beauty's joy. It transforms the longing of runaway infinity into intimacy rescue of time. *Honest* tears convert melancholy into tragic beauty's joy and brooding into prayer.

When does Hamlet's loneliness yield the solitude of Lear who sobers up in his very madness? Poets are at their most intense when sonnets of personal anguish give voice to their worldly pain. Do poets of pain pray? Prague lends her sweet sadness more to musicians and poets of the tragic than to heady philosophers. Czech-born Edmund Husserl is known for his Crisis lecture delivered in Prague three years before Hitler's armies desecrated the city's beauty with swastikas. Husserl's student Jan Patočka lamented the shared totalitarian fates of twentieth-century Europe. In Václav Havel's poetic imaginary, philosopher-poets no longer pursue rigorous science. It is as if Central Europe, with a historical destiny that never belonged to itself, were made to feel and sing, rather than just think, the pain of the world. There is a legion of Hamlets on the coasts of Bohemia—that classic geographical misnomer of Shakespeare's imagination about Slavs and Gypsies. Each time Prague's Good Soldier Švejk or Milan Kundera laughs, Franz Kafka and Rainer Maria Rilke cry. Havel's political irony causes tears to course down a laughing face.

What would convert Prague's Hamlet-like sorrow for the world into Jerusalem's psalmody, the lamentations that the prophet Jeremiah and Jesus alike shed over their city's tragic beauty? Do prophets of lamentation pray with joy?

Hamlet converses with Horatio and his ghosts about the demise of his state and about death. Lest his pain for the world transfigure self-forgetful brooding into honest tears, it remains but the tragedy of a self-misunderstood loner. Melancholy Hamlet finds no joy, brooding prophets of doom and gloom have not begun praying. In ancient and modern drama, the loneliness of fate suffered by the likes of Oedipus, Medea, Electra, or Lady Macbeth becomes converted into the uncanny of tragic beauty. The comedic sublimity of laughter transmigrates into the tragic sublime of tears. Blind fate comprehended and then repented in time is elevated into destiny. Repentance transforms the melancholy and brooding tears of loneliness into tragic honesty capable of joy and intimacy. Lonely pain for the world becomes transfigured into a redemptive act when one's blind rage is atoned. The tragic hero not only feels and expresses his or her pain, but in repentance bears it well. To bear the pain of oneself as well as of the world is not to carry it on one's shoulders as if one were Atlas carrying the fate of the globe. To bear it well is to laugh through one's tears with joy. I emerge from loneliness that is suffocated by and bonded to world's pain into solitude that is released into prayer. Coming out from my willed muteness into receptive silence, I begin to speak with the language of hope.

Witnessing the dawn of tragic beauty stirs us within; beauty's intimation and language of hope empower us to bear singular and worldly pain. Aristotle's poetics names this conversion of melancholy brooding into tragic tears as *catharsis*. In purification, the blind Oedipus at Colonus is no longer blind to himself. More akin to Shakespeare's magician Prospero, the dramatic stage of previously self-distanced suffering transforms lived actuality into *honest because atoned tears* of tragic beauty. Tragic tears are shed through beauty—the sunlit rain becoming rainbow. Then tears of joy *pray*.

MEDITATION FOUR:
BETRAYAL, FRIENDSHIP

"O my friends, there is no friend." The first *New York Times* obituary for Jacques Derrida (Kandell, 2004), by any measure no act of friendship to him, assigned this ejaculation to the late French-Algerian philosopher's clouded thinking. It somehow escaped the attention of the editors of this respectable daily that Diogenes Laertes and Michel de Montaigne attributed the sigh to Aristotle, who likewise wrote, "We need a friend who is another self, only to provide us what we are unable to provide ourselves" (*Nichomachean Ethics* 9.1169b6). Telling a group of friends that there are no friends, Aristotle waxed Derridean and uttered the paradoxical. Does not friendship, when sought to cure one's loneliness, try to resolve the paradox by betraying both oneself and another? Can friendship be sought without both betrayals? Are there no friends?

One ordinary meaning of loneliness is to have no friends to speak with; equally ordinary is the view that friendship means to find a remedy for loneliness in another. Two lonely planets join to travel together, and they might even pick up a travel guide, *Lonely Planet,* but can they cure their shared ailment? Do they speak? Can two lonely islands keep intimate silence? What could one loneliness add to another but "another self" that is lonely? What do two ailing lovers provide each other but shared self-evasion?

The fundamental confusion of my loneliness, when I have not faced it on my own, is that in search of a friend I externalize my anguish. I expect that friends are there to rescue me from myself. I am angry at the cosmos for leaving me bereft of friends. I am envious of friendships others have. Fleeing loneliness, I periodically use "another self" to give me some relief from having no self. I have not become a Buddhist no-self; I am still trying to find myself vicariously. I distract myself in the boisterousness of peers. I "enjoy" my drinking buddies as I drown sorrow by rushing to the bottom of my mug. I have not become a friend to myself. Friendship to another I can hardly provide except by doing so deceptively, bonding with another in envy or hatred of the world. Or like a prostitute I can sell my loneliness to cure the loneliness of another, if not for profit then for that quick ecstasy whose profound sorrow even a morning-after pill cannot abort. Loneliness born of an unloving embrace begets the children of sorrow. "That's what friends are for," one might say to another, "and if you are not willing to be there for me, then you are no friend." In my threat to withdraw, I reveal that I have been "using" another to do for me what I fail to provide myself.

The commonsense imperative—remain lonely or find a friend—marks the most fundamental confusion. In the ordinary use of friendship as a panacea for loneliness, there are no friends. Aristotle was just as right as Derrida, and the *New York Times* obituary is no friend to anyone. Aristotle's praise of friendship between equals in search of shared good and happiness meets its existential corrective in Kierkegaard's Climacus: "For existing ethically, it is an advantageous preliminary study to learn that the individual human being stands alone" (CUP 323). Unless I learn to stand alone, I cannot hope to find intimate joy.

In seeking a friend as "another self" who substitutes for what I cannot provide for my own self, I betray both myself and the alter. That first betrayal—evading myself by loading my loneliness on another to carry for me—is the most fundamental: I fail to befriend myself. I find no joy in being myself and being with myself. I grow mute even if I utter the most beautiful prayers. With myself, I fear to become a friend; seeking another friend or the loved one, I flee myself; with the holy other, intimate I am not. A bad friend to myself, I am using myself, I am running from intimacy with my own thoughts, prayers, and even my notebook. Social activist yet desperately lonely, I am no good as a friend or model of justice to "another." I am unable to receive the friendship of another in truth. Can social solidarity emerge among those who flee themselves? Can love of people or gods address me in my flight from the joyless self that I cannot welcome home in intimate embrace?

A cowardly lion, a social activist in flight from essential aloneness, I did not dare to befriend myself. Courageously standing as a singular self, I begin to convert my loneliness into solitude. Friendship, love, and solidarity begin in solitude. Two in solitude find their joy intimate. Then relationship with another does not intensify loneliness, sociality does not increase fraternal terror, and intimacy with another and the holy and in social solidarity *are* prayer.

MEDITATION FIVE:
PERSONA, SINGULARITY

Among the joys of being an actor, readily shared by enthusiastic audiences, are dramatic masks by which the stage personifies real-world characters. Actors time-travel in slices of infinities from one human universe to another. The dramatic persona embodies a staged self, almost indistinguishable from its actual world appearance. The actor rarely appears on stage as his or her world self. All vocations carried in excess of their finite realization carry this professional hazard. Soldiers and policemen are supposed to protect, but their uniforms may hide brutishness. Clergy, monks, and nuns are esteemed as those who yearn for the infinite, but their holy garb may hide the infinite anguish of disbelief and unsated erotic longings. Teachers educate and liberate, but, like their social activist peers, they may just indoctrinate youth. Vocational hazards mark the contradictions of the human condition, and the actor's hazard is no exception. Shakespeare had one of his masks read the drama of lived existential truth—our real world is but a stage, and everyone has in it a singular entrance and exit. Ironically, any dramatic persona, if lived in the world, could become a perfect cover for flight from oneself. Flight from self begins in ordinary hiddenness, grows into muteness, morphs into trauma.

The real-world mask can dramatize the fig leaf of shame, the persona covering the unspeakable. The temptation of artistic imagination only heightens what is true of every human journey. The tension between profession and vocation parallels the one between the persona and the singular self. One either becomes a professional—wearing social roles and conventions as so many dramatic masks—or one strives for a vocation—becoming singular in existence. It is not uncommon to meet individuals so deeply embedded into their lived persona, as if each mask were a "real" self, that one can hardly get to the self buried behind the mask. A real-world character is crafted into body posture, voice, facial expression, idioms or habits, repertoire of responses; over the years, the mask becomes etched into facial wrinkles. Like all good actors, persons living in their persona are unable to change whom they represent. There is no intermission, no falling curtain, no self-presentation from behind the mask. It would strike us as comic if Falstaff suddenly stepped out of his role and became the gentleman from Verona, though the actor's training might require just that. In daily encounters we often mistake our or another's persona for the self. Unlike the actor whose masks are many things to many people, world personae accept masks as earnest money. This makes the world masks comic in elasticity, tragic in rigidity. Drama is supposed to heighten this hazard or tension between stage and life. By presenting the comic and tragic elements of the personae, drama aims to propel us, the living characters, in choosing our singularity. Drama's tragic and comedic soundings—the *catharsis* unlocking the unspeakable—open within us our smothered words.

The festival rescues my boring and anguished passage of time. Authentic laughter and tears overcome my nostalgia and longing, each acted out on the real-world stage. I become a character capable of action and total engagement in the moment when I find courage to befriend myself. Choosing my genuine vocation, while knowing the difference between the hazards of donning a professional mask and the task of becoming myself in time, I convert the flight of my persona from myself into the motion of singularity. "When the curtain falls on the stage, then the one who played the king and the one who played the beggar etc. are all alike . . . actors. When at death the curtain falls on the stage of actuality . . . then they, too, are all one, they are human beings." When Shakespeare's magician, Prospero, reminds us that "the theater of art is like a world under a magic spell" and then lifts that spell by returning the full cycle of spring and winter dramas to us to live out in existence, we grasp that "eternity is not a stage at all; it is truth" (Kierkegaard, WoL 87). The drama of existence stages intimacy in which creating *is* joy.

MEDITATION SIX:
HOMELESS IN EXILE, AWAKE IN EXODUS

Abraham, Moses, Buddha, Mary and Joseph, Jesus, Muhammad—their great religions dramatize the call from the land of our birth and origins into the uncertainty of foreign lands and an even greater unknown. Many paths to awakening and faith exist, but all lead through an exodus from the familiar. Yet refugees, exiles, émigrés, and the homeless of our streets often suffer greater loneliness than others. Loss of a home is a trauma like muteness. An aggravated homelessness of forced exile is akin to the unspeakable that severs humans from the most intimate of homes—language. As the language of hope is joy and prayer, love songs for human lovers and gods are homes more intimate to us than our native language. This is how I can be exiled from my mother tongue and culture, albeit continuing to partake in both. The "death of God" affects civilizations in their cultural edifices and even in the grammatical *I,* where Nietzsche worries about the residual survival of the dead god. But what Nietzsche's madman does not proclaim is the excess of the "death of God." The betrayal of the grammar of hope becomes something even worse than the death of cultural gods. This lonely, hopeless language grows mute, traumatized, unspeakable. Exiled from itself, the language of gods and culture transmits meanings without intimate joy. How can homelessness point to homecoming?

The Soviet motherland would punish its political undesirables with internal exile to the Siberian gulags. Before I left my native communist Czechoslovakia as a refugee, I practiced with thousands of my compatriots the art of internal emigration into dimensions of life where the state could not intrude. Like many oppressed groups, we made a virtue out of our sorrow. Czechs called for a parallel polis or culture (a hidden city within the city), Russians invented an art of escapism (fleeing hated regimes through imaginary doors such as a matchbox or a desk drawer), and all East Europeans mastered samizdat (self-publishing of forbidden books). There were other escape hatches: lines heard between the lines in theaters, underground rock, humor, sex, and alcohol.

Kundera thinks that the Czech word for sorrow—*litost*—is untranslatable, even though he defines it as "a state of torment caused by a sudden insight into one's own miserable self" (1980:122) and identifies it with "heroism" (150). He also judges it to be beyond repair, claiming, ironically, that the Czech history of defeat invented *litost:* "A man obsessed with *litost* revenges himself by destroying himself" (150). In Kundera's novels *litost* transmogrifies into a vengeful self-destruction. Yet Czech intellectual giants, while never efficacious en masse, have pointed the way out of tragic fate into singular awakening. Jan Hus was burned at stake in the fifteenth century for standing alone in speaking truth to power. Jan Amos Komenský, two centuries later in the wake of the Counter-Reformation, died in exile while taking his abode in his opus *Labyrinth of the World and the Paradise of the Heart.* Prague philosophy student Jan Palach stood alone when he drew the lot in a student pact and immolated himself in 1969 in opposition to the Soviet invasion during Prague Spring; by that act he shook the conscience of the nation. The Husserlian-Heideggerian professor Patočka died a Socratic death all alone in the hands of the Czech secret service while spearheading the dissident movement for human rights, Charta 77. Václav Havel quixotically proclaimed the power of the powerless at the height of the normalization purges in the 1970s and 1980s. The historical revisionists of the communist era in the east, Czech President Václav Klaus chief among them fifteen years after the Velvet Revolution of 1989, share Kundera's skepticism of dissent, demeaning it as intellectual bathos and bombast.

Lonely internal exile withered in *litost,* but it found an obverse side in solidarity. As in the Polish trade union by that name, Solidarnosc, it rose against stupid power and turned sorrow into occasional joy. The dissidents' dreams of another polis were overtaken by market politics soon after the Soviet collapse. Dreamers lost escape routes from *litost* into joy. Kundera missed out on the dissidents' joy in his French exile, but he wrote a perfect work, *Ignorance,* for the postcommunist return of *litost,* a phenomenon understood by only a few in his native land. This book sheds light on the lonely odyssey and homecoming of an émigré. The dissidents' home was lost too, when their solidarity was replaced by money power, when the old communist cadres and mafias who used to persecute them began to benefit from the market. The exiles returning to their once-lost land recognized it as "home" no more easily than Kafka could imagine himself at home in America.

There is the incommunicable loneliness of a refugee who has no prospect of ever being allowed to return home. Every refugee, not just the Palestinian, imagines "a right of return." But to what do we have the right to return? Can it be one's culture, civilization, or even the once-living myth of origins? Do cultures and ethnic groups possess the right to their eternal continuation? Can even languages in this or another form claim that right? If the myth about the end of myths, with which I concluded the previous chapter, marks our sense of fragile time and place today, then "right of return" cannot be a homecoming to holy lands as usual. We can at best return to the language of hope. This would be a homecoming to the soundings of silence (*chashmal*).

There is a deeper loneliness in the passage of time between the day one fled and the imagined return home. In an archetypal story of maturity,

Odysseus grows into a wandering Jew. Unless one discovers that to be a Jew means to witness to the infinite in oneself, one has lost all paths leading to the promised land. One's conquest and settlement of holy turf comes up empty, one's longing for return home does not match the memory, one is misrecognized in the return as *this* person, one is for others but a nostalgic memory and a more or less fulfilled longing for its return.

Waking up from *litost,* my sorrowful wanderings and nostalgic promises of return convert into exodus from all sentimental conceptions of home and memory. My encounters with Kundera's literary sorrow of lost and never-attained immortality (another novel about unattainable home) yield to Kafka's metamorphosis in the midst of his and my Prague exile. One day when I visited Jerusalem, years after my exile, I was greeted by an uncanny epiphany of Prague returning to me in the ways "real" Prague never did or could. Homes are parallel infinities of each self standing alone. Infinities are irreducible singularities, and what perishes in the death of gods and decadence of origin myths and promise of homecoming leaves in its wake the sound trace of silence. My homecoming at last reveals my infinity. In exodus from nostalgia for home and longing for return, freed from their loneliness and civil wars, I am on my way. *Where is my home* but in joy and intimacy! Exodus to holy lands *awakes* in meditation without borders.

MEDITATION SEVEN:
ANOMIE, MENDING

Meaninglessness—anomie—always and already compresses all our undertakings to mute an unspeakable trauma, yet each new effort to act and speak against it in turn exceeds anomie in that it calls on hope for healing. The act of healing is expressed well by four spiritual words: *teshuvah, tikkun olam, chashmal, berakhah/barakah.* The Hebrew *teshuvah* invoked on the Day of Atonement, Yom Kippur, expresses the immemorial possibility of existential self-transformation, radical turning, true beginnings both in the sense of creation and redemption. The Sufis as well as the Jews mean by *berakhah/barakah* a blessing, breath, essence of life from which evolutionary process emerges. The early modern Kabbalist Isaac Luria called for *tikkun olam,* a mending of the world, a way for humans to aid the ongoing spiritualization of the cosmos. And the prophet Ezekiel (1:4, 27; 8:2) intimates in *chashmal* the creative and redemptive words of silence. These ancient invocations reveal what must be healed: not just material entropy (in that case individual effort and social activism would suffice to heal, and it would suffice to learn from Marx, Sartre, Marcuse, or Habermas) but spiritual entropy (we stand alongside each other alone, each one needing self-transformation in order to become capable of a community of human flourishing). Luria considered the material universe to be marked by entropy in a restricted sense; the essential entropy is the catastrophe of the trapped divine light of original creation. The human task is to help the Creator and Redeemer to free up the fragments of this light, overturning the gravity of anomie. All creation participates in the messianic event. Messiah is not to come through the phenomenological field of experience and flow of time, but rather counterexperientially. The epiphanies of the uncanny arrive always already through the messianic now-time. This is why the coming of the kingdom is always at hand and yet infinitely far from our lived human history. The messianic event, whether one awaits the first or the second or the perpetually prophesied coming under this or another sacred name, enters through all intransitive gates of the now or, like the waiting for Godot, nowhere, never, not at all.

Anomie names the unquenchable sorrow of cosmic insignificance. I can suffer from an overproduction of empty meanings. Nietzsche locates here the nihilism of all value positing. Meaninglessness announces the ongoing historical demise of received values. That "God is dead" *means* for Nietzsche that there is no value which I can safeguard by heroic or cultural projects. No values last forever, and all value positing perishes in entropy. Nietzsche hopes to find in "willing nothing" rather than not willing at all an overturning of all anomie. Will to power is neither *berakhah/barakah* nor *tikkun olam*. Nietzsche's nothing is still full of itself. Conservative and progressive revolutionaries alike believe they change the world, yet they often overproduce annihilation. Thereby they rob the victims of history of meaningful death.

Both philosophy of religion in its search for speculative ultimates and the modern destruction of ordinary human meanings jointly overproduce spiritual entropy. The loneliness borne of anomie arises from these twin highs and lows of human insignificance. After the Thirty Years War of religion in seventeen-century Europe nobody wanted to hear about "religion"; after the cataclysms of the twentieth century and since 1989 in Eastern Europe and Russia, social(ist) dreams of a more just world seem to be just as dead as Nietzsche's god. Mao's great leap forward fed millions of hungry, and yet cultural and spiritual entropy with which the leap was paid accelerates today's unhindered market-authoritarian rise of zealously materialist China. The loneliness of anomie herds religious and secular fanatics into the cold embrace of terror and the war on terror. Terror feeds on the entropy of loneliness.

The dying voice of Hal, the onboard computer in Stanley Kubrick's film *2001: A Space Odyssey*, evokes the vast empty universe and in it a depth of sorrow that does not heal. The hecatombs of the dead in the modern era, the human terror of insignificance and the terror we overproduce to flee our insignificance, can be measured by the intensity of entropy we dread. Without *teshuvah* or *Kyrie eleison, berakhah/barakah, chasmal,* and *tikkun olam,* human projects drown in anomie, plunging us into a lonely cosmic night. Just as Viktor Frankl defines the human self through its search for meaning, so Sarah Kofman, as we witnessed in chapter 1, liberates light from entropy on Auschwitz latrines through the portrait of prisoners who witness Nazi guards as all-too-human to be capable of destroying the human. The shared finitude and mortality of prisoners and guards, without erasing the horror of the house of death, converted the overproduction of meaninglessness, which was worse than dying, into laughter on the edge of annihilation. Kofman's father was killed for refusing to work on the Sabbath; her death camp ethics resists not just his but also our spiritual entropy.

Sacrilege is accepting entropy in the face of annihilation. The excess of inhumanity assigns some among us the second degree of death. This antiredemptory constellation of the second degree, because negatively saturated, calls in me and out of me the categorical imperative, or better, the new-old commandment to love against hell, to affirm that love is stronger than cruel death. Protesting cosmic insignificance, and more than that, *praying against an ever-encroaching anomie* with soundings of her father's Sabbath festival, Kofman's smothered words spoken of deep solitude bless and heal. If joy is not freed by the sparks of light illuminating even the shit houses of worldly hell, then anomie's despair will have prevailed over intimacy's prayer.

MEDITATION EIGHT:
DESIRE'S DESPAIR, INTIMACY'S FAITH

Loneliness desires, intimacy abides in faith. Desire fills too loud a solitude, intimacy sounds in silence. Desire's need surges from felt lack, intimacy rests in love's simplicity. Craving depletes desire and so smothers words, overflowing completes intimate embrace and so opens words. Desire's need knows no ultimate satisfaction, intimacy's abiding begins in receptive openness to another. Desire's need is the lack felt in the emotive self, just as doubt is the lack recognized by the speculative self. Doubt is a despairing intellect, despair is a doubting of self, but the intellectual doubt of unsatisfied desire misreads its despair and so also its healing (Kierkegaard EO 2:211). Loneliness is incurable speculatively just as it is unresolvable externally through social solidarity. Desire's lonely unsatisfaction becomes choked, mute, unspeakable. Lonely words, even when uttered, mushroom into despair. Sounding faithless words, one says nothing; one has lost capacity to speak from the self because one has lost hope of a new beginning.

Capacity for speaking is granted, intimated, and sounded in intimacy's faith. This capacity arrives as the faith of a child; in adolescents and adults traumatized by the unspeakable, that primordial faith that one can speak again becomes revitalized by hope for a new beginning. Faith's hope is granted in healing when there is forgiveness of the unforgivable; it is intimated in blessings of tragic and sublime beauty; and it is sounded in solitude's silence. Desire's need is to intimacy's abiding as despair is to faith. Desire's want produces despairing sorrow; it suppresses the self's ecstasy; faith converts desire into love's joy and its unspeakable trauma into intimacy's prayer.

Loneliness despairs because it thinks it has no other with whom to share itself. "I am lonely," so one says in common language, "I have no mate." Loneliness despairs long before it meets another; desire despairs when it possesses the other. Desire is initially sensual, autoerotic, pleasuring itself. It wants, and what it wants most is its craving satisfied. Desire's need defines the ordeal of Narcissus in men and women alike. The sociality of Narcissus produces a combustion of crowds; the political movements of Narcissus promote an activist self-seeking, and at their most intense autoerotic revolts lead to totalitarian closures of desire upon itself.

Pleasure rarely gets too far from drowning in its own self-referential yearning for intensification: "More, give me more, do me more, me more," pleads Desire's need. Desire's yearning multiplies pleasure "objects" and, with each achievement, it multiplies venues of satisfaction, always more, me more. How ironic that drugs could make sex more infinite in intensity and supply a reality show of intimacy to boot! How ironic that the sexual liberation of men and women should amount to multiplying desire's—*jouissance's*—multiplicity! Have women's and gay liberation movements, by liberating and multiplying desire's need and its many ways of satisfaction, cured individual loneliness, self-suppression, and social oppression?

Children's polymorphous play in aggravated adult games becomes the cold heat of cruelty. In cruel pursuits of satisfaction—at once unforgivable and unforgettable wounding of one's own flesh, inflicting pain and terror on another—desire's celebration of the perverse craves its own runaway infinity. The bloodsucking vampire, that myth of the never-quenched thirst for the fountain of youth and the lust for those who embody it, morphs into a grimace of death. The beauty salon mirrors and the plastic body parts become visions from hell. If I cannot satisfy pleasure, I can at least feed my pain! If I cannot drown my loneliness in pain, I can feed pleasure by inflicting pain on those I claim to love. I can play at a sadomasochistic fear and trembling as if to simulate faith: the other will give me only so much pain as suffices for my desire's pleasure; I will inflict only so much pain as suffices for simulating intimacy's faith in another whom I have in my power to hurt and make sacrifice for me. We share this horrid pretend intimacy of pleasure's dizziness. When all stops are pulled, how bottomless is the well of cruel tears! I know of no other more devastating portrait of desire run amok in multiplied cruelty than the Marquis de Sade's *120 Days of Sodom:* it is exquisitely elaborated by Horkheimer and Adorno in the darkest chapter of their *Dialectic of Enlightenment* on Enlightenment morality and the Jacobin terror infusing modern rationality. It is brought to its insane conclusion in Pasolini's last film, *Salo, The 120 Days of Sodom* (1975), a shocking allegory of sadistic fascism in a story of Italian aristocrats who kidnap a group of teenagers in whom they gradually liberate desire that, when desperately intensified in bad infinity, consumes all participants in mutual cruelty.

Is the multiplicity of pleasuring the same as the infinity of joy? The lonely craving is infinitely distant from intimacy's faith. Loneliness confuses the intensities of pleasure with those of joy. Pleasure without joy returns to its emptiness in self-suppressing anguish. I seek all the pleasure I want, but my pleasure seeking achieves neither liberation nor ecstasy. There is no intimacy in the morning when the drug *maya* wears out. Loneliness desires itself, locks itself in the cycle of desire, comes back at itself by consuming itself without rest. One prays in loneliness to one's own addiction. Pleasure knows no genuine infinite, and without it one cannot pray either.

Intensities of pleasure know only a fleeting orgasmic multiplicity or momentary release, so pleasure's search for endlessness turns into pain, only to resume the cycle of want all over again. This is a prescription for despair. Endless multiple orgasms would actually yield physiological pain. An infinity of desire's need (unlike Hegel's imaginary that views all struggles for recognition fulfilling the human desire to be desired) is not community or solidarity but fraternal terror (which so worried Sartre) and narcissistic hell. The name for hell is one's lonely inability to love—the cold fire of cruel, unspeakable grasping for self in another that yields no closeness, no intimacy, no faith, no hope. The hell is ironically unending in desire's desire of desire. Yet bereft of the single overflowing intensity of joyous intimacy, the circuit of desire gives no fruit of life. Unlike the cold desire of loneliness, Lévinas's concept of infinite Desire is a figure of a different kind entirely, for it no longer craves to be satisfied; Desire overflows in intensity of transcendence.

Intimacy abides in faith and because it is not self-suppression, its soundings of silence speak out of one's solitude. Because it abides in faith, intimacy converts the fleeting intensities of pleasure into infinite intensities of joy *now.* Joy's movement inscribes a dimension of infinity that cannot be found in anxiously multiplied variations of desire. Intimacy does not yearn to fill the felt lack; it welcomes the alter whom it receives in faith. Intimacy does not capture the imaginary self or the other, as if ego or alter were the Real to be owned. Faith yields, wonders, ceases to possess itself or another. Yielding in faith to intimacy, there is hope that opens to another; then there *are* the soundings of prayer and joy. Faith's joy and prayer lie in the infinite mystery of self and other.

MEDITATION NINE:
SORROW'S MELANCHOLY HOPE,
SORROW'S FORGIVING JOY

When the weight of memory is unbearable, one hopes to forget; when the pain of loss is unbearable, one hopes to remember. This is the despair of hope that locks the movement of sorrow into the double cycle of melancholy. Melancholy hope suffers with a sorrow that fails to begin innocently. Joy *is* innocence. Where one cannot begin innocently because beginnings were lost or burdened by the past, one suffers unforgettable sorrow. I sorrow over what is, what seems to block joy; I sorrow over what has been and no longer is. There is the melancholy of too much history, there is the melancholy of demise. Old worlds like Europe, Asia, or Africa suffer under the burden of monuments and soil drenched in unforgivable and unforgettable memory of their victims. New worlds like North America suffer from shallow memory of their ancestral struggles and genocides; they suffer from severing native roots (i.e., from deracination).

Sorrow's melancholy hopes are propelled by *anamnesis* or recollection of beginnings that are at once overburdened and lost. Social history and psychohistory are propelled by remembrance of the past. Coming to terms with the past, whether of national crimes or personal trauma, dramatizes political and therapeutic equivalents of sorrow's hope speaking against the unspeakable. But can I win my innocent words by melancholy sorrow?

Freud ascribes to uncanny hope (or he held an unaccounted for hope in the uncanny) that retelling the story of one's trauma under the receptive gaze of the therapist will cause melancholy sorrow to yield to mourning, which in turn will deliver one to hope. While hope is last to escape from Pandora's box, psychoanalysis has no resources of its own to convert melancholy hope into innocence. Its own hope is melancholy rather than uncanny, for its cure relies more on the motion of historical *anamnesis* than on works of love. Just as Sartre's human freedom announces optimistic toughness in the material world of entropy in which hope's passion must be viewed as a useless undertaking, so also Freud's talking cure at best limits the neurotic side effects of lost innocence. The mourned trauma—either too much memory or insufficient roots—delivers one from neurosis to sorrow's melancholy hope. Revolutionary projects, what we might call therapy on a grand scale, always and already suffer from sorrow's melancholy of lost moorings. Revolutions drown the innocence of their liberating words in too much memory or too much loss, and cultural revolutions leap forward by obliterating the roots of speaking in solitude and silence. Human devastation of post-Soviet Russia and traumas of modern China are legion. Is there a therapy for the lost capacity to speak? Revolutions may feed millions in one generation, yet how many generations will it take to pay for loneliness and the unspeakable wastelands of spirit?

Joy does not eliminate all sorrow; it repents its melancholy hope. Sorrow repented is not sorrow forgotten. Sorrow repented is not erased from memory; repenting remembrance *is* prayer's silent joy. What propels repentance? Unlike *anamnesis,* repentance takes its leave without being burdened by the past. Yet unlike the leap of deracination, it need not obliterate true sorrow for suffering. In repentance I leave without melancholy sorrow; in healing and blessing remembrance, I sorrow by coming back to my finitude and temporal limits. In repenting I look back (this is the movement of sorrow without melancholy) in order to begin anew. In repentance I do not recollect what was lost or still is too much to bear. I repeat my beginnings. Melancholy sorrow binds me to my anguished sympathy, my historical self, my personal or revolutionary projects. Repenting repetition lifts my historical burdens in a historical leap forward yet not by forgetting my origins. The repented self dies to melancholy hopes.

But "repentance cannot cancel sin, it can only sorrow over it" (Kierkegaard, CA 115). Repentance transcends the blind revolutionary and therapeutic cycles of melancholy hope, for example, in the enacted repentance of the truth commissions in Guatemala, South Africa, or Rwanda. Yet only the grantings of hope in forgiveness, the intimations of hope in sublime or tragic beauty, and the soundings of hope in the language born of solitude and silence create new beginnings.

It lies within human power to repent. Yet to forgive the unforgivable, to begin in the innocence and newness of creation, and to speak anew out of unspeakable trauma testifies to the uncanny. If the unforgivable, unforgettable, and unspeakable were not *negatively saturated* by what binds them (their negative modality) and *positively exceeded* by what could release them (their positive modality), there would be no uncanny phenomena available to us after the "death of God." The registers of the uncanny, both in their *personal* (what I witness as my suppressed or released self) and *impersonal* (what is blocked or granted, intimated, sounded, gifted) dimensions, thus saturate our postsecular mentality.

Social revolutions by definition do not forgive; they attempt to create anew by enacting a clean slate out of revenge or social liberation. The talking cure mourns and hopes to begin anew. The talking cure leads to the tragic doorstep of repentance, and there one's admission initiates the lifting of the Oedipal blindness. Yet therapy possesses no power of forgiveness, healing, blessing, granting of speech or gift of creating anew. Both therapy to address personal trauma and truth commissions to deal with the social trauma of genocide anticipate gifts of healing that come down like manna from heaven. Neither social revolution nor therapy has the power to impart joy's innocence. Forgiveness, joy, and love's intimacy are uncanny phenomena on which no psychological or social theory has a monopoly. All social theory fails to show how the uncanny can appear again in the killing fields of genocide.

Joy neither forgets (that is why the cosmos reveals an impersonal face of sorrow that is not melancholic *lítost*) nor revels in pain and revenge (that is why genuine creation and forgiveness give birth not out of trauma but in the silent prayer of innocent joy—out of nothing). Sorrow that acknowledges itself in forgiveness receives joy. Works of transformative love differ from both talking and revolutionary cures; they transform our melancholy sorrow by the divine sorrow that is always and already a forgiving joy. Another word for this conversion of melancholy sorrow into forgiving joy is faith in the immemorial past of the promise that the unhoped for is to come. The creative nothing of innocent beginnings *is* joy, its language are the soundings of solitude's silence. Joy does not eliminate sorrow, but forgives its melancholy mourning. Forgiveness converts repentant sorrow into joy. Sorrow forgiven *is* the answered prayer for the innocence of creation in which we all primordially share.

MEDITATION TEN:
LONELINESS, SOLITUDE

Lonely in the crowd, I am imprisoned in my solitary cell. I am confined by an abundance that leaves me empty, by relations without nearness. Loneliness is autistic inwardly, the crowd is lonely outwardly, both arrested in disclosure, so essentially entrenched in disconnection. Moving from my solitary confinement to the general prison population does me no good. How ironic to want to cure one's own loneliness through another! Mere sociality, even gregarious speech, intensifies my loneliness.

Love terrifies loneliness, for intimacy aggravates the anguish of standing alone. Lost to myself, desperate to find another, nakedness demands an account of myself: naked I am born alone, naked I bear dying alone, naked I face intimacy, naked my heart beats in prayer. Nakedness stripped of love terrifies the body's pleasure, for the body is of death; abiding love rescues the body. Without abiding love the self is neither received nor given in faith. Loneliness suffers loveless entropy. "If it were so . . . that we should believe nothing that we cannot see with our physical eyes, then we first and foremost ought to give up believing in love" (Kierkegaard, WoL 5).

Anxious loneliness bereft of abiding love matures into sorrowing loneliness. I view my solitary confinement as misfortune. I sulk, feel sorry for myself, wear loneliness as my fate and even destiny, curse my birth, seek temporary remedies, venture to assign myself some identity. Heroically, I become a monk, solo before God. Yet what monk has not faced the solitary anguish of loneliness? The hazards of religious yearnings imbibed out of the well of sorrowing loneliness are as terrifying as those of nakedness without intimacy. Religious fervor and naked embrace when each is sought out of sorrowing loneliness are like the soul and body in anguish, giving birth to a secretive, aberrant, despairing love. How lonely is the sorrowing piety of a pedophile celibate who craves to possess the infinite in the godly innocence of youth!

Sorrowing loneliness if untreated morphs into despair. To face despairing loneliness, I must sorrow not over the misfortunes of my life but over the self I have not become. I return home to despairing loneliness for the first time as *this* self. I welcome and embrace a prodigal and orphaned self— myself. My truth born of intimacy—that I wander from loneliness home to solitude—is my sole offering to another. Self-offering is prayer's love. Converting loneliness into solitude, I am begotten in and by intimacy. Joy *abides* in getting oneself back in giving oneself. Possessive self grows lonely; solitude's intimate joy *is* agape.

MEDITATION ELEVEN:
ABANDONMENT, SELF-LOVE

Orphaned youth and old age meet each other in the ordeal of their abandonment. The loneliness of those who find themselves abandoned at the very beginning is trumped only by the sorrow of the one who lives too long to have any friends left. Birth and death equally present the trauma of how to heal the unforgivable, bless the unforgettable, and express the unspeakable occasioned in us by the essential setup of life. When the comedies of youth and spring yield to autumnal tragedies, then the winter of death remains as the last single passage following our entrance onto the dramatic stage. Our entrances and exits do not come on majestic thrones or through golden gates. At birth, whether with good or bad parents and homes, we are already shipwrecked; in death we are still or yet again orphaned. The abandonment of birth recollected in death is the last station of sorrowing loneliness. How unhappy, how desperate is the winter of a life that has not loved itself in solitude! How terrifying is dying without the self-love that forgives the cosmos for one's birth and death, the first and last ordeal that makes infants wail at birth and old age bend into earth like the weeping willow!

Whether one is born into destitution, a loveless home, a brothel, or a prison; whether one is orphaned or finds oneself a refugee from one's homeland, one leaves the world alone. The anxiety of abandonment is not the privilege of those who were abandoned by their parents or country. The Jew is quintessentially defined biblically by exodus and in the modern era by diaspora and exile. In that core "Jew" is an icon of the human condition—Adam. And ironically, being a chosen people, Jews are set aside to witness to the universally human singleness of every person. A Jew in this essential witness may neither be assimilated into the crowd nor defined through hate as the one who stands apart from humanity. Jew hatred is a universally human hatred of one's own aloneness; hating the Jew, one hates oneself. A self-hating Jew marks the universal, internalized tragedy of every self-hatred. Hating myself, I flee my abandonment anxiety; I flee through prejudice I project onto the race, sex, ideas of another I decide to hate.

Adam is everyman—the cosmos chose everyone to leave a homeland and to live as an orphan, like the ice birds hovering over the deep waters. In self-forgiving of one's own passage of birth and death, abandonment's fear and trembling convert into an Abrahamic parenting of the human race. In Adam/Abraham—in exodus from self-reliance, in exile from naive home, never setting up the hubris of *causa sui*—I become a parent to myself. That parent, like Abraham offering Isaac to God, cannot hold on to the creative offspring as a possession. In solitude I and my creative deeds are all begotten in faith. Self-love that has been learning to hope is reconciled to its cosmic wounding of birth and death. Self-loathing loneliness becomes healed by self-loving solitude. Then the soundings of silence speak with the language of hope; then in the infinitely vast cosmos there *is* joy and intimacy.

MEDITATION TWELVE:
THE UNSPEAKABLE, SILENCE

Loneliness binds words with an unspeakable trauma; solitude releases them with the soundings of silence. The personal modality of loneliness is to solitude as the impersonal modality of the unspeakable is to silence. Distinct saturated phenomena (i.e., the religious after the "death of God") are disclosed in equal measure by our bondage and releasement. In bondage, loneliness negatively saturates (smothers) words, as they neither speak with intimacy nor console with joy. Other than madmen, only persons with earplugs and cell phones walk on the busy streets while shouting to an empty universe. Should one scream vocatives into the empty chaos of the world? After the "death of God," to whom does one address such prayers from hell? What is a speaking loneliness if not the noise and nonsense of addressing oneself?

Cosmic infinity is cold without intimacy. It becomes too loud to be a solitude. Empty space and runaway time fill with their echoes of nothingness the inner chambers of desperation. When loneliness gets jammed by an unspeakable trauma, its smothered words begin to exceed themselves.

Then loneliness saturates itself negatively, speaking in willed speechlessness, and it utters pain and then falls into silences of anguish.

One is not born lonely; one becomes lonely. One is born and dies alone. One need not die in loneliness. Not speaking, being a newborn infant or one losing memory in death, is not the same as *not* speaking. The unspeakable needs words to bind itself, for its bondage is not silent. The soundings of solitude dwell in silence from which words draw strength. We draw strength from intimacy, we speak out of silence. Intimacy and silence dwell in love of the loved ones even at death. Loneliness binds to a living death; solitude releases even in death to life.

Saturated loneliness exceeds itself, and so it addresses something or someone within itself. Loneliness faces itself alone—it is seeking for the first time its solitude. Loneliness cries out in hope against hope. The language of hope is silence. The unspeakable trauma of loneliness speaks out by having its willed muteness now fall silent. The sounding of hope is solitude; the grammar of silence is joy and intimacy. One prays in solitude, unlike a madman or a man with a Walkman, when joy, intimacy, and silence invoke the living cosmos.

Prayers from Hell

Chrétien (2000:147) turns to prayer as the core dimension in which "the religious appears and disappears." From the end point in our meditations this may be entirely correct, as the act with which one turns to the holy bespeaks hope, and the language of hope, once granted and intimated, is silence, and the grammar of hope that is invoked by intimate silence is what praying and making love mean. From the point of our difficult beginnings, the religious is instituted and destroyed by the possibility of radical evil. I pursued the thought that even after the "death of God," radical evil, even if not prayer, can be apprehended as the negatively saturated phenomenon. I end here where Chrétien begins. With this nuance I likewise try to answer Janicaud's objection to the theological turn of French phenomenology.

Impossible hope that is implored by all those suffering from bodily hunger, immiseration, and hopelessness, and the aggravated scarcity of hope in all acts of radical evil negatively saturate and so eclipse the uncanny. They always and already reach out to the uncanny. The unforgivable parasitically invokes the dimension of forgiveness, the unforgettable overreaches itself into the immemorial and the unhoped for, and the unspeakable addresses something or someone. The unforgivable deeds, the unforgettable suffering, and the unspeakable trauma—all are willing their own bondage.

They are willing bondage for whom and for what reason? If we bracket the madman or the passerby on a cell phone each shouting words for others to hear, then to whom does a despairing, suffering, and lonely heart pour out its anguish in an empty cosmos? I am not raising a cosmological or cosmic design question. Nor am I interested in proofs for or against God's existence. Nor, after reducing proofs to a problematic ontological argument attempting to derive God's existence from an idea of such a being in the mind of a biblical fool who claims God does not exist, am I reducing the religious to something within the bounds of mere reason. I am not interested in moral postulates of hope, immortality, and God. These classical "ways" and their post-Kantian and post-Nietzschean analytic discontents in contemporary proofs or disproofs of God's existence represent but the *aggravated despair of philosophy of religion*.

What must we learn from the form of despair that Kierkegaard calls defiance? The secret, we have seen, is hidden in the question, How is *vocative despair* possible? What does it *say* about itself? Willing one's existence through self-inflicted despair and loneliness testifies to excess. To whom in the empty universe does one address the cry, or why does one intensify such willingness—in despair to will to be oneself? If defiance is not like the mumbo jumbo of a madman, then is not vocative despair a prayer from hell?

Defiance, albeit it is a mute and unspeakably personal modality of the negatively saturated agency, is a form of communicative action. I have noted several times that devils and demons are not atheists. Yet theologies do not customarily ask whether or not one prays in hell. We know from mythologies that defiant spirit beings suffer neither Kantian nor Nietzschean doubts, nor do they suffer the despair of contemporary philosophy of religion. Spirits in hell have an addressee. That vocative defiance is a loud yet *contrarian prayer* of their unspeakable loneliness.

Yet not just the extreme anguish of the demonic but every prayer is always and already the "wounded word." In prayer, just as in acts of intimate love, one stands alone and yet this aloneness is neither a monologue nor soliloquy; one expresses one's deep self and yet does not know how to reach one's depths (Chrétien, 2002:151). Just as lovers do not transmit knowledge, so prayers do not transmit factual data. Functional or information words, seemingly, are just as useless to lovers as they are to addressing the invisible. In prayer's intimacy "the word affects and modifies the sender, and not the addressee. We affect ourselves before the other. . . . We are in and through speech made manifest to ourselves" (153). In nakedness before the lover, in our spirit's nakedness, I come to manifest myself to myself through the alter (154). This is why neither love nor prayer can build on beliefs about the other (a/theism), but rather love builds up love and prayer builds on faith in the other.

In intimacy one is "standing dispossessed of all the beliefs." As I do not know how to speak, love, and pray, I suffer the wound of unspeakable loneliness. Silence, solitude, and intimacy are my teachers. Prayer's difficult and circular beginnings mean that "it belongs to prayer itself that in it alone does the praying man learn that he does not know how to pray" (157). In love's and prayer's intimacy, I do not begin but respond to the call (158). The wound of transcendence does not vanish with familiarity and intimacy among lovers any more than with the holy one; love and prayer intensify the infinite of closeness and otherness (159). "Silence is still allocution," it is a thou. Its intimate stillness brings the other's presence out of silence. "The silence of prayer is here a silence *heard* by God" (160). Love and prayer always exceed their proper measure because one can never exhaust their infinite addressee. And even lovers drink from the infinite in their finite embrace. Words of lovers and meditation break down in whispers, murmurs of the heart, silent absorption, but they do not become unspeakable. "Prayer, like all lovers' speech, bears the weight of giving itself." Intimacy is an "ordeal," hence love is terrifying to the point that one may prefer loneliness to intimacy; prayer in solitude discloses the self as one is. "Speech appears in the attentive light of silence—the voice is truly naked" (161, cf. 167). One is not left alone, as hope prays in us in excess of loneliness saturated by hopelessness. Hope's language is silence, its grammar is joy and intimacy.

As I must be taught to hope, love, and pray, I must be given words of psalms or the song of songs just as the baby is spoon-fed nourishment. Thus the most intense intimacy is "the speech we do not invent, but which invents us, in that it finds us and unveils us there where we were without knowing it" (Chrétien, 2002:172). One does not prattle prayers, one does not say mass or have the rabbi lead the holy day services, just as one cannot have another perform or sell love to us in an erotic salon. One is made anew and released to oneself in intimacy as much as through prayer. In the religions of the Book, "God . . . is Speech" (173) as much as Love. Transcendent, infinite, inexhaustible dimensions of word and love render all human speaking and intimacy always and already wounded. The primordial wounds are inflicted by the cosmos because of the chasm between our finitude and the infinite fount of speech and love. Yet even more important is that wounds are self-inflicted by the abyss between the excess of our hopelessness and the mysterious grantings of hope that teaches us the grammar of beginnings. The language of the granting is sounded by silence; the grammar of granting and intimation is joy and prayer.

Why isn't all our primordially wounded speaking and loving also traumatized, fallen, logocentric, egocentric, violent—essentially, always already unspeakable and unlovable? Why are even self-inflicted wounds, albeit they can occasion anguish, paths that are never closed off to hope? Behold the epiphany of the uncanny in the soundings of silence. The wounds can be of

joy (174) because we are wounded primordially by what precedes our hearing or even calling out. Thus prayers of hope can be sounded from the pit
of unlovable hells and even said in defiance. Who prays to whom in the
negatively saturated excess where words have suffocated speech and love has
died of disconsolation? (What really wounds us in Nietzsche's mad cry,
"God is dead"? Is this not a prayer from our hell, yet still audible as a prayer
to the living cosmos?) It is "the prayer that would go from God to God, in a
voice, and therefore in a human body, the prayer by which God would invoke himself." Prayer is wounded because it is preceded by the one who
teaches how to speak, pray, love. Prayer becomes a wounded word in one's
self-inflicted despair; and then in crying out, one prays with a postsecular,
negatively saturated excess of one's lonely suffering. Prayer is wounded also
as it sounds the silence of those who are without a voice to cry out, as if
"wanting to give voice to all the voices that keep quiet, forbidden from
praying by the play of echoes where they address their individual and collective idols, or by the atrocity of the destiny they endure, whose despair
does not even become a cry that would incriminate God, which can be a
way of praying" (175).

Khôra knows no *teshuvah, tikkun olam, chashmal, berakhah/barakah,* it
is mute and deaf spacing without any ability to hear these blessings or to
pray them in itself or for itself or for another. If there are prayers coming
even from hell, then what do they tell us about this state of one's inability to
love and perhaps even about positively asserted yet inverted ways of praying? How does one pray without knowing the name for love's calling, love's
vocative, one's vocation or command to love? That hell is a state in which
one can still hear and respond makes it infinitely unlike the entropic,
anomic *khôra*. And alone in this ability to hear and respond in anguish lies
the margin for resistance. And hell, albeit tone-deaf to religious music of
the spheres, is not a winter night without hearing and cries. And this fact
about the anguish of defiance accounts for the iconography of the descent
of the messianic light into hell. God is spending in hell the whole eternity
of God's redemptive-though-useless suffering, in God's divine *tikkun olam*
of substitution, and this eternity is the creative interval or moment between
the "death of God" and the new beginning proclaimed already by Solomon
and Ezekiel. Despair of defiance asserts against hope that love must or can
never be as strong as death. *Khôra* that knows no such anguish or defiance
lacks the negatively saturated freedom to resist and so reveal in itself the
scarcity of hope.

If ours were either a completely secular, totalitarian or religiously cocksure, fundamentalist age, we would never discover the wounds of loneliness. Devils and other human-all-too-human agents of radical evil would
have to grow mute and unintelligible in a purely entropic universe; eventu-

ally their defiance would run out of steam. But then the unspeakable would never be able to convert into the words of silence (it would be perpetually deferred as maximized yet unfulfilled, paradoxical intention and desire). Nor would loneliness convert into solitude. And vocative defiance in its anguish could never pray out from hell. The excess of the unspeakable trauma of loneliness *is* our postsecular, negatively saturated wounds. Those wounded prayers reveal what our tragic moments have often sounded as their remnants of joy, intimacy, and hope.

TEN

Without a Why

●

There is purposeless cruelty.

Chapter 9 took us through the twelve steps into crushing sorrow and the despair of loneliness, and twelve steps into the ecstatic joy and prayer of intimate solitude. The thirteenth and last step is also the fourth epiphany of the uncanny. It reveals that annihilating cruelty can be met only with the blessing and gift of unconditional love—if love is as strong as death. If there is will to *annihilation* of spirit (impersonal modality of bondage) and thus human *cruelty* (interpersonal modality of bondage), then why is the possibility of the blessing and *gift* (interpersonal modality of releasement) of love *unconditional* (impersonal modality of releasement)?

More intensely than despair, suffering, and loneliness, cruelty saturates personal bonds with the perverse joy of hopelessness. There is nothing reasonable about cruelty. Cruel acts are so many negatively saturated phenomena. But why is there cruelty in the age of reasonableness? Why is there radical evil at the twilight of the gods? Why should one want or need to be deliberately cruel? Why add that something extra to self-and-other inflicted unforgivable, unforgettable, and unspeakable deeds? What does cruelty bring into murder that is not already accomplished by murder? How can death exceed itself in death? If one truly does not know whether one can ever pray to a living spirit or must always already pass for a believing atheist praying to the empty, unresponsive spacings of the *khôra,* then why do acts of cruelty occur with an apodictic self-assurance, zealotry, and fanaticism? This is so difficult to ponder because there is no rational "why" assignable to cruelty. Cruelty appears as a self-defeating pleasure, malignant sublime, goodwill that becomes utterly self-and-other destructive. Torture and terror are deeds without conditions; they *are* and *are not* at once: they are gratuitous acts of annihilation.

To reach depths in this difficult postsecular meditation on radical evil, I dwell on the unconditioned—the negatively saturated acts, the second-order impossible—without a why. I scaled twelve steps into the sorrows of loneliness, twelve steps into the joy and intimacy of solitude. The thirteenth meditation is suspended between falling into nothing and creating out of nothing, the annihilation of hope and the self-giving of love, uncreation and *agape*, damnation and *berakhah/barakah*.

MEDITATION THIRTEEN: ANNIHILATION, UNCONDITIONAL LOVE

I want us to return for the last time to the Nazi project for what I branded in chapter 5 as the Museum of Radical Evil, the memory site for an annihilated people. Now we can grasp with greater nuance what such space and time would represent. Genocide would be celebrated as a positive, accomplished deed of the unforgivable, unforgettable, and unspeakable annihilation. This memorialization would not have an ordinary antiquarian value, albeit the Prague museum was to gather the precious legacy of Bohemian and Moravian Jews, originally assembled by the Jewish curators of the site for its educational and historical value. The Nazis turned the precious legacy into the festival of death. This is, indeed, an act of positive annihilation. In the world *after* the "death of God" this act makes even less sense than it would in an ordinary religious or ideological warfare. The act performs annihilation or *uncreation*.

We reach at this juncture the zenith and nadir of meditation on radical evil. What makes any evil radical is its annihilation of hope. Its radicality is more than self-interest (Kant); it is a saturated excess of violence that seeks deliberate yet purposeless dissonance of uncreation, an undoing of something or someone into a negative surplus value as tangible nothing. There exists no definable rational purpose for annihilating hope except wanting to intensify despair and turn hopelessness into an accusation. In torture and terror, even the lonely prayers from hell grow silent. The unforgivable, unforgettable, and unspeakable grow into a positive void. What was found as good in coming to be, that is uncreated, and in turn it is now recreated as a negative sum. This positive void of uncreation stands as a dissonant, loud, agrammatical accusation against the granting of hope in forgiveness, a malignant sublime against the intimation of hope in tragic beauty, and sacrilege against the prayerful soundings of hope in silence.

The first mythical couple was given the power to name creatures in the Garden of Eden. One does not create what one names. Yet to name is to speak out of silence with hope, and its grammar is joy and intimacy. This primordial capacity to name grants creatures their living reality; they are sounded out of their silent solitude. In Eden speaking *is* prayer, living *is* joy, and relation with creatures *is* intimacy. Humans in Eden would be like the Prague rabbi Maharal who spoke life into the clay figure of Golem. Humans in hell would be like inhabitants in the Museum of Radical Evil. Annihilating cruelty usurps power to name creation in order to uncreate—to render as unforgivable, traumatic, mute—hope's healing, blessing, and speaking.

But Does Radical Evil Even Exist?

The polarities of creation and uncreation require me to update my meditation on religion and violence from part 2. I cited in the opening of the book the neo-Marxist protagonist of the early Frankfurt School, Horkheimer, who wrote that both theism and atheism have their martyrs and tyrants. In chapter 6 I pondered two other twentieth-century Jewish philosophers, Lévinas and Derrida. The former thinker defines religion as the site in which the violence of totalitarian closure is resisted by every face-to-face encounter. This is his fundamental ethico-religious commandment against the killing of another. The latter finds in radical evil the site in which the religious is both instituted and destroyed; yet because ontological or textual undecidability regarding the two sources of religion, either as messianic hope or as the *khôra,* structurally frames Derrida's thinking about religion without religion, in finite time and space, one is never free from conceptual, metaphysical violence. Derrida can pray at the scene of the best and the worst, because maintaining both words and silences undecidable whether they name hope or the spacing of space; and so praying one can never praise hope even while denominating hope as hidden and incomprehensible (cf. Derrida, D; Marion, 1999). This metaphysical violence of prayer that can never be sure to praise would seem to pervade both the secular and religious worlds. Thinking so at the edge of postsecular hope reveals violence in several of its dimensions. If there were an essential implication between religion and violence, and this would seem to produce invidious undecidability rather than impossibility that would condition every possibility for resisting the scarcity of hope, then neither nonviolent creation nor unconditional love would be possible.

There is *physical violence,* from pain to death. There is *mental violence,* from the conceptual framing of the world that is defined against other thought determinations, to culture that excludes other cultures, to historical forms of civilization and their institutions, all the way to ideologies. There is *spiritual violence,* from entropy of meaning to the second degree of death—despair and annihilation of hope in all relations. Every form of modern violence springs from some form of unfinished secularization or incomplete atheism, from idolatry and so from belief rather than from faith. If we hold the distinction between faith and belief firm, then cruelty, torture, and terror must be rooted in our most intense beliefs in human apotheosis. One can hardly embark on a suicide bombing mission with faith. Unlike belief, faith opens us to an unknown, unknowable, and risky venture. Violence can be traced in all its forms to idolatry, and so to spiritual violence. For this reason we live a two-edged paradox that violence intensifies with an unfinished project of secularization—with dishonest atheism—and at the same time there is nothing wholly secular about violence. Violence is always and already negatively saturated in its overreaching, and yet it is imperfectly spiritual in its annihilation of hope.

All great religions speak about suffering and death. To nourish faith in a supratemporal dimension of the immemorial and the unhoped for, we must begin with an acceptance of our finitude. That is why faith is not a romantic or drug-induced ecstasy, bigoted adherence, fanatical self-lessness. God does not await the suicide bomber any more than do virgins in the pseudoreligious utopia of an erotic salon. Great religions respond to acts of violence with faith. We find a similar response in nonsectarian thinkers of nonviolence with their promise of a radically new thinking. Long before attempts at the destruction of metaphysics and the deconstruction of culture, great religions distinguished between consciousness, in which we perceive and think, and awareness, which leads to awakening. Only modern philosophers in the West suffer from the mind and body problem, but this has little to do with the awakening from which prayer, meditation, and intimacy gather life. It would be illusory to create a department for the propagation of awakening that would comprise many a department for the propagation of doctrines. To conflate faith with doctrine or belief then becomes the catastrophic recipe for ideological violence. Doctrinal efforts—whether the new or old orthodoxy—have little in common with awakening. This is one reason why the axis of theism-atheism is much more appropriate for the matters of *adherence* to something or someone (belief, membership, form of life) than *inherence* in the cosmos, destiny, or the holy (faith, vocation, intimacy). I have stayed away from formulating the nonviolent response to evil as some version of theism not because of my preference for New Age spirituality but rather to make room for postsecular faith *after* the "death of God."

Spiritual violence cannot be resisted through greater adherence to purity of belief or purity of blood. Spiritually intense violence—the demonic —transcends the bounds of culture, orthodoxy, and mere reason. Spiritual violence aims at producing the unforgivable, unforgettable, and unspeakable. The requisite answer to this intensity of violence is the promise of possibility. When one of Kierkegaard's pseudonyms ventures the thought "that everything is possible means the being of God" (SuD 40), he touches on the mystery that hope is attacked by the most intensive forms of violence. That violence lies in will to cruelty and annihilation of another. To destroy the possibility of another is to act with powers of creation in order to undo creation.

What prompts one to become godlike in this contrarian fashion? The will to uncreate—the quintessence of spiritual violence—is unconditional, gratuitous, for it has no reasons but itself. Enter the diabolical that Kant named and feared—a doing of evil for the purposeless purpose of the malignant sublime. Indeed, such doing has no condition, and for this reason Kant denies it legitimacy. Yet could its unreasonableness or the lack of rational motive alone make such acts impossible? We must ponder the possibility of deeds that undo all possibility. In that possibility radical evil partakes in its inverse, perverse form of unconditioned freedom.

What can "purposefulness without purpose" of evil mean if it has no assignable reasons or motives, no conditions to be fulfilled or aims to be followed? Evil struggles with beauty in the naming of creation. While tragic beauty suffers, wanton destruction of beauty is no longer sublime. It is better then to speak of evil for the sake of cruelty. Evil without a why—there is something counterintuitive in wanting to be like the Creator in a godless, *khôra*-dominated universe, someone who creates flaws, creates oneself as a testament to the defect of creation, who embodies the unforgivable, unforgettable, unspeakable accusation, who becomes an anti-Job and anti-Messiah.

Kierkegaard (SuD) distills from the counterintuitive case of possible demonic will an indirect phenomenological awareness of spirit-self, offering us a paradigm case of what I call the negatively saturated phenomenon. Analyzing the forms of despair, he concedes that a truly *secular despair* could produce only two forms: unconscious despair (general cultural neurosis) and the aggravated despair of weakness or the introverted state of despair in which one wills not to be oneself; rather, one wishes to do away with self. In any purely secular age there should be no *religious despair,* the hyperconscious state of existence in which one in despair wills to be oneself. Defiance cannot but be related either to impersonal sources of creation one rejects or, personally, to someone who releases me from despair. Defiance binds me always and already in a refusal of creation and forgiveness. *Khôra* knows no despair, it neither creates nor forgives, it cannot call or respond; and so defying this faceless surd would be performing sheer madness. But defiance is not madness, and devils are not lunatics either, as both reveal a response to a call, or there would be no defiance or cruelty in the first place. Cruelty and deliberate annihilation of others both exist. Hence there is something or someone Other than *khôra* whom one's religious despair defies. The addressee to whom one prays, not just in heaven and on earth, but most of all in the hell holes of the world, is always already decidable as a Thou.

When ordinary despair intensifies into despairing over despair, ultimately anguishing over one's unforgivable state and of oneself as unforgivable, then, redoubling itself, despair morphs into a rejection of forgiveness. Thus is born the third degree of despair that requires, as its condition of possibility, a relation to the one who gives life in creation as well as in forgiveness. Albeit demonic or diabolical defiance is conditioned by this very relation—in that it is negatively saturated by transcendence—I treat it as unmotivated and so unconditioned. Life is given freely, and so its rejection has no assignable terminus except its own freedom *ex nihilo.*

Creation is undone by uncreation; forgiveness is met by the spiritual destruction of hope's possibility. Another evidence for defiance as the negatively saturated, and in that misrelation *religious* or *spiritual,* phenomenon is its false testimony against unconditional love. Only in a finite spirit can freedom to create, heal, bless, and hope produce the unconditional despair of annihilation. The divine spirit's sorrow cannot despair; it always and already creates, heals, blesses, forgives, and loves unconditionally. In a primordial incidence of unconditioned despair of finite beings in time, the key act is their refusal of creation (the impersonal modality of bondage) and of the creator (the interpersonal modality of bondage). In its consequent incidence, despair refuses the gifts of forgiveness (the interpersonal modality of releasement) and unconditional love (the impersonal modality of releasement).

Uncured self-hatred blossoms into the cruel flowers of annihilation. If the cosmos did not call me to a journey of solitude, then my vocative response to an empty universe would be an insane excess. To defy is to respond to the cosmos calling me to a life of vocation rather than empty chaos. That is why mythical vampires, devils, and demons would be comic if we portrayed them as philosophers of religion debating proofs of God's existence, theism, theodicy or the reasons for evil, but never as those who reject the living and loving divinity. No. Demons, like Ivan Karamazov and his Grand Inquisitor, opt for a lonely, that is, unloving and unspeakably mute, existence. There is no secular benefit from deliberate acts of annihilation. All phenomena of wanton annihilation supervene—they are an excess with which secular social theory grapples in vain—even the meaninglessness of entropy and hopeless despair. Annihilating acts of cruelty destroy self-love in victims already assured of their death. One is not left to die as human! No, the annihilating cruelty of meaningless death robs its victims of birth. In this perverse inversion of Genesis, the power to annihilate attests to the spiritual dimension of the human doer who acts diabolically:

the infinite creation is usurped by the doer of evil in order to undo what *is*. *Let joy be not!* The lonely self-hatred, intensified unto infinite degree in cruel annihilation, lives through a diabolical mastery of spiritual entropy—lives on the borrowed powers of *uncreation*.

Two cases assisted us from chapter 5 onward with this most difficult meditation on loneliness. The most baffling remains the intent for a Nazi museum celebrating genocide. As if mass murder were not enough, it was necessary to eliminate every redemptive memory, uncreate all possibility, and unredeem the flow of time as well as any beyond of time, whether nostalgic or longing, whether as the weight of history or as hope for innocence. If the purposeless purpose of hell (a contrarian Kantian definition of beauty) should find an earthly yet otherworldly, malignantly sublime, expression, then the museum of annihilation would witness—against the Jewish witness to the infinite—to the meaninglessness and lovelessness of all creation. The paradigm case of unconditional evil—created for no other sake than its own, yet in spite of the unconditional love of Genesis and atonement—would be the shrine of annihilated hope. By contrast, the countermemorials of human cruelty and victims of history serve as antiredemptory testimonials against wanton annihilation. They neither forgive by uncreation nor elevate the unspeakable into the void of a holy of holies nor consolingly forget the unforgettable. The voids of exile and murder are rendered without representation through a series of absences. The empty and unlit tower of the uncreation suspends the living in the gripping, negatively saturated site of the immemorial and the unhoped-for possibility.

The saturated excess of despairing annihilation is thus nothing remotely secular, and so I find it appropriate to meditate on the diabolical or demonic as the postsecular paradigm of radical evil. The classical mind-set would argue that such evil is a contradiction. Even the modern Kantian mind would define it in such a way as to judge that very possibility unreasonable: the evildoer always seeks some good, finds some pleasure. One never acts for the sake of evil; ergo, evil in the radical sense of the diabolical does not exist. Yet what the reasonable mind does not grasp is precisely the unreasonable as its paradoxically unconditioned possibility. Cruel will still wills to do good, and this is what classical and reasonable minds get stuck on. To understand this despairing, undoing, uncreating, annihilating will, the logical mind fails us. It can play games of a sort. "Radical evil" as evil for its own sake is a logical impossibility because one always seeks some good or pleasure. To grasp this inverted good will, one can no longer stay at the level of moral and rational explanations. Radical evil appears as a postsecular saturated excess that cannot be detected by moral or logical categories. Kierkegaard distinguished between spheres of existence in order to show religious phenomena to be irreducible to aesthetic as well as ethical categories. To grasp how my ethical will to be a good parent, teacher, provider, citizen, churchgoer, and so on, can bring about its own undoing means precisely to become horrified at the goodwill that could become a will to power and evil at its very core. Both despair and evil are self-annihilating, negatively saturated positions; they are not mere negations or absences. Despair is curable by positive acts of faith, awareness, awakening, abiding in hope. Radical evil is healed by forgiveness abiding in unconditional love.

But Does Unconditional Love Exist?

The figure of unconditional love is what students find the most difficult—more so than the thought of evil and despair. Not just that evidence runs against loving without any preferences or conditions, but the very idea that God loves so and commands that we do likewise strikes even the most pious among us as perverse. Human loneliness intensified unto an infinite degree produces living uncreation, a sickness unto death of which one physically cannot die. My strength to love the day of my birth and accept the hour of my death in the midst of lovelessness becomes depleted by the scarcity of hope. Yet this very courage is sought on therapeutic couches, in truth commissions telling of human atrocities, in villages where neighbors who killed and raped one another's families move back as if to resume innocent life, and increasingly on this entire planet. We await the strength and courage to face loneliness on the cruel earth and yet assume it is already in our power. That is our contradiction. Only by loving unconditionally can we experience the ultimate healing of loneliness, cruelty, and despairing will to annihilate oneself or another. Unconditional love we await from parents and homelands, yet its unconditional abiding is the gift of creation and healing. I conclude with three Kierkegaardian figures of unconditional love from *Works of Love:* love believes and hopes all things, love is merciful and forgives, and love abides.

Love Believes and Hopes All Things

One can say this of unconditional but not preferential love. One can say so when the unconditional groundless ground grounds even our love's preferences. Singular love for this or another person begins to hope against its despair by rooting its preferences in what goes beyond them. Thus single lovers too must learn the unconditionality of hope. Against the impulse to annihilate, love without a "why" creates; indeed, it already finds creation beautiful and good without needing to assign it or its love other motives. Love believes and hopes without conditions, for it answers "Why create or love?" by creating and loving. The question, Why do you love me? drives all lovers always and already into a mad despair of infinite regress of the finite "why." Unconditional love neither seeks nor procures such a why. Perhaps hell is the despair of self-hatred that cannot love or be loved without reasons. Love's motion has no other origin or *telos* than creative fidelity and hope emerging out of its depths.

Love's faith "believes all things—and yet is never deceived." Love cannot be fanatical: fanaticism establishes a cognitive relation, love decides. Thus "not everyone who believes all things is therefore one who loves" (WoL, 225). When the fanatic believes all things, love comes under erasure and certainty into foreground. "It is *love* that believes all things." Love does not adhere to a belief but inheres in another. Mistrust destroys love (233). Faithful love is not a blind faith; a fanatical drive for cognitive certainty seeks to blind itself to questions. Love is not deceived by believing in another's possibility, "because to deceive . . . is to deceive oneself" (239). To believe all things renders the believer naively gullible; love believes in the good as a possibility of another. Faith is not a blind certainty of knowledge but a decision to love (231); "*lovingly to believe* all things is a choice on the basis of love" (234f.).

I can only deceive myself. Love that believes all things cannot be deceived, though I could be deceived in fanatically believing all things or nihilistically believing nothing. If I believed nothing at all, then I would deceive myself out of the blessing of self-giving, of "the blessedness of love" (235). The greatest self-deception would be to annihilate love's motion of faith and hope. Self-deception of annihilating will lies in its will to clarity and the good. Yet as love believes in the possibility of another, so also the annihilating will abides by a decision to uproot all faith and hope. Conceptually self-consistent, even radical evil seeks pleasure and joy, and wills to do some good. The annihilating will breaks faith with itself, cuts itself off from hope. If evil were a cognitive category, then radical evil in its diabolical figures would be impossible to think and redress. One could point to its logical impossibility, yet this mental masturbation would do nothing to dislodge the form of willing that decides out of its free unconditionality against itself.

Only in unconditional love does radical evil meets its requisite match. We need not portray this duel in a Manichaean drama. Good and evil, creation and uncreation, are not divinities but modal possibilities of releasement and bondage that define a free spirit's action. Whether or not the annihilating force of evil is as strong as the creating one of love, this question raises a metaphysical, not existential, issue. The Manichaean worldview is cognitively infatuated with the great cosmic battle of personified forces. The unconditionality of radical evil reveals the spiritual core of violence; the unconditionality of love heals self-hatred in self-defense.

Evil begins in mistrust and envy and then mushrooms into "unbelief" and hopelessness. As faith and hope are not cognitive relations, one cannot harp on the formal contradiction in the concept of hopelessness. Evil, like love, is a decision not to believe, to become cut off from hope. "To believe nothing at all is the very border where believing evil begins. . . . To believe nothing at all is the beginning of *being* evil, because it shows that one has no good in oneself." Envy and mistrust "believe all evil." To believe the good in another, to keep positive knowledge of deception and truth in balance, to keep all possibilities for another person open, this "is in itself a blessing" (234). The only ground and *telos* of the annihilating will—its vanishing point—is to give up love altogether. The core of all deception lies in self-deception; the annihilating will believes all things it does as its highest good. The self-contradiction of the morally annihilating will—believing that the destruction of a race of beings is a moral duty—thus cannot be cured cognitively. Just as the addict would not stop self-abuse by getting more education about the consequences of abuse, so telling someone that his will to truth is a will to power and her will to good is a will to evil would do little to reverse that will. In the infinite conception of love, "to be deceived simply and solely means to refrain from loving, to let oneself be so carried away as to give up love in itself and to lose its intrinsic blessedness in that way" (236, cf. 244).

Hope is like the air we breathe. It carries the promise of possibility, the breakthrough of the infinite into the *now:* "Lovingly to hope all things is the opposite of despairingly to hope nothing at all" (248). Hoping always all things destroys fear of the past and the future. In hope one expects the possibility of good. Expectation of the possibility of evil generates fear (249). Hope must not be mixed with nostalgia or longing; hope decides with the infinite dimension of time invading every moment. One cannot create possibility out of heaps of nostalgic and longing instants. Hope does not have beginnings in ordinary time, nor has it history (251). An entire life lived without possibility is marked by despair. One becomes educated by possibility not to fear. Both creation and annihilation relate to possibility; both cognitively apprehend it. Annihilation destroys hope: "To give up possibility is to despair" or "to *assume* the impossibility of the good" at once fears and posits the possibility of evil (253f.).

When despair hopes for nothing, it stimulates itself by "weird phantasmal flashes of possibility" as if to distill hope from its sure demise (254). There is a semblance of justice even among criminals; there is imaginary life in prison. One's hope dies last. Defiant cruelty destroys hope in others. When I give up loving another, I lose love; when I destroy another's possibility, I lose my own hope—like for like, by annihilating another's hope I destroy my own possibility. Anger, bitterness, envy, and malicious joy are many ways that hopelessness tries to destroy possibility in another (257). Auschwitz affected not only its victims and perpetrators but also the generation of bystanders and the generations still coming to terms with it. Hope is a gift, it cannot be commanded, its fabric is fragile, and it grows back slowly. Hoping for Germany, Israel, Rwanda, Sudan, Iraq, Bosnia means to inscribe possibility into a history of suffering and destruction. Eternity's law of "like for like" applies here: to despair over another is to despair of oneself; to destroy another's hope is to annihilate it in oneself (256).

Perhaps the scarcity of hope lingering after acts of annihilation is even more devastating among survivors who cannot forgive the perpetrators, and even more so in scarce hope for the next generation. I gain nothing by giving up love for another, yet love cannot be bought or achieved by a method. How does possibility appear? We have meditated on its uncanny granting, intimation, and sounding. Ultimately wanton destruction can be met only by unconditional love, and even there the gift can be rejected. Possibility is not an idea or idol but more like an icon through which "the eternal touches the eternal in a human being" (258). While I abide in love and love abides in me, at "every moment" I renew possibility. "Love hopes to the limit, yes, to the 'last day,' for not until then is hope over." To hope is to dwell in joy. Yet without love, "hope would not exist either; it would just remain lying there like a letter waited to be picked up" (258f.). What kind of hope is neither deceived nor shamed? Hoping nostalgically or with melancholy longing, "wishing, craving, expecting," is not to hope (262). Envy stretches across the passage of time and extends from hell to paradise; its idols are put to shame (263). Hope's icon does not envy; love opens in another the transformative *now*-time of hope.

Excursus on Idol and Icon, and Roots

I want to ponder the example of Chiapas from chapter 5 in order to elucidate the postsecular hope for roots. The difference between modern racial identity and cosmological roots is driven home definitively by the Mayan struggle. Shortly after the Zapatista uprising in 1994, a controversy arose over the so-called San Andrés Accords on Indigenous Rights and Culture signed between indigenous communities and the Mexican federal government. The accords were intended to recognize Mayans as a distinct people with a right to indigenous self-governance, law, education, use of natural resources on their lands, and customs. The Mexican federal government consistently misinterpreted the Mayan struggle for recognition as a cultural and social particular that could be brought under the liberal democratic umbrella of the modern, deracinated, social and political universal. The accords do not intend to safeguard the Mayan interest in race as a democratically organized social or national identity. Their struggle is not nationalist in either the classical European struggle for sovereignty or the derivative black nationalist political struggle informing racial social formation. The accords promise to preserve an autonomous space of hope for the Mayan roots and safeguard their received cosmological sensibility and organize indigenous political and local culture. While partisan interest in racial or national identity formation is a modern secular project that complements social struggles for political and economic equality; the interest in indigenous roots underwrites how one is to think about social, political, and economic projects in the first place. In the Mayan struggle, the roots ground social identities, not vice versa. Subcomandante Marcos, an educated outsider to the Mayan culture, speaks for indigenous interests more like a poet-cosmologist than like a critical race theorist. Identity delivers peoples to a developmental, evolutionary, activist standpoint; roots embody a cosmological, transformative, and ultimately spiritual angle of vision. The Chiapas populations in resistance (they are well informed by the context of the modern world in which their struggle transpires) strive to preserve a radical memory of hope, and for this aim they nurture their roots. One can be against invidious assimilation and genocidal nationalism alike, but can one sustain either course of action by conserving hope as mere secular identity formation? Do *postsecular roots* make just a difference in degree or all the difference in kind?

The danger of ethnic cleansing, invidious assimilation, and imperial nation building, on the one hand, and the conservation of race that would not foment national, ethnic, or holy wars of terror (or those against it), on the other, persists whether or not one thinks as a secular or postsecular theorist. Postsecular thinkers engaged in redemptive critical theory are in a stronger position than either a secular Marxist or nationalist to challenge religiously inflected social integrations. A postsecular theorist can critique religious forms of invidious nationalism or fundamentalism immanently. To unmask them as social formation proffers external criticism; to speak of them as new sacralizations of identity formation exposes them at the root of false hope.

A cosmological or spiritual sensibility for racial, ethnic, or cultural roots lives at the heart of all people and also in North America. It defines the nonviolent vision of Martin Luther King Jr., as much as the transformative ethic that Malcolm X discovered on his Mecca pilgrimage. It forms the core of Cornel West's existential and prophetic articulation of race matters as well as Eduardo Mendieta's or Enrique Dussel's integration of critical theory with liberation philosophy in the interest of Latin American and Hispanic people. Native American cosmologies are among the oldest, richest roots of the continent. Even if a racial partisan refrains from examining the mythical dimensions of race or, like Habermas (2001:114), suffers from tone-deafness to religion, the secular theorist ignores postsecular sensibility today at the peril of failing to challenge the invidious claim to roots that most forms of secular nationalism and religious fundamentalism profess. The distinction between identity and roots is forced on us in the twenty-first century with terrorism and wars on terror alike, as each is an outgrowth of deracination in religious as well as secular terms. Outlaw's (2005) partisanship for DuBois's "racial formation" views nationality in a noninvidious manner of universal solidarity. Still a derooted race seems just as empty as the one assimilated into class or ideal society by white Marxists or liberal democrats.

I offer a maverick suggestion inspired by Marion's (1991) religious distinction. Hoping to improve on Heidegger's momentary nationalism in the interest of German folks, he proposes to overcome onto-theo-logy. Ontotheology, a "God" fashioned along the lines of theistic philosophical metaphysics was supposed to die with Nietzsche's proclamation of the "death of God." But Nietzsche did not end the search for roots; he only hoped to transvalue our search by giving up the notion of God as value, thus the idea of all values. At the twilight of idols, which every "God" of ontotheology always and already incarnates, our deracinated age, fearful of its nothingness, adopts secular values to replace those invented by human theistic integrations. It is at this juncture that I am interested in Marion's distinction between idol and icon (7–52).

Why not think of race or the broader categories of ethnicity and culture along the lines of either idols or icons? While idol and icon are neither pure social constructions nor biological reductions, there is a difference between what substantial and concrete humanity means in terms of social identities and what in terms of individual roots. Race, ethnicity, culture, and even religion regarded as idols signify forms of religious or secularized value-positing and linguistified, partly acquired and constructed, social identities. Idols are fulfilled intuitions of human-all-too-human intentions. Even a religiously tone-deaf critical theorist can appreciate the political dangers of theistic idolatry, whereby one's intentions—race or nation or culture—come to occupy the onto-theo-logical place of "God" in the role social, cultural, or racial supremacy. Claims to racial or cultural, even religious, supremacy express misguided claims to roots, a desire to be "God" otherwise such claims really mean nothing to worry about. Idols of one's own kind (and these can be any social identity) allow one to love one's land and people. Idolatry differs from the finite love of idols, as in the former identity formation idols becomes absolutized. Idolatry arises from self-apotheosis of human values, and religious fundamentalism, secular nationalism, imperialism, and racial supremacy are the prime examples of idol worship.

If we regard race, ethnicity, culture, and religions as icons, we open cosmological, I admit spiritual, windows through which one either discovers or apprehends one's roots. Idols represent social mirrors through which we pursue regulative ideals of selfhood or humanity; icons open faces with cosmic eyes or windows deeper than the Hubble telescope or ancient wells through which cosmos calls us to self. Hope announces a homecoming to self. As idol is to social identity, so icon is to roots. In idolatry we worship social or psychological identities, so many hopes, as if idols, even in theism, contained cosmological roots. If modern dangers of carving and conserving idols are legion, must we not conserve races, cultures, and religious symbols as icons but never as idols?

One may love one's racial, ethic, and cultural identity, all social values, in a finite, multicultural, nondivinized manner as one loves ethnic food, clothing, music, or sex. One may desire transgressing all social frontiers. Can self-love remain noninvidious when I do not know my identity as distinct from my roots? Must I not learn that the latter are never in anyone's possession? For those with spiritual or cosmological sensibility, whether among modern individuals or various indigenous peoples, roots always play a revelatory role. That is why, like icons, roots revealed in race, culture, or religion open a window beyond the social universal to the infinite. To be a Jew is to become a witness to the infinite, but neither secular nor fundamentalist Jew could say just that and no more.

Roots are to theism as icons are to idols. We must hold the distinction between idol and icon minimally to resist the genocidal impulse and the terrorist desire to become "God." We could meditate in truth about our age as follows: identity formation should replace neither the twilight of idols nor the revelation of one's uncanny post/modern deracination. Or, negatively, with the conclusion of Albert Camus's *Rebel,* humans must tell one another that none of us is God. What should one say positively about ancient roots? Once we become sufficiently and properly a-theistic and so learn to resist idol worship in our postsecular age, what icons are we to conserve beyond political projects, rap songs, sects, and received national or social identities? We may hope that any racial, cultural, religious partisanship would stimulate future generations to pursue the questions of faithful adherence and vocation to their cosmological roots in hope.

Love Is Merciful and Forgives

Love seeks love, yet its agape work is a secret effort without effort, a wu-wei revolution in one's spirit, a gift and not reparative justice (WoL, 264ff., 218). Redoubling of love creates anew, it heals what was broken, it works in forgiveness (281f.). As a "blissful confusion," love's "revolution from the ground up" confuses the economies of exchange and possession (266). This is the revolutionary secret of love: "All things are mine—I, who have no *mine* at all" (268). One finds courage to give all away, but to find love. Singularity intensifies in love, as in its intimacy one stands alone (271). To love is to help another "stand alone" (274), not to make a dependent (275). The Creator's love is everywhere and yet it is hidden. We each stand alone and yet with another's help, and this gift is like a hidden midwife. Love's forgiveness and mercy are self-annihilating, making their works "nothing" in the eyes of the one helped. But this is exactly the opposite of despairing, antiredemptory, willed annihilation of cruelty (278). The atheists among analytic philosophers of religion object to God's hiddenness, yet this lament does not yield a consolation of their philosophy but a despair of the argument. The objection to hiddenness of forgiving and merciful love misconceives love's works, for "it is every human being's destiny to become free, independent, oneself" (278).

Love remains a secret gift in creation. Love is wooing me to its ground without waiting on my petition for forgiveness and mercy. Wooing me through singular self-recovery, love works its new creation in hiddenness as well. The child who knows no evil and finds no pleasure in it is the prototype of love that forgives. Love grants forgiveness, first, by hiding a multitude of sins (282–88). Second, love forgives in silence, as if to infuse life to smothered words, as if to reverse the tongue of slander, as if to quench hate's arson (289–91). Third, love finds joy in explaining all sins away, seeking mitigating explanations. Imagine how the world would be transformed through a league of those who sought the good and mitigating explanations for horrendous evils we commit, if love stood guard next to state prosecutors and judges who bring us to justice. "Believing all things in love and hoping all things in love are the two chief means that love, this lenient interpreter, uses for the mitigating explanation that hides a multitude of sins" (294). Finally, forgiveness "blots out" sins. Just as creation makes something at the beginning, so forgiveness gifts someone who lost oneself with a new beginning. Both acts require faith, as both creation and forgiveness are invisible, unbearable, without analogy in experience, and irregardable. Creation and forgiveness burst into our lived time with the infinite in every now. This brings redemption into the messianic now-time, and if love is not discovered in time, no afterlife can teach it. Creation and forgiveness arrive in time's passage not out of its nostalgia or longing. Nostalgia lives on one's inability to forgive and forget; it keeps the future hostage to the past in ways that must not be redeemed. Longing desires absolute beginnings, and it adheres to a godlike standpoint that finite creatures can never inhabit.

Unconditional love is not stupid or naive; it suffers sin as what it is. Yet love's mercy and forgiveness alone, not the annihilation of evildoers, removes radical evil's positive claim to have the final word. Should the unforgivable of Auschwitz have the final word? Should it become the memory site of destroyed hope, the final accusation that even Job could not answer?

But then would not we always and already live in the museum of our annihilation? What is more defiant and/or offensive: to insist on the unforgivable as our scarcity of hope or to allow impossible hope that even the unforgivable may be forgiven? The former act is always and already negatively saturated, as if gazing with Job's horror at Auschwitz with but a phantom limb of piety. It is the act of forgiveness and mercy, unlike sin that has just been blotted out, that must be believed, as that healing act has been unseen. By faith one becomes aware of the invisible and supratemporal dimension of creation all the way down within the visible and temporal. By love's forgiveness one becomes aware that sin is hijacked away from the visible and temporal. "Both are faith." In this most intense modality of the uncanny, forgiveness is just as mysterious and wondrous as genesis (295).

Paradoxically, forgiveness falls under the formal category of uncreation, just as does the annihilating will. One uncreation stands at the apposite of the other. The self-annihilating secret gift of unconditional love stands to the annihilating worm of cruel will in the analogical way as the uncreation of sin in forgiveness is to the uncreation of another person in wanton annihilation. We reach at this juncture the greatest intensity of modal opposites. In uncreating the living person, the annihilating will wants to remember its cruelty. It wallows in the despairing joy of defiance, and finally it positively usurps the power of creation yet without the force of its love. Love's hope gifts with the fullness of being; it creates the person whom it finds good and beautiful. Love's forgiveness blots out sin by turning to the person rather than gazing at the sin. Unconditional love uncreates and heals what it finds broken in a person, yet without ever ignoring the act—the unforgivable, the unforgettable, the unspeakable. Love heals and restores the person to the possibility of goodness and beauty: *Kyrie eleison* and *teshuvah,* mercy of forgiving, *tikkun olam,* mending, *chasmal,* speaking out of silence, and *berakhah/barakah,* blessing the whole person. Forgetting to gaze at sin like Benjamin's *Angelus Novus* staring at human history of catastrophic progress, hope arrives to restore the person. "Forgetting, when God does it in relation to sin, is the opposite of creating, since to create is to bring forth from nothing, and to forget is to take back into nothing" (296).

Unforgiveness continues sin; it enlarges and nourishes it. In the human spiritual capacity to saturate the negative with the infinite, sin to the nth degree becomes the denial of possibility. To deny forgiveness is to annihilate hope. Negatively saturated unforgiveness *that there is no possibility* for oneself or another, this perverse faith or hopelessness becomes one's "new sin." In a weak form, addiction to the state of sin is like a jammed house of unforgiving despair. One prefers to die of one's self-inflicted abuse rather than wake up from it. In the aggravated scarcity of hope, in its defiant form, the uncreating and annihilating cruelty provides the ultimate, rather strange meaning to action in one's refusal to accept forgiveness and thus to forgive oneself (297ff.). Radical evil in the will to horrendous and cruel deeds might be a conceptually contradictory if not aporetic category. Yet if it is understood as an inward decision of the split self, then "one can speak of thriving in connection with evil." Evil acts take on love and forgiveness as their direct targets and aim at a purposeless purpose ("without a why" standing at the apposite of another). We witness this counterpoint of unconditionality as a mysterious postsecular saturation in all acts of radical evil. Unconditional evil fails to prevail against the environment of unconditional love that starves the purposeless tumor. "When the sin in a person is surrounded by love, it is outside its element. It is like a besieged city . . . it is like someone who has been addicted to drink, is placed in reduced circumstances . . . and now . . . waits in vain for an occasion to become stimulated by intoxication" (298).

Love Abides

To claim that "love abides" in the desert of hope in which the saturated phenomena of radical evil are the only echoes of the uncanny could strike many as at best counterintuitive and at worst sacrilegious. It would be the latter only ironically, to be sure, and I am not proposing a Manichaean worship of evil. Yet our sense of cruelty and annihilation is at times taken by the present age as our sole intuition that something holy has been violated. It appears that God has withdrawn and is "far off in heaven" (WoL, 301). So is it not to pontificate if one says that love abides? Does the claim violate some strange sense of the sacred whose traces were left behind by the exiled God in our valley of tears? "Meet all the terrors of the future with this comfort: love abides; meet all the anxiety and listlessness of the present with this comfort: love abides" (WoL, 301).

Love is "the third"; it is neither I nor the other. The *how* of love informs my releasement or bondage. Do I love in despair or faith? The third is the mode of my loving. That is why the cruelty of annihilation is at bottom destructive self-love. All personal modes of bondage choke love in that I love myself badly. I break myself by false love, I hate what I love, I love hatingly, I am cruel. The impersonal mode of love delivers the epiphany of the uncanny rescue with which I am restored to the immemorial past and to the radical memory of hope. God is Love, yet to me this *how* of all loving is available as the third, as a mode of my comportment rather than as a theism, that is, as a concept or idol.

God is not a concept but a relationship, and this relation is not a logical but a living one. Despair of modern philosophy of religion lies in its love of formal relations, yet God is the third and this is not even the third of the Hegelian ever-moving syllogisms.

In the divine comedy, love is a holy threesome (301, 305, 339). That love abides, *there is love,* names unconditional love's changelessness (303, 308). We must not think of abiding love's supratemporal mode metaphysically. Love is not an unmoved mover. No. Love is supremely moved. The abiding third touches the abiding in me and between us. This is love's decisive moment, always to renew faith's hope to love. Preferential loves evolve in time; their hopes break without the aid of unconditional love. Hope moves love to its ground in the infinite, its movement is not nostalgic or longing, it is not of the passage of time. Time overpowers preferential loves; its "why" collides with eternity. Agape abides without a "why" (311f.).

In chapter 7, we witnessed Jankélevitch's tragic sense of the unforgivable: one cannot forgive those who do not ask for it. Unconditional love works abidingly without waiting on a request of forgiveness, as repentance aids the one who receives, rather than the one who gives forgiveness. Unconditional love requires neither punishment nor penance for its works; the latter two are required, as moral and political thinkers from Kant to Hegel and Marx recognized, by our inward weakness or inability to receive hope. Punishment and penance are supplements of the unforgiven that require them in order to forgive itself and thus to receive healing. Yet even capital punishment, that odd supplement to Christian morality, of itself does not bring inner consolation to the survivors or the condemned criminal who accepts it as justice. Thus every execution, even of the worst offender, sends strange tremors through retributive hearts.

Will not the annihilating and cruel will prevail when its sufferers, the aggrieved, the survivors withhold all promise of forgiveness? I want to echo the great spiritual insights of two twentieth-century secular Jewish thinkers already mentioned. Arendt (1951:459) early on in her work unmasked the perversion of radical evil in any act that willingly makes human beings "superfluous." Kofman intimated that to forgive would also have to reveal the humanity of the cruel masters. From the moral point of view, radical evil can neither be repented nor repaid. It is in this sense that the contested notion of radical evil as something gratuitously cruel always escapes us. Radical evil exceeds the moral bounds at both ends, in acts committed and retributions sought. It pretends to be moral in violating the moral sense, yet it is seeking cruelty as its supramoral good and pleasure. It also pretends to be immoral in making forgiveness unavailable in repentance and normatively impossible through legislation. One cannot repent oneself back into ethical life; one cannot legislate forgiveness. Amnesty and pardon fall as short as ethical deeds seeking to repay and so heal the breach in human hope. It is *this* second-order impossibility that has drawn our attention to radical evil as the religiously or spiritually saturated phenomenon even as evil often pretends to move within the banal, moral, or paradoxical discourse. To take at their word radical evil's "good" and "pleasure," as if these aims provided evidence for the logical incoherence of evil as a malignant sublime, would be the same as to take the heroin addict's vision of paradise earnestly. Only a formal or naive talking head would rest assured by a broken spirit's pretense of operating by a will to some good or pleasure. What such will to pleasure and good embraces is a path to utter ruination. It is the very prospect that the antiredemptory designs of the cruel will might become victorious that compels me to reject Jankélevitch's acceptance of the unforgivable as a positive surd with which to make my peace.

We must pray even from hell, pray to be able to forgive and love in hell in order to safeguard the promise of hope for the victims of history, hope that they may be redeemed beyond the fate assigned to them by the cruel masters of history, hope that love is as strong as death. Unconditional love can muster the only lasting, deep response to the intensity of evil lodged in the acts of uncreation by the unconditionally annihilating will. "In the absolute sense, to forgive is not the conciliatory spirit if forgiveness is asked for; but it is the conciliatory spirit to need to forgive already when the other perhaps has not head the slightest thought of seeking forgiveness" (WoL, 336). "It would be a weakness, not love, to make the unloving one believe that he was right in the evil he did" (338). If hope for another is hoping for oneself (255f.), then to love and to forgive are the only things worth living for (376–86). Beliefs are not sufficient unto themselves, nor are philosophical arguments for or against theism (375). My forgiveness to another is always my self-forgiveness, the forgiveness received (380). The saturated mode of the holy is this "like for like" to the infinite degree: "God is actually . . . this pure like for like, the pure rendition of how you yourself are. . . . God's relation to a human being is at every moment to infinitize what is in that human being at every moment." In solitude's soundings of silence, do we hear echoes of hope or despair? "If you have never been solitary, then neither have you discovered that God is; but if you have truly been solitary, then you also learn that God just repeats everything you say and do to other people; he repeats it with the magnification of infinity" (384).

Arendt (1951:476–79, italics mine) concludes her brilliant work on totalitarianisms and tyrannies of the modern era with her secularly uncanny thoughts about loneliness and its intrinsic connection with the growth of ideology and terror. It bears rereading the way she points social theorists and activist toward the redemptory quality of human beginnings in intransitive hope for freedom found in one's recovered solitude:

> Loneliness is not solitude. Solitude requires being alone whereas loneliness shows itself most sharply in company with others. . . . Solitude can become loneliness; this happens when all by myself I am deserted by my own self. . . . What makes loneliness so unbearable is the loss of one's own

self which can be realized in solitude, but confirmed in its identity only by the trusting and trustworthy company of my equals. . . . What prepares men for totalitarian domination in the non-totalitarian world is the fact that loneliness, once a borderline experience usually suffered in certain marginal social conditions like old age, has become an everyday experience of the growing masses of our century. . . . But there remains also the truth that every end in history necessarily contains a new beginning; this beginning is the promise, the only "message" which the end can ever produce. *Beginning, before it becomes a historical event, is the supreme capacity of man; politically it is identical with man's freedom.*

In solitude, then, unconditional love speaks to each one of us in joy and intimacy from our silences and voids. In loneliness one shouts into empty space and time while desperately hiding from oneself. And so suspended between hope and abyss, we dwell huddled in homes and cities that hurry the hourglass to our sure demise. But if praying only the lonely and cruel prayers of despair, forgetting to pray for one's ability still to love even in hell, one awaits the immemorial beginning and the unhoped healing of radical evil in vain.

EPILOGUE

Job Questions the Grand Inquisitor

Dostoyevsky's last novel, *The Brothers Karamazov* (2003), offers a sharp literary confrontation with radical evil. I saw the novel staged at a Czech theater, Husa na provázku, on the second night of Passover, also Christian Holy Thursday, after I completed this book. I was invited by Petr Oslzlý, the theater director and a former adviser in Václav Havel's first presidency, to conduct an afterplay night discussion in the "Cabinet of Dostoyevsky." The series of Dostoyevskian dramatizations by the dramaturge, Vladimír Morávek, and the night discussions on the productions form part of this avant-garde theater's vocational role to speak to the heart of the dominant Czech self-irony. The theater is raising Dostoyevsky's questions of faith and unbelief, fundamentalism and religious terrorism, and what also Lévinas learns from him in this regard about the end of theodicy, hence useless suffering of innocents. In a substitution of responsibility for the other, useless suffering transforms into redemptive suffering. These questions are prophetically posed for the twenty-first century. My reflections recorded from that wondrous night, April 13, 2006, gather what I want to communicate in these meditations.

FOUR BROTHERS, ONE SELF, ONE BUFFOON FATHER, ONE FATHER IN HEAVEN

Freud discovered in the four Karamazov brothers—Alyosha, Ivan, Dmitry, and the illegitimate son Smerdyakov—inward aspects of the same self. In the Czech staging I witnessed a psychoanalytical drama of inwardness refracted through redemptive criticism. Fyodor Pavlovich Karamazov, father of the four, appears on stage from the start as a corpse, yet his presence is reincarnated through his sons in whom the father's voice and character periodically come to life in shrieks and violent personae of the old buffoon. All the brothers struggle with the internalized destructiveness of their father. Begotten by the earthly father of hatred, the fragmented self searches for itself. The stage between heaven and hell lies in human inwardness.

Just as in the testing of Job, Dostoyevsky lets God place the Karamazov self on trial by the devil. While Job's trial has a Russian Orthodox setting (all characters, particularly Alyosha, his sage teacher Elder Zossima, and the Grand Inquisitor appearing as a fictional character within a fiction, speak in a Christian dialect), it would be a mistake to miss its universal significance. Job appears as everyman in an existential drama of human suffering in which each person is drawn on stage both as witness and actor in one's own inwardness. Zossima narrates the "spiritual awakening" he experienced at the age of eight during a reading of the story of Job (377ff.). Many years later Zossima fathomed Job's fidelity to God: suffering or witnessing the demise of the innocent without falling into nihilism and despair about the reality of love and forgiveness reveals the promise of a new creation in forgiveness and responsibility for the suffering of others. The role of the devil, revealed to Ivan (820, 828), is to test Job's, indeed everyone's, lived answer to suffering and moral evil.

The central dramatic plot of the book turns on the parricide. The book concludes with Dmitry being exiled permanently to Siberia for the murder committed by the bastard son—Smerdyakov (Stinker). By killing the old man, Smerdyakov embodies Ivan's idea that without God everything is permitted, all is lawful (110, 753, 798, 808). Smerdyakov commits suicide on the eve of the court sentence, and by taking all evidence of his guilt to the grave, he brings Dmitry to an unjust sentence and Ivan to a spiritual breakdown. Ivan plans his brother's escape, whereas Dmitry accepts the unjust penalty as his assumption of greater guilt and responsibility than all others, his substitution for the other, hence as redemptive suffering (652, cf. 101, 106, 369). Dmitry's response to the sufferings of the other is quintessential Judaism in ways Lévinas comes to embody the anti-idolatrous law and ethics of responsibility in his work. At the same time, it reveals *for us*, who come later, the low Christology and the post-Holocaust ethics of suffering God of Abraham, Isaac, Jacob, Job, and Jesus. Ivan collapses mentally under the weight of having desired divine parricide (190, 782). He suffers responsibility for destroying the "idea of God" (829), to wit, for creating a world in which everything—including diabolical parricide and judicial error—is permitted.

Who was killed? Who is the murderer? Alyosha alone believes in Dmitry's and Ivan's innocence. Dmitry had reason to hate his father for disinheriting him and for courting his lover, the harlot Grushenka, whom both intended to marry. Ivan inhabits a world in which God became dead (178f.,

308, 320, 829; cf. 89). Yet neither brother committed the earthly parricide, though both mutinied against the heavenly Father. Alyosha witnesses in each brother's life the dramatic setup in which the devil instigates the inward trial. The devil appears as the variously masked character throughout the story: as father Karamazov the devil is the lying "old buffoon" (55–65), as Smerdyakov the devil is the self-loathing Judas-self hiding from itself (771–93), in Ivan's rationalist nightmare the devil is the unforgivable and unlovable Hamletian ghost (811–31). The devil never materializes as a self-standing person or god. The buffoon, the stinker, and the demonic apparition all stand for abject aspects of oneself. Smerdyakov casts the shadow of nonintegrated self. The devil murders in us by killing life and being the life killed (607, 609ff., 614, 623, 796). The bastard son commits parricide beckoned by the internal voice of the unloving father. The radical evil of defying the loving and forgiving Creator—the essential spiritual meaning of parricide—lies in one's unforgiving and unforgivable heart. The crime against heaven cannot be morally or legally repaired; it can only be redeemed in spiritual *metanoia,* change of heart, forgiveness, *tikkun olam,* the resurrection of God in the heart. Dmitry rises from the dead in himself as he is taken away in handcuffs.

Alyosha's teacher Zossima, whose dead body stinks (in this way the stinker-devil tests Alyosha to mutiny arising from his naive religious expectations of material proofs for Elder's resurrection, 423–42, 813–15), is an icon of the loving Father. Zossima defines hell not as some eternal place of damnation but rather as the "suffering of no longer being able to love" (417), self-hatred (531). Alyosha's faith in innocence lifts up all Karamazovs to the Father who creates and forgives, who thus brings into coincidence the fragmented, abject, loathing self.

THE GRAND INQUISITOR:
A FIGURE OF RADICAL EVIL

In the poem narrated by the rationalist doubter, Ivan, to his saintly brother, Alyosha, the Grand Inquisitor (GI) appears as a prophetic figure of diabolical will. The genius of the GI is the versatility of evil. Ivan's poem speaks about the seventeenth-century inquisitor in Seville intending to burn at the stake Jesus of Nazareth, who dared to show up again with his message of love, yet the story applies to all modern regimes that underwrite power with religion. In the character of the GI, official Christianity is put on trial in the role written by the Gospel narratives of the Paschal mystery for the Jewish high priest. All Christians, not just Catholic Rome, become guilty with the blood of the Redeemer. The GI has been appearing with increasing frequency in the past hundred years on the secular political left and right as well as globally across the secular-sacred divisions between theism and atheism. As a metaphorical Antichrist, the GI becomes a natural ally of Nietzsche's grammatical "death of God."

The GI appeases human conscience by taking away human freedom. While the main silent character in the story is Jesus, the GI's harnessing of the three temptations of Christ could be retold as one more rationalization for Job's suffering. Christ is tempted by the devil to turn stones into bread, fly off the highest point of the temple relying on angels to save him, and bow down to the devil in exchange for worldly power. He is told that he suffers because of hunger, anomie, and loneliness. The GI makes the following Faustian bargain with our suffering: I take away all your suffering and you give me your conscience, I eliminate hunger, fear, and loneliness, and you give me your freedom. The GI aims to fulfill Schelling's speculation that for evil not to be possible, God would have to be impossible. Pretending to better God, to wit, using power to create the world that would eliminate all suffering, the GI is bent on destroying the idea as well as the inner need for God. But is not the Promethean offer to escape the twin evil of finitude and death what ultimately motivates all deeds of radical evil and spiritual violence?

In order to eliminate human suffering, the GI corrects God's world by creating a religious-political constitution based on miracle, mystery, and authority (333–35). The first core article grants us free bread, the second provides for "a *community* of bowing-down" (331), and the third gifts us with a master to worship in order to appease our conscience. The miracle of five loaves of bread shared among five thousand will never be reproduced in a polis, as humans in their psyche are incapable of sharing material resources; they will always kill each other for them. The GI's conservative revolution is a regime change (partly socialist and partly authoritarian, prophetic of modern times in both senses) that does not require a change of heart. The GI's miracle of feeding the hungry redistributes our wealth, satisfies our need for material security, and requires vesting our freedom in the regime. While the plank based on the miracle of free food represents a socialist engineering solution to a conservative view of evil human nature, the plank based on mystery exhibits neoconservative features of elites suffering and deciding for the gullible masses. Since we do not alive by bread alone, we need to be nourished by larger meanings.

The GI's elites alone bear the true knowledge that there is no mystery and life has no meaning, but we will be spared this revelation in a community of bowing down to GI's ideology. We will be given circuses, games, and permission to sin and with this allowance we never have to suffer sin consciousness. We will kill in holy wars and come home celebrated as heroes. The plank based on authority cuts across the full political and sacred-secular spectrum, as it absorbs all debates between theism and atheism into a single diabolical solution: the GI takes the place of both religious and secular gods and so satisfies the deep human yearning to find a master to yield one's freedom and abdicate one's conscience. The most evil regimes of power unite the secular and religious authority, state and church, the roles of king and divinity.

Job questions the true nature of the GI in all incarnations. The core of his challenge is the law of anti-idolatry: If there is no God, then why are you so willing to play one as an idol? If there is no conscience and all is permitted, then why do you want to appease my responsibility? If God is so oppressive to freedom, then why do you require me to abdicate it to your authority?

The GI's defiance reveals that neither he nor Ivan could be called ordinary atheists, as they freely decide to give back the entry ticket to God's world, recognizing but rejecting the world's Creator, thereby relating to God personally yet without faith (308, 320, 797). Both Ivan's cynically nihilistic claim that "without God all is permitted" and Žižek's (2006) fundamentalist caricature of it, "with God all is permitted," show the abuse of the religious. On either side, God appears as a disciplinarian of conscience, not a God of freedom. This is how the GI's authoritarianism functions: manipulations of conscience invade one's inwardness as a stench of perversions permitting evil deeds and yet decaying with them. When I ponder Žižek's retort to Ivan, I realize how far the modern era has gone since Nietzsche first lamented the "death of God." No longer plagued by Nietzsche's question of unbelieving or reactive nihilism that arises in the crisis of values and belief systems, we are not even bothered by the matter of fashioning a post-Nietzschean atheology, such as a Tillichian God beyond the God of theism. Heidegger intensifies Nietzsche's question by a concern about the age of technology turning God into a value, meaning, or object. Faith—religious awakening—must neither be identified with a belief or value nor with reactive nihilism. Ivan's concern that with God's death *after* Easter Sunday all becomes lawful is never assuaged by fundamentalist laws, as if Žižek could be made right, albeit cynically, against Ivan. We must discern in Žižek's charging fundamentalism with holy wars of terror and wars on terror, "with God all is possible," the GI's self-apotheosis of power, a variety of deeply disingenuous and dangerously misleading atheism.

If the four Karamazov brothers stand for features of the same self, then the dramatic plot shapes the setting between God and the devil. They are the main masked characters who no longer enter the stage on flying machines but through inwardness, where they experiment with human freedom and conscience. The work in its entirety presents an either/or choice between the GI's diabolical volition, which offers happiness by silencing responsible conscience, and Job's free acceptance of human suffering, fini-tude, and death as part of life. Whether or not radical evil exists, whether the word "evil" should be used in secular vernaculars, or whether the devil requires evidential proof (813) never becomes a serious ontological or cos-mological question. *The question of radical evil is posed in inwardness that is negatively saturated by unjust suffering, deception, despair, and cruelty.* There the only sensible question for me, witness to my own as well as my neigh-bor's suffering, becomes whether or not I shall decide to live in hell or heaven. Neither Ivan nor the GI could be understood as ordinary atheists because their mutiny springs from disenchantment with God whom they know and address *personally* and yet whose world they freely reject. The GI's (and Ivan's) response to human atrocities, such as the cruel torture or suffering of innocent children, is his supramoral justification of power to appease conscience. Faking consolation, the GI whispers to unwary in-wardness and to the gullible public with a voice of radical evil.

WHY THE "DEATH OF GOD" AND "RADICAL EVIL" ARE NOT ABOUT ATHEISM

In my engagement with Kant's conception of radical evil, I found in Dos-toyevsky an ally who affirmed the cornerstone Kant rejected: the possibility of human diabolical volition. Kant shunned his own discovery of the devil-ish will with which the human agent could freely embrace a malignant sub-lime and purposelessly aim at self-and-other destruction. By delimiting rad-ical evil within the bounds of mere reason, Kant was a pre-Kantian philosopher of religion, while Job and St. Augustine have already been post-Kantian. Pre-Kantians analyze moral evil as a conceptual or metaphysical problem for any coherent conception of God or, like Hegel and Habermas, they hope all wounds of history to be healed by reason, or like Marx, they correct the wounded world by social revolution. The figure of the GI was created to warn about false rational and revolutionary hope and any naive adoration of progress—our modern sources of radical evil's return. For the post-Kantian phenomenology of religion, radical evil challenges our very capacity for free, self-transformative, and social development.

Nietzsche's Easter kerygma without resurrection and Dostoyevsky's Job-like questioning of God must be read from the post-Kantian shores; other-wise we miss the point of the existential crisis that even if God appeared to us, we might not believe in forgiveness and love. This second-degree unbe-lief is not expressive of intellectual atheism but rather of willed ignorance, buffoonery, stupidity, self-deception. As I already remarked, the devils are not intellectual atheists. The devil sees God yet does not believe (821); "in the matter of belief [read: faith] no proof is of any avail, especially the material sort" (813). Pre-Kantians rationally doubt *about* God; post-Kantians struggle with inward despair. Pre-Kantian doubt pines for evidential proofs from evil (for or against God); post-Kantian despair must wake up and so risk faith. The "death of God" reveals a crisis of faith, not speculative doubt about God. Radical evil *after* the "death of God" reveals all doubt to be already saturated by despair. These conceptions are therefore not about atheism but despair. Any philosophy of religion or critical theory that is unaware of this difference aggravates human despair. "I know it's reactionary to believe in God in our day . . . but after all, I'm the Devil, it's all right to believe in me" (819).

WITNESSES OF THE UNCANNY

Elder Zossima is Alyosha's icon of the uncanny, a window to the heavenly Father, an ongoing revelation of the core of the Torah, shared by Jews and Christians alike, the Janus-faced law to love God with all one's heart above all idols and to love one's neighbor as oneself, indeed to receive forgiveness *as* one forgives others. Whatever inward damage the "old buffoon" Karamazov inflicted on his sons, it did not tarnish the youngest, whose self had been begotten by the heavenly Father. Alyosha's face resembled that of Zossima's brother who died young, and to the Elder, Alyosha came as a prophecy and memory of hope. Alyosha is the lover and healer of the human race (29), and in that sense he is assigned by his dying Elder the mission to leave the monastery and abide as the monk in the world, "bless life, and make others bless it" with him (370, 104).

What is revealed to us in the "Alyosha" aspect of the Karamazov self? Just as Zossima witnesses the holy in all creation and in each person who comes to him, so Alyosha comes on stage as the witness dimension of the self. The Father and Son testify against the Accuser. Rather than accusing God for the suffering of the world, both are in search of the Job-like response in the inwardness of each self. Alyosha witnesses how his three brothers struggle (207, 303, 309, 687, 756, 746, 763), and he listens to the lamentations of their female companions (453). To him all persons, even his father (229), reveal some of their convoluted self and confess their fears and hopes. Alyosha witnesses self-doubt, unbelief, and stirrings of evil, as well as the search for unconditional love and forgiveness. We never find Zossima judging or Alyosha condemning anyone for personal transgressions, though each tells the truth as he witnesses it. Alyosha builds up Ivan's faith, thereby rejecting the latter's self-accusation, impressing on him that it was not *him,* Ivan's true *self,* who murdered the old Karamazov (768ff.), even though he might have desired his father's death (782). Alyosha holds out for Dmitry's healing. Less concerned with proving the latter's legal innocence, Alyosha has no moral scruples to help him escape from prison and seek higher justice in Dmitry's redemptive suffering.

The witness self apprehends the guilty and twisted self with the uncanny awareness of mercy and hope. Against Ivan's disenchantment, despair, hardness, nihilism, and rejection, Alyosha abides in steady awareness of blessing, love, mercy, grace, and forgiveness. Against the crises of belief and despair, and against the political-authoritarian solution to these crises proposed by the GI, Alyosha bears suffering and insults with the clarity of a spirit who remains unshaken in hope for the possibility of healing. What is the radically evil, the diabolical, as apprehended within oneself by the saintly witness? Radical evil is one's rejection of the gift of creation and forgiveness, one's refusal of unconditional love. Alyosha witnesses to the possibility and actuality of radical evil in oneself; he shows the diabolical in oneself a mirror. He never says that it does not exist; at the same time he attests to the gift of forgiveness and healing.

Who is this healer battling with the diabolical in us? The devil and God never appear on stage in person as representatives of a/theism. That lack of evidential argument should not be a cause for our unbelief, since they act in the inward core of human existential drama. They spar with each other on the terrain of the beautiful and uncanny (145). Just as the GI performs the diabolic in Ivan's imagination, so the devil appears in his nightmare as the author of the GI (828). If the devil did not exist, Voltaire might say of the dark side more emphatically than he did of God, we would have to create one in the human image (306, 312, 707). Alyosha incarnates the messianic promise. In the Christian Passion, he is the silent Jesus standing to be sacrificed by the GI; in the Jewish Passover, he is standing before the GI as the Job of anti-idolatry. Alyosha is not a Cartesian cogito distilled from methodical doubt, or the transcendental ego appearing through the Husserlian brackets of all mental contents and operations; as a witness of healing, he is the Kierkegaardian spirit-self free of despair. On a Jewish and Christian, indeed, in any essentially spiritual journey, Alyosha is faith, mindfulness, awareness, awakening of oneself.

RESURRECTION AS FORGIVENESS

What is hell? Is it a place and time of damnation that is always and already eternal? In Zossima's memoir, posthumously recorded by Aloysha, we are given existential adumbrations that while forgiveness is eternally extended all the way to hell, as shown on Christian Orthodox icons of resurrection, its path is blocked by self-hatred (531). Whether or not hell is a place or time, temporal or lasting, Zossima defines it as one's inability to love (417). Grushenka in her last feast with Dmitry before he is taken away does not reach deep enough when she wishes, "If I were God, I would forgive every-one" (566). Yet Dmitry's heart-stirring prayers from hell are answered be-cause in his despair of losing everything he petitions to be allowed to love even when in hell (532). His prayer opens a path to redemption.

Ivan returns the entry ticket to God's Eden because of the unforgivable tears of tortured children. Ivan's words could have been adopted by Jankélévitch about Auschwitz,

> I do not want the mother to embrace the torturer who tore her son to pieces with his dogs! Let her not dare to forgive him! . . . Is there in all the world a being that could forgive and have the right to forgive? (320)

Ivan rebels against the heavenly harmony accepting the world where hell and, in particular, religious cruelty occur (313ff.); no paradise is worth the price of the innocent suffering of children (316). Alyosha answers by point-ing to divine suffering (321).

The unforgivable are not acts that usher us to hell; it is our "voluntary and unsatiable" decision to stay in hell, to hate ourselves so intensely as to reject forgiveness. Refusal of forgiveness is unforgivable (418), as in a self-hating heart *God is dead* even when seen. The devilish will feeds on the gen-uine "death of God." Even while "seeing" God, the diabolical will is unable to hope in God's resurrection (829f.). No hope seems reserved for the devil, whose role is to criticize, negate, test, and even suffer, so that there could be a hosanna for Job, though that hard labor of critique, deconstruction, and anguish does not seem redemptive of the diabolical will, and apart from that will, the devil might not exist at all (819f., 828f.). The devilish will un-creates, and Smerdyakov's final act is suicide (831).

What is paradise? A mysterious visitor forever impresses the young Zos-sima by announcing that he knows what paradise is. "Paradise is concealed in each one of us, and now it is contained within myself, and I want it to begin for me tomorrow and to last for the rest of my life" (392). The visitor has been suffering from anguish for fourteen years. He confesses to Zossima because he killed a person but was able to escape apprehension. He could get away with murder, yet he has lived all this time in hell. He arrives in par-adise at the moment of confessing his guilt publicly and accepting suffering for his act (399). "As soon as I had done what was incumbent on me I at once felt paradise within my soul" (403).

To forgive is to allow God to rise up from the dead in one's heart. Niet-zsche would be right that "God is dead" only if there were no mercy and forgiveness in the world. Dostoyevsky's drama is so deeply moving because next to the unforgivable acts, recounted and desired as well as committed from hell's bottomless despair, there echo prayers from hell, and Ezekiel's prophecy that dry bones will rise is fulfilled every day in the smallest acts of mercy and forgiveness. Hearts turning stone are rolled over by a faith that hopes for the impossible. The unforgivable means death, but forgiveness raises the guilty from the dead, allowing the criminal to become a person capable of another life than the evil deed.

Zossima tells the woman who murdered her husband not to be afraid of her sin, and hope arises in her heart (72). Alyosha witnesses the resurrection of Grushenka when he does not see her as a common whore—who once schemed to seduce him from innocence and now orchestrates the feud between Dmitry and his father that brings both to ruin—but calls her his sister (455). Alyosha acknowledges that his brothers desired parricide when they willed the death their father in their hearts, yet his faith in his brothers melts their self-hatred. He believes that God will rise up in Ivan's dried up intellectual self if he meets two tasks, "to love life before logic" and "to raise up" his dead fathers, that is, restore his vocational roots (302).

When Dmitry prays from his Gethsemane for ability to love even in despair, forgiveness descends into his hell, and we tremble at Dmitry's heart lit up as an icon of resurrection (532, 562). After Alyosha, knowing Dmitry's parricidal intent, proclaims Dmitry's innocence, calling upon God as witness, "the whole of Mitya's face was illuminated with beatitude" (764). Indeed, Alyosha's only proof of Dmitry's innocence presented at the court was to appeal to his brother's face (864). In this Lévinasian appeal to the face of the other, Alyosha witnesses in Dmitry an atoning desire to suffer with the guilty: I want "to purify myself through suffering," even though I am innocent of father's blood (652).

> A new person has been resurrected within me! He was imprisoned within me, but he would never have appeared had it not been for this lightning bolt. . . . It is possible there, too, in the mines, under the earth, beside one, in another convict and murderer like oneself to find a human heart and to consort with him, for there, too, it is possible to live, and love, and suffer! It is possible to resuscitate and resurrect in that convict the heart that has stopped beating. . . . If God is driven from the face of the earth, we shall meet him under the earth. (756f.)

At the end of the drama, Alyosha stands as a village idiot or the Russian Juro Divy before a group of schoolboys and testifies to Dmitry's innocence. At this time the little Ilyuschechka dies of consumption. Kolya, "a desperate character" (700) of thirteen who precociously adopts Ivan's nihilistic worldview (707–14), wishing for that dead boy's resurrection (981), proclaims Dmitry's resurrection: "So he is going to his ruin as an innocent victim for truth and justice! . . . Though he is ruined, he is happy!" (975). Alyosha's parting words with the boys by the stone where Ilyuschechka wanted to be buried carry joint echoes of the Last Supper and Pentecost:

Alyosha is imprinting onto their youthful hearts "a beautiful, sacred memory" of their mutual friendship and love of the innocent Ilyuschechka. Let this memory rise up in our hearts. To the direct question from Kolya whether we shall all rise up from the dead, Alyosha ecstatically answers, "Without question we shall rise" (985).

MORE GUILTY THAN OTHERS

Emmanuel Lévinas was deeply impressed by one thought in Dostoyevsky's novel, that "each single one of us is indubitably guilty in respect to all creatures and all things upon the earth, not only with regard to general guilt, the guilt of the world, but also individually—each for all people and for each person on this earth" (216). That we are all responsible, and I am more so than others, this now central Lévinasian thought inspired dissidents to take an extra risky step by issuing a manifesto for human rights in Czechoslovakia, Charta 77, written in 1977 by Jan Patočka shortly before his death at the hands of the Czech secret police. Václav Havel carried the idea of citizens' responsibility for their past and present to his first presidency after the Czechoslovak Velvet Revolution of 1989 (more on this in Matuštík, 2007).

Ivan's mutiny against God for allowing the innocent to suffer is answered by taking radical responsibility for others. In reorienting human anguish from accusing God to accepting responsibility for the state of the world, one's Job-like suffering can become redemptive for others. Hope and paradise arrive *now* in forbearance and forgiveness for one another. "Each of us is guilty before the other for everything, and I am more than any," says Zossima's younger brother on his deathbed, "each of us is guilty before all for everyone and everything" (374; cf. 651). "Why count the days, when one is enough for a man to know all of happiness?" (375). "In truth each of us is guilty before the others for everyone, and people don't realize it, but if they did, we should all instantly be in paradise" (386). Dmitry, although not legally guilty, is guilty inwardly *more* than others (592).

In this most difficult of the Judeo-Christian messages of shared guilt and responsibility, to wit, of the unconditional love inviting us to bear and suffer for others, we receive the promise of a different world rising from the dead than the one bequeathed to us by holy wars of terror and wars against terror. With the hindsight of redemptive critique, we know why the Grand Inquisitor's ideological labeling of others as evil, the vanguard's offer to vanquish radical evil in his name, and the patriotic resources of his tool box are all a lie. Their truth, whether preached from holy shrines or propagated around some national resolve, leads to hell. By silencing our conscience, difficult freedom, and responsibility, the GI becomes the impostor of the religious in and among us. That we are all guilty and *I more* than others, this spiritual testament of Dostoyevsky raises the categorical imperative at the heart of Lévinas's ethics of responsibility. That imperative does not command, You shall not kill friends but you can torture terrorists! It requires our unconditional response to the most radical evil: you shall not murder! It is impossible to win the war on terror externally, as there is no forgiveness in the heart bent on war, for that heart lives in terror. We might not be capable of Dostoyevsky's prophetic thought of forgiving the unforgivable, of praying for love even from hell—an honest admission of which even stupid demons seem capable. But then with that minimal confession there remains a margin of hope even within its scarcity that we could no longer in good conscience call our all-too-human worlds and motives, whether they be secular or religious, by holy names.

NOTES

2. REDEMPTIVE CRITICAL THEORY

1. Blume (2004) notes that Habermas gave this "polemical lecture" at Northwestern University after Bush was reelected. His more dynamic and politically charged presentation was given to an audience in excess of five hundred at Purdue University on October 15, 2004 (see KPCL).

2. My response is in part with reference to Pensky (2005) and Owen (2005). That discussion took place on December 27, 2001, in Atlanta during the APA panel on my book (2001).

3. In November 2006 the German journal *Cicero* published a denunciation of Habermas on account of his participation in the Hitler Youth in 1944, when he was fifteen. Busche (2006) contends that Habermas swallowed an incriminating piece of paper from his Hitler Youth days that a colleague of his from that period, Hans-Ulrich Wehler, handed back to him after the war. Wehler is a well-known professor of German history and Habermas's friend. The *Süddeutsche Zeitung* printed on October 27, 2006 a letter from Wehler: "Habermas was no Hitler Youth leader. For reasons of his harelip alone [Habermas was born with a cleft palate, *Gaumenspalte*], he could never have had a leadership function under the Nazis. The fact is that at fourteen he gave first-aid classes in the Hitler Youth, for which he had been trained as an orderly. Among his tasks was to remind participants who missed classes to attend punctually with so-called call letters. These were preprinted forms in which the instructor simply had to fill in with the participant's information and then sign his name." Referring to the posthumously published autobiography of Joachim Fest, the onetime editor of the *Frankfurter Allgemeine Zeitung*, Busche insinuated that one of these "call letters" survived the war; that it recorded Habermas's youth enthusiasm for Hitler; and that Habermas swallowed the piece of evidence after the war. The fact remains that Fest was a key player in the German historians' debate about the Nazi era, a debate from the late 1980s in which Habermas boldly intervened against Fest and the revisionist historians. This latest attempt to discredit him or writers like Günther Grass showcases a generational echo of the German trauma.

I discuss Habermas's membership in the Hitler Youth in my published biography of him (2001:4, 31 n. 1, 295–97) and in a book chapter on his relationship to the Holocaust (2000). In my biography, I document in detail what I learned of Habermas's father, Dr. Ernst Habermas, regarding his membership in the NSDAP (2001:303–304 nn. 5–12). In my post-9/11 biographical article (2006:n. 5), I correct the actual year of Habermas's entry into the Hitler Youth from 1944, the year I stated in my biography on pages xxx and 4, to 1939, the year Habermas identifies as the year he joined the Nazi youth organization. Habermas made me correct that year for my *Encyclopedia Britannica* online entry after the publication of my biography of him. By 1939 membership in the Hitler Youth for boys of his age had become compulsory. There is no piece of historical evidence that between 1939, when he was ten and entered the Hitler Youth, and 1945, when he turned fifteen, Habermas did anything that requires from him a statement of public regret or apology.

3. BETWEEN HOPE AND TERROR

1. In his gadfly posture Socrates was like the stingray, which emits electric torpedo shocks.

2. A contrast with Žižek (2003:90, 140ff.) helps us fine-tune the nuance between Habermas and Derrida. Žižek locates suicidal autoimmunity in the human imaginary with its desire for absolute otherness. Žižek (2003:66–70, 86–91) *perverts* but unabashedly recenters Pauline-cum-Leninist (i.e., atheistically and materialistically inflected) Christianity against messianic Judaism. Human empathy with the divine failure of the crucified God mirrors the emptiness inscribed into our failure to possess an absolute, transcendent reality. As if anticipating and caricaturing Mel Gibson's *The Passion of the Christ,* Žižek welcomes the failure of Jesus who, abandoned by the Father, gets himself killed and thus inaugurates a this-worldly passion for justice. Against Derrida's Benjaminian-Lévinasian Judaic transcendence, the *perverse* in Christianity is the epiphany of the disconsolate "divine fool." The Messiah has come to reveal the infinite failure of the imaginary to bridge the human and divine reality. We must not wait for the messianic promise of the wholly other world than this unjust one. Žižek frowns on all appeals to Other as abstract or imaginary projections. We must accept trauma without the possibility of mourning. His post-Hegelian materialist theology—Holy Spirit as the life of community—would be an outcome of successful Lacanian therapy. Wounding continues to define the human condition after the coming of Christ. Enter Žižek's Lacanian-Calvinist rendition of original sin. Repelled by unredeemable terror yet attracted by a dying God, "in our very failure, we identify with the divine failure," confessing universal human failure. Žižek opposes all appeals to the wholly other Pauline-Leninist vision of community. The atheist lamentation of Christ who finds himself alone on the cross helps us give up the imaginary longing for the absolute Thing. How the St. Paul of Habermas's Peircean community ideal lines up with Žižek's Pauline materialist theology remains a good question; or whether, on Derrida's account, both Pauline versions of community (Habermas's communication ideal and Žižek's Leninist materialism) still involve ontotheology exposed by Kant as transcendental illusion and thoroughly discredited by late Heidegger's move beyond it.

PART 2. THE NEGATIVELY SATURATED PHENOMENON

1. The term "saturated phenomenon" is attributed to Marion's post-Husserlian, new phenomenology and to his interlocutors, such as Caputo, Derrida, Westphal, or Janicaud; even as a cognate, the term "saturated" has little to do with Allain Badiou's (2006) secular ontology or social theory. Badiou's use of the term "saturated" speaks about a closing off or burdening or exhausting of a discourse, concept, idea, revolutionary praxis. To the question, After the saturation of the class-party experiment, what next? Badiou responds:

> I think a fidelity does not really finish, but sometimes it is saturated; that is my term for it. There is a saturation; you cannot find anything new in the field of your first fidelity. Many people, when this is the case, just say, "It's finished." And really, a political sequence has a beginning and an end, too, an end in the form of saturation. Saturation is not a brutal rupture, but it becomes progressively more difficult to find something new in the field of the fidelity.

Since the mid-80s, more and more, there has been something like a saturation of revolutionary politics in its conventional framework: class struggle, party, dictatorship of the proletariat, and so on. So we have to find something like a fidelity to the fidelity. Not a simple fidelity.

For my generation, it's a choice between saying, on the one hand, "Nothing is possible today in the political field; the reactionary tendency is too strong." That's the position of many people in France today; it's the negative interpretation of saturation.

When the fidelity is saturated, you have a choice. The first possibility is to say it's finished. The second possibility is this: With the help of certain events—like the events in South America today—you find what I name a fidelity to the fidelity. Fidelity to the fidelity is not a continuation, strictly speaking, and not a pure rupture, either. We have to find something new. When I was saying yesterday that "from outside, you can see something you don't see from inside," that's merely a rule by which to find something new.

And later Badiou says:

During the entire development of Marxism, Leninism, and Maoism, the theory of contradiction was the heart of the logical framework. In my conviction, that is also finished. For the same reason as for the party, dialectical logic in the Hegelian sense is saturated today. We can no longer simply use the paradigm of contradiction. Naturally, there are contradictions; it's not a question of fact. But for the definition of a new discipline, we cannot directly use the logic of contradiction; we have to find another paradigm.

Marion means by saturation the opposite of exhaustion in the sense of getting overfed or having enough of something: he means overflowing on the side of intuition, hence the arrival of something that is not satisfied or contained by a concept and fulfilled intuition. By "negatively saturated phenomenon" I mean the opposite of Badiou's "nothing is possible."

2. Marion uses the word "saturated" throughout his earlier work (1991), but that notion is only marginal to the main distinction drawn there between idol and icon (on this use, see 17, 21, 46, 126). There is, however, one instance in which he refers to the idolatrous gaze that fixes and reflects itself back to itself in the mirror, itself invisible to it, as a negative apprehension of the iconic invisible (13): "The invisible mirror thus marks, negatively, the shortcoming of the aim—literally, the *invisable*"(that which one cannot view or at which one cannot aim, not to be confused with invisible, that which cannot be seen). Thus if the idol apprehends the iconic invisible *negatively,* as *invisable,* then radical evil marks the special existential case of lived, aggravated self-idolatry whereby the positive will to destroy, annihilate, cause harm, is negatively saturated by its aim.

4. JOB QUESTIONS KANT

1. On contemporary discussions of radical evil relevant to my discussion, see Copjec (1996:xv); Derrida (1992: 165 n. 31, 2002:48–53, 77, 100); Green (1992:64–68, 156–80, 193–95, 273n113); Gross (1992); Lara (2001); Nishitani (1982:22–30); Ragozinski (1996); Ricoeur (1995:chaps. 4, 11, 14); Vries (2002:102–22, 156, 160–75); and Wiesel (1990).

2. Kofman (1998) makes this a centerpiece of her resistance to dehumanization in Auschwitz.

3. See Matuštík (2001:139–50) for the discussion of Habermas in relation to this issue.

4. See Matuštík (2001:150–56) for the discussion of collective guilt versus liability in Habermas and Jaspers; on discourse-ethical equivalents of existential either/or, see also Matuštík (1993). On the disconsolate void of Daniel Libeskind's post-Holocaust anti-redemptory art in the Berlin Jewish Museum, see chapter 5 below and Matuštík (2001: 166); cf. Libeskind's notion of void centrally inscribed into his design for replacing the Twin Towers in New York City.

5. Cf. Allison (2001:86–100).

5. REDEMPTION IN AN ANTIREDEMPTORY AGE

1. The order by Rahm from June 16, 1942, regarding "transfer of libraries and histor-ically valuable objects from the provinces to Prague," in a letter by the Jewish Community of Prague (June 17, 1942) addressed "To the Central Office for Jewish Emigration Prague-Střešovice" (Volavková, 1968, 60, 62).

2. I draw on the summary found in Paulson (2000), the text of the accords (*Acuerdos* 1996), and the report by Thompson (2001).

3. The notion of recognition endeavors to correct for the perceived limits of the Husserlian phenomenological method, which privileges singular consciousness over social or intersubjective relatedness. By showing that no self-enclosed *I* can stabilize itself apart from being first recognized by another *you*, recognition and the accompanying co-consti-tutive primacy of alterity become phenomenologically foundational. The Hegelian strug-gle for recognition takes up the same foundational issue that runs ahead yet in parallel fashion to Husserl's search for evidence that would elucidate intersubjective relations. Only with Marx does this struggle find its decisive sociopolitical stabilization. By showing that possessive individualists cannot reach singular sociopolitical and economic aims apart from inhabiting a more just social form of life, notions of recognition and redistribution become more than phenomenologically or ontologically foundational. The struggle for recognition turns sociopolitical and revolutionary. The quest for a fundamental revolu-tionary standpoint and for the social subject of liberation reimport the noted limits of re-spective phenomenologies (the Husserlian and Hegelian-Marxist) into existential and phenomenological Marxism and the early critical social theory. When I invoke the witness posture of the redemptive memory of hope, I have in mind the limit of struggles for recognition to deliver such hope. I find those limits in the Hegelian-Marxist as well as Husserlian traditions.

6. RADICAL EVIL AS A SATURATED PHENOMENON

1. On Kant's fear of the diabolical, see Derrida (1994:165 n. 31, 2002:49); Vries (2002:171).

2. Derrida (1994:166 n. 31) traces the sense of "diabolical" cruelty and unforgivable evil that "calls for forgiveness," and which "Kant does not want to acknowledge," to *bêtise* or stupidity. Cf. with Kierkegaard's SuD, who calls sin a willed or motivated form of ig-norance—stupidity.

3. When in the fall of 2002 I posed these questions to Habermas at the Northwestern conference to honor Charles Taylor, he had nothing to say.

4. The redemptive reality does not deliver us to some messiah who signals radical apocalyptic change. Such apocalyptic change often suffuses a desire to rid the earth of all

evil, and it leads to outward heroic projects to do the same in the name of the expected change. The redemptive messianic reality has at once a prophetic and an existential structure. Humans in their drama must decide on the course of action, and they alone must learn to curb their desire for the mastery of the unknown reality. As Franz Kafka suggests in the epigraph to part 1, redemption arrives to us when we have worked out all issues of responsibility in our freedom, when in that freedom we no longer need to master the apocalyptic change by pursuing evil outwardly. Then redemption issues in concrete existence when the apocalyptic messiah no longer needs to be posited as a value or heroic project.

5. "Freedom and fear, justice and cruelty have always been at war, and we know that God is not neutral between them" (George W. Bush, September 20, 2001, to the U.S. Congress).

"We are in a conflict between good and evil, and America will call evil by its name" (George W. Bush, June 1, 2002, West Point commencement).

6. On will to power and nothingness, see Nietzsche (1967:sec. I) and Heidegger (1977:79, 1993:89–110); on religion and nothingness, see Nishitani (1982:1–45).

7. See Gordon (1997:273–90, 2000:41–61) on Douglass as an existentialist.

WORKS CITED

(Frequently cited works by Derrida, Habermas, and Kierkegaard are referenced in the main body of the text by title abbreviations that are listed below after the year of publication. All other works are cited by the year of publication.)

Acuerdos de San Andrés. (1996) Centro de Información y Análisis de Chiapas, A.C.

Adams, Marilyn McCord. (1999) *Horrendous Evils and the Goodness of God.* Ithaca, N.Y.: Cornell University Press.

———. (2001) "Horrors in Theological Context." *Revista Portuguesa de Filosofia* 57: 871–80.

Adorno, Theodor W. (1967 [1955]) *Prisms: Cultural Criticism and Society.* Trans. Samuel and Shierry Weber. Cambridge: MIT Press.

———. (1973 [1966]) *Negative Dialectics.* Trans. E. B. Ashton. New York: Continuum.

———. (1982 [1962]) "Commitment." In Andrew Arato and Eike Gebhardt, eds., *The Essential Frankfurt School Reader,* 300–18. New York: Continuum.

———. (1986 [1959]) "What Does Coming to Terms with the Past Mean?" In Geoffrey H. Hartman, ed., *Bitburg in Moral and Political Perspective,* 114–29. Bloomington: Indiana University Press.

———. (1998) *Critical Models: Interventions and Catchwords.* Trans. Henry W. Pickford. New York: Columbia University Press.

Allison, Henry. (2001) "Reflections on the Banality of (Radical) Evil." In María Pía Lara, ed., *Rethinking Evil: Contemporary Perspectives,* 86–100. Berkeley: University of California Press.

Altshuler, Linda A., and Anna R. Cohn. (1983) "Precious Legacy." In David Altshuler, ed., *The Precious Legacy: Judaic Treasures from the Czechoslovak State Collections,* 17–45. New York: Summit.

Antelme, Robert. (1992) *The Human Race.* Trans. Jeffrey Haight and Annie Mahler. Marlboro, Vt.: Marlboro Press.

Arendt, Hannah. (1951) *The Origins of Totalitarianism.* New York: Harcourt, Brace.

———. (1958) *The Human Condition.* Chicago: University of Chicago Press.

———. (1965) *Eichmann in Jerusalem: Report on the Banality of Evil.* Rev. & enl. ed. New York: Viking.

———. (1994) *Essays in Understanding, 1930–1954.* Ed. Jerome Kohn. New York: Harcourt, Brace.

Arendt, Hannah, and Karl Jaspers. (1992) *Correspondence, 1926–1969.* Ed. Lotte Kohler and Hans Seiner. New York: Harcourt Brace Jovanovich.

Badiou, Allain. (2006) "The Saturated Generic Identity of the Working Class." *Carce-laglio,* October 16, 2006. An interview with Diana George and Nic Veroli.

Baer, Ulrich. (2000) *Remnants of Song: Trauma and the Experience of Modernity in Charles Baudelaire and Paul Celan.* Stanford: Stanford University Press.

Baynes, Kenneth. (2005) "Understanding Evil." *Constellations* 11/3: 434–44.

Baudrillard, Jean. (1983) *Simulations.* Trans. Paul Foss, Paul Patton, and Philip Beitchman. New York: Semiotext(e).

Becker, Ernest. (1973) *The Denial of Death.* New York: Free Press.

———. (1975) *Escape from Evil.* New York: Free Press.

Benjamin, Walter. (1968) *Illuminations: Essays and Reflections.* Ed. Hannah Arendt. Trans. Harry Zohn. New York: Shocken. With an introduction by Hannah Arendt.

———. (1999 [1928–1940]) "N [On the Theory of Knowledge, Theory of Progress]." *The Arcades Project,* 456–88. Trans. Howard Eiland and Kevin McLaughlin. Cambridge: Harvard University Press.

Bergman, Ingmar. (1962) *Winter Light.* A Svensk Filmindustri. Home Vision.

Bernstein, Richard J. (2002) *Radical Evil: A Philosophical Interrogation.* Cambridge, Mass: Polity.

Bloch, Ernst. (1959) *Das Prinzip Hoffnung.* 3 vols. Frankfurt a/M: Suhrkamp.

———. (1972) *Atheism in Christianity: The Religion of the Exodus and the Kingdom.* Trans. J. T. Swann. New York: Herder & Herder.

Borradori, Giovanna, Jacques Derrida, and Jürgen Habermas. (2003) *Philosophy in a Time of Terror.* Chicago: University of Chicago Press.

Brandner, Judith. (2001) "Widerstandsaktion oder Masterplan der Nazis zur Erinnerung an eine 'ausgestorbene Rasse'"? *Die Gazette,* November 23.

Buber, Martin. (1982) *On the Bible: Eighteen Studies.* Introduction by Harold Bloom. New York: Shocken.

Busche, Jürgen. (2006) "Hat Habermas die Wahrheit verschluckt?" *Cicero,* November.

———. (1993) *Der Jude und Sein Judentum.* Gerlingen: Lambert Schneider.

Cahnman, Werner J. (1981) "Schelling and the New Thinking of Judaism." In *The American Academy for Jewish Research Proceedings* 48: 1–56.

Caputo, Jack. (1997) *The Prayers and Tears of Jacques Derrida: Religion without Religion.* Bloomington: Indiana University Press.

———. (2001) *On Religion.* New York: Routledge.

———. (2007) "The Hyperbolization of Phenomenology: Two Possibilities for Religion in Recent Continental Philosophy." In Kevin Hart, ed., *Counter-Experiences: Reading Jean-Luc Marion,* 67–93. Notre Dame, Ind.: University of Notre Dame Press.

———. (2007) *The Weakness of God: A Theology of the Event.* Bloomington: Indiana University Press.

Caputo, John D., Mark Dooley, and Michael J. Scanlon, eds. (2001) *Questioning God.* Bloomington: Indiana University Press.

Caputo, John D., and Michael J. Scanlon, eds. (1999) *God, the Gift, and Postmodernism.* Bloomington: Indiana University Press.

Catalano, Joseph S. (1986) *A Commentary on Jean-Paul Sartre's Critique of Dialectical Reason.* Vol. 1, *Theory of Practical Ensembles.* Chicago: University of Chicago Press.

Cooper, David A. (1997) *God Is a Verb: Kabbalah and the Practice of Mystical Judaism.* New York: Riverhead Trade.

Copjec, Joan, ed. (1996) *Radical Evil.* London: Verso.

Cornell, Drucilla. (1992) *The Philosophy of Limit.* New York: Routledge.

———. (1993) *Transformations: Recollective Imagination and Sexual Difference.* New York: Routledge.

———. (1995) *The Imaginary Domain: Abortion, Pornography, and Sexual Harassment.* New York: Routledge.

———. (2002) "The Swirling of Images: An Interview with Drucilla Cornell." *Paralax* 8/4.

———. (2003a) "Autonomy Re-Imagined." *Journal for the Psychoanalysis of Culture and Society,* Spring 2003.

————. (2003b) "Facing Our Humanity." *Hypatia* 18/1: 170–74. Special issue on feminist philosophy and the problem of evil.

————. (2003c) "The Sacrilege of Feminism." *Identities*.

————. (2004) "Adorno: Civilization, Progress, and Beyond." *Defending Ideals: Democracy, War, and Political Struggles*. New York: Routledge.

Cornell, Drucilla, and Daniel Morris. (2003) "When We Sit in the Hands of the World." Unpublished manuscript.

Cornell, Drucilla, and Sara Murphy. (2002) "Antiracism, Multiculturalism, and the Ethics of Identification." *Philosophy and Social Criticism* 28/4.

Chateau, Ladislava. (2004) "Pražské Židovské muzeum-od zavření k poznání." *Listy* 6.

Chrétien, Jean-Louis. (2000) "The Wounded Word: The Phenomenology of Prayer." In Dominique Janicaud, *Phenomenology and the "Theological Turn": The French Debate*, 147–75. New York: Fordham University Press.

————. (2002) *The Unforgettable and the Unhoped For*. Trans. Jeffrey Bloechl. New York: Fordham University Press.

Derrida, Jacques. (1955*) The Gift of Death* [GD]. Trans. David Willis. Chicago: University of Chicago Press.

————. (1978) *Writing and Difference* [WD]. Trans. Alan Bass. Chicago: University of Chicago Press.

————. (1992a) *Other Heading: Reflections on Today's Europe* [OH]. Trans. Pascale-Anne Brault and Michael B. Naas. Bloomington: Indiana University Press.

————. (1992b) "How to Avoid Speaking: Denials" [D]. In Harold Coward and Toby Foshay, eds., *Derrida and Negative Theology*, 73–142. New York: SUNY Press.

————. (1994a) *Specters of Marx: The State of the Debt, the Work of Mourning, and the New International* [SM]. Trans. Peggy Kamuf. New York: Routledge.

————. (1994b) *Given Time: I. Counterfeit Money* [GT]. Trans. Peggy Kamuf. Chicago: University of Chicago Press.

————. (1995). *Khôra* [K]. Trans. Ian McLeod. In *On the Name*. Ed. Thomas Dutoit. Stanford University Press, 87–127.

————. (1999) "The Century and the Pardon: An Interview with Michael Wieviorka" [CP]. *Le monde des débats*, 9.

————. (2000) *Foi et savoir suivi de le siècle et le pardon* [FeS]. Paris: Éditions du Seuil.

————. (2001a) "To Forgive: The Unforgivable and the Imprescriptible" [UI]. In John D. Caputo, Mark Dooley, and Michael J. Scanlon, eds., *Questioning God*. Bloomington: Indiana University Press.

————. (2001b) "On Forgiveness: A Roundtable Discussion with Jacques Derrida" [OF]. Moderated by Richard Kearney. In John D. Caputo, Mark Dooley, and Michael J. Scanlon, eds., *Questioning God*, 52–72. Bloomington: Indiana University Press.

————. (2002a) "Faith and Knowledge: The Two Sources of 'Religion at the Limit of Reason Alone'" [FaK]. In Gil Anidjar, ed., *Acts of Religion*, 42–101. New York: Routledge.

————. (2002b) "A Silkworm of One's Own" [S]. In Gil Anidjar, ed., *Acts of Religion*, 311–355. New York: Routledge.

————. (2002c) "Hostipitality" [H]. In Gil Anidjar, ed., *Acts of Religion*, 358–420. New York: Routledge.

————. (2003) "Autoimmunity: Real and Symbolic Suicides" [A]. In Giovanna Borradori, Jacques Derrida, and Jürgen Habermas, eds., *Philosophy in a Time of Terror*, 85–136. Chicago: University of Chicago Press, 2003.

Dostoyevsky, Fyodor. (2003) *The Brothers Karamazov*. Trans. David McDuff. New York: Penguin.

Douglass, Frederick. (1968 [1845]) *Narrative of the Life of Frederick Douglass.* New York: Penguin.

Fackenheim, Emil L. (1994) *To Mend the World: Foundations of Post-Holocaust Jewish Thought.* Bloomington: Indiana University Press.

Felman, Shoshana, and Dori Laub. (1992) *Testimony: Crises of Witnessing in Literature, Psychoanalysis, and History.* New York: Routledge.

Felluga, Dino. (2000) "Holocaust Iconoclasm and the Anti-Intellectual: 'Jetztzeit' as a Response to the Postmodern Impasse." *A.R.I.E.L.,* 1–13.

Fraser, Nancy. (1989) "What's Critical about Critical Theory? The Case of Habermas and Gender." In *Unruly Practices: Power, Discourse, and Gender in Contemporary Social Theory,* 113–43. Minneapolis: University of Minnesota Press.

Freud, Sigmund. (1955) "The Uncanny." In *The Standard Edition of the Completed Psychological Works of Sigmund Freud,* 17:219–52. Trans. James Strachey. London: Hogarth.

Friedländer, Saul. (1984) *Reflections of Nazism: An Essay on Kitsch and Death.* Trans. Thomas Weyr. New York: Harper & Row.

Friedländer, Saul, ed. (1992) *Probing the Limits of Representation: Nazism and the "Final Solution."* Cambridge: Harvard University Press.

Glucksmann, André. (2002) *Dostoïevski à Manhattan.* Ed. Robert Laffont.

Goodhart, Sandor. (1996) *Sacrificing Commentary: Reading the End of Literature.* Baltimore: Johns Hopkins University Press.

———. (2005) Presentation on the Book of Job and the Problem of Evil. Purdue University, April 1.

Gordon, Lewis, ed. (1997) *Existence in Black: An Anthology of Black Existential Philosophy.* New York: Routledge.

———. (2000) *Existentia Africana: Understanding Africana Existential Thought.* New York: Routledge.

Green, Ronald M. (1992) *Kierekegaard and Kant: The Hidden Debt.* Albany: SUNY Press.

Gross, W., and K-J. Kuschel. (1992) *"Ich schaffe Finsternis und Unheil": Ist Gott verantwortlich für das Übel.* Mainz: Matthias-Grünewald Verlag.

Habermas, Jürgen. (1988/1992) *Nachmetaphysisches Denken: Philosophische Aufsätze.* Frankfurt a/M: Suhrkamp. *Postmetaphysical Thinking: Philosophical Essays.* [ND]. Trans. William Mark Hohengarten. Cambridge, Mass: MIT Press.

———. (1989) *The New Conservatism: Cultural Criticism and the Historians' Debate.* [NC]. Ed. and trans. Shierry Weber Nicholsen. Intro. Richard Wolin. Cambridge, Mass.: MIT Press.

———. (1992) *Autonomy and Solidarity: Interviews with Jürgen Habermas* [AS]. Ed. Peter Dews. Rev. & enl. ed. London: Verso.

———. (1998/2001a) *Die postnationale Konstellation: Politische Essays* [PC]. Frankfurt a/M: Suhrkamp; *The Postnational Constellation.* Trans. Max Pensky. Cambridge: MIT Press.

———. (1999) "Bestialität und Humanität: Ein Krieg an Der Grenze Zwischen Recht und Moral" [BH]. *Die Zeit,* April 29, 1999, 1, 6–7.

———. (2001b/2003) "Zum Friedenspreis des deutschen Buchhandels: Eine Dankrede" [FK]. *Süddeutsche Zeitung,* October 15. Text of speech at Frankfurt's Paulskirche on the occasion of receiving the Peace Award of the German Publishers, October 14, 2001; "Faith and Knowledge." In FHN (101–115, 126–27).

———. (2002a) *Religion and Rationality: Essays on Reason, God, and Modernity* [RR]. Ed. Eduardo Mendieta. Cambridge: MIT Press.

———. (2002b) "Letter to America" [LA]. Interview by Danny Postel. *The Nation,* December 16.

———. (2003a) *The Future of Human Nature* [FHN]. Trans. Hella Beister and Max Pensky. Cambridge: Polity.

———. (2003b) "Dispute on the Past and Future of International Law: Transition from a National to a Postnational Constellation" [DIL]. Presentation at the World Congress of Philosophy, Istanbul, August 10.

———. (2003c) "Fundamentalism and Terror" [FT]. In Giovanna Borradori, Jacques Derrida, and Jürgen Habermas, *Philosophy in a Time of Terror,* 25–43. Chicago: University of Chicago Press.

———. (2003d) "Intolerance and Discrimination" [ID]. *International Journal of Constitutional Law* 1/1: 2–12.

———. (2003e) "Was bedeutet das Denkmalsturz?" [IFM]. *Frankfurter Allgemeine Zeitung,* April 17; "Interpreting the Fall of a Monument." Trans. Max Pensky. *Constellations* 10/3:364–70.

———. (2003f) "Neue Welt Europa" [NWE]. *Frankfurter Allgemeine Zeitung,* January 24.

———. (2004a) "America and the World: A Conversation with Jürgen Habermas" [IEM]. Interview by Eduardo Mendieta. Trans. Jeffrey Craig Miller. *Logos* 3/3.

———. (2004b) "The Kantian Project of Cosmopolitan Law" [KPCL]. Lecture at Purdue University (October 15).

———. (2004c) "Öffentlicher Raum und politische Öffentlichkeit: Lebensgeschichtliche Wurzeln zweier Gedankenmotive" [ORpO]. A thank-you speech on the occasion of the Kyoto Award on 11 November. *Neue Zürcher Zeitung* (11 December).

———. (2006) "Towards a United States of Europe" [TUSE]. *Sign and Sight.* Bruno Kreisky Award speech, Vienna, March 9, 2006.

Habermas, Jürgen, and Jacques Derrida. (2003) "Plädoyer zu einer Wiedergeburt Europas" [PWE]. *Frankfurter Allgemeine Zeitung,* May 31; "February 15, or What Binds Europeans Together: A Plea for a Common Foreign Policy, Beginning in the Core of Europe." Trans. Max Pensky. *Constellations* 10/3 (2003): 291–97.

Hansen, Miriam Bratu. (1997) "*Schindler's List* Is Not *Shoah:* The Second Commandment, Popular Modernism, and Public Memory." In Yosefa Loshitzky, ed., *Spielberg's Holocaust,* 77–103. Bloomington: Indiana University Press.

Hart, Kevin, ed. (2007) *Counter-Experiences: Reading Jean-Luc Marion.* Notre Dame, Ind.: University of Notre Dame Press.

Hartman, Geoffrey H. (1986) *Bitburg in Moral and Political Perspective.* Bloomington: Indiana University Press.

Hartman, Geoffrey H, ed. (1994) *Holocaust Remembrance: The Shapes of Memory.* Cambridge, Mass.: Basil Blackwell.

Havel, Václav. (2002) "The Transformation of NATO." Speech at the conference organized by Host Committee and Aspen Institute of Berlin, November 20, Prague, Sovovy mlýny.

Heidegger, Martin. (1962) *Being and Time.* Trans. John Macquarrie and Edward Robinson. New York: Harper & Row.

———. (1969) *Identity and Difference.* Trans. Joan Stambaugh. University of Chicago Press.

———. (1977) "The Word of Nietzsche, 'God Is Dead'." In *The Question Concerning Technology,* 53–112. Trans. William Lovitt. New York: Harper Torchbooks.

———. (1988 [1936]) *Schelling: Vom Wesen der Menschlichen Freiheit (1809).* Frankfurt a/M: Vittori Klostermann. *Gesamtausgabe,* vol. 42.

———. (1993) "What Is Metaphysics?" In David Farrell Krell, ed., *Basic Writings,* 89–110. New York: HarperCollins.

Hick, John. (1987) *Evil and the God of Love.* 2nd. ed. London: Macmillan.

Hillesum, Etty. (1984) *An Interrupted Life: The Diaries of Etty Hillesum.* New York: Pantheon.

Horkheimer, Max. (1972) "Traditional and Critical Theory." In *Critical Theory,* 188–243. Trans. Matthew J. O'Connell. New York: Herder & Herder.

———. (1974 [1963]) "Theism and Atheism." In *Critique of Instrumental Reason.* New York: Continuum.

Horkheimer, Max, and Theodor W. Adorno. (2002 [1944]) *Dialectic of Enlightenment: Philosophical Fragments.* Ed. Gunzelin Schmid Noerr. Trans. Edmund Jephcott. Stanford: Stanford University Press.

Howard-Snyder, Daniel, ed. (1996) *The Evidential Argument from Evil.* Bloomington: Indiana University Press.

Howard-Snyder, Daniel, and Paul Moser. (2002) *Divine Hiddenness.* Cambridge: Cambridge University Press.

Huntington, Samuel P. (1996) *The Clash of Civilizations and the Remaking of World Order.* New York: Simon & Schuster.

Husserl, Edmund. (1998) *Ideas Pertaining to a Pure Phenomenology and to a Phenomenological Philosophy.* Bk. 1, *General Introduction to a Pure Phenomenology.* Dordrecht: Kluwer Academic.

Janicaud, Dominique. (2000) *Phenomenology and the "Theological Turn": The French Debate.* New York: Fordham University Press.

———. (2005) *Phenomenology "Wide Open": After the French Debate.* New York: Fordham University Press.

Jankélévitch, Vladimir. (1986 [1956]) *L'imprescriptible: Pardonner? Dans l'honneur et la dignité.* Paris: Seuil.

———. (1994) "Dernières lignes écrites." In *Premières et dernières.* Paris: Seuil.

———. (1996) "Should We Pardon Them?" [1971] and "Do Not Listen to What They Say, Look at What They Do." Trans. Ann Hobart. *Critical Inquiry,* Spring, 549–72.

———. (2005 [1967]) *Forgiveness.* Trans. Andrew Kelley. Chicago: University of Chicago Press.

Jonas, Hans. (1996) *Mortality and Morality: A Search for the Good after Auschwitz.* Ed. Lawrence Vogel. Evanston, Ill.: Northwestern University Press.

Kandell, Jonathan. 2004. "Jacques Derrida, Abstruse Theorist, Dies in Paris at 74." *New York Times,* October 10, sec. 1, p. 1.

Kant, Immanuel. (1963) *On History.* Ed. Lewis White Beck. Indianapolis: Bobbs-Merrill.

———. (1973 [1791]) "On the Failure of All Attempted Philosophical Theodicies." In Michael Despland, ed., *Kant on History and Religion,* 283–97. Montreal: McGill-Queen's University Press.

———. (1996 [1793]) "Religion within the Boundaries of Mere Reason." In *Religion and Rational Theology,* 55–215. Ed. and trans. Allen W. Wood and George Di Giovanni. Cambridge: Cambridge University Press. Cited by marginal numbers of the German edition of *Kants Gesammelte Schriften,* ed. Royal Prussian Academy of Sciences. Berlin: George Reimer/Walter de Gruyter, 1900.

———. (1996b) *Practical Philosophy: The Cambridge Edition of the Works of Immanuel Kant.* Cambridge: Cambridge University Press.

Kearney, Richard. (2004) *Debates in Continental Philosophy: Conversations with Contemporary Thinkers.* New York: Fordham University Press.

Kierkegaard, Søren. (1962) *The Point of View for My Work as an Author* [PVA]. Trans. Walter Lowrie. New York: Harper.

———. (1967) *Journals and Papers* [JP]. Vols. 1–7. Ed. and trans. Howard V. Hong and Edna H. Hong. Assisted by Gregor Malantschuk. Bloomington: Indiana University Press.

———. (1978) *Two Ages: The Age of Revolution and the Present Age* [TA]. Ed. and trans. Howard V. and Edna H. Hong. Princeton: Princeton University Press.

———. (1980a) *The Concept of Anxiety* [CA]. Ed. and trans. Howard V. Hong and Edna H. Hong. Princeton: Princeton University Press.

———. (1980b) *The Sickness unto Death* [SuD]. Ed. and trans. Howard V. Hong and Edna H. Hong. Princeton: Princeton University Press.

———. (1985) *Philosophical Fragments* [PF]. Ed. and trans. Howard V. Hong and Edna H. Hong. Princeton: Princeton University Press.

———. (1987) *Either/Or* [EO]. Pts. 1–2. Ed. and trans. Howard V. Hong and Edna H. Hong. Princeton: Princeton University Press.

———. (1991) *Practice in Christianity* [PC]. Ed. and trans. Howard V. and Edna H. Hong. Princeton: Princeton University Press.

———. (1992) *Concluding Unscientific Postscript to "Philosophical Fragments"* [CUP]. Ed. and trans. Howard V. and Edna H. Hong. Princeton: Princeton University Press.

———. (1998) *Works of Love* [WoL]. Ed. and trans. Howard V. Hong and Edna H. Hong. Princeton: Princeton University Press.

Kisch, Egon Erwin. (1986) "Mörder bauten dem zu Ermordenden ein Mausoleum." In *Prager Pitaval: Späte Reportagen,* 331–43. Berlin: Aufbau-Verlag.

Kofman, Sarah. (1998) *Smothered Words.* Trans. Madeleine Dobie. Evanston, Ill.: Northwestern University Press.

Kundera, Milan. (1980) *The Book of Laughter and Forgetting.* Trans. Michael Henry Heim. New York: Knopf.

———. (1999) *Immortality.* Trans. Petr Kussi. New York: HarperCollins.

———. (2000) *Life Is Elsewhere.* Trans. Aaron Asher. New York: Perennial.

———. (2004) *Ignorance.* Trans. Linda Asher. New York: HarperCollins.

LaCapra, Dominick. (1992) "Representing the Holocaust: Reflections on the Historians' Debate." In Saul Friedländer, ed., *Probing the Limits of Representation: Nazism and the "Final Solution,"* 108–27. Cambridge: Harvard University Press, 1992.

Lanzmann, Claude. (1985) *Shoah: An Oral History of the Holocaust.* Preface by Simone de Beauvoir. English subtitles by A. Whitelaw and W. Byron. New York: Pantheon.

———. (1994) "Why Spielberg Has Distorted the Truth." *Guardian Weekly,* April 9, 14.

Lara, María Pía, ed. (2001) *Rethinking Evil: Contemporary Perspectives.* Berkeley: University of California Press.

———. (2007) *Narrating Evil: A Postmetaphysical Theory of Reflective Judgment.* New York: Columbia University Press.

La Revuelta de la Memoria. (1999) *Textos del Subcomandante Marcos y del EZLN sobre la Historia.* San Cristóbal de las Casas, Chiapas: Centro de Información y Análisis de Chiapas.

Lévinas, Emmanuel. (1969) *Totality and Infinity.* Pittsburgh: Duquesne University Press.

———. (1981) *Otherwise Than Being: Or, Beyond Essence.* Trans. Alphonso Lingis. Boston: M. Nijhoff.

———. (1983) "Transcendence and Evil." In Anna-T. Tymienicka, ed., *The Phenomenology of Man and of the Human Condition.* Analecta Husserliana, 14. Trans. Alphonso Lingis, 153–65. Dordrecht: D. Riedel.

———. (1988) "Useless Suffering" and "The Paradox of Morality: An Interview with Emmanuel Levinas." In Robert Bernasconi and David Wood, eds., *The Provocation of Levinas: Rethinking the Other,* 156–80. London: Routledge.

Libeskind, Daniel. (1995) *1995 Raoul Wallenberg Lecture: Traces of the Unborn.* Ann Arbor, Mich.: College of Architecture and Urban Planning.

Lieben, Salomon Hugo. (1912) *Das Jüdische Museum in Prag.* Prague: Josef Flesh.

Lyotard, Jean-François. (1988) *The Differend: Phrases in Dispute.* Trans. Georges Van Den Abbeele. Minneapolis: University of Minnesota Press.

Marcel, Gabriel. (1962) *Homo Viator: Introduction to a Metaphysic of Hope*. New York: Harper.

Marcos, Subcomandante. (2006) "The First Other Winds." Communiqué about the "Other Campaign" by the Zapatista Army of National Liberation, EZLN, from February 18–19 and March 11.

Marcuse, Herbert. (1955) *Eros and Civilization: A Philosophical Inquiry into Freud*. Boston: Beacon.

———. (1991 [1964]) *One-Dimensional Man: Studies in the Ideology of Advanced Industrial Society*. With a new introduction by Douglas Kellner. Boston: Beacon.

Marion, Jean-Luc. (1991) *God without Being*. Trans. Thomas A. Carlson. Chicago: University of Chicago Press.

———. (1999). "In the Name: How to Avoid Speaking of 'Negative Theology'," response by Jacques Derrida, 20–53. In John D. Caputo and Michael J. Scanlon, eds., *God, the Gift, and Postmodernism*. Bloomington: Indiana University Press.

———. (2000) "Saturated Phenomenon." In Dominique Janicaud, *Phenomenology and the "Theological Turn": The French Debate*, 176–216. New York: Fordham University Press.

———. (2002) *Being Given: Toward a Phenomenology of Givenness*. Trans. Jeffrey L. Kosky. Stanford: Stanford University Press.

———. (2002b) *In Excess: Studies of Saturated Phenomena*. New York: Fordham University Press.

———. (2007) "The Banality of Saturation." In Kevin Hart, ed., *Counter-Experiences: Reading Jean-Luc Marion*, 383–41. Notre Dame, Ind.: University of Notre Dame Press.

Marx, Karl. (1975) "Letter to Ruge." In *Early Writings*. Ed. L. Colletti and trans. Rodney Livingstone and Gregor Benton. New York: Vintage.

Matuštík, Martin Beck. (1993) *Postnational Identity: Critical Theory and Existential Philosophy in Habermas, Kierkegaard, and Havel*. New York, London: Guilford.

———. (1995) "Derrida and Habermas on the Aporia of the Politics of Identity and Difference: Towards Radical Democratic Multiculturalism." *Constellations* 1/3: 383–98.

———. (1998) *Specters of Liberation: Great Refusals in the New World Order*. Albany: SUNY Press.

———. (2000) "The Critical Theorist as Witness: Habermas and the Holocaust." In Lewis E. Hahn, ed., *Perspectives on Habermas*, 339–66. LaSalle, Ill.: Open Court.

———. (2001) *Jürgen Habermas: A Philosophical-Political Profile*. Lanham, Md.: Rowman & Littlefield.

———. (2002) "Contribution to a New Critical Theory of Multiculturalism." *Philosophy and Social Criticism* 28/4: 473–82. Response to Drucilla Cornell and Sara Murphy's essay, "Antiracism, Multiculturalism, and the Ethics of Identification."

———. (2003) Letter. *New York Review of Books*, January 16, 2003, 49.

———. (2004) "America's Prayer." *www.opendemocracy.com*, May 17.

———. (2006) "Habermas' Turn?" *Philosophy and Social Criticism* 32/1 (2006): 21–36.

———. (Forthcoming) "More Than All the Others: Meditation on Responsibility." In J. Aaron Simmons and David Wood, eds., *Between Levinas and Kierkegaard*. Bloomington: Indiana University Press.

McRobert, Laurie. (1989) "Emil L. Fackenheim and Radical Evil: Transcendent, Unsurpassable, Absolute." *Journal of the American Academy of Religion* 57/2: 325–340.

Mendieta, Eduardo, ed. (2005) *The Frankfurt School on Religion: Key Writings by the Major Thinkers*. New York: Routledge.

Metz, Johann-Baptist, and Jürgen Moltmann. (1995) *Faith and the Future*. Orbis Books.

Mexico Solidarity Network. (2001) "Weekly News Summaries." February 22–28.

Mitscherlich, Alexander, and Margarete Mitscherlich. (1975) *The Inability to Mourn: Principles of Collective Behavior.* Trans. B. Placzek. Preface by Robert Jay Lifton. New York: Grove.

Moltmann, Jürgen. (1967) *Theology of Hope: On the Ground and the Implications of a Christian Eschatology.* SCM Press, London.

Monsiváis, Carlos. (2001) "El indígena visible." *Proceso*, March 4, 10–13.

Neiman, Susan. (2002) *Evil in Modern Thought: An Alternative History of Philosophy.* Princeton: Princeton University Press.

Nietzsche, Friedrich. (1967) *On the Genealogy of Morals.* Trans. Walter Kaufmann. New York: Random House.

———. (1968) *The Portable Nietzsche.* Ed. Walter Kaufmann. New York: Viking.

Nishitani, Keiji. (1982) *Religion and Nothingness.* Trans. Jan Van Bragt. Berkeley: University of California Press.

Oliver, Kelly. (1998) *Subjectivity without Subjects: From Abject Fathers to Desiring Mothers.* Lanham, Md.: Rowman & Littlefield.

Paris, Jeffrey. (1998) "Impossible Hope: New Critical Theory and the Spirit of Liberation." Ph.D. diss., Purdue University.

Pasolini, Pier Paolo. (1975) *Salo, The 120 Days of Sodom.* New York: Waterbearer Films.

Paulson, Joshua. (2001) *The San Andrés Accords: Five Years Later.* Report by Mexico Solidarity Network.

Payne, Jan. (2005) *Odkud Zlo? O nezkrotnosti čili slabosti lidské vůle.* Praha: Triton.

Petrášová, Markéta. (1988) "Židovské ústřední muzeum 1942–1945." Ph.D. diss., University J.E. Purkyně, Brno.

Postel, Danny. (2003) "Noble Lies and Perpetual War: Leo Strauss, the Neocons, and Iraq." *Open Democracy*, October 16. www.opendemocracy.net.

Ragozinski, Jacob. (1996) "It Makes Us Wrong: Kant and Radical Evil." In Joan Copjec, ed., *Radical Evil*, 30–45. London: Verso.

Remnick, David. (2003) "Letter from Prague: Exit Havel." *New Yorker*, February 17 and 24.

Ricoeur, Paul. (1995) *Figuring the Sacred: Religion, Narrative, and Imagination.* Ed. Mark I. Wallace. Trans. David Pellauer. Minneapolis: Fortress.

———. (2004) *Memory, History, Forgetting.* Trans. Kathleen Blamey and David Pellauer. Chicago: University of Chicago Press.

Roberts, David. (2006) *Kierkegaard's Analysis of Radical Evil.* New York: Continuum.

Rosenzweig, Franz. (2005) *The Star of Redemption.* Trans. Barbara E. Galli. Madison, Wis.: The University of Wisconsin Press.

Sade, Marquis de. (1784) *Les cents-vingts journées de Sodome* [The 120 Days of Sodom]. Written on a continuous twelve-meter-long roll of paper while Sade was imprisoned in Bastille, the text was lost during the French Revolution in 1789. It was first published clandestinely by Max Harwitz and edited by Iwan Bloch in Berlin in 1904.

Sartre, Jean-Paul. (1976) *Critique of Dialectical Reason.* Vol. 1. Trans. Alan Sheridan-Smith. London: New Left Books.

Sartre, Jean-Paul, and Benny Levy. (1996) *Hope Now: The 1980 Interviews.* Trans. Adrian van der Hoven. With an introduction by Ronald Aronson. Chicago: University of Chicago Press.

Schellenberg, J. L. (1993) *Divine Hiddenness and Human Reason.* Ithaca, N.Y.: Cornell University Press.

Schelling, Friedrich Wilhelm Joseph von. (1860 [1809]) *Philosophische Untersuchungen über das Wesen der menschlichen Freiheit und die damit zusammenhängenden Gegenstände.* Stuttgart: Cota.

Scholem, Gershom Gerhard. (1991) *On the Mystical Shape of the Godhead: Basic Concepts in the Kabbalah.* Translated by Joachim Neugroschel. New York: Schocken Books.

Schuster, Ekkehard, and Reinhold Bochert-Kimmig. (1999) *Hope against Hope: Johann Baptist Metz and Elie Wiesel Speak Out on the Holocaust.* Mahwah, N.J.: Paulist Press.

Sherwood, Yvonne, and Kevin Hart, eds. (2005). *Derrida and Religion: Other Testaments.* London: Routledge.

Silber, John R. (1960) "The Ethical Significance of Kant's *Religion.*" Introduction to Kant's *Religion within the Limits of Reason Alone,* lxxix–cxxxvii. Trans. T. M. Greene and H. H. Hudson. New York: Harper Torchbooks.

———. (1991) "Kant at Auschwitz." *Proceedings of the Sixth International Kant Congress,* 1:177–211. Ed. Gerhard Funke and Thomas M. Seebohm. Washington, D.C., Center for Advanced Research in Phenomenology/University Press of America.

Thompson, Ginger. (2001) "Mexico Congress Approves Altered Rights Bill." *New York Times,* A9.

Tiedenmann, Rolf. (1999) "Dialectics at a Standstill." In Walter Benjamin, "N [On the Theory of Knowledge, Theory of Progress]," *The Arcades Project,* 929–45. Trans. Howard Eiland and Kevin McLaughlin. Cambridge: Harvard University Press.

Tolkien, J. R. R. (1990) *The Lord of the Rings.* 3 vols. New York: Houghton Mifflin.

Tolle, Eckhart. (1999) *The Power of Now: A Guide to Spiritual Enlightenment.* Novato, Calif.: Publishing Group West.

Tracy, David. (1999) "Form and Fragment: The Recovery of the Hidden and Incomprehensible God." Palmer Lecture, Princeton Center for Theological Inquiry.

Veselská, Magda. (1999) "Židovské muzeum v Praze." M.A. thesis, Masaryk University, Brno.

———. (2005) *The Man Who Never Gave Up: The Story of Josef Polák (1886–1945).* Prague: Židovské muzeum v Praze. Exhibition catalogue for the centenary year of the Jewish Museum in Prague.

Volavková, Hana. (1968) *A Story of the Jewish Museum of Prague.* Trans. K. E. Lichtenecker. Praha: Artia. From the Czech, *Příběh židovského muzea v Praze* (Prague: Odeon, 1966).

Vries, Hent de. (2002) *Religion and Violence: Philosophical Perspectives from Kant to Derrida.* Baltimore: Johns Hopkins University Press.

Westphal, Merold. (2004) *Transcendence and Self-Transcendence: On God and the Soul.* Bloomington: Indiana University Press.

Wiedmer, Caroline. (1999) *The Claims of Memory: Representations of the Holocaust in Contemporary Germany and France.* Ithaca, N.Y.: Cornell University Press.

Wiesel, Elie. (1990) *Evil and Exile.* University of Notre Dame Press.

Wilber, Ken. (2006) *Integral Spirituality: A Startling New Role for Religion in the Modern and Postmodern World.* Boston: Shambhala.

Wise, Michael Z. (1999) "Totem and Tabu: The New Berlin Struggles to Build a Holocaust Memorial." *Lingua Franca,* December–January, 38–46.

Young, James E. (1990) *Writing and Rewriting the Holocaust: Narrative and the Consequences of Interpretation.* Bloomington: Indiana University Press.

———. (2000) *At Memory's Edge: After-Images of the Holocaust in Contemporary Art and Architecture.* New Haven: Yale University Press.

Žižek, Slavoj. (2003) *The Puppet and the Dwarf: The Perverse Core of Christianity.* Cambridge: MIT Press.

———. (2006) "Defenders of the Faith." Op-ed. *New York Times,* March 12.

INDEX

MARTIN BECK MATUŠTÍK is Professor of Philosophy at Purdue University. He is author of *Jürgen Habermas: A Philosophical-Political Profile* and editor (with Merold Westphal) of *Kierkegaard in Post/Modernity* (Indiana University Press, 1995).